HARDPRESS.NET
HOME OF HARD-TO-FIND BOOKS

Pascarèl
by Ouida

Address:
HardPress
8345 NW 66TH ST #2561
MIAMI FL 33166-2626
USA
Email: info@hardpress.net

COLLECTION

OF

BRITISH AUTHORS

TAUCHNITZ EDITION.

VOL. 1316.

PASCARÈL BY OUIDA.

IN TWO VOLUMES.
VOL. I.

TAUCHNITZ EDITION.

By the same Author,

IDALIA	2 vols.
TRICOTRIN	2 vols.
PUCK	2 vols.
CHANDOS	2 vols.
STRATHMORE	2 vols.
UNDER TWO FLAGS	2 vols.
FOLLE-FARINE	2 vols.
A LEAF IN THE STORM	1 vol.
CECIL CASTLEMAINE'S GAGE	1 vol.
MADAME LA MARQUISE	1 vol.

PASCARÈL.

ONLY A STORY.

BY

OUIDA,

AUTHOR OF "TRICOTRIN," "CHANDOS," ETC.

COPYRIGHT EDITION.

IN TWO VOLUMES.

VOL. I.

LEIPZIG

BERNHARD TAUCHNITZ

1873.

"Se
Non Ami
Firenze,
Questo Libro
Ti
Nosera."

"Love is enough; though the World be a waning,
  And the woods have no voice but the voice of complaining,
  Though the sky be too dark for dim eyes to discover,
  The gold-cups and daisies fair blossoming thereunder,
  Though the hills be held shadows, and the sea a dark wonder,
  And this day draw a veil over all deeds passed over,
  Yet their hands shall not tremble, their feet shall not falter;
  The void shall not weary, the fear shall not alter,
  Those lips and those eyes of the loved and the lover."

TO THE READER.

WITH feminine obstinacy the Donzella sacrifices truth to pictorial effect, and justice to high-coloured contrast, touching Rome.* The love that Rome begets is different to that which Florence inspires; but it is never less strong and is even more reverent; less familiar, and more close on awe; as tender, but more solemn. In Rome, Art and Nature strain together in perpetual conflict for supremacy; a struggle of a Titan with a God that holds mortal onlookers breathless: in Florence, Art and Nature clasp hands and smile on men, and even the Mercury Agoreus, being in Florence, borrows the flowers of Dionysus to deck his scales of barter. But who, with any power of vision or soul of artist in them, can live a day blind to the vast and sublime beauties of the Capital of the World?—who can fail to grow at once the humbler and the greater by dwelling on that sacred soil?—who will not draw nearer to God himself as they see how mighty human genius can be?—who will not yield to Rome a

* Vol. I, p. 165.

homage that is a passion as well as a religion? If any such there be, let them see the sun fall once on the face of the Faun, let them see the moon shine once on the Palace of the Cæsars:—and surely they will repent.

OUIDA.

ROME, *Feb.* 12, 1873.

———

CONTENTS

OF VOLUME I.

BOOK I.

THE CITY OF CATULLUS.

BOOK II.

THE CITY OF LILIES.

BOOK III.

THE DAUGHTER OF HERCULES.

BOOK IV.

THE WANDERING ARTE.

PASCARÈL.

BOOK I.

THE CITY OF CATULLUS.

CHAPTER I.

King Carnival.

IT was the first day of Carnival.

The populace was out all over the city in a many-coloured and ever-changing swarm of human life. The gay masque reeled madly round the marble iron-bound flanks of the Duomo, and flung its hail of toys and flowers against the frowning masses of the old palaces and prisons; and surged in its foam of mirth and mischief all along the length of the green Adige in the light of the winter noon.

For a month King Carnival would reign supreme in mockery and merriment over the lives of men; his path strewn with violets, his sovereignty shouted over wine, his dynasty proclaimed far and wide—everywhere, by high and low, from the cobbler who pranked himself in the guise of Stenterello to the great lady who laughed through her velvet mask of Venice.

And at the month's end, at nightfall, just as the moon should rise, with music and many a jest and sound of horn and drum, and rioting of Arlecchino

and Pulcinello and all their immemorial brotherhood,
at nightfall the fickle people would lead the old King
out to his funeral pyre in the great square, and there
would burn him in all pomp and cruelty until the
flames should redden grim Roland standing at his
vigil at the cathedral doors, and be seen afar off,
where the last outposts of the great Alps kept watch
and ward in the quiet of the silence and the chillness
of the snow.

Burn him,—a monarch yesterday, to-day a scape-
goat, in grimmest ironic symbol of all human histories.

Poor King Carnival!

His rule has lasted longer than any other dynasty;
for though his nations burn him one year, he rises
from his ashes, and they cry All hail! to him the next.

But the axe is at the root of his throne. The old
glad days of his mumming are numbered, and the
pomp of his pageant is shorn. The world is old and
very weary.

Here "nel aer dolce, che del sol s'allegra," life is
brighter and more buoyant than elsewhere.

Here the people still laugh from clear throats, and
the hours still reel away, marked with flowers; here
they sit in the sun, and still know the priceless pleasures and true uses of leisure; and here the heart
of a child still beats in the war-scarred breast of the
nation.

Yet even here the world is older, greyer, sadder
than of yore; and even here the day is close at hand
when King Carnival will ride his last ride round the
city walls, and be burned for the last time, in all the
panoply of his historic robes, upon a pyre whence his
ashes shall never rise again.

The world is too wise to be foolish—so they say. Or is it too foolish to be wise?

King Carnival might tell us if he would. Perhaps he would answer:—

"In the days when men were so great that they did not fear to stoop, and were so strong that their dignity lost nothing by their mirth, they rode in my train and followed me—Carnivale, the old King—and laughed as children laugh—those men of those days of Dante, of those days of Lionardo, of those days of Shakspeare. Are you wiser than they? or weaker? or only more weary, perhaps? No matter. I have held high feast with the giants, and they were not ashamed to be glad. But you, who blush for your mirth because your mirth is vice, bury me quickly. I am a thing of the Past."

And the old King would speak sadly aright; for his name is almost emptiness, and his earth-swaying orb is but now an empty gourd in which the shrivelled beans of the world's spent pleasures are shaken in fruitless sport and sound.

For in the old days,—when he reigned supreme, over all men's lives, from sovereign's to serf's, for a few weeks' span of full feast and fair folly,—in the old days men lived greatly great lives to great ends.

Their faith was ever present with them—a thing of daily use and hourly sweetness. Their households were wisely ruled and simply ordered. They denuded themselves of their substance to give their gold to the raising of mighty works—*vivis lapidibus*—which to this day do live and speak.

Great artists narrowed not themselves to one meagre phase of art, but filled with all its innumerable powers the splendid plenitude of their majestic years.

And that art was in the hearts of the people who followed it, and adored its power and were nourished by it, so that it was no empty name, but an ever-vivifying presence—a divinity at once of hearth and temple that brooded over the cities with sheltering and stainless love.

Therefore in those days men, giving themselves leave to be glad for a little space, were glad with the same sinewy force and manful singleness of purpose as made them in other times laborious, self-denying, patient, and fruitful of high thoughts and deeds.

Because they laboured for their fellows, therefore they could laugh with them, and because they served God, therefore they dared be glad.

In those grave, dauntless, austere lives the Carnival's jocund revelry was as one golden bead in a pilgrim's rosary of thorn-berries.

They had aimed highly and highly achieved; therefore they could go forth amidst their children and rejoice.

But we—in whom all art is the mere empty Shibboleth of a ruined religion whose priests are all dead; we—whose whole year-long course is one Dance of Death over the putridity of our pleasures; we—whose solitary purpose it is to fly faster and faster from desire to satiety, from satiety to desire, in an endless eddy of fruitless effort; we—whose greatest genius can only raise for us some inarticulate protest of despair against some unknown God;—we have strangled King Carnival and killed him, and buried him in the ashes of our own unutterable weariness and woe.

For the old King is heartsick to hear the manful laughter that he heard in his youth; and we—we cannot laugh; all we can give is a sneer—and a sob.

CHAPTER II.

The Bird and the Fates.

NEVERTHELESS in Verona this first day of Carnival men made believe to be glad.

In the deep wintry gloom of the old sad city the gold of the alien tyranny had been scattered broadcast that the people might wear at least the mask of contentment; and on the whole they wore it, nothing loth, grinning gleefully from ear to ear.

The old stone balconies were draped with amber and rose and silver; the beautiful trecento windows were filled with eager faces; the dusky crypt-like streets were full of colour and tumult; the great marble tombs, looming white in the darkness of their sepulchres, were flecked with the pretty pallor of violets from Rome.

Verona under her taskmasters took holiday.

Under a deep porch, sculptured with vine foliage and the heads of griffins, two children stood looking on the pageantry, and not thinking very much about it; for one of them—the girl,—was full of trouble, and the boy tried his best to solace her.

"Do look at Stenterello!" the little lad murmured. "How nimble he is—look, look! the boys have caught him. No!—he slips through like an eel. Ah, ah! do look! There is Arlecchino angling for a priest's hat with a gilded fishing-hook. Oh, carina mia! to think you have no heart to laugh to-day—"

The tears brimmed over in his companion's eyes.

"How can I laugh? We have nothing—absolutely nothing. We must sell those poor little jewels of my mother's, or Mariuccia will starve. It must not be, you know; she is so old, so old! And yet to sell the jewels! See here, 'Ino. I have a voice, and I am fifteen years old, and I am good to look at, you all say. Why should I not sing in the choruses? You know how often we have laughed at them—the fat ugly women with the crowns that would always tumble off. Now I am as thin as a cane, and am handsome, and could wear a crown as one should be worn. Why might I not sing in the chorus?"

The pretty boy looked perplexed, and his little bare foot traced nervously an arabesque on the stone of the dusty stair.

"That would never do, dear donzella! Your father is too illustrious——"

"But one cannot live on being illustrious. One wants to eat—somehow. And there is nothing to eat. Nothing. We have not heard of my father for more than a year, and Florio even does not send now. Why should I not sing in the chorus? It is quite easy, all that sort of music."

He shook his pretty, curly, golden, Venetian head, in grave concern.

"Oh no, dear donzella; it would never do. Mariuccia would never allow it. It is so late at night, and the women are not fit for you: it would never do."

"Then the jewels must go? And they are all that I have of my mother's—the only, only, little thing!"

The words ended in a sob; and the whirling, many-coloured procession of the Carnival was hidden from the child's sight by a haze of sudden tears.

At home there were an empty cupboard, a cold hearth, and an old woman of eighty years, who had not broken her fast. Such things seem hard to bear when one is very young; and it is the first day of Carnival; and beneath there, in the street, all the mad and merry masque is flaunting on its way.

The boy listened wistfully, with a tender and anxious face.

"See here, dear donzella," he murmured, after a pause. "I have a thought. Sing in the chorus you must not; but why not sing in the streets? The people are all happy and good-tempered to-day. I have got my lute here, and we will sing, and then ask them frankly to help us. Why not? We have made music for them often out of pure love and goodwill. They will certainly give us a little money now, and no harm done."

"Oh, 'Ino! You never sang for money yet, nor I. It is so different——"

"We have not sung for it, because we have not wanted it. But if we do want it, where is the harm——"

"It is shameful!"

"Shameful! How shameful? When the great singer Lillo went through here last spring, do you not remember that the least atom of standing room in the theatre was worth gold, and the people took the horses from his carriage, and drew him through the streets, shouting and smothering him with Easter lilies?"

"That is very different."

"Not at all different. Except that they pay Lillo by millions and we only want a few florins."

"But why, then, will you never take money when you play yourself? You never do."

He crossed himself, and glanced gratefully at an old battered, black-faced Madonna that hung behind an iron grating high up above in the doorway.

"Our Lady has been so good to me, and I have never wanted for anything. And the people who would have paid me have always been so poor—so poor. But I would play for money rather than sell a thing of my mother's. Perhaps your mother up there says to Our Lady,—'Look at my donzella; she is proud: take that sin out of her heart.' And Our Lady says,—'We will prove her: she must love you a little, though she never looked on your face.' And so Our Lady sets this thing in your way. And your mother up there waits, watching and trembling, to see if indeed you do love her, or only care for your pride. For mothers never forget. That I am very sure. No, not though they sit on the right hand of God with His angels."

The boy's voice was very sweet and solemn, and murmured with a strange softness and clearness through the riotous laughter and uproar that rose from the Carnival crowds in the street below. He looked no longer at the antics of Stenterello and the pranks of Arlecchino, but up at the breadth of blue serene sky which stretched above where the gabled roof parted.

His companion listened, with the colour coming and going, fleeting and burning, in her downcast face; then suddenly she caught his hand and sprang down the first stair.

"Let us go, 'Ino—let us go!"

And hand in hand they ran down, and were mingled with the hundreds who were streaming in frolicsome humour, through the narrow tortuous street towards the great Piazza.

A few minutes later they also were standing in the Cathedral square.

They were a picturesque little pair—the girl taller than the boy by full a head.

He was barelegged and barefooted—a child of the populace; he wore the loose shirt and the red waist-band of the Venetian gondoliers; and slung round him by another bit of scarlet was an old ebony mandoline. She was clad in quite another guise, so that she looked like some silky-leaved flower growing out of the grey stone pavements; she had a hood of dark velvet over her head, from which great, bright, trustful eyes looked out wonderingly upon the world; her skirts were of heavy amber satin, that seemed to have been fashioned out of some brocaded train; her hands were full of flowers that she had picked up from the ground as the people of the balconies flung them downward.

As they stood together, hand in hand, the contrast of colour and the grace of attitude made a picture against the dusky pile of the Duomo and in the crisp whiteness of the sunny frosty air. Many people passing paused to look at them; the little

2 *

lad whispered to her, and then unslung his mandoline.

There was a lull in the sports of the day. Some
sporting of a band of mummers headed by a scarlet
Mefistofelo and a gorgeous Dulcamara was over and
done with: the commencement of the traditional Galà
was delayed; the crowd was unoccupied and willing
to be amused, but not impatient nor out of temper,
because it was a crowd of Italy.

The boy judged his time accurately, and touched
the cords of his lute. The girl wavered a moment with
the colour hot in her face; then with a sudden gesture
threw the hood back off her curls, and lifted up her
voice and sang.

Her song was an old familiar street-song of the
Lombard population.

Far and wide on the clear wintry air, keen with
the hard breath of the mountains, the strong pure
notes of a voice in its earliest youth rang out like a
bell over the muttering and shouting of the people.
Those nearest to her listened, and hushed down the
noise around them; the silence spread and spread
softly like the circles in the water where a stone is
thrown; the boisterous gaiety dropped to a quieter
key; in a little while all the square was still.

The hood fell back wholly upon her shoulders;
the sun shone upon the little group; the amber of her
skirts, the violets in her hands, the scarlet wool of
the boy's sash, all glowed in the light; above all
hum and buzz from the other quarters of the city the
song rose on the air clear as only the tones of childhood can be.

"L'Uccello!" the people shouted. "Go on, go on!"

A smile rippled over her face, as at some familiar word of greeting: she sang on at their bidding song after song of the sweet unwritten melodies of the nation. Now and then the boy struck a chord or two from his mandoline, but seldom; her voice was rich enough and strong enough to fill the square without aid, and it leaped aloft in the wintry air with the eager, straight, upward flight of a hawk that is loosed from its holdings.

When at length it ceased, the throng in the great square screamed, laughed, almost cried with delighted applause; the people in the balconies clapped their hands, the loungers at the caffè dashed their hands on the marble tables till their glasses rang, the masquers and merry-makers shrieked a hundred times,—"Viva l'Uccello! Viva l'Uccello!"

The boy marked the propitious hour. He took the red berretta off his curly head, and advanced amongst the multitude, and with the infinite grace of his nation, the grace which is so perfect because so utterly unconscious of itself, stretched out his hand to them for charity.

"Some little thing, signori, for the love of God. There is an old woman at home who wants bread."

He was generous, and he sought to bear all the shame of the alms-seeking for his own portion. But his companion saw his purpose, and sprang to his side. Her cheeks were flushed, the tears were bright on her lashes, the winds blew the heavy gold of her hair and the snow off her courtly skirts; her voice had lost its strength, and trembled a little.

"It is not for him, signori!" she cried. "It is for me. For himself, when he plays and the people

would give him coins or cakes or confetti, he will
never take payment for his music. He says it is God's
gift, not his. The money that he begs now is for me.
I am illustrious; oh yes! but I am very poor. I have
an old nurse at home who wants bread, and sits by a
fireless hearth. She is so old, so old. And we have
nothing to sell but a few little jewels, and they were
my mother's, who is dead. Will you give me some
little thing, if my songs pleased you?"

The answer came from a hundred hands at once
—from above and around, on every side.

Paper money fluttered to her feet; loose silver rolled
like sugar-plums; here and there a piece of gold flashed
like a star through the air; flowers and toys and gilded
horns of sweetmeats, and ribboned playthings of the
pageantry were all showered upon them from the balconies above and from the throngs around, until their
arms ached with stretching for the gifts, he his red
berretta, and she her amber skirts.

Great ladies, leaning in the draped galleries of old
palaces, cast down money with lavish hands; white-
coated soldiers, laughing over their wines at the marble
tables, tossed bright florins to swell the store; a child-
noble in his gala-costume of white and gold and powder
and jewels, ran down some palace steps and shyly
thrust a roll of notes into the singer's hand, and hastily
lifted his soft smiling mouth to kiss her cheek; the
poorest of the people sought in their leathern pouches
for some copper pieces to give.

In vain the boy and girl, being honest, protested,
laughing and crying both at once—"Basta, basta!—
enough, enough!"

In vain; the golden shower did not cease until, in

the distance, as the first of the patrician pageantry appeared on the entrance of the square, there rose a glad shout,—"The Galà! the Galà!"

And the populace, kindly of heart, but fickle of temper, turned to the new pastime, and the little noble ran to his people, and the great ladies looked the other way, and the golden chariots rolled under the historic walls, and the sea of the bright masque surged outward; and the children were forgotten where they stood.

Then to them there came one who had listened and watched all the songs and all the payments where he had leaned in the shadow of the cathedral wall.

He uncovered his head as he approached, and the sun fell full on his face—the dark, poetic, historic face of Florence.

"Ah, cara donzella," he murmured softly with a smile. "Money I have none to give you, until I make some more to-night. I too am an artist; and so—it goes without words—I too am poor. Nevertheless, let me thank you."

He dropped a ring into her amber skirts, amongst the violets of Parma and the daffodils of Tuscany, and turned away and vanished in the throng.

The girl sought for the ring amongst the flowers and toys and money and sweetmeats with which her skirts were full.

It was a very old seal ring—an onyx, cut with the heads of the Fates.

She looked at it long and curiously, with a dreaming look on her face; then thrust it into the bosom of her dress. Then she gathered closely up about her the heavy brocades of her garments, and turned to the boy.

"Let us run, 'Ino. The people are not looking now.
We shall lose the Galà, but Mariuccia is so cold at
home."

So they turned away from the square, and went
back into the old, irregular, gloomy streets where even
at mid-day there was no gleam of brightness.

But now they could not run; their fleet feet were
powerless to bear them swiftly; they were too heavily
laden with the spoils of their prosperous efforts; it was
of no avail to try and move quickly; at every step they
trod upon a knot of violets, or trampled a bright narcissus under foot.

They were forced at last to go very tranquilly, with
bent heads and with cramped limbs, along the cold
and dreary passage ways.

"Oh 'Ino!" the girl cried. "When we sang for love
and goodwill, we were so light of heart and of foot.
But now——"

She sank down upon a flight of steps, her skirts
glided from her hands, her treasures rolled to the ground
and were scattered. She sobbed as if her heart would
break.

"That is ungrateful to the people, cara mia," said
the little lad softly. "Is it that stone with the Fates
that has chilled you?"

"Nay she is right," said a voice above them. "Count
art by gold, and it fetters the feet it once winged."

He who had given the ring spoke the words, passing swiftly in the shadow so as not to be delayed nor
questioned.

After him ran a gay and giddy throng of masks,
thrashing each other with coloured bladders, and chas-

ing him with tumultuous shouts as of a band of mummers to their chief.

The shouts in their hoarse vibration filled the tunnel of the narrow twilit street as the parti-coloured group of the masquers reeled down it like a score of anemone leaves blown heedlessly upon an autumn wind.

They all cried one word:—Pascarèl.

I,—the child who sat on the stone stair, weeping over my fallen violets and my scattered wealth,— treasured the name in my heart on which the carven Fates were resting.

The masquers reeled on out of sight, a cloud of misty and tangled hues; over the high grim roofs and the sculptured buttresses the name came back flying gaily in glad echo on the air—

"Pascarèllo!—Pascarèl!"

CHAPTER III.

By the broken Donatello.

THE first thing I remember is of how poor we all were; how horribly poor, how terribly poor!

When I went to take my first dancing lesson at four years old, I had holes in my little lace frock, and a pair of faded blue shoes nearly out at the toes. I cried bitterly for very shame sake.

"Never mind, carina," said old Mariuccia, my nurse. "Never mind. If you dance away with a light heart, what does a tatter or two in the dress signify? It is better to have holes in the shoes, little one, than a leaden weight on the feet, believe me."

Oh! and what a fool I thought her! Though she was sixty and I was not six.

But when my father's man Florio came in and lifted me up before the old battered silver mirror, and murmured in his soft tongue, "Ah! what does a shabby frock matter when one has an angel's face like the signorina's? The other little ladies may be all hung with rubies and pearls if they chose; nobody will look at them if the signorina be there"—then, indeed, there seemed some sense in the argument, and Florio appeared to me a person so discerning that I consented to be pacified and to be led away to the vast bare frescoed dancing-hall, where one little shrill fiddle was piping and shrieking to a score of Lombardic babies, all more or less noble, I believe, in descent.

We were at that time in Verona. Poor old Verona! World forgotten, though having given so much to the world.

The city of Lesbia's lover is but a sorry desolation now, despite its hidden treasures, that no man remembers once in a score of years.

Those narrow sun-baked streets, those grim dust-covered fortifications, those little lines of stunted sickly trees, those simooms of lime dust, those bitter piercing mountain winds, those pale grasses, all alive with brown lizards, those lofty desolate houses, palace and prison in one, those straggling vines choking the strangled maples, the dreary weary "waveless plain,"—how miserable it all is now, how miserable it all was then!

Verona never seemed like Italy to me. Perhaps because I saw it always under the dominion of those white-coated stranieri, who pampered its greedy priesthood and bribed its lazy proletariate, and who waltzed themselves into favour with me by swinging me round many and many a time to the gay measures of their regimental bands, and spending on me floods of sweet-meats and pretty phrases, although old Mariuccia, whenever she saw me thus polluted, would snatch me away from the barbarian's arms with fiercest flashes of her still eloquent Tuscan eyes.

Mariuccia told me many a tale of the old gran-deurs of the city of Can Grande; and I used to wan-der about it gazing at its amphitheatre and its acacia hedges, and its green Adige and its two Paladins at the door of the duomo, and dreaming of Marius and Theodoric, of Catullus, and Carolus Magnus, of Romeo, and Ezzelino, of Vitruvius, and Paolo Vero-nese, in the strangest confusion of fable and truth, in which my little brain floated as on a gorgeous, but misty, sea.

I never loved Verona.

The four first years of my small life had been spent with Mariuccia on a farm on the distant Ro-magna.

There I had lived in the open air, rolled in the grass, gleaned the gold of the millet, got drunk in my innocent fashion off the grapes at vintage time, and filled my hands with wild wood flowers all the whole year round. There I had owned all a child's delicious riches of freedom and sunlight, of chains of daffodils, of fans of chesnut leaves, of friendships with birds and beasts, of long, happy, heedless days in which the sky seemed always blue, and the angels of God always near.

When at four years old I was taken and cooped up in the dusty duskiness of Juliet's birthplace, I re-belled bitterly, and at first pined constantly, refusing to be comforted. I fretted for the free air and the

glad light, as many a prisoner had done before me in
the days when

"Death and sin played at dice with Eccelin."

Of course after a while my sweet first memories
paled a little, and I grew a little reconciled. But I
never forgot that bright beloved Italy of mine, away
there southward in the blue ocean of the distant
Romagna; I never grew to care for these grim streets,
these filthy courts, these parching heats, these frozen
winters, these masses of frowning stone, these labyrinths of palaces and prisons, which seemed always to
my fancy, as I grew older, to have still upon them
the mark of the scourge of Attila, the grip of the
gauntlet of Scala, the scorch of the crimes of Romano.

At the time when the little shrill fiddle played to
me in my little shabby shoes, we were, I say, in Verona
for no better, or lesser, reason than that having got
in there we had not the means to get out again.

We had the second floor of an old palace; such
a palace as you used to rent for a song in Italy, before Italy changed her proud "Farà da Sè," from a
boast and a dream to a heroism and a truth.

A palace with superb staircases reeking in filth;
courts which would have held a troop of men, armed
and mounted, given over to lizards and centipedes;
chambers with tapestries of Rosts, from the cartoons
of Bronzino, ancle deep in dust and dirt; and walls
that were due to the designs of Fra Giocondo, hung
with the padrona's ragged garments, drying in the sun
after their wash in the Adige.

"Peintures aux plafonds; ordures aux pieds." It
is Georges Sand, if I remember aright, who wrote that

bitter line, or something like it, upon Italy. It is terribly bitter, for it is at times terribly true.

Our palace was no exception to the rule.

It was magnificent as a dream, even still abovehead, where some wondrous-eyed woman, worthy almost of Leonardo himself, laughed down from her frescoes of roses, or where some apotheosis or cenacolo by Gentile, or Pisanello, still kept its radiant colours, despite all ravages of time, and neglect, and fire, and dust. It was magnificent too from that beauty of proportion, in which, as by some almost unerring instinct of symmetry, so many Italian buildings have a beauty that cannot perish whilst one stone is left upon another, even as in so many Italian faces there is a perfection which, being born not of hue but of outline, is unharmed by age, and endures even after death itself, as did that golden loveliness of Faustina that was found a century after death unharmed in the dusky depths of Santa Croce.

But it was also unutterably dreary, dirty, ghastly, dismal, comfortless; bats rustled through its passages, and downy owls haunted its roof timbers. The upper rooms were all tenanted by working people, or rather by people who affected to work, and in reality lived on the Austrian doles; and the lower halls were the abode of the padrona and her eight children. She was a stout-built, black-browed, comely soul; the most good-natured creature in existence; and her children lay in the sun, or played boccetta, or fought for the chesnuts on the stove, or did whatever seemed best to them all day long in an endless strife and riot.

The padrona was poor enough; she beat her own in the river, and baked, and swept, and cooked unaided, and added to her scanty means by stuffing mattresses with grass and wool, at which she was an adept. But it was owing to the padrona very often, and to nobody else, that Mariuccia had a meal to give her beloved little illustrissimi.

There were four of us; the others were boys; beautiful boys, who might have come out of a Tiziano or Giorgione canvas; gay, kindly, saucy, daring creatures, popular with the people everywhere, and caring nothing how their linen blouses were torn, quite content to sit and eat polenta for their only dinner with the woman below and her dirty children.

My poor brothers! They were so bright and so bold, so mirthful on nothing, so full of goodwill to all the world; and they all died so young; mere children. One of fever in Verona itself; another of a knife-thrust in a street scuffle in Rome; the last in a white squall off Cagliari, that swamped the little felucca within sight of land.

But at the time of which I now write, whilst they were all three around me, they were the pride and torment of Mariuccia's life, the delight of the padrona's, and the wonder of all the town, for the skill with which they—bambini inglesi—poured quips and cranks upon the people in true Veronese tongue and fashion.

The padrona would stand in her great arched doorway, with her arms akimbo, rocking to and fro with laughter at their encounters, whilst her onions frizzled neglected in her frying-pan. They were quite happy teasing the market-women, riding in the bullock waggons, driving the ball at pallone, fishing with the boatmen, dancing the tarantella in the wine shops, playing at dominoes with Pepe and Zoto and Giàn, and all the rest of the padrona's brood. It was only into my soul that the iron of our degradation entered.

With the male children in the market-place, they were still the young signori, whose shabby clothes could not lessen their distinction, so long as they threw the ruzzola unerringly, and had a lightning-like skill in morra: but for me it was otherwise; with the feminine aristocrats in embryo of the dancing-lessons I was only a little detestable forestiera, who had shabby shoes and a torn frock, and who had nevertheless the intolerable insolence not to be ugly in proportion to her poverty, and also to dance very much better than they did themselves.

"Look at the signorina, little ladies, all of you," the old dancing-master would say a dozen times in an hour, suspending the screams of his fiddle to point at me with its bow. "Look at her! only a month in this room, only half the age of most of you, and look at her! What grace, what accuracy, what lightness; the sweep of the swallow, the poise of the sea-gull! And such a baby! It is wonderful. Are you not ashamed to carry yourselves as you do, with such an example as the little Uccello's before you?"

Dear old Fortunato! He taught me, out of pure good will; having met me often in the street, and having at last succeeded in persuading Mariuccia that not to initiate a woman child into the ways and wiles of Terpsichore was to fly in the face of all the designs of Providence. He taught me from sheer love of his art, and some touch of love I think for me; but he did me an ill service with the little Lombard ladies by his praise.

They dared say nothing; for Fortunato could rap both feet and hands sharply enough with his bow, when he was irritated by contumacy or clumsiness; but they eyed me askance very evilly and munched their chocolate chicchi, grouped all together at the top of the room, muttering scornful things of me and mine in an offensive and defensive alliance.

Unhappily, there were few scornful things which could have been said of us that would not have been sufficiently true to hit us hardly. We were all of us handsome; in all times, they say, the race we came from had had the gift of the "fatal face;" but we had very little else.

It was the old, old story; I used to make Mariuccia tell it me as far as she knew it, over and over again, when she used to sit of an evening shelling beans on the great staircase, under a half ruined statue that they said was by Donatello.

I can see her now,—so plainly,—as she used to sit there, with a big round brass basin in her lap; she had a dark red skirt and a yellow kerchief; her costume never varied; she had a huge silver pin in her white hair; she had the noble frank face and the changeful kind eyes of her country people; she was weather-beaten till she was as brown as a chesnut, though she had the broad flap hat of the country spreading its roof over her head to keep her from the blaze that streamed through the vines that hung over the grated casements.

The sunbeams and shadows used to play on the old marble stairs and the old grey statue; a passion flower had somehow thrust itself through the stones from without and blossomed there at her feet on that chill bed; the brass bowl used to glitter like gold in the light; above at a vast height there was a lunette with frescoes of the labours of Hercules; from below there rose a smell of garlic, of fried meats, of coriander seeds, of stabled cattle; the crack, crack, crack of the beans used to sound on the silence regular as the ticking of a clock; the huge straw hat would shake itself slowly and sadly as she spoke:

"Do I remember your mother?" she would say. "You ask me that so often, 'Nella. Surely I remember her. I was with her at the birth of every one of you. I was an old woman then. At least as you children count age. She was beautiful, yes;—else your father had never looked at her. You are more like him. Oh, you are handsome enough; I do not deny that; you have a face like a flower, and you know it, though you are such a little thing. The people spoil you: they will turn your head with praise. You will end just like that wicked Speronella of Padua whom they sing about to this day in all Romagna. It was a name of horrid savour, of ill omen, for you; I always said so; but your poor mother would have it; it had been her mother's, she said. It is no use teasing me to tell you more; I have told you all I know a hundred times, and none of it is any good. When I first went to your mother she had not been long wedded; she was happy then; they always are,—for a week! There were difficulties; that I saw the first hour; but they did not press much. He had met her in Florence; she was an opera singer; he was a great signore, in his own country, so they said; it is always a mistake. He was double her years; but he was so handsome,—

Milordo Maurice. You only see the wreck of him. But you may see that still——"

"And I am like him!" I cried where I sat at the feet of the mutilated Donatello, shedding my quota of beans into the brazen bowl.

Mariuccia nodded.

"Yes, you are like him," she said gravely. "In more ways than one, signorina. When you get older, take care you do not throw your life away as he has thrown his. A noble in his own country; and I have to beg a meal for his children from the woman below!"

My father was not a nobleman, though Mariuccia, in the common continental incapacity to understand insular titles of courtesy, always called him so. He was only the fourth son of a northern marquis:—God help him!—but even so much as this I scarcely knew at that time.

Now I adored my father with very little reason for it, for I saw him perhaps six days in the year, and each time I saw him received about six careless words. But he was so handsome, so easy and good-humoured, so indifferent to every created thing or any possible fortune, that he seemed to me the very perfection of humanity.

I adored him, at a distance indeed, for it was chiefly when I was eating figs on the stairs or cracking walnuts in the court yard, that I ever saw him at all; but adore him I did, and with the inconsistent ingratitude of human nature, I cared more for a slight or a reproof from him whenever he deigned to notice me by one, than I did for all the untiring goodness of Mariuccia.

She, dear soul, was very wroth against him always, and could not forbear letting out her wrath to me.

Mariuccia did not think very much of filial duties; her own parents had been a travelling cobbler and his paramour, who had rid themselves of her in her baby-hood by the simple process of leaving her at the Innocenti; and she considered that she broke no moral canon when she inveighed against the shortcomings of her master to me on the old grey stairs. Indeed, I think she honestly believed she only did her duty in trying to turn me from my unreasonable worship of a false god; a god moreover who provided next to nothing, and left her to puzzle her brains as best she might how to find bread for three hungry, healthy boys, and how to turn my poor mother's costly faded wardrobe into decent attire for my use.

"He broke your mother's heart," she used to say with a sharp crack of a bean; and I used to feel a certain pang, yet also a certain incredulity. My mother was a mere vague name to me; I had not even a portrait of her. "What did he do?" I used to persist, and Mariuccia would respond in anger:

"What did he not do, rather? He did as he does now. He went and amused himself, and threw away the little he had in gambling, and left us for weeks and months to starve in some hole, whilst he feasted in gaming-towns and winter-cities, and spent such gold as he might win on creatures as bad and as useless as himself. Oh, it is no good your curling your lips and getting on fire like that, signorina. It is the truth, as you will know to your cost one day. Why do you ask me of your mother if you do not believe what I say! You are always angry that you are so poor; pray

3*

whose fault is it if not your father's, and how should
he be worth anything, I would be glad to know, when
not a soul of all his own people ever takes notice that
he lives, but every one of them leaves him alone as
men pass by a trodden fig, or a dead dog on the
causeway."

That used to silence me, for I knew it was true;
and I could only sit in mute rebellion shelling the
beans with a swelling heart, while the bright golden
lizards darted to and fro on the stairs, and the radiant sunset lights poured down from the frescoed
lunette.

Then Mariuccia, whose temper was as close a
mingling of sour and sweet as the core of a ripe
pomegranate, would relent, and would suspend her
bean-shelling to lay her hand on my head.

"Carina," she would say tenderly, "why will you
vex yourself about your father? Little one, he cares
as much for that lizard as for you. Do your duty by
him; that is proper, of course; but do not make a
god of him. Fret yourself for some good love, not
for a foolish one. It is all very well for the maple to
be choked for the vine's sake; but it is rubbish for
the maple to die for the nightshade."

Which hard saying she left for me and the lizard
to digest as best we might, whilst she went into the
cavernous gloomy little crypt which served her for a
kitchen to fry her beans in oil, or set them to stew
with a cabbage. That, or something like it, was our
daily meal; dainty little birds and tempting little pots
of chocolate went in for my father when he was there,
procured and prepared by Florio, who was a sort of
universal genius; but we children never tasted of such

fare. We thought ourselves in wondrous luck if we got a big dish of eggs and macaroni in the Pasquà Week, or could have a handful of sweet ciambelle or a lump or two of pan giallo for the Befana night.

As for envying my father his quails and thrushes and mullets, I should have thought it as blasphemous as Mariuccia would have thought it to envy the Madonnas in the churches their weight of jewelled garments and crowns of beaten gold.

At such times as Florio was with us, which was but seldom, I had more success in my endeavours to hear good of my idol.

Florio, in Italian fashion, had attached himself to us, and having once done so was not to be separated from us by anything that adversity could do to him. Once on the staircase I heard the padrona ask him how he could waste his years in service, so little lucrative, so often indeed, actually only repaying him by privation.

Florio shrugged his shoulders with the most expressive pantomime in the world.

"Eh! what would you?" he replied to her. "I have got to love them,—it is all said."

Florio would acquiesce in all my enthusiasm for his master, though he looked a little grave sometimes. But when I would fain have learned from him how my father spent those innumerable long absences of his, Florio would tell me nothing. He would pretend to laugh and show his white teeth.

"No, no, no," he would cry. "In good time the donzella will see for herself how men live; but she could not understand it yet;—no, no, no."

Once again also I overheard him say to Mariuccia,

"It is almost always such bad luck with him now; sometimes he has a good vein, and then we live like quails in the fattening coops; but it is very seldom now. They are all scared of him. At Nizza this very winter they warned him privately from the Masséna. And to be too bad for the Masséna——!"

Florio threw up his hands in the air with a gesture that concluded his sentence more eloquently than any speech.

Florio was about forty years old at that time; a little plump man, as round as a ball, with merry eyes, and the frank, tender smile of his nation.

He was a charming creature. There was very little he could not do. He could put on a white apron and cook to perfection; he could talk most languages, more or less correctly; he could draw inimitable caricatures; he did not disdain to wax a floor, and skim on it with brushes for skates; on occasion he has woven Machramme as well as any woman lacemaker along the Riviera; he could string a lute and sing on it in a very pretty tenor; and he would go to market with a big basket and bargain for butter and cheese with a terrible acuteness that was feared by the stoutest shrew that ever sat under a green or crimson umbrella on a sunny piazza, with her live hens screeching in her old mule's panniers.

As far as his principles went, looking back to that time, I should say he was absolutely innocent of even knowing the existence of such things.

He would lie with the sweetest smiling serenity in all the world, and he would cheat—in our service at least—with the most exquisite dexterity. Yet in other ways he was as frank as a babe, and if moved to pity he gave with both hands, withholding nothing from any thought of self interest. Yes,—Florio was a charming creature; the most perfect mixture of intense shrewdness and entire simplicity that I have ever met; and wholly and entirely devoted to a service in which his multifarious talents were utterly lost and almost utterly unrequited. And yet even Florio blamed my father!

It was a terrible perplexity to me. What evil could my father do?

Night after night I used wearily to wonder over the problem, lying awake on my truckle bed, in a vast room painted with the loves of Orpheus and Eurydice, while the bats beat against the lofty windows and the beautiful white moon sailed past them backed in clouds.

To the condemnations upon him I attached no idea of gambling, despite Mariuccia's invectives.

I saw everybody gamble; the children in the court below, the people in the streets and at the public lotteries, the men in the coffee houses and taverns, the boys in the market-places, the old beggars on the church steps: they all gambled, with cards, or dice, or balls, with nuts, or little cheeses, with dominoes on the pavement, with the gay painted cards at taroc, or by means of their fingers alone, at morra, if they had no other method available. That a pastime so universal in the broad daylight could be in any one criminal never occurred to me.

And having a strong and entirely reasonless adoration of my father, who fascinated me into love for him by his mere look and gesture, as he fascinated Florio into his service by a mere surface kindness and gracious trick of manner, I came to the conclusion as I watched the clouds and the moon, that my father was a man deeply wronged by his world and his relatives. It was very easy for me to solace myself thus, for I knew nothing of either one or the other.

He was called Milordo, and our name was Tempesta —as the Italians had it—that was all I knew: and I had mingled my ideas of him vaguely and oddly enough with that great Tempesta, who has left his sign on so many frescoes and canvases throughout Italy, and who fled to Isola Bella with his fatal love and all its crime upon his soul, and dwelt there between sea and sky.

Such small obstacles as centuries and probabilities were nothing to me, lying awake under the smile of Eurydice, and watching the bats in the moonlight beat their wings against the painted casements.

One winter in Verona he stayed longer than usual. He was not well in health Florio told us; and he had found some Austrians who amused him. He used to go out every evening and return at dawn; that I knew, for I could tell his step and listened for it. I do not think he rose all day; for Florio was perpetually in and out of his master's rooms, with some frothing cup of chocolate, some sparkling cool drink, or some dish of dainty flavours, compounded by his skill.

One evening I was upon the stairs as he came down them.

Our stairs were very dark. One little poor oil lamp burning under a hapless Madonna who had lost her nose and hands was all that illumined the immense depth of it from hall to dome. I had been to my lesson with Fortunato; it was cold; I was muffled in a little purple-velvet hooded cloak that Mariuccia had made me out of one of my mother's dresses; my cheeks were warm with the run home; I had in my hands a silver laurel-wreath—Fortunato's yearly prize —with which he had just presented me, for the fourth time, in all solemnity and honour.

In the deep shadows I saw my father descending the steps; involuntarily I paused; my heart gave a great bound; if he should notice the laurel-wreath, I thought?

By a miracle he stopped likewise.

"Is it you, 'Nella? Let me look at you."

He drew me up under the lantern which was hung a step or two above, and bent his eyes in studious scrutiny upon my face; I trembled from head to foot; I was a bold child enough, but I was afraid of him because I loved him, and because he was to me such a majestic mystery, unapproachable, and inscrutable.

He looked at me long; my hood had fallen back; my hair was blown about me by the wind; I felt my cheeks changing in colour every second under his gaze.

"Heavens! how like you look to your mother," he murmured. "And yet you are like us too;—how old are you?"

I told him that I was nearly ten years old—at least so Mariuccia said.

"I daresay, I daresay," he said, carelessly. "You have grown very much of late. You will be a beautiful woman, 'Nella. Do they tell you so?"

"Many people do," I murmured; my limbs shook under me; my face was scarlet; my heart beat like a wild bird's:—he had praised me!

He laughed a little, wearily.

"Already? Very well! Good-night, little one."

He slipped a little gold piece into my velvet mufflers, and, for the first time in my life, touched my lips lightly with his. As he went out of sight into the gloom below, I sat down on the filthy marble stair under the Madonna and her poor dull lamp, and burst into tears,—tears of passionate joy.

When Mariuccia found me, she found me sobbing bitterly, the laurel-wreath neglected on the stones.

CHAPTER IV.

With the Popolani.

THAT small gold piece I treasured ever afterwards; piercing it, and hanging it round my neck. I used to be often hungry in those days, but no temptation of coriander cakes, or anchovy pastries, of Neapolitan *confetti*, or Florentine *dolci*, ever allured my little precious five-franc from its hiding-place.

The next day Florio summoned Mariuccia into my father's room; he gave her a sum of money, and bade her get me with it such education as she best could in Verona. She had taught me to read; Fortunato had taught me to dance; Florio had taught me to sing ritornelli to a mandolin; but these were all my acquirements; at ten years old I was barbarously ignorant, and knew nothing, except such quaint old stray pieces of knowledge as I had gleaned from some odd volumes of Vasari and Ammirato, of Villani and Muratori, and the like, which I had found left by some former tenant in our chambers, and which made me conversant with some art-lore and with the heroical histories of

"Le donne, i cavalieri, le armi, gli armori,
  Le cortesie, le aydaci imprese"

of the by-gone centuries.

"It is the Tedeschi's money," grumbled Mariuccia, with her face dark, and full of reluctance. and of abhorrence.

Florio showed his white teeth.

"What is that to you?" he responded. "All your business is to spend it. That is enough."

Florio theoretically hated the Tedeschi as much as she did, but practically he thought the best use Tedeschi could be put to was that of spoliation.

"They are foreigners; they are hateful; they are our tyrants and our oppressors; and we will make them fly one day," he would say. "But while they are here, we may as well get what we can out of them. That is the true patriotism."

It was the true philosophy, at all events; and one that served its professor exceedingly well.

As for me, I could not understand how my father's money could be said to be the Austrians' also.

"It is not much, anyhow," I heard Mariuccia say, when she busied herself over her pots and pans while Florio plucked a Piedmontese partridge as plump as himself. "As I had the chance to see the signore, I spoke up the truth a little. When he had given his commands for 'Nella, I said to him, "And the boys, excellenza? What of them? They are growing tall, strong, dauntless lads, and they live with Pepe, and Zoto, and Giàn, and the children of the people; and they are as ignorant as so many young mountain bulls. Will vossignoria deign to say what is to be done about them?"

"He only laughed a little. 'They must do as they can,' he answered me. 'When they are old enough, your Tedeschi friends will give them rank in some regiment, I daresay; and there is very little learning wanted for that.' Did ever you hear such an answer, Florio? As if the blessed children would ever draw a sword against Italy? But he would not say anything better; he bade me begone in that gentle way of his which, as you know, there is no gainsaying. But was it not horrible?" she went on lifting the lid off her stewpan. "The noble lads! I am sure they would be cut in a thousand pieces before they would wear the white, and help to enslave Italy, who has been a foster-mother to them from the very days of their birth."

Florio smiled, as having plucked, he proceeded to truss his partridge.

"To be sure; to be sure. Of course we none of us would. Nevertheless, the Vienna beer tastes very light and good in the caffès, they say; especially when it costs nothing; and I have seen a good many of our people with their noses buried in the tankards."

Mariuccia poured her stew into a dish with a charitable wish that an "*accidente*" might strangle forever all Italians who so far forgot themselves as ever to drink the horrible barley brew of the accursed stranieri; it was to be as vile a traitor as Judas, she averred, when God himself had given the Italians the juice of the vine.

So it came to pass that I had such teaching as Verona could afford, whilst my brothers ran wild like young colts.

Mariuccia locked the sum my father had given her

away in a stout bronze coffer, and eked it out, with religious fidelity, as long and to as good purpose as she was able. Every atom of it she spent loyally, as she had been bidden; and shrewdly as became her Florentine citizenship.

She wanted many things direfully, for he and Florio went away with the first months of spring, and left her but a miserable pittance for all household purposes. But to take the smallest note from that money to procure rice, or wood, or onions, or flour, or oil for her daily needs, would have been a falseness to the trust of her stewardship which I am certain never even tempted in imagination that good, sturdy, honest soul of hers.

She laid it out to the last in the culture of my worthless little brain; if I did not profit by it as I might have done, it was no fault of hers. It was the fault of the saucy impatience of restraint, and the indolent love of basking in the sun, doing nothing, which the country and its habits had fostered in me. For I was decidedly a naughty child; I loved my own way and generally took it; and my sins of omission and commission were so many and various that with every Eve of Epiphany I listened in fear for the tinkling bell in the streets, and dreaded the bag of ashes and the long cane with which the black-faced Befana punishes the wilful.

Mariuccia went very wisely to work; she would have nothing to do with women teachers or schools; there were many old professors, old scholars, in the town whom she knew were terribly poor, and yet full of erudition, and not too grand to take something for imparting it. To these men she went, and so she secured me the means of getting a knowledge much more worth the having than the convent-culture which the children of my sex ordinarily obtain; that I profited too little by it was, as I say, no fault of my dear old nurse.

For the only teacher amongst them all to whom I really gave attention and obedience was my singing-master.

I adored music; it is impossible, I think, not to care for it, if you are reared in Italy. Everything seems to sing, from the cicale upwards. All that unwritten music of the populace whose scores no hands have ever penned, is exquisite; and every now and then in the streets, or from some high casement in the roof, you hear the notes of a divine voice, and you seek it out through filthy courts, up cut-throat stairways, into dark, dismal, foul-smelling chambers, and you find that it is only Pasqua the washerwoman singing at her tub, or Gillo the facchino amusing himself as he carries up the wood.

I had my mother's voice—so Mariuccia said. It seems that she had been of infinite promise as a singer when my father, desperately enamoured of her for the moment, bore her off from the stage in the second season of her public appearance, and the first of her performances at the Pergola. What my voice was to others, I do not know; I only know that all my life long song has been as natural to me as to any thrush or bullfinch.

The Veronese used to call me L'Uccello, the bird; and where there were so many uccelli, all more or less musically-throated, the name was in itself a distinction. Many and many a time, in Verona, when I have been out alone, I have found myself the centre of an eager little crowd, which followed me because I was singing aloud as I went; and to pacify them, I have vaulted on a parapet or a ledge, or anything that was convenient, and repeated the stornelli to an enthusiastic circle of blacksmiths, and horse-boys, and porters, and fruit-sellers, and beggars;—Mariuccia knowing nothing.

And then they would escort me homeward, humming the choruses of the songs themselves, delighting in me with that mingling of charming familiarity, and yet perfect respect, of which the Latin nations alone seem to know the secret; and saying nothing to me, that a little princess might not have heard, but waving their caps to me, and tendering me, by the hands of some old butcher, or some young ostler, a knot of china roses, or a plume of lilies and verbena, with the prettiest grace, and the sweetest smiles in all the world.

Ah! dear people, dear people! when I think of you, I repent me that I have said I hated your ugly town; for of a truth I loved you, and you me.

My music-master was an old man, by name Ambrogiò Rufi; he was most wretchedly poor; he lived in a little square den in the roof of a tumble-down house; he was very dirty, very shabby, very ugly; the world had never heard of him, and he got a bare living as first violinist at the theatre. In his youth he had created things that the world would never listen to; and he had become instead the interpreter of other men's creations.

He was inexorable as a master; but he was also admirable. His severity had an enthusiasm, and even a tenderness, underlying it which made it endurable. One knew that he was only harsh, because he would allow of nothing slight, or mean, or slurred, to be put forward in the guise of his art. Himself, he was a great master;—yes;—though he had never made a name, and had barely wherewithal to get a daily meal. I have seen the sums of a princely fortune, and the homage of a fastidious society, poured out upon artists who were not fit to hold a candle to my old master for him to read his score.

Circumstance is so odd and so cruel a thing. It is wholly apart from talent.

Genius will do so little for a man if he do not know how to seize or seduce opportunity. No doubt, in his youth, Ambrogiò had been shy, silent, out of his art timid, and in his person ungraceful and un-lovely. So the world had passed by him turning a deaf ear to his melodies, and he had let it pass, be-cause he had not that splendid audacity to grasp it per-force, and hold it until it blessed him, without which no genius will ever gain the benediction of the Angel of Fame.

Which is a fallen Angel, no doubt; but still, per-haps, the spirit most worth wrestling with after all; since wrestle we must in this world, if we do not care to lie down and form a pavement for other men's cars of triumph, as the Assyrians of old stretched themselves on their faces before the coming of the chariots of their kings.

Ambrogiò had a few pupils—not many. Most of them were young choristers of promise, whom he had sought on hearing them at some office in the S. Zanone; and whom he taught for pure devotion to his art, as Fortunato had taught me to dance. His method of instruction was wonderful, strict, and inexorable, as I have said, and giving infinite labour, infinite repetition to the scholar, but it was of an unapproachable excellence, and sifted the grain from the chaff amongst his aspirants with unerring accuracy.

There was—there is—an academy of music in the old city of Catullus, but such was the blindness of its direction, or such the rabid envy of its professors, that no effort was ever made to secure for it the inestimable value of Ambrogiò's lessons. Mariuccia's payments for myself were, I verily believe, almost all the remuneration that he ever received. All the rest were so poor; the children of coppersmiths, and coopers, and vine-dressers, and pottery-painters; boys and girls who had fair voices, and who sang in the choirs of the churches.

We used to stand in a semi-circle before him, a dozen children or so, and sing the scale simply hour by hour. You had to be far advanced before he would permit you to leave that first arduous exercise.

It used to be bitterly cold in winter in that little den of his, with its cold stove and its brick floor; and stiflingly hot in summer there amongst the red and grey roofs, the cupolas, and the towers. There was nothing picturesque or poetic in it; it was all hard work in a wretched little place before an ugly old man who flashed fury upon you through his spectacles if you dared to torture his ear with a false note. And yet we all went to him faithfully; and seldom or never rebelled.

There were in him the sincerity and the excellence which impress themselves upon children long before those children are old enough to reason on what they are awed by and admire. I tormented my other masters sadly enough: but I am thankful to think that I never added to the many pains and the infinite disappointments of Ambrogiò's life.

I was a favoured pupil with him—I and Raffael Baptista.

Raffaello was the son of a coppersmith in the town, who lived hard by the cathedral, in a quaint old vaulted place filled with coppers of all sorts and sizes, which used to blaze quite red in the sunset.

It was the workshop as well as the dwelling-house, and was full all day of the clash of hammers on metal as well as the discordant noises of the church bells and the people's cries.

Yet amidst all that clangour and uproar, the child had been born with the most subtle and perfect instinct for melody. One would have thought that all that clanging and clashing of copper and iron all the livelong day, from the time he had cried in his cradle, would have deadened his ears to all perceptions of harmony; but it seemed as though it had produced the contrary effect, for he detected an incorrect note, and shivered under it as quickly and as painfully as the Maestro himself.

Raffaelino as we called him, when I met him first at our music lessons, was just eight years old when I was ten; his mother came of a Venetian race, and he had the Venetian look and accent; he was a small, slender lad, with eyes full of dreams and a mouth full of smiles; his fair hair clustered thickly round his head; he had dark, straight brows and a curious half-shy vivacity of expression that changed twenty times

in an hour. He was the most picturesque figure in
all our little group, with his brown legs bare, and his
shirt loose about his throat, and a scarlet woollen sash
girt in Venice fashion round his loins.

It was not in song that the little Baptista excelled.
His voice was pure and true, but of no great compass.
It was for the violin that he showed the extraordinary
talent which won old Ambrogiò's heart to him, and
one day when he had played on his own little viol a
charming little *capriccio* full of life and grace, and I
asked him whence it came, he hung his head and
coloured, and confessed at last that it was of his own
invention.

He implored me not to tell the Maestro; he was
quite sure that Ambrogiò would look up with that
frown through his terrible spectacles which we all
dreaded, and bid him in tones of thunder go back to
his scale practice, and not tempt the wrath of dead
Cimarosa and Palestrina, and all the immortal brotherhood with such impious audacities. I thought differently; but Raffael had a right to his own secret, so I did
not betray him. Which was unfeminine I suppose;
but the only two women I had ever had aught to do
with had been the padrona and Mariuccia, both simple
people as the world went.

I liked Raffaello the best of all the children in
Verona; he had an infinite tenderness for his mother,
who was blind and whom he tended with untiring
patience; and he had a profound homage for myself,
—the *donzella* as he called me,—and would never
meet me without some spray of roses, some bough of
lemon, some knot of violets, or some cluster of ches-

4*

nuts, for which he had rifled the hedges or had begged some neighbour.

In my way I was very proud; Mariuccia continually reproached me for it; but I was not the least beset by that sort of pride, which would have made me regret Raffael Baptista's companionship, because his father was a coppersmith, and he ran about the streets without shoes. I had lived too much amongst the people; and I had too much of the bohemian in me for that.

Indeed I enjoyed vastly, when I left Ambrogiò's attic, drawing my little velvet hood over my curls and running home hand in hand with Raffaelino, past the dancing hall, at the hour when Fortunato's pupils, of whom I no longer needed to be one, were coming forth from his lessons.

The little feminine respectabilities,—my born foes, —glorious in starch and ribbons, and coral and silk stockings, would recognise me by a solemn stare and a general drawing together of themselves for mutual protection, and I would laugh in their faces and flash by them holding 'Ino's hand the tighter, and shaking the rose petals all over my little weather-stained purples, which like all purples fared ill when brought down into the streets.

Mariuccia never objected to my complaisance for Raffael. There was much of the old genuine, sturdy Florentine democrat in her. His mother, too, was a gossip of her own.

"It is a rare good lad," she used to say; and that he ran the streets with bare feet was no social sin in her eyes.

At such rare times as Mariuccia allowed herself a

spare hour from her incessant baking and washing, spinning and sewing, she used to cross the piazza to the coppersmith's workshop, under the sign of the Spiked Mace, and drink a cup of black coffee with the blind woman, not losing her time, but whilst she gossipped going on with her weaving of rough linen garments for us from the little distaff which in true old Tuscan fashion was seldom absent from her, being hung round the waist with its hank of flax in readiness for any unfilled moment of her rare leisure.

I used to go with her, and Raffaelino and I used to sit on the threshold and play dominoes on the bottom of some big copper turned downwards to serve us as a table; or at other times he would bring out from its corner his little old quattrocentiste viol, which he had found amongst some lumber, and we would play and sing stornelli whilst the white moonlight was flooding the pavement, and the marbles of the buildings turned to silver in its lustre: Mariuccia beating time with her spindle, and his blind mother nodding her head to the measures.

One of the young painters then in Verona made a little picture of Raffael and of me, playing and singing thus in the moonlight, with the background of the huge arched doors and the innumerable coppers with just the glimmer of a brass oil-lamp behind us where Mariuccia sat and span.

It was a pretty little bit of *genre;* he was delighted to sell it for twelve gulden notes to a German Jew dealer. I have seen it since in a great collector's galleries; and the holder of it told me he had given for it some fifteen thousand francs.

One of the saddest things perhaps in all the sad-

ness of this world is the frightful loss at which so
much of the best and strongest work of a man's life
has to be thrown away at the onset. If you desire a
name amongst men, you must buy the crown of it at
such a costly price!

True, the price will in the end be paid back to
you no doubt when you are worn out, and what you
do is as worthless as the rustling canes that blow together in autumn by dull river sides: then you scrawl
your signature across your soulless work, and it fetches
thrice its weight in gold.

But though you thus have your turn, and can
laugh at your will at the world that you fool, what
can that compensate you for all those dear dead
darlings; those bright first fruits, those precious earliest
nestlings of your genius, which had to be sold into
bondage for a broken crust, which have drifted away
from you never to be found again, which you know
well were a million fold better, fresher, stronger, higher,
better than anything you have begotten since then;
and yet in which none could be found to believe, only
because you had not won that magic spell which lies
in—being known?

I was great friends with all those youthful artists
who lived in nooks and corners all over the town,
and who got their living by copying or by counter-
feiting the old masters.

From the time that I had been old enough to
climb up their steep stairs unaided, they had made a
pet of me always, and often a model. I liked nothing
better than to be perched on a table in any one of
their big barns, arrayed in peacock's plumes, or old
laces, or ancient brocades, or any other of the pic-

turesque useless dusty lumber: and I think the dealers and buyers in the old town must have got very tired of my dark-eyed, golden fringed little face, which these students were wont to use for every allegory or childish subject that was ordered of them.

But painters, if one chance to please them at all, always see so many types in one's face, all more or less contradictory of each other, that one comes to the irresistible conclusion that it must after all only be typical of the poor human nature which makes us all akin,—when it does not set us all at strife.

They were very good to me all those poor lads; though they quarrelled often enough amongst themselves, and not seldom got into trouble for fierce wrangle with the invader. They all of them lived high up in the air, amongst the open rafters of the unceiled roofs; with wondrous lights streaming in through the vast bare garrets and magnificent views of limitless horizons, southward to the plains and northward to the mountains.

They used to be very good to me. They would dance with me unweariedly at the open air balls; they would take me to laugh my heart out over the dear delicious rheumatic burattini; they would play me all sorts of sweet little mad *canzoni*, rippling all over with a very phrenzy of mirth; and when I sat to them they would run out at noonday down six pairs of stairs into the street to fetch me a noonday meal of coffee, simmering in its brass pipkin, and little patties crisp in their white papers. I fear they must often have spent on me the only coins they had for their own dinners, for they lived on about three soldi a day, two of which would go for the theatre and the nightly smoke at their clubs.

To my coming and going with them, Mariuccia having once satisfied herself that they were honest lads, offered seldom any opposition. The Italians are not a people who think evil of every trifle, and Mariuccia had a good deal in her of the stanch, uncompromising republicanism of old Florence.

We amused ourselves; that seemed to Mariuccia the right and proper thing for childhood and youth; and moreover, as she used to say, with a laugh and a frown together, the "signorina is proud enough for six; how she queens it over them, the little imperious thing."

No doubt a nurse duly reared to a sense of her duties would have thought the judgment of heaven would have fallen on her had she allowed a little "illustrissima" of ten years old to clamber up into the roof of houses to sing stornelli amongst paints and pots, and cans and lumber, with a circle of bearded bohemians, or clamber down again in company with some stout-limbed peasant in gold ear-rings and scarlet kirtle, with a grand head like the Donatello Judith's, and a profession which was frankly and undesignedly that of a model.

But the songs had never a line in them for which I could have been the worse, and the model was a good gentle soul who had babies at home that she loved, and whose only care was to get broth and polenta enough for them. And dear old Mariuccia was too straight and simple a soul to be on the watch for evil; besides, as she sometimes mumbled to herself as she unlaced her bodice at night before coming to her small straw bed in my chamber, she thought it might be well if I should take to the people alto-gether, and be happy and marry amidst them in due time, for of a surety money there would be none for me, and my father's people made no sign.

But when I heard her breathe these wishes for me, she standing over me perhaps with her dull oil lamp and fancying me asleep, I used to laugh her to scorn in silence under the rough hempen sheet.

"Never, never, never!" I used to say in my heart.

Mariuccia used to close her soliloquies by kneeling down to a picture of the Mother of Many Sorrows, and praying to her for my future; but I, silent beneath the sheets, used impiously to think, "what use is it to be handsome if one cannot do for oneself without the Madonna?"

The Madonna was all very well no doubt, for these poor lean old folks who had not a friend in the world, or those pale foolish lovesick girls who could not keep their lovers, but could only kneel down and pray for them in the chapels; it was very well to have a Madonna, no doubt, when one was ugly or old, and when with one's life all was finished: but for me! —there was a little triangular mirror hung in the corner of my room to which I am afraid I said many more orisons than I ever offered to Mary.

I loved the people: who would not in Italy?—the dear, graceful, sunny-natured people, whose very selfish-ness is more engaging than other nations' virtues.

Where else but in Italy, when you give a franc for an armful of roses will the seller cast to you in free gift of pure good will his choicest magnolia flower?

Where else will the old porter to whom you offer

two sous for his trouble in hobbling up and down the stairs for you, limp off to his snuggery and bring you thence a bough from his lemon tree with a courtesy and a smile that courtiers might envy?

Where else will the facchino who has toiled after you on a summer's day with a heavy load, put his hands behind his back and shake his curly head, and steadily refuse reward, crying:—

"No, no, no! it is pleasure enough just to see the signora!"

Where else, if you pause at a little music shop in a bye street, will the master of the shop come out and hum you the songs that you seek harmoniously in a mezza-voce, whilst your coachman turns round to correct a change to the minor, and the baker-boy pauses to join in the refrain, and a girl, mending her shoe at a window, chaunts her share in the measure, and every mortal leaves off his or her occupation to loiter out and join the chorus with sweet singing rhythm, till the whole narrow street is filled with the melody?

Where else, indeed?

True, if you fail to buy roses next day, the seller may petulantly wish you an accidente. True, the porter next week may keep you languishing for your letters while he gossips over your affairs in the street, and allots you more lovers than there are days in the year. True, the facchino may expect you to nod and smile and be *buon amico* with him all the rest of your life. True, the music-seller may feel not the smallest scruple in giving you imperfect copies at six times their due value.

But all the same how genuine were the grace and

the courtesy and the vivacity and the kindliness! how genuine they will be again a million times over! how they smooth and illumine the rough and dark pathways of life! how easy they render the cordial intercourse between far-sundered classes! how pleasantly they make melody amidst our rude human nature, like the singing flower-sown brooks amidst the hillside stones!

"Italians cheat one as much as other nations do," said a shrewd Frenchman to me, the other day. "Oh, yes, no doubt; some say they cheat one a little more. But then they alone know how to do it amiably; they alone save one's self-respect."

Such was his verdict (a very superficial one, for, except Stendahl, where is the Frenchman who ever could understand the Italian?); but myself I would go farther than he did.

I would much sooner say, and surely more justly, that the Italian, to the fine subtleties of civilisation and the keen astuteness of his natural intelligence, unites a rare simplicity and a joyous frankness which he alone of all people has retained amidst the artifice of modern life.

No, I loved the people; I had enough soul in me for that; but all the same, even in my happiest hours, I never dreamed for an instant, as Mariuccia dreamed for me, of being content to dwell amidst them for ever.

And happy hours I had; though my brothers and I sat at night reading Vasari, or old Pulci, or the Chronicles of Compagni, or Ferreto, or the wonderful stories of Croce, that Bolognese "Homer of Children," by the light of one poor little miserable lamp; and though in the winter sometimes we had barely charcoal enough to heat the small brown jars, and though even on most summer days we had little else to eat than a roll of bread and a broth of herbs, a few ripe figs from the old tree in the court, or a slice of the padrona's polenta.

CHAPTER V.
The Peacock's Plumes.

WE were happiest when we were alone with Mariuccia.

We were children, and strong and well, and there was the bright, broad, living sunlight about us, and all things were possible for us in the future. But when my father came and Florio it was different. We did not reason on it, but we were vaguely affected by their presence, vaguely depressed by it. Some breath from a world we knew nothing of blew in on us, and chilled us in our bare old home in the mellow Lombardic heats.

"Oh, Dio mio! but it is terrible!" Florio would say, lifting his hands as he peered into the faggotless cupboard, the empty stewpans, the ill-furnished bread pot, and then we became sensible of the privations which we had scarcely perceived before, and alive to that vital truth of the old Condottieri, that "*Senza soldi non possono fare.*"

"It is terrible," Florio would say, cooking a couple of little larks and some toadstools out of the woods in such magical fashion that they would have deceived any epicure in the country into belief in them as ortolans and mushrooms. "It gets worse, you see, every year; of course it gets worse. He wins less often; and he takes more brandy when he loses. It is always the way. It is a puzzle to live at all, and half the cities are shut to us. Debt—debt—debt. It slaps the gates in our faces. There is hardly anywhere that they will trust him now. It will end in that,—some day,—and soon."

With "that" he gave a gesture as though he drew a knife across his bare throat. Mariuccia shook her head.

"End in that? End?" she echoed. "And, say you, Florio, what pray will then begin for them? For the dear little ones? It is very well to say 'end,' as if he were the only one concerned in the matter. Four of them: and not a farthing except the few notes he leaves with me when he comes and goes, which the Holy Mother knows would be hardly enough to feed up a goose for San Giovanni's day, let alone feeding four big hungry children from one Lent on to another."

Such discourse as this we used to hear between them in stray fragments; and they left on us a subtle, indistinct sense of some impending evil; and even I, despite the innumerable illusions and indestructible faiths in which the name of my father was involved for me, grew by degrees dimly sensible that he only returned to us at such times and seasons as it had become impossible for him to live elsewhere.

The old barren dusky palace was the cheapest roof that we could have found all the world over to cover our heads, and when he came thither for a temporary refuge, the fidelity of his two servants still contrived to sustain around him some show of ceremonial and some sense of comfort. How they did it I cannot tell, nor even at this day can I imagine; but do it they did; with surpassing patience and with unwavering self-sacrifice.

An Italian can subsist on almost as little as an Arab; and if he only offer you but a couple of dates he can serve them on a majolica plate with a few lentiscus leaves and a little myrtle in such fashion that they will lack nothing in grace of service that any king could desire at his banquet.

Such a man as my father was could not be anywhere wholly without companions.

The native nobility and gentry never came nigh him; but the Austrians used to flash their white uniforms on our dark staircase many and many a night. They used to pass within the doors of his room and remain till daylight; and all night long Florio used to be gliding to and fro with glass jars of chartreuse, or fresh flasks of brandy.

They were my old Tedesco acquaintances who had waltzed me round a hundred times to the swell of their military bands; but as I grew older my father sternly bade Mariuccia take heed that I was never about upon the stairs at evening, and she kept me imprisoned by her side under the lamp, weaving the lace, which I hated, or studying the scores of Ambrogiò Rufi, which I loved.

Other of my pleasures came to an end too about this time.

It was a lovely spring in Lombardy, mild even as though amidst the Sorrentine orange woods.

Everywhere the meadows were white and hyacinthine-hued with a million crocuses. The violets followed them in countless hordes amongst the grass tufts underneath the vines. The maple and mulberry trees were pushing forth their tender leaflets, and in the dark old city there were soft blushes of colour where the yellow daffodils and the home-reared carnations blossomed in the casements and the balconies.

And away to the northward was the silvery cloud of the Alps, and the students would go outward thither and come back with the fresh winds blowing in their hair, and with their hands full of blue gentian flowers.

In the spring, even, our level plain of the Adige, which had not the beauty either of the mountain or the valley, had a certain charm of its own under the budding vine boughs and amongst the delicate acacias; I used to be in the fields all the day long, with my brothers and Raffaelino, playing till we were tired, and then, lying down to rest, watching the blue sea, of those immeasurable distances beyond which lay the world.

One day when I had filled my arms with masses of wood violets, I clambered up the stairs to the bottega of one of the students. He was very fond of flowers, and introduced them in all his sketches, and I was accustomed to take him a share of my field-spoils. He was a swarthy, large-limbed, tender-hearted creature; a son of peasants of an Aquillian village, whom we always called Cecco.

One day, when I was about twelve years old, I went my round as usual amongst my friends the painters. It was a fine bright day in February; I had been out in the woods by daybreak with my brothers and the padrona's boys gathering violets; the great odorous purple violets that, like so many other flowers, smell surely sweeter in Italy than ever they do else-where.

We came home by noon laden with them; the padrona's lads went out to stand with their share of the forest plunder at the corners of the streets, and see if they could get a penny to play with at boccette; I filled Mariuccia's pots and jugs with some of mine, and took the rest to my friend Cecco, who loved flowers, as I say, and so often introduced them in his pictures that the students nicknamed him Il Squarcionino, or the Little Squarcione, from that old Padovan who was the first of the Early Masters to paint flowers and fruits in arabesque.

He lived at the top of a lofty old house in a gloomy bye-street.

I climbed the hundred and odd stairs with labour, for they were rotten, twisting, and slippery from over much dirt; and, with my arms full of violets, purple and white, darted into his painting room, that was as bare as a barn, and not half as cleanly.

With Cecco there were three or four other lads, smoking and laughing, and talking as they worked. He had an admirable light in his great, ugly work-room; and those comrades of his who were not so fortunate in that respect were wont to set up their easels beside his, and labour together all in their various manners.

They welcomed me with enthusiasm, went on their knees to me and my violets, and abandoned their work that they might sketch me.

"Just as you are, signorina!" they called to me. "No! do not touch a thing; it is perfect. Look at her now, with the light on all that ruffled hair, and the little gay skirt full of the violets, and the colour all hot in her face from the wind: ah, bellina, bellina!"

So they cried around me in twenty different forms of admiration—the artists' admiration, which is so curiously compounded of fancy and of fact, and which they were accustomed to pour out on me as unthinkingly as though I had been a porcelain figure.

I was so accustomed to it, that it hardly hurt me more than it would have done the china; I knew Nature had made me good to look upon and picturesque. Altro! I used to shrug my shoulders and think no more about it except to give a passing pity to the unfortunate ones who were not similarly gifted.

So that day they hoisted me up upon the wooden dais where their models were accustomed to stand, and, with their four easels in the four corners of the room, set to work to paint me as I was, with my load of violets, and my hair all blown from the rough mountain breezes.

In a couple of hours they had all contented themselves more or less thoroughly with a first sketch, and simultaneously laid down their brushes.

"I have made her the Genius of Spring," said Bernardino Scalchi, surveying his workmanship with his head on one side, like a robin's.

"And I have made her 'La Primavera della Vita, La Gioventù dell' Anno,'" said Beppo Lavo, who wrote very pretty verses, and could sing them, too, not ill.

"And I have made her the Renaissance of Italy; the type of the Dawn of Freedom, the Symbol of the

Future," said Neri Castagno, who was a patriot and a red republican.

Old, swart, clumsy Cecco laughed a little as he turned round to them:

"I am very prosaic after you. I have only made her what she is—a child."

And yet, when all the sketches stood side by side, in the dying light of the late afternoon, it was Cecco's, they frankly admitted, which had the true poetry in it, after all.

A child with a skirt full of violets, with a rough wintry sky behind her, with a fresh wind tossing her hair, and with her feet gaily flying over the wet earth already green with the coming of spring: that was all that Cecco had made of it; but beside his picture the others looked false in sentiment, strained in fancy, and garish in grandiloquence.

Their work over, they made me jump from my throne; they thrust the violets in a bowl of water; they insisted that I should stay and have a little feast with them. Cecco had been in luck that day; a small panel of his, a girl's face in a garland of roses, had sold for the enormous sum of twenty florins; he was a millionaire, at least, for a day, in his own estimation.

He ran downstairs into the street, and in a few minutes came back in gay triumph with a couple of flasks of chiante, with a pan of steaming chesnuts, with a round sweet-almond cake, and a big bundle of cigars.

Then he thrust me in an old oak chair draped with dusky tapestries; he cast over me a magnificent old brocaded robe that the Jews would have bought of him to cast in the fire for its gold to melt out of the threads, but which he would never part with, because it had belonged to his father, who had been an artist before him; he gave me a sceptre of peacock's plumes, and a diadem of silvered paper with which models were crowned when they had to sit for Madonnas; and then our feast began.

How we enjoyed ourselves! how we chattered! how we laughed! how rich the wine tasted! how crisp were the chesnuts! how we shouted the "Fuori gli stranieri!" how we sang every song that occurred to us, from motives of Rossini's and Bellini's to the last chorus of the newest street song!

We were merry at heart, and full of zest, in the deepening twilight and the clouds of smoke, while a ruddy light from the setting sun glanced on the swarthy face and kindling eyes of Cecco, and lit up the peacock's plumes of my thyrsus and the gold stitches in the brocade: so merry, indeed, and so full of zest, that we never heard the door unclose or perceived that anyone besides ourselves had entered the painting-room.

Only at the sound of a strange voice did Cecco tumble hurriedly up from the floor where he was stretched, and, with eager apologies and bewildered haste, strike light to a lamp and welcome three strangers, who, going the round of the ateliers, had come in its turn to his.

I, seated on my brocaded throne, with my Madonna's crown on my tumbled hair, and my pewter plate of chesnuts on my lap, paused in my singing, and looked up; two of the strangers were Austrians, the third was my father.

5 *

Trembling, I slid down and stood like a little culprit, with the folds of the brocade curled like many-coloured serpents round my feet: it was not that I had any sense of doing what was wrong, it was only that he was to me a mystery so full of awe, and wonder, and attraction, that to see him suddenly there appalled me.

It was the first time in my life that I had ever met him in Verona out of our own old home.

His eyes glanced across me and he knew me in a moment; that I saw; but he gave me no recognition.

As chance would, however, have it, one of the Austriaci looked at me by the flickering lights of the lamp and the sunset.

"A charming little figure!" he cried. "Fantastic but very charming. A model, of course, in all that tinsel and brocade."

Dumb and perplexed, and glancing at my father in a vague terror, I stood still, with the silver crown upon my curls, and wished to sink into the depths of the old brocades; but he, hearing his friend speak, came forward and looked at me coldly.

"A pretty little beggar," he said, with a cold, swift glance of his eyes. I knew his meaning in a moment: he chose to affect to avoid all recognition of me.

My face burned, my heart rose, my fear of him was forgotten. I threw off my silver diadem and the old robes, and stood up straight before him, the poor neglected peacock sceptre trailing on the bricks.

"If I be a beggar, it is not my fault, nor yet Mariuccia's," I said, boldly, with a scorn for him that thrilled me with a horrible sense of guilt and of humiliation. "We are very hungry and very cold—all of us—very often. They do not dare to tell you. But it is true. And if I can forget it a little while laughing here, where is the harm? I am not ashamed."

My father's face, haggard and cold though it was, flushed deeply, whether with anger or any more tender sense of shame, I cannot tell. He thrust me from the room.

"Whatever else you be, you are too young to rant so glibly," he said, as he closed the door upon me.

I ran down the street to fling my woes at Mariuccia's feet, and sobbed as I ran, the poor bedraggled peacock's plumes still trailing from my hand, and gathering in their course the dust and ordure of the uneven and uncleanly stones.

I fled along under the darkling shadows of the grim fortresses which overhung the pavement, burning all over with a sense of outrage and of indignant scorn.

My father was not ashamed to starve me, but he was ashamed to acknowledge me because I sat and laughed and sang, and was glad in a garret, in a paper diadem, over a horn of cheap wine, and a handful of chesnuts, and a bowl of wood-violets.

I had a passion of scorn for such shame: and yet the weight of it was heavy on my child's heart, for I had a vague, shapeless, unreasoned-on sense of foreboding that, as my father had judged, so would the world judge likewise.

Mariuccia comforted me in her tender, homely fashion, and washed clean the peacock's plumes, and set them up over the stove with a palm-sheaf blessed for good luck in Holy Week.

But at evening-time she told me sadly that my father had forbidden her to allow me ever again to visit any of the students.

The loss of that cheery, good-natured, chivalrous, riotous companionship of theirs cost me many and many an hour of rebellious tears, and from that moment I ceased to be loyal to my father.

I would look at the peacock sceptre again and again, and think to myself—

"If you had been of gold and ivory, he would have praised you."

And I loved my feather-thyrsus all the more tenderly for other's neglect of it; and for my father a settled scorn fired itself in me, and killed love.

CHAPTER VI.
Mater Dolorosa.

So things went on, until I reached my fifteenth year. I was tall, but I was still,—for I had the open-air life which develops the limb and strengthens the body,—I was still in my ways and my tastes quite a child.

Raffaelino grew apace, too, and his people talked of his entering the priesthood; they did not know what to do with him; he had no taste for any hand trade; he was for ever haunting the churches; and to his mother, who was a religious soul, there seemed no life more beautiful or blessed than life amidst the silent marble cloisters, and the perpetual calm of Certosa or Camaldoli.

One of my brothers long before had died of fever in one of the hot, nauseous, pestilential summers of

.

the uncleanly town; another had gone of his own will off with a Genoese sea-captain, whom he had met by chance, and who had dazzled him with stories of the sea, and he had been drowned on his first voyage; a third had kissed us, and clung round Mariuccia's neck, and confessed, shamefacedly, that his heart was breaking with monotony and inaction, and so had also gone his way to see the outer world with some other young students, as poor and hopeful as himself, who talked of immortality and starved upon a dream; and of him, also, we had heard that autumn that a knife-thrust in a students' scuffle had ended his short life just as it had opened into manhood.

She and I were left alone in the old home.

We closed the great rooms, and lived through a dreary winter in one little chamber abutting on her kitchen, and looking down into the stone court where the fountain that year was frozen, and the cold killed even the hardy bitter-orange-trees.

We had not heard of my father since the previous Easter-term.

Twice or thrice, Mariuccia had gone to the little dark den on the piazza, where the letter-writer of the poor people sat, ready to indite an amorous effusion or a summons for rent, a proposal of marriage or a butcher's bill, according to his clients' requirements; and thence she sent a letter each time to Florio or to her master.

I suppose she did not care for me to know of it, since she did not avail herself of my aid to pen them. Twice or thrice, in answer, Florio sent a little money, as from my father; but I have had many doubts since that Florio had contrived to gain it by some one of his innumerable talents, and robbed himself for our sakes. From my father, directly, we received no word.

The winter was terribly dull.

Mariuccia was getting very old, and wept sadly and often for the loss of her boys.

They had been as the very apple of her eye; she had toiled for them from the very days of their births; she had spent many a sleepless night and weary day beside their sick-beds in their wayward infancy; she had gone without her morsel of meat many a time to feed better with it the young lion cubs she loved; and now—one was dead, and the other two had thrown their arms about her neck, and laughed, and talked of the future, and gone gaily away, thinking only of the worlds they had never seen, and of the dreams they were sure would come true.

That was all her reward: it was hard.

I saw those firm-shut lips of hers quiver often as she sat and spun by the dull lamplight; and I heard her many a night murmur on her knees to the Mater Dolorosa, "Do not forget them, thou Blessed One. They will forget thee—children will—but mothers are not angered for that."

"What has made you stay with us, Mariuccia?" I asked her once, smitten suddenly with some remorseful consciousness of the enormous debt we owed to her. "Why have you stayed with us? It has been a hard life always; and we have been only a trouble to you and no reward?"

She looked at me with a steady look that had a certain pathetic sadness in it.

"One must love something," she said, simply.

I pondered darkly on the saying.

CHAPTER VII.
A Twilight Tale.

THE winter was very dull. My father's forbiddance had taken from me many of my old pleasures; and the failure of funds had arrested all continuance of my education. There was only Ambrogiò Rufi to whom I still went, and in whose attic I was solaced by the strains of Cherubini and the melodies of Gluck.

It was bitterly cold there.

The snow was thick on the roof, and the wind from the mountains poured through and through the unprotected place. The old man could afford no such luxury as a stove; and the bare brick floor was like ice to the feet. I used to shiver as I sang.

And yet when I think of the sweet sigh of the violin melodies through the white winter silence; of Raffaelino's eager, dreamy eyes, misty with the student's unutterable sadness and delight; of old Ambrogiò, with his semicircle of children round him, lifting their fresh voices at his word; of the little robin that came every day upon the water-pipe, and listened, and trilled in harmony, and ate joyfully the crumbs which the old maestro daily spared to it from his scanty meal—when I think of those hours, it seems to me that they must have been happiness too.

"Could we but know when we are happy!" sighs some poet. As well might he write "Could we but set the dewdrop with our diamonds! could we but stay the rainbow in our skies!"

During this sad time of privation, I saw a little way into the closed past of my old music-master.

Verona perceived nothing in him but a meagre old man, who took his toilsome way noon and night to the theatre; who chaffered in the market for a pinch of charcoal and a bit of goat's-milk cheese; who wore his clothes so long that they fairly dropped asunder; and who made their boys and girls cry bitterly at many a sharp word and blow of his fiddle-bow when they sung not to his liking.

But I had always felt or fancied—fancy is so much feeling with every child—that there was something sadder, wiser, nobler in Ambrogiò than the townsfolk credited.

Perhaps he liked me better than he did the others, or he liked my voice better; all human creatures were only counted as so many voices by him; at any rate he now and then let fall, in my hearing only, brief sentences which seemed to me born of a mind higher than most of those with which I came in daily contact.

Mariuccia would not listen to any idea of the kind. She was a little jealous of my regard for him.

"Those music-mad people," she would say, "are just like that big sea-shell the dear lads brought me from Genoa. The sea-shell sings all day long if you put it to your ear. Why does it sing? Just because it is empty. Just because the heart that used to beat in it is dead and gone. It is just so with them. They are all melody because everything else born in them is withered up—che-e-e!"

One night, as it grew dark, I ventured, contrary to usage, to go and see my old maestro.

I was dissatisfied with my tiresome fate; I was ill at ease and impatient; I wanted I knew not very well what.

I climbed up his dark staircase, and found him in his chamber.

It was a night when there was no performance at the theatre of which he was one of the orchestra. He sat alone in the cheerless, fireless attic scanning some old scores by the light of a miserable little oil lamp.

He looked up as I entered; I think that he was always glad to see me, though he said nothing in welcome at any time.

"It is late for you to be out," was all his greeting.

I told him the Ave Maria had only just then rung; and asked him to explain again some obscure instruction in counterpoint which had been hard for me at his last lesson.

He went through and through the passage lucidly with me; he was always willing to smooth difficulties to a patient student, and in music I had patience, though in nothing else.

When the point was so clear to me that I had no longer excuse to linger over it, I still loitered by him, sitting there at the old bare table, leaning my elbows on it, and my face on my hands, and gazing at the red, dull wick of the ill-fed lamp.

"Talk to me a little, maestro!" I said, suddenly.

Ambrogiò took off his spectacles slowly, and gazed at me in stupefaction.

"Talk!" he echoed: it never happened to him to be asked for words; such things as he had it in him to say he said through the strings of his violin.

"Yes! Talk," I repeated, with the insistance of a spoilt child, — for poor Mariuccia had spoiled me sadly, despite all her warnings. "You must have seen the world sometime. Tell me a little about it."

"The world!"

He said the words with a startled, heavy breath. He looked like one who hears the long, unuttered name of some dead thing.

"Yes. The world," I said again. "What is it like?"

"Go in a convent, and never know," he answered, with a bitter brevity.

"Is it so bad, then?"

He looked at me across the deal table in the dull, yellow lamplight; a dreary, grey, shrunken figure, very old, very poor, very hopeless, with his great hollow eyes burning bright with the fires of awakening memories.

"Bad? Good? Pshaw! Those are phrases. No one uses them but fools. You have seen the monkeys' cage in the beast-garden here. That is the world. It is not strength, or merit, or talent, or reason that is of any use there; it is just which monkey has the skill to squeeze to the front and jabber through the bars, and make his teeth meet in his neighbours' tails till they shriek and leave him free passage—it is that monkey which gets all the cakes and the nuts of the folk on a feast-day. The monkey is not bad; it is only a little quicker and more cunning than the rest; that is all."

I sat silent; it seemed to me but a dreary prospect, this monkeys' cage which I should be doomed to enter when once I should be across the mountains.

"Tell me a little more," I urged to him. "You must have seen so much when you were young."

"No," he answered me. "I never saw very much. The man who is poor can only look out of a garret window. He sees the skies, and the sun, and the moon, and the changes of the clouds, better than anyone else; but it is all he does see."

"But he can walk abroad?"

"Can he? Shoeleather costs money; and though bare feet might safely tread the sands of deserts in the days of saints, they go but ill upon the flints of the king's highways—now."

This I felt was true; indeed I knew it by many a painful moment when my little worn-out shoes had click-clacked sorrowfully over the scorching stones of Verona in midsummer.

I grew cold with a sort of sickly fear of this new world into which a second earlier I had been all eagerness to plunge.

"But you must have seen so much to what I have seen," I urged, after a pause, again with a child's persistency. "Do tell me something—some story I mean—of your old life?"

His eyes were full of pain beneath his shaggy brows as they met mine across the dim light.

"Child, you should never open dead men's graves," he said, drearily, with a sort of shudder. "I tell you

I was always poor. It is a kind of blindness—poverty. We can only grope through life when we are poor, hitting and maiming ourselves against every angle."

"But you had genius?——"

He shrugged his shoulders in a pathetic, hopeless gesture of resignation that went to my heart through all my thoughtless selfishness.

"I have been most unhappy," he answered simply. "Yes; you are right."

I felt that I knew his meaning, vaguely though his words shadowed it.

"And how then," I said under my breath, "how then—not great?"

He smiled a little, very wearily.

"How? Well, I loved Art, and not the world, and, in my way, was honest. Time was, when I was young, that I dreamed a little of being, as you call it, great. At twenty-five, I was—yes, even I—was happy.

"I was poor indeed; in winter I had to keep my bed lest I should die of cold, and in summer I was glad to dispute the acorns with the swine. But I was happy. I had my Art, and I had a friend closer than a brother.

"He was a German, Karl Rothwald; together we studied music at Milano. He had no strong talent, only a graceful taste. I—well, I had genius, God help me, and of the most arduous study I was never tired.

"At twenty-five I trusted myself to commence my first great work—an opera upon the theme of Alkestis. I was two years engaged upon it. They were the two happy years of my life.

"Rothwald and I dwelt in the same chambers together; we walked abroad in the daybreak and the evening times, and we sat up late into the nights, I all the while dreaming of Alkestis, and giving shape to the creations that haunted me, and calling on his sympathy and joy each time when my composition was good on my own ear and satisfied my own desire. He never was fatigued, nor ever failed to rejoice with me.

"Often and often as we went through the millet-fields at sunrise, or sat in our garret through the long moonless nights, and the power of song that was in me broke forth and arose triumphant, and filled me with its own exultant strength, he—my friend—would laugh and weep in his boyish fashion and fling his arms about my shoulders and cry out how beautiful and strong my music was, and prophesy I should rank with Bach and Gluck and Palestrina.

"Those two years I was quite happy,—quite,—though I was but a starving scholar, and had often to go without bread to be able to buy paper for my scores.

"All the world was full of hope and of beauty to me; everywhere I heard delicious melodies in leaves, and waters, and bells, and winds, and all the things that moved, and my friend was with me,—close as a brother,—dear almost as a mistress. I wanted nothing more, and was sure of fame.

"My opera was barely finished when Rothwald was summoned from my side; some illness in his northern home, he said.

"I begged him to return swiftly; I pledged my word to him not to submit my opera to the direction of La Scala until he should return. 'My triumph would be robbed of half its joy if thou wert not with me to rejoice in it;' so I spoke to him as we bade each other our farewell. It was then autumn.

"The delay was sad for me, for I had hoped to have seen the Alkestis produced that winter; but I never thought of putting it forward in his absence. I loved him only second to my work; and I had pledged him my word that he should be present whenever it should be given to the public.

"The first months of winter are bitter in Milano; they were very cheerless and desolate to me; but I had many tender letters from him to keep warm my heart, and I occupied myself fondly in touching and refining the creation on which all my future hung.

"No one had ever heard a chord of it, except himself, but I had not much fear that it would not be accepted. At the great Scala, they knew me; and the conductor of orchestra, who was powerful with the direction, had a liking for me, because of my execution upon the violin.

"Rothwald had been gone four months; there were snow and ice in Milan; one day I sat shivering in my garret, yet with my heart warm still, because so much hope abode in it. The chief of orchestra paid me a visit; he was, as I say, good to me; I could not have maintained my life at all without the place he gave me amongst his musicians.

"He spoke to me of myself this day. 'Ambrogiò,' he said, 'it seems to me that you have too much genius to sit behind my bâton all your life. I hear that you have attempted original composition. Is it true? Then let me see your score. It should be something great. You are a master of counterpoint.' He argued with me so kindly and so long, that in the end he prevailed, and I drew out my Alkestis, and bade him judge of it.

"'Alkestis? Alkestis?' he murmured, as he heard the name. 'Is that your theme? It is unfortunate. There is a new opera this very week produced in Vienna on that same old story.'

"I was pained to hear that I had been forestalled; I asked him by whom it was composed.

"'Nay, that I forget, and am not sure if I have heard,' he answered me. 'But, anyway, you had best go thither and judge of it for yourself. If it be poor and fail, you can still produce yours; but if a triumph, as I am told, we must needs fit your music to some other narrative. Ah! I know how you love your first thought—your first poem,—but still we might manage to alter the libretto without much injury. Well, go you to Vienna—nay, nay, do not be so proud. Take my gold for the journey, and we will leave the matter as a debt to be paid me when La Scala first brings out your opera. Nay, do not argue. Go. You must, of necessity, judge your rival for yourself.'

"So I took his gold and went through the bleak white winter over the mountains at peril of my life.

"It was night when I reached Vienna.

"The gay city was all ablaze with light. I had travelled far and fast; I was exhausted. Nevertheless, before I changed my clothes, or broke my fast, I made my way to the opera-house. There they played Alkestis.

"I paid my entrance-money, and went into the heat and glare and stood and listened. The house was shaking with thunders of applause. When the clamour ceased, the music rose again—it was my own.

"Phrase after phrase, chorus on chorus, solo and septuor, and recitative, I heard them all like one made stupid by a blow. They were all mine.

"The curtain fell; the rapture of the people cried aloud, 'Rothwald!' 'Rothwald!' 'Rothwald!'

"Then I understood;

"I fell like a stone; so they say; they took me up as dead.

"He had stolen it all—all—all: stored up in his notes and his copied score.

"It made him a great name. You may hear of him now in the world. He has done nothing great since; the world wonders; but it is possible to stretch one triumph over a lifetime so that it covers every after failure. To make a name is hard; but once made, to live on it is easy.

"As for me—I say—I was dead. My heart, my brain, my genius were all killed. It is only my body that has dragged on life ever since.

"I never denounced him—no. For I had loved him. And if I had denounced him, where had been my proof? None would have been found to believe."

As the last words died on his lips, his head sunk on his chest; a film overspread the weariness of his hollow eyes; the silence of the innumerable years that he had passed, mute and alone, amidst his kind, stole afresh over him.

In vain I knelt before him; in vain I caressed his withered hands; in vain I spoke to him, begging his forgiveness for my thoughtless cruelty which had thus torn open rudely this deadly wound so long concealed from every human glance.

In vain: he answered nothing; he heard nothing; his dulled eyes only gazed at the gleam of the lamp; his hands only moved vaguely as though straying over the chords of some half-remembered music; his lips only muttered now and then under their breath:

"He betrayed me; yes; he stole all,—all,—all. But could I denounce him? He had been my friend."

And this he said again, and again, and again, many times; not knowing rightly what he said; and murmuring between whiles softly to himself sweet broken snatches of sad melodies—the melodies, doubtless, of his lost Alkestis.

I stole away, awed and afraid, for I was but a child, and went out into the flood of moonlight, into the bath of cold and luminous air, and there in the streets I sat down and wept bitterly for a woe not my own—for a life that was ended.

On the morrow he did not seem to remember the confession he had poured out to me, nor ever again did any allusion to it pass his lips, or mine. But he had become sacred to me; every time that I stood before him I could have kissed his hands for very love, and reverence, and pity.

From that hour I loved and honoured, and never dared be wayward with him.

He was only an old withered man, very bent and broken and poor, ill clad, and taking snuff with trembling hands in the bitter cold of his fireless attic, but to me from that night onward he was a hero and a martyr, and whilst he lived I never told to anyone what he had told to me, not even to Raffaelino.

6*

When a man's eyes meet yours, and his faith trusts you and his heart upon a vague impulse is laid bare to you, it always has seemed to me the basest treachery the world can hold to pass the gold of confidence which he pours out to you from hand to hand as common coin for common circulation.

It was Mariuccia who had reared me in that manner of thinking.

"Child," she used to say, "if they gave a diamond in trust to your safe keeping, would you run with it to the goldsmith's shops in the public streets? Well, is not human faith of more sanctity than diamonds?"

She thought so; being an old stanch republican of Florence and a woman very poor always, who knew little of the world or of its ways.

CHAPTER VIII.

The little red Box.

AT this time the winter set in with an almost unexampled severity.

All over Italy it was cold; so they said; and poor Verona lying in her open plain receiving full upon her defencelessness the strokes of the alpine storm winds, seemed to crouch and perish under the driving of the hurricanes; her huge old houses were riven through and through with cold, and her high leaning walls whose shadow was so precious in the summer noons, seemed now like barriers of ice.

That winter was a very terrible one to Mariuccia and to me.

Poor we had always been, but that winter we had absolutely nothing. Of my father we had not heard for nearly twelve months, and the last of Florio's letters was already half a year old.

Mariuccia earned a little, a very little, by spinning and by selling the work, but this was all. We lived on the very barest food that could keep life in any human creatures.

Of clothing there was no absolute need, for my poor mother's wardrobe had been costly and almost indestructible. But even in this we had come to the very last, and I was forced either to wear rustling silks and lustrous velvets, which made me look like a figure out of a masked ball, or else go without covering in the bitter alpine blasts.

Happily it did not matter so much in Italy as it would have mattered any where else; yet I used to feel absurdly and cruelly out of keeping with my fate as I wove lace to get a pennyworth of bread to stand between me and starvation, whilst all the time my brocaded skirts swept the brick floor, and a boddice sown with gold thread and seed pearls imprisoned my aching and hungry heart.

I was fifteen; and old enough to know that it was very terrible to be without friends or money in the world; and very bitter to sit endlessly crossing and knotting the threads of my lace all the while wholly powerless to untwist one of the threads of fate.

If I could only escape from Verona, I used to think—it seemed to me it would all be quite simple then, once beyond the gates:—just once.

The Christmas week came, and kept the bells of all the churches ringing all day and night.

The dark, black-faced Befana had her feast day, and the people rejoiced and ate and drank and sang

at the midnight mass, and exchanged compliments
and confetti, good will and generous wines.

And all this time Mariuccia and I had not so
much as a log of wood for the hearth, or a slice of
meat for the soup pot; we were cold, poor, alone.

We went to mass all the same; and no one looking at her in her ruddy serge kirtle and her great
Tuscan hat, and at me in my satin skirts and my
velvet hood, would ever have dreamed we were in
want of anything.   For Mariuccia in her way was
very proud; and so was I in mine.   Nevertheless, so
utterly did we want that we besought the Madonna
humbly to send us a crust of bread.

But no doubt the Madonna hears this cry of
"bread, bread, only a little bread," so very often that
she has got deaf to it.

Be that how it may she sent us nothing; and in a
little while it came to pass that for one whole day
we did not even break our fast, and must have gone
supperless to our chill beds, had not the padrona,
from whom we could never quite conceal our dire
needs, toiled up the stairs in the dark with a smoking
pan of maccaroni lentil flavoured, and besought us to
partake of it for the love of God.

Mariuccia accepted it with tears in her fearless
old eyes, which for more than eighty years had never
failed to open at dawn to the day's labour.   Mariuccia would take a gift as frankly as she would give
one; yet to eat the meal of charity was very bitter
to her; she had done her best so long to live without alms; it seemed to her, I think, hard not to have
died a little earlier, so as to have escaped this degradation.

That night she prayed very long to her Mother of Many Sorrows; I sobbed myself to sleep shivering and without a prayer.

In the morning, when we rose, there was not a thing in the house for our hunger; not a drop of milk for our thirst. Mariuccia set out the cups and plates by sheer habit, but they remained empty; there was not so much as a dust of charcoal with which to heat any water.

It was a very cold day, but very bright. The sun was shining. The bells were ringing. Already in the streets below there was a crowd of quickly moving feet and of laughing voices. The Carnival had come. It was the first day of the corso di gala.

Mariuccia and I looked at one another with the dry eyes of an absolute despair.

After a little space she went to a drawer in an old walnut-wood press, and took out a little red box. She brought it to me where I sat with the pillow of my work lying idle in my lap. She took out of it a few trinkets; corals and mosaics.

"These were your mother's," she said tenderly. "She had a great mass of jewels when I went to her first. After her death your father took them away, and sold them all no doubt. I have never seen them again. He kept these few little things; they are not of much value, though they are good of their kind. I have kept them for you. I could not think it right to sell them. But now it is a question whether they go or you starve. You are old enough to choose;— say."

I held them in my hand whilst she spoke; there

were earrings and lockets and a bracelet, all—in mosaic.

My poor young mother! I had never felt such pity for her, such nearness to her as I felt then.

My eyes grew wet with a rush of tears. I threw my arms about Mariuccia's throat.

"Keep them to-day," I murmured. "Dear, dear Mariuccia!—just to-day. I have thought of something. I am going to Ambrogiò."

I had flung my velvet hood over my head, and was out of the chamber and down the stairs into the street before she had time to question me; moreover she had no fear; I went every other day to Ambrogiò.

The sun was shining radiantly upon the frosty pavements as I went out upon them. It was the fourteenth day of the new year and the first of the carnival.

In the teeth of the cold people were all astir; hugging close their charcoal braziers, and wrapping their faces to the eyes in their cloaks; and although it was scarcely noon, in many a dark doorway there flashed some gay mummer's disguise.

The chimes of all the churches were ringing madly; there were bursts of music here and there; a set of the Tedeschi flashed by me, driving in the Tirol fashion; muffled with scarlet rugs and brown sables, their horses in belled harness stretched like greyhounds; from a balcony above, there fell on them as they galloped by a shower of house-reared violets and roses, a woman laughed gaily as she cast the flowers; their Tirolean postilions roused the echoes of the old gateways with a tarantarratara upon their tasselled bugles—how pretty and bright it all was!

It was the first gala of Carnival, and although the procession had scarcely commenced all the city was out in holiday attire, and in holiday humour.

There was a wonderful glow everywhere of many various colours.

In the great multitudes that thronged every square and street and passage-way, and shelved upward like banks of flowers against the huge stones of the palaces and prisons, there were beautiful half tones of crimsons and greys and ambers, with here and there a broad flash of white from a woman's coif, or a glisten of golden spangles from a mummer's gear.

Here and there about in the throngs ran Stenterello or Arlecchino, or some other of their quaint, gay, bespangled and beribboned brotherhood.

Now and again the ranks of the people parted with shouts to let through some group of masks in all the colours of the rainbow, or some conjuror all aglow in scarlet, striking at 'them with his magic rod.

Through the swarming masses there began to sweep the gorgeous equipages of the patriciate, ushered forth in all the old-world pomp of Carnival; with the child-nobles clad in the costumes of their ancestors, powdered and jewelled with their rapiers at their side.

The draped balconies and the deep embrasures of the casements were filled with bright-eyed children, dark browed women, and old men with grey and noble heads, like a painter's studies for Prospero or Bellincion Berti.

Sometimes there was a burst of music, sometimes some glittering troop of cavalry clanged and clattered through the press, sometimes there rose the blare of trumpets, the tinkling of mandolines, the cries of the vendors of confetti, the shouts of little lads baiting the pantomime; and above it all, the laughter of the populace was always murmuring like an unresting sea.

I ran eagerly through the twisting passages to Ambrogiò's. I had an idea that he might get me some employment in the chorus of the opera house. I found his attic empty; the people of the place told me he was gone to a rehearsal at the theatre of Don Pacheco.

I ran then not less quickly to the coppersmith's under the Spiked Mace; I thought I would ask Raffaelo's mother to take a little coffee and bread for pity's sake to her poor old gossip and friend. But there was not a living creature in the workshop: even the blind woman had gone forth with her children to hear the echoes of the festivities she could not see.

I thought of poor Cecco, who would I know share his last soldi with me, but he and all his heedless tribe would be I knew as surely out in the town, busily helping or hindering the preparations of the mumming and the harlequinade, and all the gay street shows with which the Carnival would be welcomed in its royal pomp.

Broken-hearted and hungry, and with my cheeks wet with tears, I wandered carelessly about the streets, unwilling to return; the time stole on, the people began to pour out in throngs that grew merrier and larger with every moment; even the very cripples and beggars looked glad and triumphant, and had garlanded their crutches or adorned their rags with wreaths of leaves or knots of ribbons.

I only was all alone and most unhappy.

All at once a flute-like voice called out to me:

"Oh, dear donzella, come up here, come up here. I have looked for you everywhere. My mother is gone with my big brothers, and I have been to the house to look for you, and you had been out quite an hour and more, so the padrona said. Come up here; it is such a good place. One sees everything, and the crowd is getting large."

It was little Raffaelino who called to me, standing on the topmost edge of a flight of marble steps in one of the arched doorways of an old palace.

I joined him where he stood; and so it came to pass, that day, that I sang to the people in the great Piazza in my violet hood and my amber skirts, and that I heard the band of the maskers and scaramouches running down the street, with their coloured bladders, crying, in eager chase:

"Pascarèllo!—Pascarèl!"

BOOK II.

THE CITY OF LILIES.

CHAPTER I.

The Gifts of Gala.

"WHAT is Pascarèl?" I asked of Raffaelino as they passed away, and I gathered my fallen treasures and rose to go homeward to poor Mariuccia.

The little lad did not know; he said that he would ask his brothers. He thought that it must be the name of some new-fashioned game of the Carnival.

At the entrance of my dwelling, 'Ino poured all his own spoils into my arms, and before I could refuse them or arrest him, he had fled off down the street again as fast as his fleet, brown, bare limbs could carry him.

He wanted to avoid being pressed to take a share; and, moreover, altogether to lose seeing the gala would have been a trial too bitter for his pleasure-loving Italian temper to endure to contemplate. He loved me, and had sacrificed himself to serve me; but now that he could no longer benefit me, the gala resumed all its supremacy.

The tears were still wet upon my cheeks, but my heart bounded joyously against the grim, graven stone of the Fates as I crossed the courtyard and flew up the staircase.

The house was quite empty; everyone was gone to see the Corso; there was no sound but the drip, drip, drip of the water in the stone fountain, and the wailing of little Zoto and Tito, the padrona's youngest children, who being too small to go out by themselves without being trampled on, and too troublesome for their mother to spoil her festa by looking after them, had been locked in, in the lower part of the house, and left to console themselves as they could with a few chesnuts and some curls of wood shavings for playthings.

I ran like a greyhound up the stairs and across the bare chambers to the little inner den where Mariuccia always sat and span under the high turret window that was stained in many colours with the life and miracles of S. Bruno.

I was covered with violets and confetti; they had lodged everywhere, in my hood and my curls, in my skirts, in my gathered-up dress which held, like a great yellow pannier, the heaps of rosettes and bouquets, and crisp bank-notes, and florins, gold and silver, and sweetmeat-papers, and knots of carnations.

My old nurse glanced up, startled, as I appeared before her like the very genius of the Carnival incarnated and filled with gifts, for, as I threw open the door, a flood of high noonday sunlight streamed in with me, and danced upon the yellow daffodils and the rosy knots of the other flowers, and the bright bands of the ribbons that streamed away from me in all directions.

Breathless and wordless, I poured my gleanings into her lap before she had fully seen that I stood before her.

"Here is enough for weeks and weeks and weeks!"
I cried to her. "You need never be cold any more,
and the stew-pots shall always be full. Just a few
minutes in the square, and it is done! We shall never
want to sell the mosaics!"

Mariuccia looked, stupefied, down upon the confused heap of gold and of silver, of bank-notes and
of cakes, of fruits, and of sugared dainties. I dropped
down on my knees before her and laughed in her
face with delight; a delight to which tears lay close.

"Are you so astonished, Mariuccia? You never
thought the people would care so much? It was Ino's
thought, not mine. He would not take a thing for
himself, not so much as a candied chesnut. But are
you not glad, Mariuccia? Only think how we can
live now! Just a song or two in the streets, and we
are rich!"

Mariuccia's strong old frame shook with a sudden
emotion that vaguely awed me; a glance that was
stern and yet piteous flashed on me from her dark
eyes; a quick sad-stricken cry escaped her:—

"In the streets!" she echoed; "in the streets? for
money? And for me? ·O child, O carina! What
shame!———"

"Shame?"

I rose to my feet chilled, silenced, mortified. I
had used the one little gift with which Nature had
dowered me, and the people had only given me what
they would in return for the song that I gave them.
Where was the harm? It was simple and fair, and
honest; how could it, then, bring any shame?

So I pondered, being but a child.

Meanwhile Mariuccia covered her face with the

hem of her garment, and, rocking herself to and fro, wept bitterly.

"In the streets? for money?" she murmured again and again. "Oh, carina! the shame of it, the shame!"

I said nothing; I felt the tears swell to my eyes, but I would not let them fall.

I took up my poor treasures from the floor, on to which they had fallen in a disordered heap, and carried them to the head of the stairs and sorted them.

The notes and money I put away in the little old oak coffer that always held our riches when we earned any: then I leaned over the deep well of the staircase and called the names of Zoto and Tito.

The poor little lonely babies came tumbling and tottering to me at the summons from their old playground in the snow-filled court; I filled their little dirty eager hands with all the ribbons and roses, and sweetmeats, and pretty painted toys, which no longer had any beauty in my sight, or flavour to my mouth.

"Take them—all, all, all!" I cried to the astonished children who stood before me open-eyed at my sudden wealth and their good fortunes: they wanted no second permission to seize on all they saw; in another moment I had nothing left, and they, rapturous and shouting loudly in over glee, toddled down again in the court below, keeping high carnival amidst the snow.

As for me, I sat cold and still and sorrowful exceedingly beside the broken Donatello. Against my heart I still held the Fates.

I was wrong when I was proud, so they said; and now, when I had conquered pride for honesty's sake, I was wrong too;—the perplexity was a knot I could not unravel.

Mariuccia, the dear tender soul, soon found me sitting there, and came to me, and laid her hand upon my shoulder and kissed me between the eyes.

"'Nella mia, I was wrong to be so quick with you," she said, whilst her voice still shook. "You did for the best, dear, and it was good of you to think of me at all. But, all the same, it must not be; you must never go out in the streets again — never, never."

I sat silent upon the marble stairs; I was pained, angered, mortified, perplexed. She spoke to me, I thought, as if I had robbed in the streets instead of simply using the gifts with which Nature had dowered me, and taking nothing but what the goodwill of the people had joyously cast to me.

Mariuccia kept her hand on my shoulders where she stood before me, trying to see down into my dropped veiled eyes.

"Promise me you will never do such a thing again, 'Nella!" she said, anxiously; "I love you for it, carina; dearly, dearly. But it is so shameful!"

I shook her hands off me, and rose. I felt my face burn with anger; anger that was not perhaps so very unjust after all, for I had tried honestly to do right.

"Shameful!" I echoed. "I see nothing shameful in it. You speak to me as though I were a thief. I think it is much more shameful to sit still and see you starve of cold and hunger, and live myself on the padrona's charities. Sell the mosaics, if you like, if you think that better. But they will not last long, and what shall we do then? Altro! I am not a baby now. I know we have no money at all, and that you cannot tell where to write to my father. Are we to die of famine like caged rats, then, because you will not let the people pay me of their own goodwill for pleasing them? I am fifteen now, Mariuccia; and something or other I will do with my life; I will not mope and moulder for ever in this old prison-house. I will go away, as my brothers have gone."

My heart smote me as soon as the words had passed my lips. I saw her sturdy old frame shrink as if I had struck her a blow.

No doubt it was hard—harder than in my thoughtless youth I realized—to have given so many years, so much patience, such long unchanging care to the rearing of us motherless things, only to have us all as we reached our strength and stature impatient to escape her hold and pass from out her sight.

She was silent, and so was I; down in the courtyard the children played with their spoils in riotous glee; a sound of trumpets and of laughter came, deadened, through the closed casements from the distant streets.

"Do you hear them?" I cried to her at last in impotent impetuous pain. "Everywhere there are mirth and riches, and ease and pleasure; why am I not to have my share? I am handsome, so you all say; I have a voice; I am not a fool; I could do something in the world, I think. Anyway, can one do worse than die of cold and of want of food here?

Let me go, as my brothers have gone. Whatever the worst may be, it cannot be worse than this."

Mariuccia grew very pale, with that strange terrible pallor of age when the emotions come and go so slowly and with so much pain.

She looked down into my eyes which now met hers speaking, no doubt, the longing that possessed me with more eloquence than my words could hold.

Her strong withered hands shook where they still rested, on my shoulders.

"Wait a little," she said, at length, "wait, and let me think. The boys, at the worst, can only die; but you——"

She left the phrase unended and went from me, and passed away into the gloom of the passages.

Where I sat, under the broken Donatello, a shiver, that did not come from the chillness of the marble solitudes, or from the winds that blew from over the mountains and the snow, ran through and froze the bright current of my warm young blood.

What was this calamity, worse than death, which could not come to my brothers, but to me alone?

The rest of that day Mariuccia and I spoke not at all to one another; we sat silently as two strangers in the little square dark room with its smell of dried rose leaves and of the onions that keep off the evil eye.

She sat and span on at the distaff at her girdle, for she came of the class that cannot lay aside its daily work however much it may endure or may lament; but I sat aimlessly doing nothing, leaning my forehead against the grated window and watching the

Carnival throngs far down beneath me in the white piazza.

Once as the twilight closed in, Mariuccia called me to her; her voice sounded a little feeble. I could not see her very plainly, the shadows were so dark.

I bent to her to hear what she would say; her hand went up to my forehead, and passed over my hair in her old familiar gesture.

"Bambina mia," she said, eagerly, quite in a whisper, as she held me there; "promise me you will not sing in the streets again. Promise me! What should I say to your mother in heaven?"

"I will promise," I answered her, for there was an accent in the words that vaguely awed me, and almost vanquished the angry rebellion that was astir in my heart.

"Our Lady be with you ever," she muttered, softly and wearily, like one who is half asleep from fatigue, and speaks but on unconscious instinct. I went back to my place by the grated casement and fretted my soul in mute repining.

Now and then people flung up at me crowns of evergreens or showers of sweetmeats, but these all struck against the barred panes and fell back again into the street below.

I did not care to reach my hand and open the lattice so that they might enter.

The day went dully on its course; the duller in that little room of ours because of the mirth and mischief in the town below. It was the first day of the first Carnival in which Mariuccia and I had not clothed ourselves in the best and brightest apparel that we could and gone down to wander through the crowded

7 *

ways laughing at every step, giving gay greetings, and lingering until with the grey of night the lamps had glittered by their tens of thousands all over the lines and domes of the green old city.

It was the first day in which we sat within and let the rejoicing throng flash by without us.

The hours were very slow, very cold, very dreary; there was no charcoal in the stove; there was no bread in the pot; the padrona and all her flock had gone forth to the popular mirth-making; in the old house all was dark, and still, and melancholy.

The twilight came early; there was no oil for our lamp; no food for our hunger; it was night very soon; we sat quiet in the darkness, which was only broken when some torch-lit procession or some blaze of fire-works flashed a fitful reflection into the chamber from the streets and squares of Verona.

We should go, cold to the bone and supperless, to our chill beds; yet neither she nor I stirred to take the money I had gained in the morning from its place in the oak coffer.

I looked at Mariuccia. She was still asleep.

At length, the rebellion and the weariness in me vanquished every other feeling. Why should I not go and enjoy with the rest? Why should I sit and mope here like an owl in the market-place, because a foolish old woman had quibbles and foibles about the good blood in my veins and the dangers of girlhood?

So I reasoned in the wickedness of my heart until the revolt in me ripened.

I stole again a glance at Mariuccia. She did not stir nor seem to hear. I stole noiselessly across the room, trimmed the lamp afresh, reached down my hood, and went out on to the stairs.

There was no one to say me nay. Every soul in the house was out that night, except the two bambini, who were fast asleep curled together on a heap of pine shavings, the emptied sugarplum-horns and the broken toys strewn all around them.

I was soon in the streets and squares, that were all alive with throngs of people, bent hither and thither, laughing and talking, some singing, others dancing down the gloom of the solemn passage ways.

It was quite late.

Time had glided away unperceived as I had sat in that monotonous vexation and quietude. They were setting fireworks in the cathedral square, and the great bells were ringing the tenth hour of the night.

CHAPTER II.
The Veglione Masquer.

LONG familiarity with the Veronese ways had made me quite able to take care of myself in a crowd; and the Italian crowds, though often riotously mirthful, are never rough or rude.

I got in a coign of vantage just under the grim old stone Roland, and seated myself comfortably and carelessly to see the girandola.

The fireworks were very fine, and shot upward in streams and clouds of glory on the frosty night air, shedding their many colours on the sea of upturned faces, and flashing over the darkness of the Duomo pile. I yielded myself eagerly and with utter zest to the enjoyment of them.

I was very hungry, to be sure, and cold still; but it was much better to be hungry and cold but well amused than to suffer the same thing in loneliness and gloom.   I had not been born in Italy without being born to as much philosophy as lay in this simple reasoning.

So I gave myself up to the girandola sitting aloft under the paladins, laughing, and shouting "Bellissima!" and "Brava!" with the throng around me, and for the time utterly oblivious that I had wept such bitter tears under the Donatello, and, alas, equally forgetful, I shame to say, that Mariuccia sat at home alone in her sadness and her patience.

The bands of the Austrian regiments were playing in the piazza, to keep the Veronese in good humour; and the music, the fireworks, the picturesque chiaroscuro of the thronged square, as the various fires illumined it, all combined to make me forget my woes, and to rouse me into an exhilaration which was all the more excited and unreal because I had fasted for so many hours.

I was in no mood to go home and creep to bed in the cold supperless. It was now midnight, I knew, but I was indifferent. Mariuccia would scold; but then— had she not done so when I had tried to please and help her in the forenoon?

So I hardened my heart; and when the last sheaf of coloured flames had died out, and the streams of people began to pour outward, this way and that, I strolled on also, looking to see if by any chance there might be other amusements still forthcoming.

The Stranieri spent their gold lavishly in diversions for the populace; and the Veronese Carnival at the time of that foreign dominance, if its mirth were hollow, was, at least, as brilliant in festivity as any in Italy.

Mariuccia would scold, of course, when I went home, but what of that? Words break no bones.

So I said to myself, in my wilfulness and revolt. Alas! that hour has been a remorse to me ever since.

As I have said before, I was never very good and often very bad in those days, so far as waywardness and daring went. As a child—and I was still no more than a child—I was affectionate always; and courageous, when my imagination was not affected by fear; I told the truth, and I would give anything I possessed, however much I might want it myself.

But there my virtues ended. I was disobedient to a headlong rashness; and I was in a mood to be so to-night.

As I went out of the piazza, there was a little laughing group of sightseers, cloaked and hooded in an odd fashion. They looked like monks, but they were waltzing down the pavement, and singing a tavern song very popular then in Verona.

"Pascarèllo! Pascarèl!" they screamed at the top of their voices, as a flash of red went by under an old archway; and they set off running swiftly, their monkish robes showing beneath them women's little feet with rosetted ribbons flying.

This mystical name fascinated me; the desire to know its meaning grew stronger and stronger.

I flew in their wake, and ran too. The gleam of scarlet had vanished into the gloom of the arch.

Soon I came upon a throng of people standing before some columned steps and some wide entrance doors. Above, many lamps glittered, and against the wall there fluttered on a scroll, in great white letters on a scarlet ground, the word of Veglione.

From the belfries of the city midnight was sounding. The stream of people was passing within the building; they looked very strange to me; they made me think of an old painting that hung in our old palace entrance-hall, and that was called the "Gates of Hell."

But I pressed on to enter with them; I was not afraid; it was the Veglione by the writing on the wall.

I had heard strange and wonderful things of that saturnalia, and I imagined many more; moreover, here had entered those veiled figures who had been seeking Pascarèl.

I ran eagerly up the steps, and was carried by the press of the pleasure-seekers into the body of the hall. There was a barrier at which they stopped me for payment.

I stood helpless, with the rushing sound of the many footsteps on my ears; a man's hand, stretched over my shoulder, cast down the money for me, and a man's voice laughed in my ear, "So handsome, and not masked? Pass in, pass in, carina."

The pressure of the onward moving throngs swept me through the barrier, and away from my deliverer. I was borne into the very midst of the strange torrent of colour and tumult, of laughter and of music.

I stood still and looked, the blaze of the light half blinding me; my face was uncovered; my hood fell back; my feet were bare; my yellow skirts were stained with many a crushed fruit and bruised flower, in the old glad days of my wanderings; my little hot hands held between them the onyx ring against my breast.

There was a broad piece of mirror before me in the entrance-hall; I saw my reflection in it, and was charmed and yet ashamed.

My cheeks burned like wild poppies; my hair was in a lustrous tangle: my eyes looked like great burning lamps in the thinness of my hunger-worn, small face; my mouth was scarlet and parched with excitement; and yet I knew so well I looked handsome— so well that the people would look at me and cry, "Bellina!"

I was frightened, and yet I was fascinated. There seemed some horrible evil about me, and yet it was so vivacious, and so gay, and so full of pictures, that I could not help being allured by it.

Pascarèl I did not discover, and, truth to tell, I forgot all about that mystery.

I was too absorbed in it all to be conscious that I was singular in going thus bareheaded and unmasked amongst the dominoes.

It was a pageantry to me, nothing else; and I moved on as I should have done in the streets; the people supping at their little snowy tables in their boxes; the quaint, glittering costumes that leaned over the panels; the stir and colour of it all, the headlong flight of the mad waltzers, the white mousquetaires wringing the champagne from their long moustaches; the gorgeous eighteenth-century dresses crowned with powdered hair; the crowd of black monk-like figures that served only to intensify the gaiety of colour—all these were so many pictures to me.

I wandered on enchanted, and unheeding the observation that I gathered in my course; the only thing that I noticed was the intentness with which I was followed by the eyes of a Florentine Florindo, who wore that traditional dress with an easy grace that was in a manner familiar to me. But the Florindo did not approach me, and I soon ceased to think about him in the midst of the masquers.

For me, I never doubted that it was pandemonium itself; and yet the fantastic charm, and the lurid brilliancy of it bewitched me. It was horrible, and yet it was beautiful.

The women's eyes, as they glittered like snakes' eyes through the blackness of the masks; the cloud, and flutter, and tumult of colour; the furious speed of the dancers whirling, stamping, shouting, reeling in all the maddest ecstasies of folly; the sombre darkness of the gliding dominoes passing silently with little low, sneering laughs, as the arrows of their whispered speech hit some blot or some wound in men's strength or women's weakness; the intoxication of the loud, gay music crossed every second by the wild war-whoop of the revellers; the dazzle of innumerable hues and shine of countless jewels in the great semicircle full from floor to roof, whilst here and there some masquer, ablaze with diamonds, flung her flowers from above, and some noble, powdered and jewelled, leaned down to pledge a dishevelled, panting dancer, in rosy, foaming wine; the wonder, and chaos, and glow, and tumult of the scene bewitched me as I gazed on it.

It was only the masked ball of the Carnival; but to me it was beautiful as paradise and horrible as hell.

It all swam giddily before my sight, and the music rolled like thunder above my head.

As I stood, a dancer, in the dress of the Louis Treize musketeers, flung his arms about me, and swept me into the circle of the waltzers with a force that bore me off my feet.

"Cara mia," he cried in my ear, "you are in strange guise for the Veglione, but what matter that? I paid for you at the doors. You shall reward me up yonder."

He never ended his phrase. I struck him on the mouth blindly with both hands on the mere instinct for freedom, and broke from his hold, and ran through the maze of the dancers without sense or sight of what I did.

Shrill cries rose round me; the people parted hastily to let me through, and many fled from me in terror; a shout arose that I was mad, and had broken loose from the hospital. The sense of the outcry came to me dully as voices ring over water from a far shore to a drifting boat.

Suddenly I stopped, and flung my head upward like a beaten stag, and looked across the blinding blaze of colour, vaguely seeking help.

Fronting me was the red glow of drooping curtains, a great knot of carnival camellias, a little group of men and women, like a picture from the Decamerone, a medley of violet and gold, and scarlet and black, and diamonds and pearls; it was an opera-box, in which five dominoes leaned and laughed, and drank and jested.

The central figure of them all stood erect, with a red plume tossing in the light; he was in a flash of ruby colour and of white; he wore the dress of the Florentine Florindo, and had a dark oval face like that of an old picture; his hand was on his sword-hilt; he laughed gaily with the masked and mirthful women.

I do not clearly remember what ensued.

A band of debardeurs surrounded me; a hideous cock crowed at me; a clown grinned and gabbered; a set of black masks hooted and threw their limbs hither and thither in wild contortion.

The Mousquetaire seized me afresh; lifted me from the ground, and plunged into the wild gallopade that was rushing down the boards like a troop of riderless horses on San Giovanni's day in Florence.

I shrieked for help and release.

My tormentor, screaming with laughter, held me the tighter. There was a moment's pause; then a crash of sound, a loud outcry, a tumult of the masquers, and the Florindo with the scarlet plume had sprung from the box above, had struck or tossed the arms away that held me, and had hurried me through the maze of the dancers out of the heat and the glare into the cool white moonlight that was streaming through the darkness of Verona.

"Pascarèllo—Pascarèl!" the people had shouted as he came; and there was no pursuit, and no offence taken against him.

He stood and looked at me in the silvery light; a bright and many coloured figure, flashing with the grace and glitter of the old dead centuries under the gloom of the walls of the Scala.

"Well, my singing bird," he said, with a smile in his eyes, "what were you doing there, may I ask?

It is a place for kites and hawks, and all manner of evil birds; but not for nightingales. You did not seem as if you liked the air?"

The voice was the voice of the giver of the onyx. I burst into tears, and told him what had drawn me thither.

He heard me with a gentle amusement in his eyes; dark eyes, tender and poetic, such as Sordello's might have been here in this very same Verona.

"The best thing I can do for you is to take you homeward quickly," he said, moving onward, and bidding me show him the way to my home. "To be abroad on a Veglione night is not the best thing for you, donzella. Courage is very admirable, but a little prudence is needful too in this world.

"It is to make your cake all of coriander-seeds— to make life up of rashness only.

"Tell me—why were you singing in the streets this morning? You look like a little princess, Signorina Uccello. Nay; never mind. You shall tell me to-morrow. You will let me come and see you to-morrow.

"You want to get out of Verona? Oh, fie, for shame. That is not poetic at all. To get away from the Stranieri is always good, I admit, but surely Verona has a charm of her own still, if only you will look for it.

"She is not like my Florence, indeed; it is not given to every city to be born out of fields of lilies, and keep their sweetness with her for ever, as Florence does; a woodland fragrance always amidst the marble and the gold.

"But Verona,—oh, yes,—Sordello's song is here,

if only you listen, and it is the same moon that Giulietta saw from the balcony, and those great Scali —they seem to daunt and to awe the place still,— and do you not see Adelaïda ever bending her terrible brows in the shadows?

"Nor Cunizza, the faithless, with her 'strong, cruel star,' that ruled her life so ill, and her lovely eyes burning with the madness of the Romano, and at her side her gentle Troubadour, Ser Folco? Do you never see them? They lived and loved here in this old Verona that you despise because you are so ignorant of all its beauties.

"And then, far away,—so far away in the dawn of the poets—the pretty Lesbia twisting the roses in her lover's locks in their gardens yonder, while at a bow-shot in the circus the citizens shouted, 'Ad leones?' Oh, you should not hate Verona. It is so ancient, and it was so mighty once, though it never used its might for any very good purpose."

He talked on thus merely of course for the purpose of banishing my fear, and reconciling me to the strangeness of my position, in wandering the streets thus at night, with an unknown masquer in the dress of Florindo. There was that true and kindly delicacy in him which would not to prolong his own amusement, and gratify his own curiosity, increase my embarrassment, or cause me pain.

His voice was so beguiling, his eyes so frank and tender, his whole bearing so full of a certain gentleness and carelessness, that I was attracted into an irresistible sense of confidence in him.

He was an utter stranger; he was one of those mad carnival mummers who had imbued me with a vague sense of unspeakable, intangible evil; he was only a Veglione masquer, gay and grotesque in his vari-coloured disguise in the white Veronese moon-light; and yet I trusted him, and felt a sense of security in his presence, and spoke to him as simply and as naturally as I could have done into the ear of little Raffaelino.

"But this was very naughty of you," he said, still with the smile in his eyes, as he heard my sins.

"I am never good!" I confessed very piteously. "I am like that wicked Speronella of Padova, whose namesake I am—so my nurse says, at the least."

He laughed indulgently.

"Oh come! not quite so bad as that, I trust. And you will grow wiser in time. Let us hope rather that you will end like that good Nella whom her husband, even in a better world than this, if poets may be credited, quoted as a priceless perfection. But what possessed you to go to that place to-night? A freak of mischief no doubt, but what promoted it?"

"I wanted to see what Pascarèl was! That was all. That was all indeed!"

He paused a moment in the silent street, and laughed outright.

"Well," he asked, "did you find out?"

"No! Do you know? Pray tell me."

"I have tried to find out too," he said, with the laugh on his lips. "Tried all my life, and never succeeded yet."

"Is it something so wonderful?"

"Oh, dear, no. No wonder of any sort in it."

"Is it an enigma then?"

"Well—yes—a little. Probably the answer lies

in nothing deeper than in the one word with which
Œdipus answered the Sphinx. Do not trouble your
head after it. It is not worth your while."

"Why? The people seem to care."

A tender and saddened shade swept over his face.

"Ay! the people, perhaps, a little."

"What is it then? Do tell me."

In my eagerness I paused midway in the street;
the snow lay lightly on all the roofs and stones and
balconies; the icy Alpine air had frozen it into all
sorts of lovely and fantastic shapes.

The masquer broke off one of the pretty snow
flowers off an iron scroll, and held it in his hand.

It slowly melted and vanished.

"That is what Pascarèl is; nothing more!" he
said, lightly. "Do not talk of it; tell me about yourself."

I had not space to tell him much, for the old
palace was at a stone's throw from the opera-house,
and he and I stood in a few moments' time before
our huge, cavernous, arched portals, whose nail-studded
ancient doors stood forever wide open, night and
day, for we were all too poor there to have fears of
theft, having naught amongst us all to lose.

At the entrance he paused and uncovered his
head.

"I will bid you good-night, donzella, and go back
to my pranks and my follies. To-morrow, if you will
let me, I will come and see you. Gratitude? Oh,
altro! you have no cause for that. It is I rather who
am grateful to the Fates. By-the-way, I wish that I
had had something brighter and fairer to give you
than the old grim onyx; they are an ugly portent I

am afraid, those stern sisters. Never mind, I will try
and get you some roses to-morrow. They will be
very much fitter for you. Nightingales and roses have
belonged to one another ever since the days of paradise. Addiò!"

He kissed my hand with easy grace, and turned
away down the deep shadows of the street; in the
moonlight the red and white of his dress—colours of
Florence—glistened as the moon-rays caught them; he
went singing, half aloud, the catalogue of the Loves
from the Giovanni.

I watched him until he was lost to sight in the
darkness that fell from the lofty palaces, half fortress
and half prison, the twisted galleries, the marble balconies, the frowning stones of Romeo's city; it was a
little scene from the Tre Cento, from the Decamerone,
from Goldoni; the old dead amorous poetic life
seemed suddenly to breathe and move again amidst
the decay and the despair of old Verona.

I went slowly up the staircase, past the ruined
Donatello, and fancied that the broken, dust-strewn
stairs were the steps of the Capulet palace, and that
I was Giuliettà in that tender daybreak, when the lark
sang all too soon.

CHAPTER III.

The Last Sleep.

As I entered the chamber where I had left Mariuccia,
and groping for a match lit the little lamp, I saw that
she was still in her oak chair by the fireless hearth.
Her hands were folded, and her chin had sunk upon
her breast. I knew that she was used to allow herself

a little rest and slumber after her long day of toil, and I imagined that she had dozed on and on, not noticing my absence, nor the flight of time.

I slid down quietly upon the floor at her feet, and did not speak lest I should waken her.

I was glad that she could in sleep forget the hunger and the cold. I was glad, too, to have escaped the reproaches and rebukes that my conduct merited.

I leaned my head against her knee as I had done so often in my babyhood, and sat there, very quiet, with her hands resting heavily against my shoulder.

It was deadly cold; my limbs were frozen; my brain swam a little from long fasting and excitement; it was quite dark; from the streets below there came the hum and outcry of a city in its holiday; Mariuccia did not waken.

I think that I also must have slept a little or at the least lost consciousness of time, for I started as one starts when suddenly roused from a bad dream, as the last fireworks of the night's pageantry rose with a rushing sound above the roof, against the moonless sky.

A great girandola shot its fountain of many-coloured fires up above the black outline of the Duomo, fired most likely by the last revellers of the Veglione, and the reflection from it fell, golden and reddened, through the little grilled window into the chamber; its light fell upon Mariuccia's face.

Something in the look of its closed eyes and silent mouth made my heart tighten with a breathless fear.

"Mariuccia!" I cried to her. "Mariuccia! You frighten me! dear Mariuccia—are you still asleep?"

She was indeed asleep.

The brief and fitful fires of the girandola died away, and left behind it the blank of an utter darkness; the dense impenetrable darkness that precedes a winter's dawn.

Upon the old quiet patient face there was a look of rest, and the withered hands on which I rained my kisses were yet warm. Yet I, who never before had looked on death, knew well that death was here, and that whilst Verona laughed on her first night of Carnival, I sat in the silence of the old palace, alone with the dead body of the sole friend I had on earth.

CHAPTER IV.
At Ave-Maria.

THREE days from that time Mariuccia had gone to her last home.

The wooden shell had been jostled in the common hearse and buried in the common resting-place where the poor lie. The padrona and Raffaello and his blind mother and I had toiled after it through the driving cold of the early morning, and heard the heavy clods fall on it one by one.

It was all over—all over: the strong, pure, honest, tireless life had gone, spent in obscurity and toil, unrecognised and unrecompensed to the last.

I was but a thoughtless, wayward, and selfish child. I had been heedless always, cruel often. I had taken the countless sacrifices that she made to me with all a child's reckless, tyrannous, unconscious egotism. I

8*

scarcely even now knew the immeasurable debt I had owed to her.

Yet a vague heavy pain, that was almost remorse, weighed on me, and on some insufficient yet pregnant sense.

I realised all that this one lost life, old as it was, and humble and poor, had yet been to me from my birth, with its buckler of stanch fidelity held ever between me and the evils of the world.

The dreary weeks went by; to all the rest of Verona they were gay with all the zest of Carnival.

Night after night the fireworks would blaze against the skies, and the music would roll through the sad old streets, and the mad and merry maskers would scamper and frolic under the shadow of prison and fortress and monastery.

The echoes and the reflections of the noise and the lights would come to me where I sat in my dismal little chamber, but that was all the share I had in them.

The padrona, though so poor, would have some friends to laugh with her in her dim old kitchen, and would find some copper pieces to give her a sight of the puppets and the shows that enlivened for Verona those long and chilly days when the winds swept down like dragons whose breath was ice from the deep Tirol valleys and the desolate Dolomite range.

But I was all alone, except when Raffaellino came and tried to while away my sorrow by his innocent fanciful talk and the tender strains of his viol.

With the sad morrow my Romeo of the Veglione never returned.

Even in my passionate remorse and grief I could not but think often of him that day.

When we returned from our dreary errand in the snow, there was awaiting me a great cluster of roses, red and white, that must have come from Tuscany or Rome.

Little Giàn, who had been upon the stairs when they arrived, said that a boy about his own age had brought them, saying nothing whence they came.

I knew.

I set the beautiful things before me against the dismal grated window, and wept my heart out over them. The grief was most for the loss of dear dead Mariuccia; but a little also for the broken faith of the Florence masquer.

What could I do?

I knew no more whither my father was gone than whither the crows flew when they passed in a black cloud over the Adige; and though the good padrona served for me, cooked for me, and bade me be as welcome under her roof as were the rains in summer, I was too proud to think a moment that such depen dence on another could ever long endure.

The desire to escape from Verona grew stronger on me with every hour. I had no notion of what I should do elsewhere: but all good things seemed possible to me if once only I could cross the dreary plain and seek the sunrise of the south.

I said nothing; for I knew that Raffaello would weep and protest and the padrona take fright, and the priests would be spoken with, and some means perhaps be found to detain me, if ever they knew that I wished to take wing.

But all those winter days, when the Corso was at its gayest and the streets were full of masks and mummers, I sat in my dull little stone chamber and revolved again and again a thousand schemes for my freedom.

As the first step towards liberty, I went out one day at the close of the Carnival to see the scrivere whom Mariuccia had been wont to employ for her communications to Florio.

A certain sense of reluctance to trench on anything that seemed like a secret of the dead had held me back from asking this letter-writer any questions; but as the weeks of silence succeeded one another, I argued that not to try and find my father would be a folly and a fault, and in the last hours of one wintry day I crossed the square to where Maso Sasso held his councils at his little worm-eaten desk.

I thought sadly as I went of the homely old figure that had always been at my side spinning and talking as she hobbled over the stones; I thought a little too of that gay red and white masker whose eloquent eyes had smiled on me in the moonlight of Juliet's city.

Why had he not followed his roses?

He was not a man to me, nor a stranger; he was a poem, a picture, a thing of grace, a shape of the cinque cento; Sordello, only not so sad; Romeo, only not so boyish; Ariosto, perhaps, that gayest of lovers and poets; or one of those patrician improvisatori who spent half their lives in a court and the other half in the marketplace.

I was thinking of him still as I crossed the piazza to the hole in the wall where Maso Sasso sat.

When the Ave-Maria was rung he used to close

his office by a bronze wicket and his day's work was done. Then he would pass methodically across the piazza to his favourite trattoriâ; and in front of it, taking his frugal repast, would make himself amends for the long silence of the day by detailing to an interested audience such of the sayings and doings of his clintela as he deemed it proper to reveal.

He was known to be a miracle of propriety and discretion; nevertheless he was a good companion when the sun was set.

Indeed, they were used to say if you brewed him a bibita to his liking, there was very little that you might not hear concerning your neighbour in Verona. But a public that has to recount its joys and sorrows aloud to its penman cannot be very scrupulous about secresy, and the popularity of Maso Sasso never waned on that account.

He had his office in a little dark stone loggia; curiously black and still in the midst of the changeful life of the piazza.

He was a little meagre, yellow, shrivelled old man, who sat all day long in his den and heard all the comical comedies and tearful tragedies of the city, and never seemed to be touched at all by any one of the innumerable idyls and the pathetic obscure heroisms which came hourly before him, as the citizens and the contadini flocked around his stall eager to have had some good tidings sent to some absent one, or to unfold some stiff and blotted scrawl from over the mountains and the sea.

There was a crowd of people around the loggia in which his desk was placed when I drew near it; it was nearly four, and it was known that no press of public necessities would ever make him prolong his sittings after the Ave-Maria.

I had to wait patiently my turn.

A broad-shouldered crimson-kertled contadina wanted a love-letter sent to a soldier away in Piedmont; she did not care what was said so that it was all as sweet as sugar.

A poor wife held out a dirty miserable scrawl, and fell down in a loose lifeless heap upon the stones, as she heard that her husband had been drowned off Ischia.

A jager of the Tirol, with his green plumes dangling in his saucy black eyes, dictated an offer of marriage, giggling and grinning as the pen flew.

An old meek, timid creature tendered a paper with a trembling hand, and turned away with a heartstricken moan as the slow changeless tones of the scrivere read aloud to her that her only son was sentenced for life to the galleys far away in the Regno.

What an epitome was Maso Sasso's den of human nature and of human fate!

I stood and listened with my hood drawn over my face: when my turn came I had forgotten my own sorrows.

"Oh how can you bear it—every day and all day long—like this?" I cried to the wizen, immovable, indifferent old man.

He spread his palms outward over his desk in a gesture of silent contempt.

"Signorina—it is life!"

"But the sorrow—the joy—one against the other —the comedy—the tragedy—it is horrible!"

The old man smiled grimly.

"What does that matter to me?—joy or sorrow— tragedy or comedy—I get my scudo for my trouble."

"But how can you bear it?" I cried again, "day after day, year after year—always those terrible things, side by side with all this laughter."

The old man shrugged his shoulders and took off his horn spectacles to wipe them free of dust.

"Signorina—whether it is woe or laughter, what does it matter to me? I get my scudo, and have something to gossip about. That is all that concerns me."

In later years I have found that the world is very much of opinion with the scrivere. It scans the mass of human life through its spectacles, and whether it reads a fiat of death or dishonour, or a jest-story of love and of lightness, it cares nothing so that only it can take out of both its scudo's worth of scandal.

He asked me for the third time what I needed; I was keeping more profitable customers from his stall. I inquired of him whether Mariuccia had addressed her letters to my father. Maso Sasso shrugged his shoulders again, and sought in the full stores of his memories.

"The letters were to be left at the post, anywhere," he said at last. "Sometimes Nice—Paris— Vienna—the last time, I think, Florence. Yes; Florence. But always the post-office. Nothing more."

"You are sure it was Florence the last time?" I cried, entreating him tremblingly.

"Yes, quite sure. But the last time was eight months ago. Will the Signorina please to move aside? People are waiting, and the sun will soon set."

I moved aside mechanically, and walked dreamily

across the square and sat down on the steps of a great church, where the beggars were wont to sit.

Florence seemed a long way off; and the chance but a very slight one. Nevertheless, it was all I had.

The evening was cold still, but bright and windless.

It was at the end of February; there were lovely roseate lights in the sky, and all fresh mountain scents on the air. Women went by with large baskets full of crocuses and daffodils.

In the beautiful pearly hues of the late day the old gaunt city was transfigured.

Its roofs and domes gained a spiritual light, and vast dream-like shadows swept its plains. It was for once possible to believe in Giuliettà and to muse on Catullus.

At least, so it seemed to me; but perhaps it was only lovelier that night because I knew that so soon I should look my last on it,—perchance for ever.

CHAPTER V.

The Feast of Faustino.

AN hour passed away with me sitting there, dreamily watching Verona.

I could see my old home; the dark gruesome stone pile of it rose sheer as a rock against the blueness of the sky, unchanged since the days when Henry the Seventh had slept beneath its roof, and the bright Conraddin ridden forth from its court yard.

I had never loved the place. Indeed, it had been as a prison to me all my years. And yet my heart

ached now to leave it. We are so bitterly ungrateful
to the present, so blindly grateful to the past,—always.

The Ave-Maria slowly swung from all the bells of
all the churches; the bronze gate of the loggia was
shut with a clang, the scrivere hobbled across the
square to his place of gossipry; lamps were set one
by one in the doorways; the oil wicks were lighted in
the iron sconces of the streets; the little charcoal
stoves of the chesnut sellers began to glow ruddily in
the coming gloom.

As I turned away from the sunset to go homeward, whilst those colours of glory faded over the
silent city, a hand touched me, a voice startled me.

"Pregiatissima Signorina! have the Veronese no
eyes that you are left to stray their streets alone?"

It was the voice of the Mousquetaire, from whom
the Florentine Florindo had rescued me at the Veglione;
a voice with a strong and harsh foreign accent. The
shudder of disgust and dismay with which I recognised
him made an impatient and displeased shadow sweep
across his face.

"Wait. Hear me a little," he said eagerly as I
turned my back on him and went with quicker steps
out of the piazza. "I am a friend of your father's.
I have spent many an hour with him. You have
nothing to fear. I have pitied you many a time,
poverina, sitting up there, all alone, at that grated
window; so fair a singing bird in so dark a cage."

I twitched my purple mantle from his grasp.

"I do not want your pity. Let me be."

But he kept step with me.

"Nay, why do you bear me such ill will?" he said,

with a petulance in his laugh that served ill to reas-
sure me.

"Listen, carina mia; you are a beautiful child.
Did no one ever tell you so before? I have seen your
golden head at that grating many a day, and been
sorely tempted to enter your door; only that direful
dragon whom you have happily buried for good and
all, sat on guard so very grimly."

I shook him off as best I could.

"Respect the dead at least, and leave me!" I
cried to him; I hated the sound of his voice, the look
of his eyes, and the street into which we had passed
was so empty, and now that the after-glow had faded
the city was so dark.

He laughed lightly and pursued his way.

"Oh no, cara mia! I let you go that night because I liked you too well to raise a scene around
you. But I mean soon or late to have all that I there
surrendered out of chivalry to you. See here, my
pretty signorina, you were out on a freak, and no one
knew, of course, and it was I who passed you in to
the Veglione. Well, that is very harmless if you trust
in me; I shall be silent, that you may be sure. But
otherwise, if you provoke me—if you carry that handsome sunny head of yours aloft in that fashion, why
then—— "

I paused and faced him.

"Well?—What then?"

"What then? Why then—every one will know
that the little Tempesta stole at midnight to the opera
ball with me, and she will be very glad to give me
whatever I please to take—"

He threw his arms about me, and bent his face to

mine; but with all the strength I had I struck him on the mouth, poured on him all the epithets of injury and of disgust with which my knowledge of the Veronese streets supplied me, and shaking myself free of him, ran as swiftly as a hare through the twisting passages to my home.

The insult of this stranger had decided me. I did not dare to stay another day longer in Verona; I was pursued with the dread of him, and the disgust that he inspired was the last touch of impulsion needed to make me take wing into the unknown lands—into the unknown world.

I reached my own room unobserved; and put together the few clothes I possessed and counted my little store of money. I had changed all that I had gained on the day of Galà into gold with a childish idea that notes were of little comparative value; and so liberal had been the people to me, that when Mariuccia's funeral and my own expenses for the last weeks had been paid, I had left me sixteen broad gold Austrian florins.

I put the money with my mother's mosaics into a leathern bag, and strapped it about my waist. The onyx Fates were round my throat. I had a fancy that they would bring me fair fortune.

I took too a little dead rosebud from the great clusters that the Florentine masquer had sent me; and tied it with the onyx close about me. I had a fancy that it would propitiate the Fates.

My purple and amber costume was an absurd one for travel, but I had no other that had any warmth against the mountain winds, and I was forced to wear it.

I looked longingly around the long, familiar chambers, dusky and grim, with grated windows and deep vaulted roofs and floors of marble; desolate and prison-like though they had been, they were yet all I knew of Home.

With sobs that choked me I kneeled and prayed to the Mother of Many Sorrows, where her picture hung above Mariuccia's bed, then with a last look of farewell I drew the velvet hood over my head and stole down the stairs.

I met little Zoto and Tito, and kissed them.

I could see the padrona in her kitchen wringing out washed linen by the light of a little oil lamp, under a picture of S. Sulpitia. A contadina from the plains sat chatting with her and plaiting straw as they talked.

My eyes filled with tears, and shut out the little picture. In another moment I had crossed the threshold, and was running hard and fast towards the south gate in the twilight.

On my way, I passed of necessity the coppersmith's workshop under the Spiked Mace. I glanced wistfully through the open entrance.

The light of a large wood fire was leaping about all the brazen and copper vessels. The blind woman sat in its warmth. The coppersmith moved to and fro with bare sinewy arms. Little Raffaellino sat reading a score, with his lithe limbs twisted under him, and his lute by his side on the bricks. I dared not let him know that I was going away, lest he should raise, far and near, opposing clamour.

I prayed mutely, in my heart, to the Madonna for

them, then went on my way to the dull crooked passage in which Ambrogiò Rufi dwelt.

I dared not bid anyone farewell, lest they should find means to stop me in my course. I knew well that they would all say I was too young to stray alone over Italy. I dared not speak to anyone else, but I could not bring my heart to quit the city without some word, some look upon the face of my old master.

I stole upward to the desolate garret, and entered it unheard by him.

He was sitting leaning over the little brazier, which was all that he could afford to warm him in the bitterest weather.

It was the feast of the Martyr Faustino, and all the churches were calling to vespers.

The attic was quite dark.

The moon had not yet risen. It was so high in the air, that all the metallic clash and clangour of the bells seemed to beat through its silence like the clamour of a thousand hammers on a thousand anvils.

I went and kneeled down by him without his hearing me. I ventured to touch him gently.

"Dear master, does not the noise of all these bells tire you sometimes?"

He did not lift his head from his chest.

"I am always tired," he muttered. "What of that?"

"But if you lived where it is quieter?—here it is so close to all the belfries."

"It does not matter," he answered me, absently. "They drown the music in my brain. I am glad of them—sometimes."

"But if you wrote the music down?"

He shivered a little where he leaned over the brazier.

"To feed the stove? Not I—not I."

I dared not urge him farther. The utter hopelessness, the terrible apathy of this lost genius, which all its life long had woven beautiful things to which the world was forever deaf. What could I say to these?—I, a child, to whom every sun that rose was as a promise and a smile from God?

I waited a little while, kneeling before the brazier at his side. My heart was very sore to leave him, though he so seldom seemed to note my presence.

"Maestro," I murmured, at the last, "speak to me a little. I am going away."

"Ay, ay!" he echoed, drearily. "To be sure—to be sure. You all go away. Why not?"

I was silent.

How many hundreds of us he must have seen pass away, bright-eyed, flute-voiced children, who stood around him for a little space, and then drifted out of sight, out of knowledge, into the darkness of the unknown world; while he, the old man, changed in nothing, but remained always by his cheerless hearth under his lonely roof.

I pressed a little closer to his side, timidly.

"Maestro," I murmured again, "I have no one in the world, and I am going away. Will you bless me once—just once, for fear I never see your face again?"

He roused himself from his lethargy with a strong shudder. He looked at me a moment with a startled, awakened look in his dim eyes. He laid his hand upon my head, and, as it rested there, it trembled greatly.

"I dare not bless you—I have doubted God; but I wish you well, poor child. That is—I wish you without a heart, without a soul, without a conscience, so that you may deal unto men as surely they will deal unto you."

His hand sunk from my head; his chin dropped again upon his chest. He had fallen once more into his old dreaming stupor over the charcoal fumes under the roar of the bells.

I rose to my feet sorely afraid. It was a dread benediction with which to commence my pilgrimage.

In another moment I was again on my way to the south gate of the city. I looked back once. The old palace was black and full of gloom against the clearness of the skies. I shivered a little, and set my face again to the south-east.

Who could say how the sun might rise for me there?

CHAPTER VI.

Fuori.

HALF-AN-HOUR later I was rolling underneath the stone vault of the gate which faced towards Tuscany, in the old heavy, cumbrous, leathern-curtained diligenza, which thrice in every week droned on its way to Padova and Bologna.

Rich people travelled otherwise, I knew; but I had only sixteen florins in the world.

The soldiers at the gates looked hard at me, but

said nothing. The man with the horn, on the step of the clumsy vehicle, took my money and asked no questions. I was safe on the road to Florence. It seemed a terribly long way off, across those unknown mountains; but the name of the City of Lilies allured me with a strong sweet spell.

Mariuccia had told me many glories of the place of her birth; and my young mother I knew had there won her bright brief fame. And with what love my Florentine masker had spoken of it,—he whose tenderest little rose I had saved when dead with the rest, and had brought away with me where the stone Fates were hidden.

It was a queer, capacious, ill-scented old waggon —this conveyance, which was dignified by the name of diligenza.

There were three peasant women, smelling strongly of garlic, and hugging great baskets of woollen stuffs, of pizzicheria goods, and of live hens that they had purchased in the town. There were two old priests, a burly fattore, and a young Tirolese in the picturesque garb of the Unterinnthal.

The vehicle was as full as it could hold, and no one looked with much favour on me as I entered, except the young mountaineer.

No doubt I had appeared to them, starting up in the heavy gloom of the night, strange enough as they had thundered slowly over the stones in the gateway; all alone at my age, and dressed as I was in my mufflings of velvet, and my most absurd yellow skirts of rich brocaded satin fit for the wearing of any queen.

They made place for me, however, with pleasant good-humour.

The old waggon settled heavily on its way over the plains.

It was a dark, moonless night. An oil-lamp hung in the roof, which gave us very little light. We rolled on with a creaking droning noise, only varied by the crack of the whip.

The contadina and the priests went to sleep; the fattore took out his accounts and reperused them; the good-looking Unterinnthaler and I were alone wide awake, being young, and on a journey that was strange to us.

They had told me that it would be day and night again before we reached Bologna; and to Bologna, as the farthest stage of all, I had said that I would go. The others were to be set down midway at Padova and other places on the route.

I had never been out of Verona since our residence had begun there in my fourth year.

My head was in a tumult, my brain was in a whirl, with the strange movement, the throbbing noise, and that odd sense of jumbling on into the darkness of the night which was but too true an emblem of the obscurity of my fate.

I could with difficulty keep my sobs quite silent as I thought of the old deserted, familiar chambers, of the old bronze lamp swinging by the broken Donatello, of the little quiet, nameless grave in the cemetery of the poor; of the homelike nook amongst the coppersmith's huge, shining vessels, where Raffaellino would still be sitting with his blind mother, scanning some ancient score by the dim light of his bronze lucernata.

9*

It was all gone—all gone forever, never to come back.

Yet I felt with it all a curious sense of liberation and of exultation. If I had been alone I would have laughed and cried aloud.

The pit-a-pat, pit-a-pat of the horses' feet on the hard road seemed to me to beat out an everlasting trisyllable,—"Fuori, fuori, fuori!" Yes, I was "fuori" now,—fairly out of the gates and away. So I told myself again and again, and took an odd, unsatisfactory, remorseful and yet intoxicating pleasure in the freedom of it all.

I must have looked very strange, doubtless, as I sat there with my cheeks changing to red and white in my excitement, and my lips twitching in my longing to cry, and my hair all ruffled by the haste with which I had run, and the ridiculous yellow skirts crushed up between the tattered black robe of a priest and the grey woollen petticoat of a contadina.

We thundered on in perfect silence for a time, with a little light flashing in upon us now and then from some village post-house or some lamplit wayside Calvary.

The nights were still cold, being so early in the spring. Sitting there, I grew very stiff and chilly. The priest was stout and so was the contadina. Both were soundly sleeping, and sometimes swayed heavily against me.

My heart began to sink. The sense of the "fuori" to be more pain than glory. I thought wistfully of the little bed where I had slept for so many years under the sheltering shadows of Mariuccia's Mater Dolorosa.

I was roused by a sheepskin being placed about my knees, and by the gentle rustic voice of the young Tirolese, who prayed me to accept its covering. He was sure, he said, the signorina was very cold.

I looked up and thanked him. In the dull light of the lamp I saw his gentle honest eyes fixed on me, whilst he blushed hotly at his own temerity.

I took his sheepskin. It was roughly dressed, but warm; and emboldened, he asked me if I was all alone.

"Yes," I told him, glad to hear his voice in that horrible gloom and that unceasing gallop. "And you too?"

"I too, signorina? Yes—but then for a man it is nothing," he answered. "Besides, I go to people I know in Este—an uncle of mine married and settled there. But the signorina, does she go to friends too?"

"Oh, yes," I assured him, being too proud to say otherwise. But my heart rose in my throat at the little lie. I knew how far, far away was the only hope to which I clung.

The young Unterinnthaler looked at me wistfully. I think he knew that what I said was not very true.

"It is cold to-night, signorina," he said, gently.

"Yes—very."

"And you go far?"

"To Bologna."

"Your friends meet you there?"

"No."

"Then you go farther still?"

"I am not sure."

Do what I would the great tears brimmed over

in my eyes; his questions made me realise my desolation.

With kindly courtesy he busied himself with rub-
bing off the mist of our breaths from the glass window
nearest him, so that we might see the dark maple-trees
fly by us in the shadows of the night.

"Do you know my country, signorina?" he asked
me, to divert my thoughts, no doubt. "My country,
across the mountains. I am a farmer in the Unterinnthal. No? Ah, that is such a pity!"

"Is it so beautiful, then?"

"Beautiful? Ay, God knows it is beautiful. Not
flat like this, with nothing but these weary olives; but
all so great, so superb, so wonderful; all pine forest
and endless alps, and then the waters that flash like
so much light, and the snows that lie so high; and
then the clouds that are always about the mountains,
and the rich green woods and the yellow maize-fields
all below—beautiful? Ah, indeed!"

"You would not leave it, then?"

"To live in Este? The holy saints forbid. I should
be a dead man in a year, signorina. Away from the
mountains? I will tell you who did that. It was Andrea
Zafùr; he was older than I, but I knew him. He was
kapellmeister in our burgh. When he led the choir it
was enough to make one weep; it was like the singing
of the angels in heaven. Well, some day some people
came who persuaded him that his voice might be a
mine of gold to him if he would only leave the mountains and go into the world along with them. In an
evil hour Andrea listened. He was poor, you see, and
they told him fine things; so he went. Whether the
world cared much for him or not I never heard; but

I know that they shut him up in cities over there, German cities and French. And one day, two years later, they came for his old mother, and told her that Andrea was dying and prayed to see her. She went at once; but even then she was too late. She found him in Paris, but he was out of his mind; he did not know her at all; and all he kept saying forever was 'Take me back to the mountains! take me back! take me back!' He had made a great deal of gold; the old mother was rich when she returned; but he died, crying aloud to see the mountains once more. Nothing had been any joy to him; he had always been cramped and stifled, and sick to death away from the mountains. It must always be so. Love them once, you can never leave them—and live."

His voice was very hushed and quiet as he spoke, and there came a dreamy look into his eyes—the faraway look that men always get who dwell amidst the heights.

I hardly understood him well; for, though he spoke Italian it was not our Italian; yet there was something so gentle and simple in him that it pleased me to hear him talk.

I was glad to have him to speak to in that oppressive endless gloom, with the surging noise of the horses' gallop always on my ears, and only now and then some break in it when a lantern flashed its red glare in upon us, and hoarse, shrill voices piped discordant orders at the doors of some roadside posting house.

Finding that I listened to him, he went on to tell me all about himself—how his name was Marco Rosas; how he was of Italian race; how he was left fatherless in infancy; how his twin-brother and himself lived together on the little farm on the green slope of the Berg; how he was twenty-two years old, and well-to-do in his own way, and indeed quite rich for a farmer of the Tirol.

He described all his treasures to me; his châlet of pinewood, shingle-roofed against the hurricane and avalanche, in autumn hung over with the great yellow ears of the millet; the herds of small dun cattle, with their antelope-like eyes, and flocks of silvery hill goats; his stout little horse, with its peal of musical bells; his vines, that yielded such sweet huge purple grapes as were never ripened save in that clear, lustrous, buoyant air; the painting of the Holy Trinity that was fastened in his wall, over his house door, in an iron grating, to be a blessing on the place; his orchard, and his pastures that stretched in such perfect vivid green up the hillside, whilst above all the great snow slopes towered.

Most of all he talked of his mother—a woman whom, if all he said were true, must have been one of those who are far above rubies. A tender, homely, noble soul as this mountaineer sketched her, such, indeed, as those great silent hills produce not seldom—a woman with the life of a saint and the heart of a hero, though she neither read nor wrote, but span her own linen, milked her own herds, and had had the sweet strong breath of her own mountain air upon her all her years.

So we journeyed on our way, and, like Conraddin before us, passed "per Lombardia e per la vià di Pavia," into the Romagna country.

The day was one long bright flood of sunshine with

beautiful flakes of clouds floating before a fresh mountain wind.

The broad plains that have been the battleground of so many races and so many ages were green and peaceful under the primitive husbandry of the contadini.

Everywhere under the long lines of the yet unbudded vines the seed was springing, and the trenches of the earth were brimful with brown bubbling water left from the floods of winter, when Reno and Adda had broken loose from their beds.

Here and there was some old fortress grey amongst the silver of the olive orchards; some village with white bleak house-walls and flat roofs pale and bare against the level fields; or some little long-forgotten city once a stronghold of war and a palace for princes, now a little hushed and lonely place, with weed-grown ramparts and gates rusted on their hinges, and tapestry weavers throwing the shuttle in its deserted and dismantled ways.

But chiefly it was always the green, fruitful, weary, endless plain trodden by the bullocks and the goats, and silent, strangely silent, as though fearful still of its tremendous past.

Day came and night again, and all the heavy, chill, bitter, lonely hours jumbled themselves away in some dreary chaos. The journey had become horrible to me. I was stiff and cold and miserable. I lost all heart to look out at the spaces between the leathern curtains on to the country beyond. I had lost all power to watch for the first outline of Tasso's "grand' Apennino."

We had passed through Padovà in the darkness.

and I had not noticed the young Tirolese descend there. But I found the sheepskin left about my knees, and was touched by this little gentle wayside flower of kindness.

I suppose I must have slept some portion of the time, but the beat of the horses' hoofs never ceased to thunder through my brain.

There were red flashes of lights on my eyes as we stopped to change at a posting-house; wonderful purple and rose sunsets and sunrise; a sense of endless gliding green distances that never grew any one whit the nearer; a confusion of cruel noises; a continual sense of pain and of unrest; and then at length the cumbrous vehicle paused under an immense vaulted gateway; a sentinel challenged; a guard looked in, holding up a lantern; the gates unclosed and closed again; and as we rolled over the stones I heard the tired travellers mutter the name—"Bologna."

I trembled, and felt afraid as the tired horses toiled wearily over the pavement underneath the ink-black shadows of those vaulted footways.

It seemed to me as though they would never end; their silence, their gloom, their architecture, the enormous height of the walls, the vista of the interminable arches, the hollow echo of the stones that had been trodden for fifteen hundred centuries by the feet of men and beasts—all terrified me with a vague poetic awe which yet was, in a sense, delightful.

Every old Italian city has this awe about it—holds close the past and moves the living to a curious sense that they are dead and in their graves are dreaming; for the old cities themselves have beheld so much perish around them, and yet have kept so firm a hold upon tradition and upon the supreme beauty of great arts, that those who wander there grow, as it were, bewildered, and know not which is life and which is death amongst them.

To enter Bologna at midnight is to plunge into the depths of the middle ages.

Those desolate sombre streets, those immense dark arches, dark as Tartarus, those endless arcades where scarce a footfall breaks the stillness, that labyrinth of marble, of stone, of antiquity; the past alone broods over them all.

As you go it seems to you that you see the gleam of a snowy plume and the shine of a straight rapier striking home through cuirass and doublet, whilst on the stones the dead body falls, and high above over the lamp-iron, where the torch is flaring, a casement uncloses, and a woman's hand drops a rose to the slayer, and a woman's voice murmurs, with a cruel little laugh, "Cosa fatta non capo ha!"

There is nothing to break the spell of that old world enchantment.

Nothing to recall to you that the ages of Bentivoglio and of Visconti have fled for ever.

The mighty Academy of Luvena Juris is so old, so old, so old!—the folly and frippery of modern life cannot dwell in it a moment; it is as that enchanted throne which turned into stone like itself whosoever dared to seat himself upon its majestic heights.

For fifteen centuries Bologna has grimly watched and seen the mad life of the world go by; it sits amidst the plains as the Sphynx amidst her deserts.

CHAPTER VII.

Under the Garisendà.

I SEEMED to awake roughly from some marvellous dream, when the vehicle stopped at a post-house with a great gilded sign of a golden boar projecting far out in the dull lantern light across the shadow of one of the narrow streets.

The entrance to it was through a deep archway into a paved court; from within there was the feeble light of oil wicks burning in iron sconces; beyond I could see the kitchen, with the glimmer of its copper and pewter and the sturdy padrona in a kirtle of orange and green, who was sending her people right and left in her eagerness to retain for the night all travellers by the stage.

The diligence stopped for good at the Cignale d'Oro, and I thought that I could do no better. The inn folk came round me eyeing me with some amazement and with some suspicion; but an Italian's first impulse is always one of ready kindness; the vociferous padrona softened her voice for me, her household smiled on me, and when I asked them for a little bed where I could sleep in peace, a black-browed damsel showed me up a wooden stair to a little bare chamber with a radiant gleam of her white teeth and laughter of her dusky eyes, such as might fairly have made sunshine in the shadiest place.

That sunny smile of Italy!—it has in it all the youth of the earth's golden ages—all the faith of man's first dreams of God.

My little chamber was very bare, very narrow, with

a floor of red brick and a casement that looked only on to a pigeon-house in the roof. But I had been used to simple ways of living, and I was very tired; I wanted nothing but rest; and being young, rest came to me as soon as I stretched my limbs out and closed my eyes upon the hard grass mattress.

I slept all night dreamlessly; and when I awoke with the sun shining full on my face, and the pigeons, white and grey, pluming themselves upon the roof outside, I sprang up refreshed and fearless; eager to begin again this strange new story of life, whose first chapter I had read and turned down for ever when I had looked my last at sunset on Verona.

There is nothing in any after times, however radiant with pleasure or success those latter times may be, so perfectly happy as the buoyant and fearless ignorance of the creature who has just left childhood for youth, just first thrust out its head from the shell of dependence and ventured alone to survey with dazzled and de-lighted eyes the illimitable domain that lies in the mere Possible.

To any other than myself it would have seemed, as it had done to the Tirolean, that nothing in the whole range of human fate could be more desolate or more appalling than my fate; there was a child of fifteen years let loose upon the world with a dozen gold florins for her solitary possession, without a friend, without a refuge, and with no relative in all humanity, except a father who had abandoned her, and of whom she knew not even so much as whether he were living or were dead.

Nothing could well have been more lonely or less to be envied surely than I; and yet when I had flung the cold water over myself and tossed the hair back over my shoulders, and looked out of the window to say good morrow to the pigeons opposite, I laughed quite happily in the face of the bright day and was not afraid.

It seemed to me that nothing could long go very ill in that fresh spring air, in that warm living light, in that pleasant murmur of birds' wings, and of drowsy bees, that rose upward on the stillness of the city from the little garden court below.

It was early as I unslid the wooden bar of my door and ran downstairs in the mirthful sunlight; but the padrona was up and about, and all her stout damsels at work with her, coming and going in their many-coloured garments to and fro in the brightness and the shadows of the open court and the sombre archways.

Great turkeys were ruffling and strutting about the passages, hens were squatting by the stoves, a big white owl blinked his eyes on a butter tub, and grey rabbits ran between the swiftly flying feet of the inn-maidens as they vied in haste to obey the shrill commands of their mistress.

In the square court they had set out the winter-housed store of lemon trees.

There was a thread of water bubbling from a sculptured Medusa's mouth into a huge earthen amphora; on the door sill an old woman was slicing carrots; above her in the carved lintel was a Lucca della Robbia worth its weight in gold: it was such a scene as might have stayed there unchanged since Guido had first dipped his brush in oils.

I had all the forenoon before me, and not liking

to take up room there in that busy tavern, I wandered out to look a little at the city.

A winding passage-way led from the court-yard straight out in front of the two leaning towers, with their coppersmiths' workshops beneath them and above the clear blue sky of the Romagna.

It was about nine o'clock and a market day, and all the town was astir; throngs of busy, laughing hurrying people were crying their goods aloud, or lustily chaffering for the goods of others; whilst around them were those old sun-burned walls, those dim gigantic frescoes, those austere arcades, those mighty stones that had borne the fires and the furies of a thousand years of sack and siege.

Mules brayed, dogs barked, poultry cackled, the charlatan screamed his sing-song recitative, the hawkers vaunted their dried pumpkin seeds, their little fried alardi, or their barrowful of many-coloured woollen socks and kerchiefs; the bells clanged sonorously, the old scriveri held solemn court within their dens, the peasants rode in on their asses laden with cabbages or with poultry; the ringing hammers of the countless coppersmiths and pewterers resounded from a hundred workshops; and it was all life, mirth, tumult, business; and amidst it all rose the old unfinished mournful pile of the Duomo, the ancient palaces with beggars' rags fluttering from the balconies, the slanting shafts of the twin towers, the arched footways brown and sear with the passing of a thousand generations.

In the gay sunlight it was not so terrible as in the darkness of night; but it was perhaps more melancholy still.

I wandered on and on, looking now at the contention of some buyer and seller under the leathern awning of a market-stall, and now at the grandeur of some decaying fresco dying slowly of neglect and age above on the sculptured houses.

I stood gazing up at the Garisendà, where it leaned above against the delicate blue of the immense Romagna skies, whilst beneath in their dusky workshops the brawny bare-armed coppersmiths beat the ruddy metals, their hammers rising and falling with steady and deafening rhythm.

I stood gazing at the Garisendà and the Assinelli that in their day had seen the slender hands of Properzia de' Rossi at work upon the monumental marbles; and had heard the last Bentivoglio called from his workshop to a crown; and had watched the scholars come from all far countries—from wild Ireland, away in the mists of the northern seas, as from fountain filled Damascus rose-girt on the edge of the desert,—trooping by thousands and tens of thousands to pace the stones and learn the lore of the great Academy.

I loitered long in the old stone labyrinths of the Bentivoglio's city. It awed me, it oppressed me, yet it allured me.

The Past is very gaunt and grim in the old University, but it is noble for all that. It is like the lofty skeleton of a dead knight wrapped in the black cloak of the Misericordia.

The people chattered with me gladly; and told me where to find the Raffael, the Guido, the Domenichino, the Tarini, above all their darlings — the Carracci.

In Verona I had felt but little the genius of the place. Verona had forgotten so much; the foe's heel had stamped out her brain; and besides, her great Paolo, ages ago, was stolen utterly from her by wanton Venice.

But here in Bologna it was beautiful to find how dear and living to them their three Brethren were.

Stendahl was astonished to find his cobbler in Bologna able to tell him all sorts of traits of the Carracci, and really full of sorrowful reminiscences, because Luigi had died of grief at some bad drawing of his own in the angel of the Annunciation. Stendahl adds that a cobbler in Paris would have had a gilt chair in his shop, but would have told you nought of Greuze or of Gros.

It is just this tenderness of the past and knowledge of it, which make the Italian populace unlike any other under the sun:—in these peoples' eyes there are always dreams, and in their memories there is always greatness.

Wandering full of these thoughts, vivid and yet confused in my brain, the hours sped away uncounted by me.

That there was pain or danger or singularity in my position, I had utterly forgotten. I was only glad to be free and to be amidst these places which had lived so long for me only in the light of imagination and of history.

I was standing under the Garisendà picturing that old academic life and thinking how good the days of a student must have been in those times when the meaning of scholarship had just touched the world with its light; I was just standing there, when the

voices of men and women beside me caught my ear,
speaking of an opera which had been given the previous night with unusual pomp before all the great
people of the Romagna.

Its name arrested me; for it was the Alkestis.

"A German opera!" said one with a shrug of his
shoulders. "We have to swallow it."

"Nay, it is fine music; music that has held all the
stages of Europe forty years," said another. "And it
is more Italian than anything; the man studied always
in Milan——"

"But what good thing has he written since?"

"Mere *roba*," grumbled the first speaker. "It is
that which beats me; and he gets such prices!—he
is as rich as all the Ghetto — whilst look at our
Rossini."

"Those German hogs get all the truffles of Europe,"
said the other with a sigh. "But there is this Rothwald, the guest of the Grand Duke, to-day, and to-
morrow of the Cardinal, and what not, and good
Italians starving their naked bones over a pinch of
charcoal in their garrets, with more melody in their
do, re, me, as they sing to themselves as they saunter
about, than this fellow in all his long lifetime."

"Caro, caro, be just," laughed the others. "The
Alkestis is perfect, quite perfect; our fathers settled
that long ago; but then of course it is due to Milan,
since he studied there. Rothwald is a great old man,
that we are bound to confess, and his music is as
fresh to-day as though some youngster had just penned
it. The chorus people sang his great Cora degli Dei,
under his window in the Palace this morning early
He was quite touched; he came out into the balcony

and there threw down a handful of gold whilst they tossed him carnival flowers."

I heard, and my cheek burned, and my heart beat high with hatred: I thought of Ambrogiò Rufi as I had left him stooping over his wretched and solitary hearth.

"They honour Rothwald like that?" I cried to the students, heedless who my hearers were, as it was my careless childish fashion to be, everywhere and always.

They looked at me in surprise, and no doubt I had a strange enough aspect, glowing in my purple and yellow against the darkness of the coppersmiths' dens, and above me the quaint Garisendà.

"Why not, signorina?" they cried gaily to me, possibly amused at the rage of disdain that doubtless quivered over all my face. "Because he is a Tedesco? —a good reason, we grant."

"Because he was a traitor!" I said to them, and then could say no more, but turned away with a burning face and a swelling heart, for there seemed to rise before me the broken-hearted, weary, death-stricken form of my dear old master, and the thought of this man who had betrayed him was unbearable to me; this man, who dwelt in princes' palaces, and scattered gold broadcast, and received the songs and the flowers of the nation he had robbed.

In the fury against injustice and the passion of longing to redress it, which are part and parcel of all youth that is at all generous or at all unworldly, I felt strong enough to force my way to the palace itself up high on the hill there amongst the cypresses, and fling the truth in the face of this perjurer whose lie

10*

had been for forty years fair and fruitful before the world.

"Oh! why does God let such things be?" I cried in the rebellion of my heart against the cruelty of creation, as I dropped down under a little shrine in a twisting passage-way out of the public square.

Bologna had lost its charm for me; it seemed only a great dark, dusty, noisome, cruel place, with its strange city of the dead walled up beyond its gates.

What was it to me that my old master sat alone by a wretched hearth whilst the man who had betrayed him was feasted by cardinals and honoured by nations? What was it to me?

Nothing indeed.

And yet I sobbed bitterly as I turned from the streets into an old dark church, ashamed that the people should see the tears upon my cheeks.

CHAPTER VIII.

The Maidenhair.

THE church was quite empty: an immense naked marble desolation, with a white Christ looming vast and sad above the altar.

I sat down on an oaken bench and cried my heart out, as the children say: most for the cruelty of Ambrogio's fate, but also a little for the utter loneliness of my own.

I had little hope of finding my father; and if I found him, how could I tell he would not disown a little travel-stained penniless wanderer, as he had disowned the child with the peacock's plumes in the painting chamber of the Veronese students?

I dreaded his calm cold smile; I dreaded his icy incredulous response; I resolved within myself, if I found him not at Florence, to seek him no more, but to go on and try my fortunes at Rome.

For once, when I had sung in the streets to a little knot of people in Verona, an old man had come up to me and had told me he was the director of the Corea, and had bidden me, if ever I had a mind to appear in public, to betake myself to him there in the Eternal City.

"Might I not help you a little, illustrissima?" said a gentle, timid voice. I started, and saw the young Tirolean, the bright colour in his costume glowing in the gloom of the dusky aisles.

I was not sorry for companionship, yet I was wounded to be seen in my sorrow. I stared at him stupidly through my tears.

"You did not stay at Padova, then?" I asked him at length, seeing that he seemed more ashamed than I.

"No, signorina," he answered shyly, and then was still.

"You have business in Bologna?"

"No."

He spoke with downcast eyes, and swept the dust of the pavement with the long plumes in his hat.

"I was sorry for the little eccellènza," he stammered humbly. "And it seemed so terrible for her to be alone; so young, and with such a face as that; and so I dared to travel on with her. I was on the roof of the diligenza all the way from Padova."

Then he was silent; lifting, timidly, his brown, honest, dog-like eyes, that were wistful like a dog's that dreads a beating.

But I was too used to the comradeship of Il Squarcionino and all his boyish brethren to be in any whit embarrassed by this act of the young mountaineer. I took it as a kindly piece of thoughtfulness, no more.

"It was very good of you," I said, brightening a little, "and—and—it is true, I am all alone. But no one would hurt me—why should they? I am not afraid."

"The little illustrissima is hardly more than a child," murmured Marco Rosas, with a pity in his look I did not comprehend. "It is so damp and cold in this church. Would the signorina come a little in the country? There is a great Madonna here to see, they say, and the day is long."

I hesitated a moment, then consented. What harm could there be? And anything was better than being alone; and the young man was so gentle, so simple, and so frank, that he seemed to me only like a bigger Raffaellino.

So out of the gates I went into the white wide country, with the sun on its dusty roads, along which the bullock waggons were crawling.

Anywhere else I should have been stared at—in my yellow and violet, with the hood lying on my shoulders and my hair uncovered to the sun, and the young Unterinnthaler in his picture-like dress of velvet, and broad red sash, and hat with the drooping myrtle-green plume.

But in Italy—blessed Italy—no one noticed.

There is such immunity from observation in a country where colour is a household fairy brightening every rent and ruin, in lieu of an unknown god at once dreaded and derided.

So I went on in the sunshine along the road that leads to the Madonna of S. Luca high on her green hill.

We made our obeisance at her shrine, and gazed through the wonderful breadth of the plains with their countless cities and towns, and the low lines of the circling mountains lying curve on curve in endless undulation.

Then we came down from the height and wandered whither we knew not exactly amongst fresh-turned fields and vines just set with leaf, and orchards of olive and mulberry, where many a little quiet paese nestled with white-walled houses and red-roofed dove-cotes. At one of these poderi there was a woman with a merry handsome face and a scarlet kirtle sitting spinning on the top of a flight of steps under a dark archway hung with convolvulus.

Marco Rosas asked her if she could give us a draught of milk.

She assented joyfully, and brought out not only milk but honey and pomegranates and black sweet bread, and set them out on a stone bench on the top of the step under the convolvulus; and would have us eat there and then, she spinning all the while and telling us her own history and her grandmother's before her, looking across the great sunny plains that stretched away like the sea-green ocean, some white tower rising here and there out of the sun-mist like a seagull on the wing.

She was a cheery, good-hearted creature; she lived on the most wondrous battle-field of all Europe, but she knew nothing of that; she only knew that her eggs sold well in Bologna market, and her bit of land was fruitful, and her husband was a good man though careless, and her olive-trees had been bit by the frost and would bear ill that summer.

We had a pleasant hour with her there on the sunny steps facing the low tumbled crests of the Apennines, hyacinth-hued in the clear spring weather.

We bade her farewell with many good wishes on either side, and went on our way to the city. The sun was not far from its setting.

During those long sauntering walks the Unterinnthaler had told me still more about himself and his birthplace in the high mountains.

As we drew under the city walls he began to speak again, and a little confusedly, of his country, of his home, of his people. His millet-fields and his mountain cattle were dearer to him than all the dead glories of Bologna.

"The châlet is large," he told me, "and Anton, my brother, is a good, gentle lad. There is a great store of linen, for my mother and her mother before her were great spinners; and there is some little silver in the plate chest, for our people have been there for generations. It is not so very cold in the winter-time, for everywhere we have double windows, and we can afford to burn as many oak logs as we like. And then in the spring it is so beautiful—all the waters leaping as though they were mad, and the loose snows rushing, thundering down, and the cattle lowing with delight to get once more up on their pastures, and

the hyacinths and gentian springing up everywhere—
oh, signorina, you do not know how beautiful it is
upon our mountains then!"

"No doubt," I answered him, dreamily, my thoughts
not being with him.

"Much more beautiful than all this!" he said,
with a sweep outward of his hand to the country.
"Here it is just maple and mulberry, mulberry and
maple, over and over again, and those endless vineyards everywhere—so flat, so pale and tiresome."

"No doubt," I said again to him, indifferent,
watching the white bullocks come through the gates
with an open waggon of the past year's hay.

He was silent a little while; then he spoke again;
his voice was swift and low.

"Signorina, did ever you hear of a tale that our
priest told us once? There were terrible times across
the mountains, amongst the Francesi, I think, and
the peasantry rose against the aristocrats, and everywhere they slew the nobles; and at one place the
nobles were drowned by thousands in a river. Do
you know?"

"You mean the Noyades of Nantes?"

"It may be. I cannot tell the name. It was in
some time of revolution, and they did not spare even
the women. All the wives and daughters and mothers
of the nobles were bound and flung into the water.
There was only one way that anyone of those young
noble maidens could be spared; it was if one of the
men of the populace asked and took her in marriage——"

He stopped abruptly. I, gathering some tufts of
maidenhair off the city wall, laughed a little.

"The waters were better, I should think. Well?"

"Signorina," he began once more, and as I looked up, astonished at the tremulous sound in his voice, I saw his eyes fastened on me in pathetic entreaty, still as of a dog that prays of you not to beat him. "Signorina, I have been thinking. It is almost as ill with you as with those young noble Francese maidens. You are all alone, and you have no home and no friends—you have told me so; and surely your father cannot be amongst the living, or he had never been silent so long. Now, I am only a mountaineer, I know that, and ignorant, and altogether beneath you, and yet if you would let me give you my home so long as ever—as ever—you want one. The world is bitter and bad for a motherless child."

He paused and grew very red, then hurried on with his explanation.

"I meant—if you would come to us—my mother is so good: the little illustrissima would get to care for her; and the place is humble indeed, but sweet and wholesome—and safe. I would go straight back with the donzella, and not rest till she was safe with my mother on the mountains. And I—I know well the donzella would never look at me, never think of me —I should never dream of it. But if she would only let me be of use to her, only let me put a roof over her head, I should be so thankful! I would serve her like a dog. For—for—in this one little short day I have got to love her so well!"

Then he stopped abruptly, and grew very white, and I could hear his quick hard breathing as we stood together outside the gates of Bologna in the red sunset light.

My first impulse was that of ungrateful waywardness.

What! escape from Verona only to end my gorgeous dreams in a peasant's shieling on northern mountains! I, who had set my face to the golden south, dreaming of my Sordello of the winter's masque, of my Romeo of the fairy roses.

I am ashamed to say that, like a spoilt and cruel child as I was, I flashed on him a contemptuous glance and laughed aloud.

The moment my laughter had struck on the evening silence I was sorry. I shall never forget the look on the frank fair face of Marco Rosas.

"The donzella is right and I was mad—no doubt," he murmured, humbly; then he fell behind, and followed me in silence through the gates into the grim old town.

My heart smote me a little as I went. He had meant so well; perhaps it was cruel in me to wound him.

I heard his slow firm tread behind me until I had passed into the open court of the Cignale d'Oro.

Then he stopped, and his voice—quite changed in tone—muttered in my ear—

"Signorina, I will never see your face again. Say you forgive me once?"

I turned and looked at him, relenting a little. It was so absurd; and yet some sense of his thorough goodness, of his perfect simplicity and sincerity, stole on me and moved me despite myself.

I stretched my hand out to him with the little shaking maidenhair as a peace-offering.

"You were very good," I said to him, half laughing, half crying. "I thank you very much indeed; only, it was so absurd, you know;—go away and forget me; pray, pray do, or I shall be so sorry!"

He took the little tuft of grasses and looked at me with a wistful sadness in his eyes that haunted me for many an hour after.

"I shall never forget, dear signorina. Never—till I die."

Then he bent his head very low, and turned away and left me.

One little short day, and a life was won!

I felt a strange thrill of conscious power, yet a sense of some wrong thing done by me, as I watched him pass wearily through the entrance passage and disappear into the blackness of the shadow.

I let him go in silence, and went upstairs to my little room under the eaves.

CHAPTER IX.

The Snow-flower.

I WAS pained and yet incensed.

It seemed as though all the cares and sorrows of mature years crowded in on me in one moment. I had been so happy in my heedless goodfellowship with any one who smiled on me, and was willing to be idle and mirthful with me for an hour.

I do not know how others have been moved by the first utterance of love to them; but to me it brought a weary sense of burdensome power and of lost liberty. All the golden hazy glory of my future seemed to have faded suddenly. The future was only now to me a blank uncertainty, which might hold anything—or nothing.

All the gay elastic hopefulness of the previous day was gone from me. I leaned on the edge of my little casement, tired, and with an aching heart.

It was another red and gold evening.

The voices were merry in the cortile below. The little boy of the house played dominoes with his granddam on the stone steps. The padrona and her maidens hurried in and out, for the inn was full of travellers passing through towards Padova and Venice and Milan.

The whole was a little bright busy picture in the sombreness of this great old city, which had seen so much bloodshed, so much genius, so much woe, so much splendour, and now lived on, on its past, as childless greybeards do alone amidst their palaces.

I had no heart any more that day for the streets of Bologna. I shut myself in my little chamber and watched the pigeons plume themselves upon the roof, and heard the chattering, laughing voices down below, and vexed my soul as young things will over the perplexities and the cruelties of human life.

The warm sunset was just tinging the solemn greys of the city into all manner of tender hues, when above the clatter of the voices I heard the little shrill voice of the child of the inn crying as he ran out into the court,—

"Oh, mother, mother! give me a scudo—just one to spend to-night."

"Fie, you naughty soul!" grumbled the mother; "you are always spending money. You will come to no good, Berto. The Frate says you do not know your alfabeto, and you with those blessed Scolopì Fathers over two years!"

"Give me a scudo, mother!" pleaded the little lad. "Only one! I will win it back at ruzzola to-morrow."

"Oh, I daresay," sighed the padrona; "all my dear little cheeses bowled away down the streets. You are a wicked one, Berto, and you my only child, and I a widow; seven years old too, as you are!"

"Give me a scudo!" cried Berto, clinging to her skirts, and, in fine, helping himself without more ado from the leathern pouch that hung at her girdle.

"What is it for, Berto?" she asked, catching the child by his long hair.

"Pascarèl, mother mine!" shouted the little scape-grace, who might have seven years at the uttermost. "To-night—just to-night—and then on to Florence. Will you come too? Do, mother!"

"I do not mind if I do," said the padrona, cast-ing her lace veil about her head. "There is only that little donzella in the house, and two traders from Ferrara. I do not mind if I do. Pascarèl is as good as a winning number at lottery. Here, Pasquà, Gilla, Marta,"——

She called her maidens round her, and set them their tasks of cooking, spinning, poultry-feeding and the like, standing in a circle of red light in the black and white paved court under my casement, and then went out with her little son down into the dusky tun-nel of the passage-way.

Pascarèl! the name bewildered and yet comforted me. What would it be, I wondered; a game, a show, a dance, or the name of a living creature?

The name of the man who had chosen the bright melting snow as its emblem?—the snow-flower that glittered a day in the light, and then vanished?

Anyway, it had a solace for me when I leaned there in the red evening, while the place grew quite still as the pigeons went to roost, and the old chimes called to vespers, and the inn maidens ran to chatter within-doors to the Ferrarese as soon as their mistress's back was turned.

Whatever it might be, this mystical Pascarèl, it went before me southward to Florence. If it were only a snow-flower that would melt at a touch, it seemed to me better than all the deathless flowers of Paradise.

As I leaned there watching the silvery birds fly against the reddened sky, I thought—why I do not know—of Properzia de' Rossi.

I knew her story. I had often pondered over it, and looked at the delicate sad face of her, with its drooped lids and its Madonna's eyes. She had dwelt here, in this mighty Bologna; and Bologna had made her its saint and sovereign whilst her short life lasted, and in her death had mourned her almost as Rome Raffaelle.

A slender, dainty, girlish thing, she had a name of power even in that age of giants. She dared to wield, and to wield well, the chisel and the burin in the days when Michaelangelo and Marcantonio held them as their sceptres. Her city honoured her, and the envy and injury of Amìco gave her the surest warranty of triumph.

And yet,—she had no joy in any of it; she won one by one all the laurels only to find them bitter on

her lips; the marbles chilled her as though they were
dead children, and the shouts of the Romagnese
homage was dull and without music on her ears. For
why? for this;—so little and yet all. That one, only,
in the city's width, saw no beauty in her, and no won·
der in her deeds: and this one,—alone of them all,—
she loved.

And he, not knowing, and when knowing, caring
nothing, but turning away his beautiful cold face into
the light of others' smiles, Properzia grew weary of
her work, and changed to hate her lavish gifts of
nature; and left undone the public sculptures she had
sought so eagerly; and would not for all the city's
wooing use her power again, but drew herself in from
life and light like a sea-flower that is thrown by
tempest on the rocks. And so, when Clement came
into Bologna to crown great Charles, and asked, as
the first of all the wonders of the place, for that Properzia whose fame had spread from sea to sea in
Italy, the Bolognese, weeping bitterly, could only lead
him to the hospital to look upon the fair dead body
of a girl.

I thought of her wistfully as the tawny evening
colours spread themselves like an emperor's pall over
the desolate city.

I only saw the beauty and the sadness of the story.
What there was of evil in it passed by me; the passion
and the shame shadowed out in that terrible sculpture,
which was the last her genius wrought, had no meaning for me; of the poison of unrequited desire which
had burned up and ruined all the delicate grace and
innocent loveliness of her nature and her life, I had
no sense or suspicion.

I was only sorry for her—dead all those centuries before—here in the city of Guido. And a strange new wonder awoke and thrilled in me;—what could it be, this marvellous thing called Love which had thus killed her?

And then I thought,—I knew not why,—of the dark and tender eyes of the Florentine Masquer.

The owl had awoke from his watch-tower on the tub, and had begun to boom to and fro hunting bats through the shadows of the angles and roofs.

The deep bell of the Misericordia boomed over Bologna in the stillness. The old woman, spinning at her wheel, stopped to cross herself and say a prayer or two for the poor passing soul.

I saw the stars come out, and thought of how they were shining there away across the plains on those lowly graves beneath the shadow of the Alps; and then I threw myself wearily on the little bed, and cried myself to sleep.

At daybreak I rose and went down and paid my slender score. Then I bade them farewell, and went out into the white and glistening light that heralds morning in the Italian plains.

An hour later I was on my way across the wild gorges of the hills to Florence.

CHAPTER X.

La Reine du Moyenage.

ALL day long, and all night long, the heavy diligenza creaked and rolled upon its course over the grey heights, and through the dusky ravines of the Apennines.

I slept and dreamed, and woke and gazed, and
slept and dreamed again; it was all blent to me in
a confused tumult of light and darkness, rest and
pain.

It was again daybreak, when, with a shock and a
dull crash, the great vehicle reeled over on its side
and fell broken and crushed upon the stony way, the
poor beasts struggling under their entangled weight
of leather, rope, and links of brass. It had been urged
too swiftly down a steep and angular slope.

I rose with a confused sense of pain, but I had
received no hurt.

There were stir and strife and lamentation.   Then
some one told me that it would be hours ere the
vehicle could be again upon the road, and that it
were better to go on foot to Florence: we were on the
hill-side, not a league away, and very soon night would
have fallen.   They pointed me the way; I followed it;
a rough road winding between high stone walls, descending always abruptly, and without beauty, white
with dust, and rugged to the feet; above, a wondrous
sky; sapphire blue in the zenith, all to westward glowing with a million cloud-flecks of intensest rose; the
rose of the deep carnation buds when they blush into
life with the spring of the year.

I followed patiently the windings of the path, always between the pale stone walls, a little solitary
figure, purple and yellow, as though the violets and
crocuses of the woods had dressed me.

Suddenly, with a sharp bend, the road sheered
downward into a wide valley, white and grey with the
blossoming woods of the olive.   In the midst of that

silvery sea was stretched the fairest city of all the empires of the world.

The sun was setting.

Over the whole Valdarno there was everywhere a faint ethereal golden mist that rose from the water and the woods.

The town floated on it as upon a lake; her spires, and domes, and towers, and palaces bathed at their base in its amber waves, and rising upward into the rose-hued radiance of the upper air. The mountains that encircled her took all the varying hues of the sunset on their pale heights until they flushed to scarlet, glowered to violet, wavered with flame, and paled to whiteness, as the opal burns and fades. Warmth, fragrance, silence, loveliness encompassed her; and in the great stillness the bell of the basilica tolled slowly in the evening call to prayer.

Thus Florence rose before me.

A strange tremor of exceeding joy thrilled through me as I beheld the reddened shadows of those close-lying roofs, and those marble heights of towers and of temples. At last my eyes gazed on her!—the daughter of flowers, the mistress of art, the nursing mother of liberty and of aspiration.

I fell on my knees and thanked God. I pity those who, in such a moment, have not done likewise.

My eyes were dim, but my heart was strong, and beat high with hope as I rose and stumbled down the rugged way, onwards, to the entrance of her gates; always with the great dome shining before me in the golden haze; always with the clouds light as a breath, scarlet as a flame, hovering above me in the windless air.

The afterglow was still warm in the heavens when I reached the city walls and entered the shadows of her historic streets.

I wandered all the evening, unconscious of fatigue, until the streets were all ablaze with lights, and all astir with people. I remembered then, for the first time, that it was the last Domenica of the year's Carnival.

The great white Seasons of the Santa Trinità rose like snow against the golden air. Monte Oliveto towered dark against the rosy glory of the west. There was a sweet sea wind blowing which fanned out as it went all the spiced odours of the pharmacies, and all the scents of the budding woods. The shops of the goldsmiths, and mosaic sellers, and alabaster workers gleamed and sparkled in the light. Everywhere there was some beauty, some fragrance, some treasure; and above it all rose the wondrous shaft of the campanile, glancing like gold and ivory in the sun.

Where lies the secret of the spell of Florence?— a spell that strengthens, and does not fade with time?

It is a strange, sweet, subtle charm that makes those who love her at all love her with a passionate, close-clinging faith in her as the fairest thing that men have ever builded where she lies amidst her lily-whitened meadows.

Perhaps it is because her story is so old, and her beauty is so young.

Behind her lie such abysses of mighty memories. Upon her is shed such radiance of sunlight and of life. The stones of her are dark with the blood of so many generations, but her air is bright with the blossoms of so many flowers; even as the eyes of her people have in them more sadness than lies in tears, whilst their lips have the gayest laughter that ever made music in the weariness of the world.

Rome is terrible in her old age. It is the old age of a mighty murderess of men. About her there is ever the scent of death; the abomination of desolation. She was, in her days of power and of sorcery, a living lie. She called herself the mother of freed men, and she conceived but slaves. The shame of her and the sin cling to her still, and the blood that she shed makes heavy and horrible the air that she respires. Her head is crowned with ashes, and her lips, as they mutter of dead days, breathe pestilence.

But Florence, where she sits throned amidst her meadows white with lilies, Florence is never terrible, Florence is never old. In her infancy they fed her on the manna of freedom, and that fairest food gave her eternal youth. In her early years she worshipped ignorantly indeed, but truly always the day-star of liberty; and it has been with her always so that the light shed upon her is still as the light of morning.

Does this sound a fanciful folly? Nay, there is a real truth in it.

The past is so close to you in Florence. You touch it at every step. It is not the dead past that men bury and then forget. It is an unquenchable thing; beautiful, and full of lustre, even in the tomb, like the gold from the sepulchres of the Ætruscan kings that shines on the breast of some fair living woman, undimmed by the dust and the length of the ages.

The music of the old greatness thrills through all the commonest things of life like the grilli's chant through the wooden cages on Ascension Day; and, like the song of the grilli, its poetry stays in the warmth of the common hearth for the ears of the little children, and loses nothing of its melody.

The beauty of the past in Florence is like the beauty of the great Duomo.

About the Duomo there is stir and strife at all times; crowds come and go; men buy and sell; lads laugh and fight; piles of fruit blaze gold and crimson; metal pails clash down on the stones with shrillest clangour; on the steps boys play at dominoes, and women give their children food, and merry maskers grin in carnival fooleries; but there in their midst is the Duomo all unharmed and undegraded, a poem and a prayer in one, its marbles shining in the upper air, a thing so majestic in its strength, and yet so human in its tenderness, that nothing can assail, and nothing equal it.

Other, though not many, cities have histories as noble, treasuries as vast; but no other city has them living and ever present in her midst, familiar as household words, and touched by every baby's hand and peasant's step, as Florence has.

Every line, every rood, every gable, every tower, has some story of the past present in it. Every tocsin that sounds is a chronicle; every bridge that unites the two banks of the river unites also the crowds of the living with the heroism of the dead.

In the winding dusky irregular streets, with the

outlines of their logge and arcades, and the glow of colour that fills their niches and galleries, the men who "have gone before" walk with you; not as else-where mere gliding shades clad in the pallor of a misty memory, but present, as in their daily lives, shading their dreamful eyes against the noonday sun or setting their brave brows against the mountain wind, laughing and jesting in their manful mirth and speaking as brother to brother of great gifts to give the world. All this while, though the past is thus close about you the present is beautiful also, and does not shock you by discord and unseemliness as it will ever do elsewhere. The throngs that pass you are the same in likeness as those that brushed against Dante or Calvacanti; the populace that you move amidst is the same bold, vivid, fearless, eager people with eyes full of dreams, and lips braced close for war, which welcomed Vinci and Cimabue and fought from Montaperto to Solferino.

And as you go through the streets you will surely see at every step some colour of a fresco on a wall, some quaint curve of a bas-relief on a lintel, some vista of Romanesque arches in a palace court, some dusky interior of a smith's forge or a wood-seller's shop, some Renaissance seal ring glimmering on a trader's stall, some lovely hues of fruits and herbs tossed down together in a Tre Cento window, some gigantic mass of blossoms being borne aloft on men's shoulders for a church festivity of roses, something at every step that has some beauty or some charm in it, some graciousness of the ancient time, or some poetry of the present hour.

The beauty of the past goes with you at every

step in Florence. Buy eggs in the market, and you buy them where Donatello bought those which fell down in a broken heap before the wonder of the crucifix. Pause in a narrow bye-street in a crowd and it shall be that Borgo Allegri, which the people so baptised for love of the old painter and the new-born art. Stray into a great dark church at evening time, where peasants tell their beads in the vast marble silence, and you are where the whole city flocked, weeping, at midnight to look their last upon the face of their Michael Angelo. Pace up the steps of the palace of the Signoria and you tread the stone that felt the feet of him to whom so bitterly was known *"com' è duro calle, lo scendere è'l salir per l'altrúi scale."* Buy a knot of March anemoni or April arum lilies, and you may bear them with you through the same city ward in which the child Ghirlandajo once played amidst the gold and silver garlands that his father fashioned for the young heads of the Renaissance. Ask for a shoemaker and you shall find the cobbler sitting with his board in the same old twisting, shadowy street way, where the old man Toscanelli drew his charts that served a fair-haired sailor of Genoa, called Columbus. Toil to fetch a tinker through the squalor of San Niccolò, and there shall fall on you the shadow of the bell-tower where the old sacristan saved to the world the genius of the Night and Day. Glance up to see the hour of the evening time, and there, sombre and tragical, will loom above you the walls of the communal palace on which the traitors were painted by the brush of Sarto, and the tower of Giotto, fair and fresh in its perfect grace as though angels had builded it in the night just past, "*ond' ella toglie ancora e terza e nona*," as in the noble and simple days before she brake the "*cerchia antica.*"

Everywhere there are flowers, and breaks of songs, and rills of laughter, and wonderful eyes that look as if they too, like their Poets, had gazed into the heights of heaven and the depths of hell.

And then you will pass out at the gates beyond the city walls, and all around you there will be a radiance and serenity of light that seems to throb in its intensity and yet is divinely restful, like the passion and the peace of love when it has all to adore and nothing to desire.

The water will be broad and gold, and darkened here and there into shadows of porphyrine amber. Amidst the grey and green of the olive and acacia foliage there will arise the low pale roofs and flat-topped towers of innumerable villages.

Everywhere there will be a wonderful width of amethystine hills and mystical depths of seven-chorded light. Above, masses of rosy cloud will drift, like rose leaves leaning on a summer wind. And, like a magic girdle which has shut her out from all the curse of age and death and man's oblivion, and given her a youth and loveliness which will endure so long as the earth itself endures, there will be the circle of the mountains, purple and white and golden, lying around Florence.

Who, having known her, can forsake her for lesser loves?

Who, having once abode with her, can turn their faces from the rising sun and set the darkness of the hills betwixt herself and them?

CHAPTER XI.

The Midnight Fair.

So beautiful was it all, so strange, so wild, so fantastic, that all hunger, fatigue, and fear were forgotten by me in its curious delight. I wandered on and on, asking nothing, only for ever looking and looking and looking. I thought that I had strayed over the border land that parts us from the past, and was amidst the breathing burning life of the Cinque Cento.

By many and various streets—all made noble with frowning fortress, carven statues, walls massive and lofty as alpine slopes, ornament delicate and wonderful as frost on woven aspen boughs,—I came at length into a great square, which I needed none to tell me was the place where the soul of Savonarola had been sent forth on fire. For there the standard of the people rose on the tower of the Commonwealth, and the lustrous moonlight lay calm and broad about the feet of the bronze Perseus.

The Hercules and the David stood white and serene against the darkness; the battlements of the magisterial palace were set like jaws of iron hard against the night; the moonshine caught the colours on the blazoned shields that edged the walls; the beautiful Judith knit her brows against the world from under the black arch of her loggia. How still it was there, where only the shapes of marble and of bronze kept watch and ward in the gathering-place of the Republic.

Yet—a stone's throw, and all Florence laughed,

and danced, and reeled, and sang, and gamed, and
shouted in the open gallery of the Uffizi. A stone's
throw, — and in the very shadow of the Vecchio
standard, under the very gaze of the Donatello,
Florence in her wildest gaiety held her riot and her
revelry.

It was the midnight Fair of the Carnival.

All the length of the arcade was filled with the
bright and motley throng. In open spaces on the flag-
stones the people were dancing to shrill clamour of
fife and drum. Here a white Filatrice with powdered
face was whirled down by a scarlet Mephisto, and here
an Arlecchino all ablaze in squares of colour, spun
round a black domino ready masked for the Veglione.
There a débardeur, sunny-faced and stout-limbed, toyed
with a Neapolitan Pulcinello; and there a lithe contadina, with eyes of jet, galloped like a Friuli filly down
the pavement, tiring out a panting and piteous Stenterello.

On either side in the niches between the marble
figures were ranged the little gay canteens and stalls
of the traders; wines and straw work, and flowers and
woollen goods, and all the merchandise of the whole
contado, were decked out with coloured lamps and
painted devices, and streaming ribbons, and all fanciful follies of gay ornamentation.

Aloft on a barrel, the charlatan, in a flourish of
scarlet cloth, screamed forth the praises of his pharmacy and of his life-pills; whilst his compeer of the
lottery, in tissue of silver and a conical hat an arm's
length high, with flaunting peacock's plumes, rattled
his dice and shouted forth the winning numbers. Peasant
girls with penthouse hats of straw, grave fattori watch-

ing the selling of their wares, little children hugging loads of stracciataunta, maskers flying in a blaze of crackers, the people everywhere, in crowds, pushing, shouting, anticking, sporting, but always in glee and always in good humour, while here and there amidst them some patrician idler sauntered with some mistress of the hour, masked, upon his arm, smiling together as they watched the humours of the fair.

Amidst it all stood the white statues; here the quiet face of Arretino,—there the bold brows of the Uberti; here the austere sadness of Dante,—there the old man's smile of Sant' Antonino.

And away at the far end of the great gallery the white arches crossed each other high above against the blackness of the night; and in the gleam of the tossing lamps the drooping banners of the Lost Liberties hung, crimson as the blood of Campaldino and Custozza; and out further in the stillness beyond the stone parapet rolled the broad moon-lightened Arno water; and above all were the clear skies, breathless as in summer, the eloquent luminous purple skies of a Florence night.

This is how I saw the city first; this is how she will lie in my heart and in my memories for ever.

I was but a child; I was entranced by the goodly chaos of mirth and colour, by the beautiful outlines, by the zestful masking, by the gaiety and the grotesqueness that were framed in that stately setting.

I found a quiet nook under the marble shelter of the figure of old Taddeo Gaddi, and rested there and watched the whims and vagaries of the Florentines.

It had grown quite late. I heard all the chimes of the belfries striking and ringing the twelfth hour of the night.

Acrobats were tumbling, musicians were braying, the dancers were flying faster and faster, the swift crackers were running along the stones like stars, the buyers and sellers were raising shriller and shriller their clamour, the winners at the lottery were darting hither and thither triumphant, hugging their prizes of wines and capons and kerchiefs and sugar-loaves; and every now and then, amidst the noise and uproar, there would come a sweet, short ripple from a lute that broke in the air like sea spray; or there would pass through the crowd young, barefooted, with dreaming eyes that saw heaven afar off, and were blind to all the stir around him, some monk, with the head of Fra Angelico.

For in Italy life is all contrast, and there is no laugh and love-song without a sigh beside them; there is no velvet mask of mirth and passion without the marble mask of art and death near to it. For everywhere the wild tulip burns red upon a ruined altar, and everywhere the blue borage rolls its azure waves through the silent temples of forgotten gods.

As I stood against the stone figure of old Taddeo, a man went by me swiftly, laughing, and chased by the people. He was clad in the gay and many-coloured dress of the Neapolitan Pulcinello, bound, no doubt, later on, for the Veglione.

He had a scourge of bladders and little gilded bells in his hand, and he struck his pursuers deftly, casting amongst them wild words of the shrewd Tuscan wit that is sharp and silver like the leaf of the Tuscan olive.

The people flew after him, laughing, tumbling, shouting, frolicking, and as they chased him called out, "Pascarello! Pascarèl!"

It was he who had given me the onyx. It was my Romeo of Verona, my Florindo of the scarlet plume, and unconsciously I sprang forward and tried to touch him as he flew.

Alas! it was in vain.

He passed me like the wind, and caught a girl of the Casentino about the waist, and whirled her into the maze of the waltzing. He did not notice me where I leaned in the grey shadow of old Gaddi; and I soon lost him from sight in the mass of blending hues, and the strange chiaroscuro of that shadowy ballroom, with its torch lights flaming amongst its banners and the blue night sky for its roof.

A sense of deadly chillness and of blank disappointment stole over me.

He was but a stranger, and I had seen his face but twice, and yet I was stung to a passionate grief and humiliation to think that he had passed me by and gone to fling about in the wild dancing that black-browed, red-kirtled contadina.

The beauty and the frolic of the fiera were all over for me.

CHAPTER XII.

With the Wild Crocus.

I LEFT it with my eyes dim and my heart beating fast with a sickening pain; left it in the height of its revelry, the people streaming in faster and faster to join the merriment and take their chance at the lottery.

I had no knowledge whither to go or where best to rest the night. I moved across the piazza without quite well knowing where I went, and casting one look behind me at the Judith where she knit her dark brows in scorn against the folly of it all, I left the square by a little dusky passage way.

Some man accosted me as I turned into the gloom, but I hurried on, my hood well over my face, and he was in haste to reach the Uffizi and let me pass. *In the street that is named of the vine I saw a little homely-looking hostelry called the Silver Melon. I was very tired and sad now that the excitement of my entry into the city had passed by. I asked them if I could have a bed there, and when they assented I crept up to the little chamber that they offered me, and, after a little space, cried myself to sleep with the shouts of the populace and the strains of the music in the gallery hard by keeping the air astir all night and mingling with my dreams.

When the daylight came, a certain hope and gladness came to me with it.

There was so much to see in this wondrous city, and I was so young,—and, after all, things would surely go well with me.

The people had always said that I was fair to see; and those who knew had told me that I had a fortune in my voice. After all, I was in Florence, and I had a dozen broad florins in gold, and I was a child, and I was not afraid.

When I had broken my fast, I left my little load of clothes in pledge of my return, and went.

"Where, white and wide,
Washed by the morning's water-gold,
Florence lay out on the mountain side."

It was past ten by the clocks and belfries, and a flood of sunlight streamed on the Valdarno. In its delicious brilliance I moved on and on and on, enthralled, entranced, in rapture of the present, in meditation of the past.

> "River, and bridge, and street, and square,
> Lay mine, as much at my beck and call,
> Through the live translucent bath of air,
> As the sights in the magic crystal ball."

And of my magic crystal I was never tired.

All the town was astir, eager to make the uttermost of the last days of Carnival. The bells were ringing madly, in as much tumult and confusion of metal tongues as ever called the Trades together in the old days for a raid upon Oltrarno. The long, covered gallery of the Medician tyranny hung in the air like a black cloud. I thought of the day when to build it they had pierced through the cobbler's dwelling, and had laid bare to the tyrant's eyes the beauty of Camilla Martelli. One seems to see her sitting there in the little, dusky den, with the smell of the leather and the tic-tac of the shoemaker's hammer, her only companionship all through the weary hours, until the crash of the axes and mallets broke down the wall of the chamber, and, with the flood of the daylight, let in so wondrous a blaze of changed fortune. Beneath it, on the old bridge, the penthouses of the jewellers and of the workers in gold and silver sparkled with colour and glistened with treasure, whilst the men and the mules pushed by, and to right and left through the arches shone the sunny stretch of the river, the trireme-like group of the boats cutting sharply and darkly against the gold. I thought of that awful morning when over that bridge there had ridden the gay young bridegroom of Buondelmonte, with the white garland on his golden locks, whilst at

the feet of the statue of Mars the avengers had waited
with naked blades and souls set hard on the slaughter.
One seemed to hear the shiver of the steel against the
marriage jewels, and to watch the Easter lilies fall,
trampled on the blood-red stones.

Everywhere the people were about, they had
danced till daydawn at the Veglione and the Fiera,
what of that?—they tossed down a little red wine, and
fastened new signal ribbons to their shoulders, and
swept out in troops into the sunshine, ready again for
the masquing and motley. There were bursts of
music; notes of mandolines; ripples of laughter; chattering at all street corners; great clusters of scented
roses torn from castello walls beyond the gates; sweet
clusters of rosy cyclamen blushing faintly like sea-
shells; baskets of yellow muscat grapes and great
black figs, and the red hearts of cut pomegranates.
And above all the warmth, and stir, and glare, and
mirth, and tumult, there rose the spiritual beauty of
towers and spires, such as sculptors see in cities of
their dreams, and on the high standards there
flashed the scarlet cross of Florence that once had
burned triumphant above even the walls of Rome
herself.

It was past noon as I came out on to the river's
side, and saw to right and left of me, far as the eye
could strain, the lovely reaches of the sun-burnished
water, the near hills silver with olive, dark with ilex
and cypress, and, far, far away, the green plains, the
lines of Lombard poplars, the golden sea of light, the
purple shadows of the mountains, sown with their
countless villages and villas as a lake with the whiteness of its summer lilies.

So near they looked, so ethereal, so worthy to be some mystic border land of Paradise, those soft Apennine and Carrara ranges, lying fold on fold in their loveliness, that my steps were irresistibly drawn towards them until I had passed out through one of the city gates, and was in a wooded place upon the river, with deep ilex shadows above my head, and near me thickets of acacia, with their budding branches quivering in the light; and in the distance always those soft, dreamy hues of the Carrara marble flashing in the noonday sun.

Then, being tired and warm, I sat down upon a stone bench where the trees grew very thickly and bordered a meadow sown at every step with crocuses, until the grass was pale and purple with them.

I did not think what was likely to become of me, nor of how little probable it was that I should find trace of my father and of Florio. I was only dreamily happy, half-stupidly conscious of the charm of the soft southern air and the spell of the stretching mountains.

All was quite still: a rabbit scudded swiftly amongst the crocuses, nibbling here and there: a hawk flew by: beyond the canes that grew thick by the water there were some sweet bells ringing away there where the grey shadows of Monte Murello sloped upwards against the sun.

After a while an old creature, with a basket full of Roman lilies and Parma violets, came across the place where I sat. She cast some lilies into my lap, and called me her dear signorina, and begged of me a coin for the love of God.

"What bells are those?" I asked her, lifting the lilies, with their long green leaves, doubtfully, for I was too poor to buy them.

"Perretola, dear signorina," she said, sadly. "I was born there eighty years ago. It is hard to live eighty years only to sell flowers for a bit of bread. It is a little place. Step out, and you can see it across the vines. Yes, the bells are fine. They rang when I was married. I thought marriage a fine thing. He was a worker in stone. He got into trouble in the old Duke's time when the French were about the place; and was in prison, and what not; as if married men should do aught but find charcoal to boil the soup-pot—but it was the way of them all at that time. And now he is dead; dead a matter of twenty-five year, and we are no nearer all the fine free things he used to be mad to talk of, at least so they prate; and I sell lilies for a bit of bread. It was better in the old Duke's time—better in the old Duke's time—so I say."

Poor soul! It was "better in the old Duke's time" to her. To her, nothing the liberties of Italy, the rise of the People, the expulsion of the Gaul, the rebound from bondage into aspiration and free-drawn breath. It was "better in the Duke's time"—when she had had youth and health, and love and dreams, away there where the bells were ringing in the white village just across the vines.

I felt sorry for her, she was so old, so old: and to stand in the sun when one was as old as that, and hear the very bells that once rung in one's bridal hour and find no music in them, but only desire to mumble a crust in one's toothless jaws—it seemed horrible to me, very horrible.

"Give me something—some little something, dear signorina," she murmured, holding out her withered hands. "The lilies die so soon in the sun, and I have walked in from Perretola without bit or drop!"

Wisely or unwisely, my heart was won. I slid my hand into the little leathern pouch bound round my waist by a thong, in which all my little worldly store was kept. Oh Dio! the horror of that moment. The purse was empty!

In lieu of touching coin either of gold or of copper, my fingers slid down the bag, meeting nothing in their way. I sprang to my feet with a scream; I tore the pouch off my girdle; I pulled it inside out with the horrible vehemence of a deadly terror; not so much as a brazen scudo fell upon the ground. In the chamois leather there was a straight slit, as though cut through by a knife: the pouch was empty. No doubt I had been robbed the previous night in the press of the Carnival Fair.

I did not cry out; I stood like a frozen thing, in cold, gazing at my empty hands. The sunshiny country reeled before me; the white road seemed to heave to and fro like a sea. Everything was sickly, and blinding, and unreal.

I knew the meaning of poverty too well not to measure in one moment the whole extent of the ruin that befell me. The old contadina stood still and looked at me, appalled, no doubt, by the despair of my face and of my attitude.

"The signorina has nothing?" she stammered, thinking, doubtless, poor wretch, of her own empty

hearth and her own aching hunger. The words broke
the spell of the terror that kept me motionless and
silent.

"Nothing!" I echoed, and I know I laughed aloud
—laughed wildly, in riotous hilarity, in my unutterable horror. "Nothing—nothing—nothing in all the
whole world. My God!"

Then I threw myself down prostrate at the foot of
the marble bench, whilst the old peasant, aghast and
bewildered, stood and looked on, silent and appalled.
I could not speak nor weep; I felt as though some
huge stone had been flung on me and had stretched
me half dead beneath its weight.

With my little store of golden florins, I had felt
myself strong enough and hopeful enough to meet all
accidents of life and vanquish them, but penniless, I
was nerveless, hopeless, homeless. The extremity of
my dire despair stifled me, as though some suffocat-
ing hand were at my throat.

Alone, without a coin in the world to get me
bread! I thought how much more mercy the robber
of my little all would surely have shown to me if only
he had drawn his knife across my throat.

I do not know how long I lay there, crushed and
stunned, down on the beautiful crocus-filled grass of
the pasture.

The old woman stooped and touched me gently.

"Have you, indeed, nothing, signorina? Is it stolen,
or what? Do not lie like that—you frighten me."

I raised my head, and looked at her. A mist swam
before my eyes. The whole green expanse of the
meadow eddied giddily about me like a whirlpool.
But in the midst of my misery a vague remembrance

of how bitterly I must have disappointed her arose to me: she was not poorer than I was now; but then she was so old.

"I am sorry," I murmured, brokenly, "sorry for you; but they have robbed me—I have nothing in the world."

The poor old creature sighed; to her also the blow was heavy. She had argued from my face and my youth some liberal gift. But the generous and tender heart of her country beat in her withered breast.

"Never mind, dear signorina," she said, softly, "you wished to give; Our Lady will remember it to you just the same—just the same. And you love the lilies."

She laid another cluster of the flowers on my lap as she turned away. Poor soul! I hope that act has been remembered to her likewise.

How Italian it was! the little simple sunny kindness done in all the darkness of poverty and age and pain.

I could not speak to her again; vacantly I watched her figure, brown and crooked, pass across the blossoming meadow in the full blaze of the shadowless light. No doubt she went to sell her lilies at the gates.

On the road, which ran through trees beyond the field with all the vast panorama of the Apennines unrolled along its length, I saw a bullock-waggon creeping towards me, and farther yet a little cloud of people, bright against the sun as gold-winged demoizelle.

Instinctively, to avoid sight or sound, I rose and

wandered into the wood which bordered the meadow; it was of ilex and pine, dusky even at noon. I plunged into its shadow, holding the lilies to my aching heart.

I moved on and on through the trees, unconscious of what I did, until I struck my breast against the trunk of a tall fir with a shock that brought me to sharp consciousness of where I was. I sat down beneath its shade, wounded by the momentary pain.

I was all alone. I looked around me with a curious sense at once of apathy and desperation. I knew not what I feared; but I feared everything—I in whose daring eyes, a moment earlier, all heaven and earth had seemed to smile in the smile of Florence.

I dropped my head upon my hands, and crouched there at the foot of the pine. I sobbed as though my very heart would break.

As I sat thus there came the little white scudding figure of a scampering dog; he ran before a little troop of people: they all stopped at some distance from me at the end of one of the aisles of pine.

They were talking and laughing gaily. I could hear the indistinct bubble of their mirthful chatter; they had three dogs with them and a monkey; .they threw themselves on the grass, and took some food and wine from a basket, and one of them built up a fire with dry sticks; all the while the dogs frisked, the men laughed, the woman sang little fresh passages of song; they were all so glad and so gay, it seemed to make my misery unendurable.

The sun came down on them where they were stretched upon the turf; I sat alone in the shadow. I saw them; they seemed not to see me.

They had no doubt come out to breakfast in the Cascine woods, as Florentines will do on spring and summer days.

They seemed gay as the grilli in the grasses, and their dress was light and full of sunny hues; and from the broad hats of the men long scarlet ribbons floated. They had only bread and herbs, and some purple wine; but their laughter all the while was like a rippling brook, and they seemed not to know nor to want any better or fairer thing under heaven than thus "in sweet Valdarno to forget the day in twilight of the ilex."

They had a lute with them, and now and then one of them, the one who seemed leader amongst them, sang to it. His voice had the clear, sonorous, far-reaching vibration, like the chords of some stringed instrument, that belongs alone to Italian voices.

I sat there in a sort of stupefaction, listening to them, wondering dully how much longer the sun would only fall on other people and the gloom alone be mine. The slow tears dropped down my cheeks; my sobs had ceased; I had passed into the passive exhaustion of a great grief.

After awhile I think they caught sight of me, for they whispered together in lower tones. The woman with them rose and came towards me—a little pretty figure, plump as a little rabbit, blue, light, and gay, with twinkling feet and a small brown face under the lace headgear of Genoa, that seemed to me as bright and rosy as any tulip-bell amongst the wheat in Maytime.

She came towards me with a fresh charming grace, and paused before me.

"The signorina does not seem happy," she said, hesitatingly. "Has anything gone ill?"

I could not speak to her; I was ashamed and full of pride. I tried for her not to see the tears that were wet upon my face.

"I am sure there is something ill," she persisted. "The donzella is weeping, and all alone; if she would tell us, perhaps we might help?"

I turned my face to the trunk of the pine; but I could not keep from her sight the great mute sob that shook me from head to foot as I leaned there.

Perhaps it frightened her, for she was silent some time, though she did not move away; then, turning a little, she called to her companions.

I heard the step of a man brush through the grasses and approach her.

"Speak to her, caro mio," said the girl, in a low voice. "There must be something amiss with her, I am sure—and she so young too!—only a child!"

"If the signorina will not speak we can do nothing," said the voice of the man. It was very rich and flute-like. It was he who had sung the songs to the lute.

It conquered my pride. I turned and answered without looking at him.

"I had only twelve gold florins in all the world," I cried, in the despair of my heart. "And they have taken them, every one—every one!"

"Who have taken them?"

"A thief—how can I tell? In the fiera, last night, it must surely have been. They were safe when I came into Florence, and now—see here!"

I turned and showed them my poor little slit pouch.

I did not look up in the face of the speaker, for my eyes were blinded by their rain of tears.

He took the bag and examined it.

"Cut through with a knife, no doubt," he said, after awhile. "And you are very sad for the loss of this money, signorina? Someone will scold you if you go home without it, is that it?"

"Oh no!" I cried, with a fresh passion of weeping that I could not repress. "If it were only that! It is all I have in the world, I tell you—all—all—all!"

"But your friends?"

"I have none."

"What! You were adrift on the world with twelve florins—*you?*"

"Yes. Why not? I have no one to give me anything. I made that money honestly; it was all mine. It would have lasted me till I should have got to Rome. And now I have not a farthing in the world— not one—not one. I can sing a little, indeed, but then I promised Mariuccia never to sing in the streets, and I dare not break my word, for she is dead, you know. And I am all alone here in Florence. I do not know a soul. And my brothers are all dead; and no one can tell where my father is. But nothing of that frightened me so long as I had the money. But now I *am* frightened, oh Mother of God! for I have nothing in all the world, you see; I must just starve and die; perhaps even they will not believe what I say, but will take me for a thief, when they find that I have nothing! And if I had only died in Bologna!"

The passionate stream of the words had coursed from my tongue unbroken when once my pride had given way and found a refuge in speech; when my voice dropped in very weariness I stood before them heart-broken and striving with my piteous sense of shame; my cheeks burned dry my scorching tears, and my sobs died silent in my throat.

The man standing above under the ilex leaves laughed, but the laughter was tender and gentle.

"All nonsense, nonsense, *cara mia!*" he cried lightly. "No one ever dies in Bologna that can help it. It is not pleasant, you see, to be walled up in a square of bricks, and labelled dismally in the lump, with a thousand other '*vagabondi,*' or '*ladri,*' or '*briccóni,*' just as it may please the good town complimentarily to classify you. Take heart, signorina, and come and breakfast with us. Your gold florins, after all, may perhaps have been left at the house you slept in —who knows? You may mistake, or the thief may repent, or be found out, which is indeed the same thing. Come along and see my dogs, and taste my wine, if there be any left. Do not be afraid of us; we are none of us very respectable perhaps, except the dogs, but we will do you no harm."

Something in his voice and laugh, something of silvery resounding clearness, "*com' il dolce suonar d'una lira,*" ringing on a metal plate, thrilled through my heart familiar and full of solace. I dashed the blinding mist from my eyes and my falling hair from my forehead, and gazed up at him breathless and entranced.

"And you never came the next day!" I cried to him in passionate reproach. "And you never saw me last night! Do you not know me now? I have kept one of the roses—look!"

I took out of the folds of my dress one of the

dead white roses of Verona. His face flushed darkly; he laughed; but his beautiful eyes looked dim.

How had I been a moment without knowing him! partly, because absorbed in the terror of my grief I had paid hardly any heed to anything around me; chiefly, because on the two nights when I had seen him he had been disguised in the gay masquerade of the carnival costumes.

And yet his was a face not commonly seen, nor once seen lightly forgotten; the Cinque Cento face, the face of the old Renaissance when the features of men bore the reflex of the artistic and heroical life which was in its full flower in their midst. The face with aquiline outline, dreaming lids, thoughtful brows; profoundly melancholy in repose, and in mirth gay as a young child's; with eyes sad as death, and a smile frank as sunlight; the face which is the most historical and purely idealic of all human countenances.

Be the reason what it may, lie as it will in climate, race, or breeding, it is a fact that the Italian physiognomy retains as no other nation's does, the impression of the past upon it.

The noble comes to you down the bare stone galleries of his old palace, and it is still the noble of Tintoretto and Tiziano that salutes you with that cold and lofty grace, which can change at will to the joyous and caressing softness of a woman. The peasant of the contado flings his brown mantle across his mouth to screen himself from the mountain blast in the market place, and it is still the model of Angelo and of Sarto that laughs aloud from those glancing teeth, and saunters through the braying mules and bleating kids with those supple and sinewy limbs, and that unconscious harmony of gesture.

Were it not too fanciful one would say that those great centuries, while they gave an immortal soul to the pagan graces of art and produced human genius in its most complex and complete form, had so entered into the blood and bone of these people that their influence is deathless. The sun of that wondrous summer noon of art has set indeed; but the after-glow of its rays shines still in the regard of the living sons of Italy.

Such a face was this which had laughed on me in the moonlight in the streets of Verona, and now in gentle compassion was before me in the City of Lilies.

CHAPTER XIII.

The Great Magician.

I slid the rose back into its hiding-place a little shyly. The black-eyed girl was gazing at me with wide parted, astonished lips, and a little jealous wonder in her eyes.

"And you never knew me, last night?" I murmured to him. "Last night I almost touched you, and you never saw——"

"Last night! no;" said he, frankly. "When I go mad at the Carnival fair, I know nothing and nobody. But to-day, donzella, oh yes, I recognised you the instant you sat down under the cypress. That you have a genius for adventure is self-evident. How come you here all this way over the mountains?"

"But you never kept your promise!" I cried to him, intent on my one especial wrong.

"But you never came to me!" I cried to him, "You only sent the roses!"

"No, for the best of all reasons, signorina," said he, with a smile. "I had talked sedition that day, or so the stranieri construed it. I had lashed thy people with more than bladders, and had salted their soup with more than jokes; and to crown it all, in the Veglione, after I left you that night, I made an harangue which to Austrians' ears savoured of down-right treason. So, in the grey of the daybreak, as I went home singing and dreaming no evil, the good Tedeschi seized hold of me, and marched me out of the gates, and gave me not a second to pack my knapsack or send a word to my people, but set off with me for the frontier in the sleet and the teeth of the wind. They were fifty to one, so there had been no sense in resistance. Hard by the gates I spied a flower shop, just opening its shutters; I asked the soldiers to let me stop and light my sigaretto. Then I picked out a knot of roses, the best I could see, and paid for them, and bade them take them to you. I am glad they did so honestly. It was very cold tramp-ing across Lombardy, at a horse's tail, in that Florindo masquing dress, which looked absurd enough in the midst of the grey and white plain; and it snowed hard, and the tramontàna blew like a knife, but the sharpest thing about it to me was the thought that you would believe I had broken my promise."

He smiled a little as he spoke, that wondrous Italian smile which has so much mirth in it, so much tenderness, so much pathos. Surely that smile of

Italy is the loveliest thing left in all the width and weariness of the world!

Something in his accent made me turn and gaze at him. I breathed quickly in a happy excitation.

"Then you had not forgotten me really?" I cried. "I thought you had; I quite thought you had last night."

He laughed.

"Certainly not. I knew you, cara mia, at my first glance at you under the cypress yonder. You sang too well in Verona that day to be forgotten, and that wonderful black and gold dress, and your hands full of the Carnival roses, and that hair of yours with all the yellow lights in it;—yes, I saw you, and a pretty picture you made, that I grant I should have stayed a little to find you out; but your Tedesco friends and I have no love for one another. They say I excite the people. So I was fain to go out of Verona, not knowing your name, signorina."

"They have not stolen the onyx," I cried, breathless, standing still with the red sun in my eyes, whilst I tore the little silk cord from about my throat and drew the ring from its hiding place.

A flush of pleasure swept, like light, over his expressive face.

"Ah-ah! you kept that stupid thing? Too large and clumsy for your pretty little fingers, and no use to you at all. What did you do with the rest of the treasures? You had a fine lapfull that morning."

"I gave them away," I said, dreamily, not very well knowing what he said, gazing at him in the lustre of that crimson flash of the red and fading light in which we both were standing.

The little plump brown rabbit of a maiden peeped with her pretty, shy, raven-like eyes over my shoulder: she saw the ring with the Fates.

"Why, Pascarèl, that is your onyx," she cried to him; "the onyx you lost in Verona that first day of the Carnival when I was not with you, you remember?"

Pascarèl looked a little impatient.

"Did I ever tell you I lost it? At any rate the donzella found it, and it is hers now by every law of possession. Cara mia, those dismal old immutable Parcæ do not look fit dispensers of the Future to *you.*"

"Would you not have it again?" I murmured, seeing that he now wore no ring.

He repulsed it with a sort of gentle impatience.

"Would you insult me because I am poor? Keep it, signorina; though it be a grim and gloomy fashion of gift to you."

I hardly heard him, I was so bewildered at his recognition of me. I slipped the onyx fondly back within my dress. I looked at him, glad and astonished.

"How strange it is!" I murmured.

"Forse il destino!" hummed Pascarèl, in a soft mezza voce, as if in answer.

"Do you believe in destiny?" I asked him, wistfully, in a little awe.

"To be sure!" he answered me. "But it is always feminine, cara mia, whatever our grammarians may say to the contrary. And, now, will you tell me your story a little?"

"What could he be, I wondered, ceaselessly; of

what grade, what habits, what pursuit? A scholar in every accent, a gentleman in every gesture, with the pure inflexions of voice, with the slender delicacy of form, with the indescribable ease and indifference of manner which only come of birth and of breeding, he lived solely, as it seemed, amongst the populace; his white linen garments were worn and threadbare; his meal was of the simplest and most frugal; and his companions were nothing more than populace, little more indeed than vagrants.

Perhaps he caught and understood the speculative wonder in my gaze at him. At any rate, what could he be, I wondered. He did not leave me long in doubt.

"We are strolling players, at your service," he said, with his bright laugh, casting himself down beside me. "She who was so terrified about you is called Brunótta; that short lad with the round head is little Toccò; and the other one owns the time-honoured name of Cocomero. The three poodles are Pepito, Pepita, and Toto. The monkey is Pantagruel. Toto in especial is the star of my troop. Now you know us all. As for me, I am Pascarello or Pascarèl. If you are not afraid of such disreputable companionship, will you narrate us something of your own history, signorina?"

He had made me drink a little of his red Chiante wine and break a crust of bread; it was a solace only to be able to speak of my immense calamity; I told him willingly all my story, warming to the recital of my woes and of my wrongs.

He listened, stretched on the grass and leaning on one elbow; the girl Brunótta lent an eager ear, her little round brown face flushing and growing pale in sympathy; the two lads leaned against a tree open-mouthed and breathless; flattered by my interested and reverential audience, I grew a little calmer under my loss, and waxed more and more fluent in the narrative of my sad adventures.

My tale ended, Pascarèl sent the youth, whom he had called Cocomero, into the city to acquaint the guardia with the theft, and make enquiries at the locanda; that done, he threw himself again upon the turf. I wondered if he were sorry for me—he had not said so. All the ejaculations of sorrow and compassion had been Brunótta's.

I was full of passionate sorrow for myself; the sight of these light-hearted people only made my sense of utter desolation weigh the heavier upon me; when the excitement of the relation of my miseries had passed away, a very horror of despondency possessed me; and, without reasoning very much upon it, to find my Romeo of the Veglione nothing more than a hedge-comedian cast a shadow of bitter disappointment over the romance of my vague dreams.

"So you are absolutely all alone, cara mia?" said Pascarèl, bending his luminous eyes down on mine.

"All alone—yes!"

"And if we cannot find this thief, have not a copper paul in all the world?"

"I have told you so!" I cried with a desperation of pain at being driven to repeat my degradation.

"Altro!" he said, breathing gently that wonderful expletive which comprehends in itself every shade and variety of human emotion.

"Do you know what it is to be all alone and penniless in this best of all possible worlds?" he said, slowly, cruelly, as I thought. I almost burst out sobbing afresh under the torture of the question.

"If I do no harm, can I be hurt?" I asked, wistfully looking in his face.

He laughed, in a kindly compassion.

"Ah! if one does no harm, it goes very ill indeed with one in this world. We are suspected—for ever!"

In the stupefaction of my sorrow the irony was too fine to reach me.

"Is it right to do wrong, then, ever?" I asked, bewilderedly; for I knew that Mariuccia had been my only teacher, and that she, poor soul! had known nothing of the world. Besides,—in Ambrogiò's story, was it not Rothwald who had done the wrong, yet who had thriven?"

"There is only one thing wrong in the world— poverty," answered my new friend briefly.

"It is much the same in the country too," the little Brunòtta murmured.

"Assuredly," said the player, stretched on his back in the sun. "The country is only human nature washed in buttermilk; the town is human nature soaked in brandy."

"Why will you talk as though you were a cynic, Pascarèl?" said Brunòtta in petulant expostulation.

He held up the ragged sleeve of his old white jacket; it had been, I saw, of finest and silkiest thibetti.

"Every one is a cynic who has a hole at his elbow," he answered her.

"But—as if you cared!"

He laughed, and pinched her pretty rosy ear.

"We do not care; but then we are very disrepu-

13*

table. All respectable people care. It is only scamps
who smile."

"A smiling scamp is better than a frowning miser,"
said the girl; and she set the two white dogs, Pepito
and Pepita, to waltz round with each other, whilst she
waltzed too, singing a dance tune, down the avenue.

Pascarèl sprang up and caught her round the waist,
and set himself whirling likewise; the boy with the
fiddle struck out a wild waltz measure: the dogs capered, the monkey chattered loud, the man and the
girl span round and round laughing, with their hands
on each other's shoulders, and their feet flying like
leaves blown in circles by the wind.

The fiddle grew louder and wilder and faster; the
ape screamed in chorus; the dogs jumped over each
other and sank panting on the ground. Pascarèl and
Brunótta danced and danced and danced, with the
grass beneath them and the leaves above, and every
now and then a blaze of sunshine catching the blue
tassels at her skirt and the scarlet ribbons on his hat.

Then, at last, exhausted and laughing, and panting
like their dogs, they cast one another aside, and
dropped down on the turf in the shadow.

"How well it is to be poor!" cried Pascarèl. "If
we were dukes and duchesses we could not scamper
like that in a wood! we could only go masked, in the
gas, to an opera ball."

As he spoke he laughed, and fanned himself and
her with a sheaf of chesnut leaves. I, sitting alone in
the depth of the shadow from the cypress, watched
them, wondering, and envying their glad content.

Brunótta of the bird-like eyes seeing me sitting

there alone in the dark, rose and crossed to me, and touched me again gently.

"Pascarèl says it is always well for those who love to be poor?" she whispered.

I shivered a little. The double trouble was mine, to be poor without any love to help me under it.

"If both are content, perhaps," I murmured aloud. But I was very doubtful.

"He is;—I don't say I see it so myself," said the little player, as she dropped down by me and wove a plait of grasses, and talked in a cheery, quick, babbling voice like the tinkling of a brook; "we are poor —so poor—but then we are so merry. Pascarèl was not always so poor. He is a great comedian; only the people are all he will play to, and he does not care to be great. Coco's father was a Harlequin and never had any money; and they used to travel much as we do now. He danced for his own bread when he was three years old; and then, when he grew older, he played. He is eighteen now. Pascarèl has a talent —such a talent: I have none. I never did anything until three years ago, except milk the goats and take the insects off the vines, and plait straw, and spin, of course. I can only hop about. We have travelled with three or four companies, but Pascarèl never could get on with the directors; one director made love to me; and another one was cruel to poor little Toto; and a third one failed and ran away in debt to all his troop, and so on and so on; so we are as we are, and we have a merry life. The two lads and the animals love us, and we go about where we like; and Pascarèl can always make the people laugh, and we always get enough to live upon; and it is much better

than being at any tyrant's beck and call; and now
and then we have a holiday in the woods—like this.
In the winter it is a little harder, of course; but even
then the little towns are bright and warm, and the
people are always glad to be made merry; and before
one has romped through Carnival—presto!—the winter
is gone! A hearty laugh makes one forget that one
could eat more maccaroni, and when one's toes are
cold in the snow a dance warms them quicker than
anything. Sometimes I am sorry Pascarèl cares nothing at all to make himself great, because he has
such a talent; and if he were great one would have
such good things to eat every day, and fine clothes
and real jewels; but he says one should not care for
such things—but then to be sure he does not trouble
his head whether he eats a ciambello or a cucumber,
a swan or a sparrow! But how selfish I am to run on
so!—you are unhappy?"

The little actress saw the whiteness that came over
the face above her, and paused in the weaving of her
braid of grasses, and said softly again:—

"You are so unhappy?"

"Of course; but it does not matter."

"Yes, it does. Everything seems so unhappy—
except just Pascarèl and myself, and the dogs; and it
is such a pity, in a sunshine like this, when everything
ought to live like the crocuses, being glad and taking
no thought. You are unhappy because you are alone,
no doubt. Will you come with us? I am sure Pascarèl would be glad! It will be so much better; and
we will not teaze you to know what you do not wish
to tell—if there is anything——"

"But you know nothing of me——"

The girl laughed.

"Ah bah! We are not great people that dare not taste a pear till they know what stem it was grafted on. We are only poor players; we have nothing to lose; and if we take a liking to a face we are not afraid of its fellowship. There is so much liberty in being poor, you see!"

"Is there?"

I could not see it; it appeared to me that poverty was an ass's hobble, with which one was tied miserably to one place that we had long browsed bare.

"It is the difference between an old shirt and a new," said Pascarèl, rising and lounging near. "The new is embroidered perhaps, and very white and handsome, no doubt, but it is tight and the stitches gall; that shirt is respectable, admirable, and fit for a palace; but comfortable—no. The old is ugly maybe, and looks bad, and in it you will not be asked to a noble's table or a bishop's feast; but it is so easy to wear, and it has so many recollections, that dear old shirt: you pawned it here, and you danced in it there, and pretty fingers darned it in one place, and a rosy-cheeked laundress cobbled it in another; it is picturesque, it is memorial, it is venerable; above all, it never scratches. Those two shirts are Wealth and Poverty."

"Will it not be much better?" said Brunótta, eagerly interrupting him,—"much better, if the signorina come with us for a little space?"

Pascarèl swept the turf with his ribboned sombrero, and declared his willingness in flowery phrases.

"Only—only," he said, at the end of his graceful and gracious sentences, "you forget one thing, Brunótta.

The signorina is gentle-born and gentle-bred; our mode of life would be but a sorry one for her."

"But what can she do?" cried the little Brunótta.

"Ah! what, indeed?" I thought; and I threw myself down face downwards on the earth in a very paroxysm of despair.

Pascarèl threw one gentle look on me, then turned and walked up and down under the trees in meditation.

"Brunótta!" I heard him call; she went to him, and I heard their voices, low and earnest, in conversation at some distance from me, too far away for their meaning to be intelligible.

Then they ceased, and all was quite silent in the wood except the joyous and wild bark of the dogs as they chased a bird or a rabbit. I lay still there with my face pressed on the dry, hard earth.

"If they would only kill me," I thought, "and make an end of it all!"

A little picture rose before my memory of Raffaellino sitting at the coppersmith's door at sunset playing on his mandoline, while his mother and Mariuccia gossiped within over the lamp, and the light shone on the huge red coppers, and the stars came out over the dark quiet piazza.

"Oh, why! oh, why!" I thought, "cannot we know when we are happy!"

I would have given away twenty years of my young unspent life only to have been back once more in that old, despised, safe home in the city of Can Grande!

Pascarèl aroused me, touching me on the shoulder.

"Rise up, cara mia," he said, gently. "That is

not the way anyhow to get back your florins, or to win yourself new ones."

I rose as he bade me, and looked him in the face; my own face I felt was white with pain and desperation.

"I have been very foolish," I said to him, "and you have been very good; you are all strangers, and can care nothing for me. I will go now; I thank you very much—you and yours."

I put out my hands to him in farewell; his eyes were so beautiful, and he had been so kind, I could hardly keep the tears from flooding my own eyes as I spoke to him, and yet I knew I must not trouble them any longer—all strangers as they were.

Pascarèl took my hands and kissed them lightly with the easy grace of all his actions.

He looked troubled and almost embarrassed.

"Not so fast, donzella," he said, gently; "wait awhile; Coco is not back yet with any news, and even if he find your florins, it cannot be said that you are in very fair case for wandering over the country all alone. See here, we are not of your grade in life; we are poor strolling Bohemians; we are not, as I tell you, very reputable people, and we are poor as the devil—altro!—and yet, if you would like to stay with us as—as—Brunótta said, it might be safer at any rate for you than to stray about Italy by yourself as helpless as my little Toto would be if I lost him. We are a sorry resort, I know, but perhaps we are better than nothing, and I may be more able to find your father than you. Say, will you wait with us a little?"

Ere I could answer him, the youth Cocomero burst

through the bushes breathless from having run to and from the town.

"There is no news," he panted, gloomily. "They knew nothing at the Silver Melon, and the guards say there have been many foreign cutpurses in the city of late. They have had a score of such robberies this winter."

Pascarèl shrugged his shoulders and lifted his hands with that indescribable gesture in which an Italian expresses consummate disgust and resignation.

"It is destiny!" he murmured, resting his eyes on me with a look I did not understand. "Well, signorina mia, will you stay with us?"

"I should be glad!" I said, with a little sob in my voice. "It is so horrible—so very horrible—to be alone!"

"Of course it is horrible," he echoed, as he took my hands afresh within his own, and cast himself down upon his knees before me where I stood, in that easy unstudied abandonment of himself to each impulse and emotion of the moment which makes grace of posture as natural to an Italian as it is to a deer or an antelope.

"You will stay?" he murmured, still lightly holding my hand in his. "That is well—at least for you it shall be well; that I swear. Riches we have not, and glory we have not, and the ways of our life will be hard—for you. But all that we can do we will."

"You are very good!" I said to him, scarcely knowing what indeed to answer him.

He was a stranger, seen but half an hour before, and yet already he seemed like a familiar friend.

A shade of sadness and impatience swept over his speaking face.

"Che-che! Wait to praise us till you know us. We are good for very little, cara mia. We will make you laugh sometimes, that I can promise, and perhaps that is much in this life."

"But if I stay with you?" I said, a sudden fear and remembrance striking me with its shame, "if I stay—I have nothing; I will not be a burden to you; never, never! Is there nothing I can do to get my bread? My voice is good——"

"Yes! You sing like all the angels."

"About the angels—I do not know. But anything;—always."

"But you are so young——"

"Not too young for that—only I promised dear dead Mariuccia—— But I will not stay with you unless you tell me of some way to get my bread."

"Bread? Nonsense! You eat, I daresay, as much as one flings to the swallows. But, if you are in earnest, you might be one of us."

"A player! I?"

I echoed the words half in affront half in delight. My pride rebelled, my fancy was allured.

"Why not?" said Pascarèl. "Do you know aright what it is to be one?"

"Surely!" I answered him, with a little gay contempt—had I not seen them scores of times in Verona? "It is to be no longer a man or a woman, but only a mere wooden *burattino* that has to dance or die, to swagger or shrink, just as its master chooses to make people laugh for a copper coin. A fine thing, certainly!"

Pascarèl released my hands and sprang to his feet erect. His mobile face flushed darkly; his changeful eyes flashed fire.

"Is that all you know?" he cried, while his voice rang like a trumpet-call. "Listen here, then, little lady, and learn better. What is it to be a player? It is this. A thing despised and rejected on all sides; a thing that was a century since denied what they call Christian burial; a thing that is still deemed for a woman disgraceful, and for a man degrading and emasculate; a thing that is mute as a dunce save when, parrot-like, it repeats by rote with a mirthless grin or a tearless sob; a wooden doll, as you say, applauded as a brave puppet in its prime, hissed at in its first hour of failure or decay; a thing made up of tinsel and paint, and patchwork, of the tailor's shreds and the barber's curls of tow—a ridiculous thing to be sure! That is a player. And yet again,—a thing without which laughter and jest were dead in the sad lives of the populace; a thing that breathes the poet's words of fire so that the humblest heart is set aflame; a thing that has a magic on its lips to waken smiles or weeping at its will; a thing which holds a people silent, breathless, intoxicated with mirth or with awe, as it chooses; a thing whose grace kings envy, and whose wit great men will steal; a thing by whose utterance alone the poor can know the fair follies of a thoughtless hour, and escape for a little space from the dull prisons of their colourless lives into the sunlit paradise where genius dwells;—*that* is a player, too!"

His voice trembled a little over the closing words, and, ashamed of the passionate eloquence into which the sting of my idle slighting phrase had hurried him, he turned away and began to romp and laugh and gambol with Pepito and Pepita.

I listened; ashamed myself; moved, I knew not very well why; and regretful to think that I had wounded him.

I waited a little while; then I went up to him where he stooped over his dogs, and laid my fingers on his arm.

"I spoke idly," I murmured. "I did not think. And—and—I will try and be a player too."

He lifted his head, with a flash of light over all his face, and touched my hand caressingly with his own.

"Altro!" he said. "It is a fate. Come with us. But as for being a player;—wait and see. You must not choose your future in blind haste."

Then he bade me sing to him, which I did, and Toccò touched his violin in quaint accord with me; and Pascarèl himself raised the echoes of the wood with half the popular songs of Italy.

So, laughing and singing, and pausing to watch the dogs at play, we idled time away under the black pines and the budding chestnut trees.

I was only a child; I was almost happy again. Sometimes I started and wondered if indeed I had been so wretched, there, in that very place, an hour before.

Was he a magician, I wondered, this Pascarèl?

I was ungrateful to the supreme magician—Youth.

BOOK III.

THE DAUGHTER OF HERCULES.

CHAPTER I.

Under the Red Lily.

THE day rolled onward, growing chill something early, for it was still but the very first commencement of the spring.

I seemed to have known them all my life long—this little gay, good-humoured band; and the poodles frisked and fawned upon me as impartially as on Brunótta.

She—this pretty little brown thing—was not jealous of their sudden transference of caresses; she was about six years older than I—a girl of the people, no doubt, but with something so good-natured, so confiding, and so gay about her that one could not choose but trust in her and like her. She was so fond, too, of her brother, that one could see at a glance, and very proud of him, and a little afraid of him also.

He was very different in mind and manner to her; though a strolling player, as he said, he had the tone and the temper of a scholar: whilst little Brunótta confessed to me, half in glee, as one who had escaped a gruesome penalty and peril, that, like the padrona's son at the Golden Boar, she knew not her alfabeto.

What did that matter to me?

Raffaellino only knew it just enough to carry him

through the offices of the Church: it never seemed to me a science indispensable in people ere I took them for my friends, which, no doubt, was a grave error on my part, and due to my running loose in my baby-hood amongst these Bohemians at Verona.

The shadows and the cold came early in that dusky wood; we were almost in darkness, whilst the road and the plain were still in full sunlight. Pas-carèl gave the signal for moving towards the city.

We emerged from the ilex groves on to the high-way—Brunótta and I, Pascarèl and his dogs, and the two lads following us with the monkey and the fiddle.

"You have seen good players?" he asked me, as we walked on towards Florence, whilst the silver bells of Perretola and the deep toll of the city churches crossed each other ringing the Ave-Maria.

"I have seen the Burattini hundreds of times, and the Personaggi too, in melodrama," I answered him eagerly, proud of my experience, which was due to Cecco and the rest of the students.

Pascarèl gave his charming gesture of ineffable disdain.

"Fantoccini and melodrama! Oh, cara mia! how much you have to learn,—and to *un*learn,—which is much the harder of the two at all times! No wonder you think little of the stage."

I thought that I was willing to be great as Lillo was great, who had had the showers of gold and of lilies in Verona; but I could see no possibility of any greatness in a strolling player, as we passed over the white dry road, out of the rosy reflex of the sunset, on into the shadow of the Florentine walls.

"Even Destiny loses the light out of her hair here," said Pascarèl, with a laugh, as we passed into the deep gloom of the Borgognissanti.

He looked as if he meant to call me Destiny; but how could I be that, I wondered—I who was but a poor little stray leaf blown and buffeted by the hazards of every breeze of fate?

As we crossed the Carraia bridge and entered the heart of the city, into the twisting streets that curve all around the red dome of the Santo Spirito, and the frowning front of the Pitti, we passed by a cobbler's stall planted against the roadway; the old man, who was stitching at his leather by the aid of a dim lantern, called out gladly to him:—

"Che-che! is it you, Pascarèl? You are welcome as figs in summer!"

Some urchins standing idly near caught up the name; the street became quite noisy with the cry of "Pascarèl! Pascarèl! eccô il Pascarello!"

The people were all sitting in their doorways, or half out in the street, after the manner of Italian dwellers and traders, with little lights burning before some pile of faggots, some stall of chestnuts, some tray of amaretti, some stand of pizzicheria fare, or some image of San Giovanni. They incontinently left their trades and their pastimes and clustered round him in vociferous homage—whom would he sup with?—where would he drink?—did he play to-night beyond the Prato Gate? Beppe and Pippo had been fighting in the Sdrucciolò, he had been wanted badly;—had he heard?—who was that pretty purple and yellow thing he had got with him?—a new dancer? So their stream of questions poured out rapid and mellifluous as olive oil from a tilted flask.

But he shook himself free of them, and leaving the laughing, clinging, delighted crowd as best he might, he took me into the little tavern where they tarried in the town. It was a smaller place, and humbler than the Golden Boar; a great fig-tree climbed over it, just coming into leaf, and on an iron stanchion swung its sign of two crossed halberds, a relic, no doubt, of old Bianchi and Neri strife. But it was clean, and its people worshipped Pascarèl; and their laughter and their welcome, and the colour and pleasantness of the little place made it bright and cheerful in the midst of the dusky old age of grim Oltrarno.

There we dined frugally, as became Italians, whilst the brass stands of the lùcernati threw a feeble light over the pretty black head of Brunòtta, and the golden folds of my poor Court dress, and the Florentine face of Pascarèl.

It was only a poor little tavern; the chamber we dined in was only parted from the kitchen by an open arch.

We saw the food stewed and fried ere it came to us, and near at hand to us were some smiths and tapestry-workers playing dominoes and drinking innocent bibiti; and yet——I do not know how it might have been in other countries——but in Italy it was not vulgar, was not even common, but was only a homely, picturesque, pretty scene, full of colour, and movement, and mirth; a noble might have shared in it, an artist would have been happy in it.

They have suffered so much, these people, and yet through all they have kept their hold on so much; for they have kept the smile on their eyes and they have kept the grace in their limbs, and they have kept the poetry in their hearts.

When our meal was over, the clocks chimed the half-hour after six. Pascarèl rose, and we went out into the clear and cold evening, where the young moon was rising above the immense dark masses of the city buildings.

"You play to-night, caro mio?" cried the smiths and the weavers, and they flung their dominoes in a heap, and rose and followed us, talking and laughing with him.

I gathered from their talk that it was his habit to stroll through the country, taking the large towns and the little as they came, sometimes even pausing in the smallest villages, and setting up for himself a little theatre of canvas and wood, in the midst of any breezy pasture on the plain or sheltered nook upon the hills that took his errant fancy.

Brunótta and he and the two lads were all the little company which wandered as it would, subject to no dictation except that impulse of the moment, which was always law to Pascarèl.

By the enthusiasm displayed to him, he seemed to have a strange power to charm, or, at any rate, to amuse the people; and as I listened, the seduction of this nomadic, changeful, careless, adventurous life bewitched me, as it has bewitched so many in their youth.

From their discourse and the confidences of Brunótta I gathered that Pascarèl was always a bohemian, often a beggar; he led an idle, roving life, and preferred it to any other.

His stage had often been any plank across a cart or any board in a fair booth that might offer to him; he wrote the pieces he played that they might serve for his little troop, of which the dogs and the parrot were the stars; he rarely knew one night where he would lay his head another; he often ate his supper at a trattoria, trusting to his skill that same evening to pay off the score; when he made money, as sometimes happened—for he was popular everywhere, except with the directors of theatres—he spent it royally in a mingling of revelry and charity that left him as poor as ever on the morrow.

He was a stroller and a vagabond, so far as social status went, an idle rogue, and a dissolute; but at his heart he was a great artist; and in many a little village, and township, and country fair, and wayside tavern the people had found it out, and the cry of "Pascarèl" brought men and maidens, old women and young children, poor students and day-labourers, in a great eager crowd round any place where his changeful face, with its speaking eyes and its flexile lips, laughed out its mirth upon them.

"He studies nothing; he outrages all traditions; he violates every precedent and canon," said the directors whom he quarrelled with.

The people did not care for that; they only knew that Pascarèl, with a dog for his sole supporter, and a rag of carpet or a broken bough for all his scenery, could make them laugh or cry, hate or love, be miserable or be in ecstasy, whichever he chose in the irresistible dominance of genius.

At a stone's throw from the Cascine woods was an open space; the moon was already shining clearly

14*

upon it; a large tent, braced with timbers, was set up
in the centre of the place; the canvas was fluttering
in the cool evening breeze.

"There is my theatre, donzella," said Pascarèl.
"Oh, your Burattini have finer abodes; I know that.
When one only hangs on wires and has wooden legs,
one must have a fine house, or who will come and
look at one? But an artist, if he be worth his salt,
can make his temple in the minds of his audience,
if he have only the roof of a barn over his head and
theirs."

These were not the golden showers and Easter
lilies of Lillo! and a little contempt for this nomadic
drama rose up in me.

It stood on a breadth of meadow land outside the
Prato Gate, with the shadow of the mountain sides
behind it, and around it the scents of growing grasses
from the fields that had been sown for hay.

The people were trooping to it eagerly; townsfolk
of all trades and crafts, cobblers, tinkers, smiths, alabaster workers, mosaic workers, conscripts, carabineers,
market women, mule drivers, heaven knows what not;
and in from the villages of the Val de Grève there
were coming in the opposite direction many country
women who plaited their straw as they walked, and
contadini who had stuck a flower behind their ear as
evening dress.

It was a pretty little wooden house, light and
cleverly put together; sometimes its walls were open
to the sky like the old Basiliche of the Latins, sometimes its canvas roof fluttered over spectators as close
packed and as eager as ever the canvas roof of the
Coliseum shaded.

It had the flag of Florence with the red lily flying merrily above it, and above its entrance place was painted in gay letters the words "Dell' Arte."

I asked Pascarèl what the name meant.

"Oh, I broke a flask of wine against it, and named it so ages ago," he answered me. "Why? Because the first wooden home of Pulcinello and his brethren was called so when it rolled one fine Carnival day into Venice.

"A presumptuous name? Oh, I don't see that. We are all the arts in one, if we are worth anything at all.

"And besides, when they grew up in Italy, all that joyous band,—Arlecchino in Bergamo, Stenterello in Florence, Pulcinello in Naples, Pantaleone in Venice, Dulcamara in Bologna, Beltramo in Milan, Brighella in Brescia, masked their mirthful visages and ran together and jumped on that travelling stage before the world, and what a force they were for the world, those impudent mimes!

"'Only Pantomimi?' When they joined hands with one another and rolled their wandering house before St. Mark's they were only players indeed; but their laughter blew out the fires of the Inquisition, their fools' caps made the papal tiara look but paper toy, their wooden swords struck to earth the steel of the nobles, their arrows of epigram, feathered from goose and from falcon, slew flying the many-winged dragon of Superstition.

"They were old as the old Latin land, indeed.

"They had mouldered for ages in Etruscan cities, with the dust of uncounted centuries upon them, and been only led out in Càrnival times, pale voiceless frail ghosts of dead powers, whose very meaning the people had long forgotten. But the trumpet call of the Renaissance woke them from their Rip Van Winkle sleep.

"They got up, young again, and keen for every frolic—Barbarossas of sock and buskin, whose helmets were caps and bells, breaking the magic spell of their slumber to burst upon men afresh; buoyant incarnations of the new-born scorn for tradition, of the nascent revolts of democracy, with which the air was rife.

"'Only Pantomimi?' Oh altro!

"The world when it reckons its saviours should rate high all it owed to the Pantomimi,—the privileged Pantomimi—who first dared take licence to say in their quips and cranks, in their capers and jests, what had sent all speakers before them to the rack and the faggots.

"Who think of that when they hear the shrill squeak of Pulcinello in the dark bye-streets of northern towns, or see lean Pantaleone slip and tumble through the transformation scene of some gorgeous theatre?

"Not one in a million.

"Yet it is true for all that. Free speech was first due to the Pantomimi. A proud boast that. They hymn Tell and chant Savonarola and glorify the Gracchi, but I doubt if any of the gods in the world's Pantheon or the other world's Valhalla did so much for freedom as those merry mimes that the children scamper after upon every holyday.

"And we players are all their sons and their successors; and so I baptize my house after them 'Dell'

Arte.' Why not? If we be not artist we have no business to profane a stage at all."

And therewith he bade mè adieu, and ran in his room to dress.

We entered the booth—for in truth it was hardly more—as the Florentine clocks tolled the quarter before seven. The people were already gathering thickly in the meadow, and he could only break free of their vociferous welcome by reminding them that if they kept him there without, he could not play within; a sober fact which they recognized at last, though with some reluctance.

Pascarèl drew me to a place where I could see both actors and audience, unseen by the latter; the portion of the tent where the stage was made was divided from the public part of it by a curtain; behind this I was stationed.

They all left me and disappeared; Toccò ran round to light the oil wicks which were to illumine the performance. In an incredibly short space, so brief that it seemed to me Pascarèl must first have whisked a sorcerer's wand to change them all, Brunótta in short skirts of tinsel, and white and rose, and Cocomero in the vari-coloured dress of Arlecchino, and the dogs in quaint little brilliant coats—Toto pre-eminent by cap and plume—all bounded pell mell on to the boards together.

The curtain swung aside, the violin of Toccò thrummed a gay melody, whilst a drum, ingeniously beaten by his foot, rolled now and then its deeper melody.

They commenced one of those pretty and unintelligible dumb dramas of gesture, which are so popular in Italy, and hold the stage longer than opera, or tragedy, or comedy of voice, whether in their grander form of ballet at the Pergola or the Fenice, or in their humblest species such as that in which Brunótta and Cocomero now danced.

Brunótta danced with all the agility and vivacity of a girl who had spun round in the fairs and feste from the earliest days of her existence; Cocomero was a comic and untiring harlequin, and the quaint tricks and astounding intelligence of Maestro Toto were beyond all praise and would baffle all description.

The spectacle was received with glee and good humour by an audience which was by far too large for the limits of the theatre, and stretched far out into the open air in a sea of out-stretched throats and eager faces, in a curious chiaroscuro from the dark without and the oil lamps within, whilst they hummed the melody of the dance tunes all the way through themselves—a detestable mode of testifying musical delight, from which the most patrician musical audiences of Italy unhappily are not free.

The curtain fell, Toto as primo-uomo was thrice summoned and received a shower of sweet cakes and sugar, plaudits which were to his comprehension.

Then loud and imperious rose the cry:

"Pascarèl! Pascarèl! Il Pascarello!"

Pascarèl soon obeyed the summons, amidst the tumult of delight that greeted him from the throngs of coppersmiths, and carpet-weavers, and craftsmen of all kinds, and students, and beggars, and idlers of every sort who made up his motley clientela.

The little piece he played in was called "Le

miraculose fortune e gli amori pietosissimi del Calzo-
lajo e del Conte."

It had been written by himself, to suit the re-
sources of his scanty company; a thing of the slightest
and the simplest, in which he played himself the two
chief parts, those of the cobbler and the count.

It was only a trifle; but it abounded in wit; it
sparkled with irony, it contained epigrams worthy of
the palmy days of Pasquin, and every now and then,
amidst the rippling exuberance of its play of nonsense, it deepened and had an exquisite pathos hidden
in it; it was like a blue forget-me-not that the rains
have just dashed where it lifts its blue eyes in the
sunshine.

With the utmost ingenuity, the play was constructed so that the old man and the young, the
cobbler and the noble, whilst rivals throughout for the
love of a contadina, never met one another in all the
accidents of their fortunes.

His transitions from age to youth, from youth to
age, were so sudden, so marvellous, so perfect, each
in its kind, that none who had not known him could
have told which years were the real with him or which
the assumed.

Other actors in their youth have counterfeited as
wonderfully the age of Richelieu or of Louis XI.; but
they have been elaborately prepared by costume and
by paint, and have sustained the one part unbroken;
but here Pascarèl changed from youth to age with
scarce breathing time between the phases, and made
his personification a vivid living fact by no aid but
that of his own consummate powers.

It would have been impossible to say with which

impersonation the sympathies of the public were the stronger; each won them in its turn.

The youth of the young noble was so charming, so full of happy insolence, of generous impulse, of audacious ease, of irresistible assurance, of gay, good-tempered grace.

The age of the old cobbler was so full of sad genuine irony, of wistful loneliness, of pathetic fear of mockery, of trembling tenderness that scarcely dared be uttered; no slippered pantaloon, no palsied dotard, shrunken target for the gibes of fools, but Age—faithful, venerable, true to its own self-respect; but Age—unutterably sad because—alone.

It was a trifle, unaided by any scenic deception, or any delusion for the senses; but it was perfect as only the exquisite delicacy, the unerring truthfulness, and the supreme histrionic instincts of a great genius could make it; and as such it swept away to itself, with the rush of the storm wind, all the pity and all the passion that throbbed in the countless hearts of its audience.

When it was over, and the "Fuori! fuori! fuori!" of the enraptured people had brought him for the last time before their hurricane of applause, he came to me where I stood.

"Well?" he said, with the smile in his eyes.

I trembled before him, burning, breathless, entranced, amazed; so wondrous did his power seem to me, I could have cast myself at his feet and worshipped him for the divine force of the Art that was in him.

"Well?" he said again; but his voice shook a little,

though it had a laugh in it. "Well?—say—is it better than the Burattini?"

I could not answer him; but I burst into tears.

When we left the wooden Arte that night where it stood, with its flag dropping in the quiet air, and its gay scroll facing the line of the Apennines, we were escorted in royal honour homeward by a half hundred or so of sturdy popolani, singing, laughing, shouting, dancing in universal acclaim and fellowship, as only Italians can sing, and laugh, and shout, and dance, when the moon is high, and a mandoline is making tinkling melody before their steps.

It was late, and a beautiful, lustrous, cold night, full of the smell of the young spring, as the breeze blew in from over the budding contado.

We passed through the Porta al Prato, and glanced up at white Fiesole, and went on under the limes of the piazzone and along the edge of the glancing water.

The music of the mandoline drew the steps of the loiterers, of whom there were many about in those luminous, tranquil night-hours.

A youth with a guitar slung across him joined us, and a man with a violin ran out from under an archway, and caught the strains, and skipped before us in many grotesque capers; some people above, on a lighted balcony, threw some violets and daffodils at us as we went by; the moonlight lay broad and white upon the river; all the towers and spires rose clear against the stars; the music passed on, glad as the singing of Pan.

So we went homeward through Florence.

CHAPTER II.
The Rose and the Florins.

WHEN we reached the little tavern, our escort utterly refused to let him enter it.

They claimed Pascarèl as theirs by every human right, and insisted on bearing him off amidst them to supper to a noted wine-house, where the alabaster workers that night were about to hold high revelry. Pascarèl laughed and consented to go with them, but before he turned away, he swept the earth with his sombrero in a good-night to me, and murmured some parting counsel in the ear of his sister.

Then off he went; the rapture of his comrades no longer restrained by the presence of the "donzella," at whom they had glanced as a new and not altogether welcome addition to his little party.

They lifted him fairly off the ground and bore him along aloft on the shoulders and backs of half a dozen sturdy craftsmen of Florence, the mandoline twanging cheerily before them, and all their far-reaching voices blending together.

It was not the white lilies of Lillo; but it was a homage full as genuine in its way.

I stood in the doorway and watched them pass down the sombre, darkling ancient street; the moon shone whitely here and there upon their path, the grim arcades and the mighty walls were upon either side; above, between the roofs, was the dark blue sky of night. Their riotous glee died softly in the distance as they turned out of sight by the base of the old Guadagni Palace, and the last echo I heard was the shout of their homage, "Viva il Pascarello! Pascarèl! Pascarèl!"

How long I stood there, lost in a dream of this strange and wonderful life which had opened upon me, I cannot tell; Brunótta touched me in kindly impatience:—

"Do not dream in the moonlight like that, signorina. It makes people mad, they say. I have some hot soup here; come and drink it, and let us get to bed."

"When will he be back?" I asked, as I followed her withindoors.

"Pascarèl? Oh! not till daybreak, I daresay. He is often out all night long. Come, do not let the soup get cold. And so you thought him wonderful, did you? Ah! did I not tell you only the truth?"

She sat opposite me, with the little brass soup-kettle between us, toasting her feet on an earthen scaldino; she had not changed her pretty short white and rose skirts; she had still her little starry crown on her forehead. She was a little gay, rosy, cheery soul, and yet I thought she seemed hardly worthy to be of the same race as this marvellous Pascarèl.

"I never could have dreamed of anything like him!" I said, under my breath, for I had been too deeply moved to be able to talk of it easily: "but the whole world ought to know it; he ought to play before kings!"

"He likes this best," said Brunótta, keeping her airy skirts off the hot charcoal of her footstool. "He is so free, you see. He does just as he likes: in the world fame would be bondage. So he says, and no doubt he is right. Besides, I do not think he cares so much as this brown pot would care for either riches or fame. He loves his freedom, and he loves the people, Pascarèl."

"But he wrote that piece himself?"

"Oh, yes. He writes everything that he plays."

"But that is genius!"

"I do not know what you mean. He is very clever, no doubt, wonderfully clever; there is no one like him. But then he is a great scholar, you know; he took his degree at Pisa."

"At Pisa? And you do not know how to read!" I cried, forgetful in my astonishment of all laws of courtesy.

"No. I cannot read," said Brunótta, with a little confused laugh.

"But a degree at Pisa, and not to know the alfabeto—that is a great difference."

Brunótta coloured; perhaps she was vexed.

"Yes. No doubt it is a good deal of difference. But then I was always a very lazy little thing, and never cared to do anything but to dance in the streets, whilst Pascarèl,—oh, you cannot imagine what wonderful things he has it in him to do. He might be very great—very great—there is no doubt, if he liked."

"It is odd he should not like?"

"He has no ambition, I suppose—that is it: he likes to be free."

"But who can be free if they be poor?"

"Anybody, signorina," laughed Brunótta, with the philosophy which she had acquired from Pascarèl; "that is, if they do not try to be rich, you know. Of course, if you be always struggling to be something you are not, you never can be at ease—rich or poor."

There was a profound wisdom in this, no doubt; but it was too profound for me.

"Pascarèl might have made an enormous deal of money, no doubt," pursued the little dancing girl, "but he would never bind himself; that is where his fault is; and people will not pay you, ever, unless you will put yourself into harness for good and all. He is happier as he is; playing just as the fancy moves him.

"And you cannot think the good that he does, for all he looks so careless. That poor little Toccò there; he was the son of one of the brigands at Pæstum. The law took the father and the whole gang. They shot some, and sent some to the galleys, poor wretches! and little Toccò they turned adrift on the streets, for he was only twelve, and nothing proved against him. Of course, in time, he would have been a thief like his father, but Pascarèl got hold of him and kept him; and now there is not an honester or better little soul in the whole length of Italy than Toccò; and I am sure he would be cut in a million pieces for Pascarèl.

"At the great flood, too, two winters ago, in Tuscany, when the whole land was under water and the bullocks and sheep drowned by thousands, and the people were only saved here and there by getting up on the tops of the towers, and the great stacks of hay and corn, and the trees, and often the roofs and very bodies of the houses were tossing down the great yellow sea of the flood like so many little cockle-shells in a gutter, you should have seen Pascarèl that

day: we happened to be up high on the hills where
the flood did not reach, but he heard of it at sunrise,
and down he went and he got a boat, and he rowed
about hither and thither on the white horrid face of
the torrents, shaming the cowards that dared not stir,
of whom there were hundreds and hundreds; and ever
so many times he was within an ace of being swept
to his grave, and not a whit did he care—not he.

"He worked on and on till the night fell and the
force of the waters abated, and the men and women
and children, and the flocks and the herds that he
saved, you would never believe if I told you.

"There was much talk after that of some public
reward for his goodness and courage, and some of
the towns wanted to make great feasts in his honour
and have jubilees in their churches, and give him
money.

"But when Pascarèl heard that, he fled out of the
country as though the black death itself were after
him, and went along the Corniche into France, and
would not return into Italy till time had gone by
long enough for the people to forget what they owed
to him. It does not take very long for people to
forget a benefit, you know, signorina.

"But it is nearly midnight, donzella mia," said
Brunótta, rising after a pause in her chatter, and
shaking the embers in her earthen pot, "and Pascarèl said .you were to sleep early and wake late,
because you were tired and not used to our life.
Let me show you your room; it is a very poor and
small place, but it is clean; and I hope you will not
mind it."

Then she led the way with a lantern, and we

climbed a rickety ladder-like stair, and I found my little chamber—a mere nook in a wall as it were, and bare of comfort, but still clean, as she had said, and on the little hard bed was cast a cloak of skins.

"That is Pascarèl's; he thought you might be cold; the nights are chilly, and so he told me to put it there," said Brunótta, busying herself in a hundred kindly girlish fashions after my comfort as well as she could.

After she had bidden me thrice good-night, she stood, with her light in her hand, looking at me wonderingly as I unloosed my bodice and shook down all my hair, and took my shoes and stockings off my tired feet.

"The donzellina is beautiful to look at," she said, meditatively, with a sort of astonished inquiring pleasure in her voice: "and what white little feet, though she is so tall, and what a white skin!—it is wonderful! I wish Pascarèl could see you now. He says he never saw anything like you. He says you would do for the Angelica in that poem he is so fond of, you know? He is always running his head on that kind of rubbish, as if it would do one any good."

"You are very flattering, Brunótta," I said, laughing, as with some vanity, I fear me, I displayed to her all the thickness of my hair, which always delighted Italians, because of the yellow lights it had in it, which never darkened with the sun as their own did.

"I only say what is just true. Is that generous?" said the good little honest soul, as she turned at last fairly away with her lantern, and drew my door close behind her.

For myself, I was so confused, so excited, so full of a mingled pleasure and pain, that, though I threw myself at once on my bed, it was long before I could sleep.

When I did at length fall asleep, the grey streak of the dawn had already begun to stray through the narrow casement across the bricks of my floor; and I dreamed feverishly of rushing floods, of drowning cattle, of dancing harlequins, of the onyx with the Fates, of old forsaken Verona, and of Pascarèl.

It was broad day when I awoke; the iron rod on a wall opposite, which served for a sun-dial, showed that it was ten o'clock. I heard a voice that I knew —a voice with a clear, careless laugh in it.

"Oh, good little soul," it said, as in a mirthful expostulation, "what possessed you to go aside in that wood yesterday? We were so well as we were; and women will never let well alone. They will always paint their lilies, and, of course, the poor lilies die of it. We were content as we were, and now—. What possessed you to bind up with our hedge-row flowers a stray hothouse rose like this?"

"You saw it before ever I saw it," the voice of Brunòtta replied to him. "And you must have liked the look of the rose, Pascarèl, or you never had given away for it your onyx."

I heard him laugh, self-convicted:

"That was for the pure love of music, carina. Don't you believe that? Oh, little sceptic! Nay I will make no bones of it; I will say the truth. The donzella is too noble for us; it is that which troubles me. When I saw her standing first in the square of Verona, I said to myself: What can she be, that young

princess, with her golden skirts, singing in a crowd
for a few baiocche! I could not understand it; and
it troubles me now. She is too good for our life, and
we have no other."

"Let her go her own way, then, and go we ours,"
said Brunótta, with tranquillity.

"No, by heaven, never!" retorted Pascarèl, with
a fiery force in his voice. "What! Leave a beautiful,
fearless, innocent thing like that adrift by itself in the
world? Fie for shame, little Brunótta!"

Brunótta laughed; but there was a little sadness
in the ripple of the mirth.

"Do you remember, Pascarèl, in the great flood
that winter, when everyone was safe, as far as one
could know, and it had grown quite dark; you could
just see the outline of a young bull drowning far off;
and nothing would do but you would launch the
boat afresh, and ride the flood again, and go for it?
And you got to it as it was sinking, and dragged
it into the boat, and came to land with it with such
a struggle that everyone thought all was over with
you, and you were indeed half dead. Do you remember?"

"Yes. What of that?"

"Well, do you not remember, too, that as soon
as the bull had strength enough to stagger up on to
his legs alone he rushed at you, and struck you in
the breast with his horns, and scampered off to the
hills as fast as he could go? And you were very
ill for many days; and they said if the blow had
been an inch nearer to the heart, you might have
died of it?"

"Well?" said Pascarèl.

15*

"Well," answered Brunótta, "I was only thinking
—if the signorina should be like the bull!"

Then their voices ceased, and I heard a casement
shut; they seemed to have been speaking in the
chamber next to mine.

I sprang off my bed, a little indignant and a little
touched, too.

Like the bull! I thought—no, never, never.

Brunótta seemed a traitress to me only to have
breathed the possibility of such a parallel.

I dressed quickly, threw my hair back loose over
my shoulders, and ran down the stairs into the common room. Pascarèl was there alone, standing by the
window, looking thoughtfully out into the open air,
with Toto at his feet.

It was the Berlingancio — the Mardi gras — the
maddest madness of Carnival; all the fury and frolic
already were ringing all over the city with deafening
clash and clangour.

He turned swiftly, and saluted me with that cordial
and easy grace which characterised all his movements.

"Ah, good day, my donzella. I have good news
to shine on you with the sun. We have got your
golden florins."

"My florins!" I echoed, doubting my own joy.
"My florins! How? — when? — where? Can it be
possible?"

"Very possible," he said, gaily, and he proceeded
to count out on the stone seat of the window a dozen
round, bright, golden Austrian florins. "How? Oh,
never mind how. It is always an ugly story—a thief's.
You know I told you the rogue would repent as soon

as he should be found out; they always do.   You see
the guardia of the town went to work in earnest for
you.   But you must be more careful of your wealth
in future."

I was too enraptured to heed much what he said.
He might have told me the most improbable romances, and I should have credited them at that
moment, so supreme was my ecstasy over my recovered treasure.

He watched me with a certain melancholy in his
handsome eyes.

"So now—you are free again, you see," he said,
after a pause.   "You can go away from us when you
like, cara mia — if you like; what do you · say?
Twelve florins, even when they are of gold, are not a
large patrimony with which to scour the earth.   But
still, you thought them enough for you rashly to run
away from Verona on the strength of them alone."

His words clouded the heaven of my restored happiness.   I had been kissing my florins, laughing and
almost crying over them.   As he spoke I stopped,
and looked him full in the face.

"Signor mio, — I ought to tell you, — I heard
what you said this morning in the room next mine to
Brunótta."

His face flushed hotly.

"By heavens you did!   How much did you hear?
What about?   Tell me quickly."

"I heard you from the time that you called me a
hothouse rose to the time when your sister said that
I should be like the bull you saved out of the flood."

Pascarèl laughed; his face was a little flushed still,
but he looked relieved.

"Is that all, carina—honour bright?"

"Quite all. But—you seemed sorry she spoke to me in the wood yesterday; you seemed to think that I should be some trouble or burden to you. If that be so indeed, tell me the truth; I will go."

Pascarèl stood before me, with the lights and the shadows swiftly succeeding each other on his changeful countenance.

"You do not wish to go, then, signorina?" he asked at length. "I thought you might, now you have back your florins."

"No, I do not wish to go; I wish to be one of you, and to learn your art."

I could not trust my voice to say more, for my heart was full at the idea that I should be again adrift by myself with those poor florins, which no longer seemed to me the brilliant safeguard and the omnipotent possession which they had done ere I had lost them.

Pascarèl rolled towards me a little table spread with a white cloth, on which coffee and wheaten rolls were set ready.

"Breakfast first, cara mia; then we will talk. Do you mind my smoke? No? that is right."

Therewith he stretched himself out on the stone sill of the window embrasure, and rested at his ease, sending the smoke into the air in almost absolute silence, glancing now out into the street, already filling with processions of the Berlingancio fooleries, now glancing back at me where I broke my fast with pleasure, knowing that I could pay for what I took.

The radiance of the sunshine came through the open casement and bathed the large square red bricks of the floor; from without there came the smell of tossed flowers, and the noise of many bells, and the sound of countless feet pacing over the stones of the streets: above everything, there was the sweet, youthful scent of the Spring that dreamily breathed itself from the vineyards and fields, even through the dark and blood-stained old age of the Medicean streets.

When his spagnoletto was smoked out, and my coffee ended, he came across the room, and sat astride on an old walnut-wood chair, with his arms crossed on its back, and so gazed at me long and gravely.

"What do you wish for most in this world, cara mia?" he asked, at last.

"Money, of course," I answered him, with widely opened eyes and a little impatient laugh of wonder. Was it not what I had missed and wanted all my life long—always?

"You have no genius in you, then!" he said, with a dash of scorn.

My answer had offended all the artist's instincts in him. No doubt it seemed half puerile and half vile to him—so true an artist in every pulse and fibre of his being, that so long as his audience laughed or wept with him, he could not bring himself to consider whether gold pieces or copper bits filled the box at the door of his play-house.

"Perhaps not," I said, in my own turn a little offended. "But——"

I glanced at the queer little bit of mirror which hung on the rough stone wall between a waxen Jesù and a portrait of the last brigand known in the Valdarno.

He followed the gesture and laughed.

"Oh, you have the best genius for a woman, no doubt. I would not deny that. But I thought you might, perhaps, have a touch of the other too."

"It is a large word," I said, more humbly. "And no one ever seems to know very well what they mean by it."

"No. Some people say it is all your days to carry about with you a torch which illumines every-one's path except your own."

"Perhaps. My old music teacher used to say that to have genius was to be a fool."

"That I deny. It is to be alone amidst fools— a thing much more bitter. And *such* fools! Dio mio! But, after all, what does it matter? If the world were only human, it would matter hideously; but, thank heaven, the world is so much else besides. When one is choked up to the throat with fools, one can always get away to the woods, to the mountains, to the birds, to the beasts, to the hills in the rain mist, to the sea when the sun breaks. If it were not for that, one would go mad straightway, no doubt. And even with that one feels small sometimes — choked, fenced in,—Do you not know? One wants to push back the clouds, to thrust away the skies, to see beyond the horizon, to look close at the sun. If one only had wings!—but let us talk of yourself. You want money, you say; well, that certainly will not come to you on the stage for a long time. To many —to most it never comes at all; and myself, I always think that whether it does or not matters very little, after all."

"But money is everything!" I cried to him—I, who

knew so well by the want of it all that its possession must imply.

"Is it? Well, no doubt, to those who think so it *is* everything: I am not amongst them. But you are a woman-child; I am a man. We shall never think alike on that theme.

"A man, be he bramble or vine, likes to grow in the open air in his own fashion; but a woman, be she flower or weed, always thinks she would be better under glass. When she gets the glass she breaks it —generally; but till she gets it she .pines.

"As for my art, the art of the stage needs much study, though, I dare say, to you, as to all lookers on, nothing seems easier than to rattle through a part.

"The actor must be born, like the poet, the painter, the sculptor, no doubt; but also, like them, he must be made perfect by study. Gesture, glance, feeling, passion—all these come by nature: but accent, knowledge, oratory, effect—all these are the mechanical parts of the whole, which only long application will acquire.

"To the art of the stage, as to every other art, there are two sides: the truth of it, which comes by inspiration—that is, by instincts subtler, deeper, and stronger than those of most minds—and the artifice of it, in which it must clothe itself to get understood by the people.

"It is this latter which must be learnt; it is the leathern harness in which the horses of the sun must run when they come down to race upon earth.

"Do I talk nonsense? Never mind, if you know what I mean."

I think my face showed him I knew, for he went on without pausing for my reply.

"We Italians have always needed less of this harness than men of other nations. The French and the Italians are the only great actors that the world ever sees. The northern races cannot act, just as they cannot paint.

"After all, both acting and painting are a matter of colour, and the northern peoples have no feeling for colour, no sense of it. Perhaps because it is not about them in their daily lives, nor visible in their landscapes. They are great in very much, but they are not great in art.

"The French are great, but they are three-parts artifice; it is a very perfect study, but it is a study always. With us we do hold closely that *ars est celare artem;* and we are infinitely more natural than the French are upon the stage. This is national in us, no doubt; we are always ourselves at home and abroad, and we concern ourselves very little as to what other people may think of us. We carry this happy immunity on to the stage with us, and the result is, that on the stage Italians are without rivals.

"But, with all this, it is not the happy-go-lucky hit-or-miss sort of thing that you may fancy it. No art can be good unless into it be brought something of all other arts.

"A man may be a passable actor if Nature has given him the trick of it; but he will not be a great one unless he study the literature of his own and other nations, unless he know something of the intricacies of colour and of melody—above all, unless he can probe and analyse human nature, alike in its health and in its disease.

"To be a great artist one must be a student, and a sincere and humble one, at the foot of every greatness—ay, and every weakness—which has preceded us.

"The instrument on which we histrions play is that strange thing, the human heart. It looks a little matter to strike its chords of laughter or of sorrow; but, indeed, to do that aright and rouse a melody which shall leave all who hear it the better and the braver for the hearing, that may well take a man's lifetime, and, perhaps, may well repay it."

He paused, while a dreamy thoughtfulness cast its shadow over his features; he had been speaking rather to himself than to me, I saw. I thought of what Brunótta had said of him, that he had been a great student of many sciences once, away there in old Pisa.

And yet he had no ambition: it seemed to me very strange.

"You are a great artist, surely," I said, slowly. "And yet—yet you play only for the people."

He looked up with the quick, contemptuous flash of his eloquent eyes.

"Only for the people! Altro! did not Sperone and all the critics at his heels pronounce Ariosto only fit for the vulgar multitude? and was not Dante himself called the laureate of the cobblers and the bakers?

"And does not Sacchetti record that the great man took the trouble to quarrel with an ass driver and a blacksmith because they recited his verses badly?

"If he had not written 'only for the people,' we

might never have got beyond the purisms of Virgilio, and the Ciceronian imitations of Bembo.

"Dante now-a-days may have become the poet of the scholars and the sages, but in his own times he seemed to the sciolists a most terribly low fellow for using his mother tongue; and he was most essentially the poet of the vulgar—of the *vulgare eloquio*, of the *vulgare illustre;* and pray what does the 'Commedia' mean if not a *canto villereccio*, a song for the rustics! Will you tell me that?

"Only for the people! Ah, that is the error. Only! how like a woman that is! Any trash will do for the people; that is the modern notion; vile roulades in music, tawdry crudities in painting, cheap balderdash in print—all that will do for the people. So they say now-a-days.

"Was the bell tower yonder set in a ducal garden or in a public place? Was Cimabue's masterpiece veiled in a palace or borne aloft through the throngs of the streets?

"I am a Florentine, donzella; and I have enough of the blood of my fathers in me to know that the higher and truer the art, the more surely should it belong to the people.

"It is the people that make your nation great or vile in the sight of the universe. Shall you nourish them, then, on the garbage of ribald feebleness, or on the pure strong meats of the mind? As you feed them, so will be their substance and sinew; as you graft them, so will be the fruit that they bear.

"How would it have been with Florence if she had not perpetually borne that vital truth even as the very marrow of her bones?

"Her great men gave their greatest—not to the empire, not to the pope, not to princes only, whether temporal or spiritual, but into the very midst of the populace, into the very hands and hearts of the people, so that through the blackest ages of oppression and superstition, through the deadliest losses of liberty and of peace, she was still as a shining light in the face of the nations, and still held fast, to bequeath them to others, the unquenchable fires of freedom and art."

The rapid words coursed like fire off his lips in passionate enthusiasm; then, as his habit was, he laughed at his own emotions.

"Forgive my vehemence, cara mia," he said, as he lit another spagnoletto. "As I told you, I come of Florentine race."

"What were your people?" I asked him, expecting from him any one of the great names of the great Republic.

"My father was a tinker," he said brusquely, but with the shadow of a laugh about his mouth.

"A tinker! Impossible!"

He laughed outright at the accent of my voice.

"Not impossible at all. An Italian tinker, mind you; that is something very different to a tinker anywhere else. You know us; we are never vulgar."

"But a tinker!" I murmured, in unconquerable disappointment.

Pascarèl laughed on, radiantly and inextinguishably, and busied himself with his little paper roll of tobacco.

"That is why Brunótta cannot read, I suppose?" I said, after a pause, trying to shake off the curious coldness of disenchantment which this announcement of his cast upon me.

He got up, and walked to and fro about the room.

"Of course! A poor devil of a tinker has to mend several millions of stew-pans and braziers before he can solder the alphabet to the empty heads of his children.

"I went to Pisa? Yes: who told you that?

"Poor blind old Pisa! She was very glad to be rid of me, I fear. I won all her honours, but I played her very sad pranks.

"Poor old widowed Pisa! she always seems to be lamenting, Dido-like, her lost lover the Sea. She is unutterably sad; and yet I am never abroad on a moonlit night without wanting to watch it shine on her wonderful palaces, on her empty desolate squares, on her perfection of desolation.

"Do you remember how the Florentines went forth in arms to guard the gates of her, when her walls were weak because her sons were all away on the high seas subduing Minorca? She was their old hereditary foe, but they defended her honour for her in her day of weakness. I doubt if there be anything in all history manlier than that is.

"But to talk of yourself, mia bella.

"Is it indeed true that, lacking all better friends, you would like to wander awhile with us? Nay, no fair words. Let us speak honestly. I know that it is not the least likely that if you had any other sort of protection you would seek that of a set of strolling players. But you have no other, and so——"

He came back, and cast aside his cigar, and stood

by the table looking down on me; his eyes grew almost melancholy, and his voice was very grave when he spoke.

"See here, donzella; you are but a child, as one may say, and know nothing of life but its dreams. It is but fair to warn you; to be a player for the populace with us may hurt you in time to come. I told you yesterday we are not over reputable people.

"We are honest, and we hurt no one, it is true; we may, perhaps, even do some little good in our way; but in the very nature of things we cannot be respectable. We could not be if we wished, and I am afraid we don't wish. Well, all this may hurt you in some time to come. I dare not say it will not. At any rate, it is only fair that you should know so much.

"You are much above the life that we lead; you heard me say so; above it in temper, and tastes, and, no doubt, by your birth. On the other hand, friendless and lonely as you are, worse may easily befall you than to stay with us.

"You shall hear no evil, and shall see none that I can keep you from; that I swear.

"We owe no man anything, and we do the best we can that no creature shall go out from our little house of canvas baser than he entered by even so much as a licentious thought. We are poor, indeed, but, as you have seen, we are none the less glad and gay for that; and we find, perhaps, a fairer side to daily life and human nature than do those whose honey of gold draws the thieves and panders and liars to lick them over with tongues false and foul. As

you are now, your fate is a very terrible one for your
sex and your age."

His voice had a sweet, persuasive force in it, and
lulled me into a dreamy silence; I did not answer to
him; I listened as to some delicious music.

"I have been thinking, donzella," he pursued, after
a while, "that it may be ill for you to associate yourself with us.   Association, you know, is like a burr
off the hedges; it clings ere we know it, and we can
scarcely free ourselves of it without losing something,
be it only a shred.

"The life of the stage—it is only fair you should
know—at its best has a certain slur in it.   You spoke
thoughtlessly, but you spoke as the world speaks,
when you uttered your scorn for us living Burattini.
At its greatest the life of the player has only false
glitter in it, and never true honour.   We are toys for
the rest of mankind; and the world, having done with
us, laughs and then breaks us.

"Why not?   We are only its playthings.

"Yesterday, when you said this, I rebuked you,
for you wounded me more than you knew.   But, to
be frank with you, as it is only just I should be, I
confess that your gay disdain had its grim root in
fact, whilst my reproaches were baseless and worthless, because they were only the fanciful utterance of
a fanatical enthusiasm.   Sincere, indeed, in its way,
but, for all that, self-deceiving.

"Perhaps we never so fatally deceive others as
when we are ourselves the first dupes of our falsehoods.

"Altro!   I love the life that I lead, but I will not
wrong you by saying that it is a fit one for you.

Nevertheless, perhaps a broken crust is better than no bread whatever at all. You must choose for yourself. I have said all there is now to say."

I stood and thought bewilderedly, withheld from him by my pride, drawn towards him by the nameless seduction which existed in all his words and ways.

The brightness of the sun shone across us; the brazen tumults of the bells filled all the air; the people streamed past the casement, laughing, chattering, dressed in their best, and eager to enjoy.

The fulness and gladness of human life was all about me; I had not courage enough to turn away from them and go out into the darkness and the loneliness by myself. I was but a child, and I was afraid of gloom, of solitude, of misfortune. This man, with his passionate tones, with his radiant courage, with his eloquent eyes, had an influence over me that I hardly attempted to resist, and attempted not at all to dissect.

What matter if he were only a bohemian, an adventurer, a strolling player, a tinker's son; he was an artist, a poet even; it was surely better to laugh with him than to perish miserably all alone in the very onset of my warfare with the world.

So the thoughts drifted vaguely and restlessly through my brain; self-centered as the thoughts of all young creatures are. He spoke of my future, but it was not of that I then thought; the present was enough for me.

"If I remain with you, can I earn enough to pay my way?" I asked him, suddenly.

He gave a gesture of impatience.

"Certainly.   Your florins will last for all eternity
in so simple a life as ours; and even if they do not,
we can find a place for you, no doubt."

"Then I will stay," I said, on an eager impulse
that I did not dream of defining; and I remember that
I held my hands out to him with a little triumphant
laugh.

That wonderful luminance, which gave so subtle a
charm to his face at such times as it lightened there,
flashed over his features.

He caught my hands and touched them lightly
with his lips, as one may brush with a kiss the leaves
of a rose or the curls of a child.

"Altro! So be it!" he cried, with a laugh which
covered, I thought, a deeper emotion.   "Ah, dear
donzellina, did I not give you the Fates?   For me it
was ill, very ill, I fear; but for you it shall be well, if
the will of a man count for aught in this world."

"Does it not count for much?" I asked him.

And he answered sadly:

"I have lived to think not; for in this world there
is—Woman."

CHAPTER III.
The Golden Celandine.

My future being thus determined, Pascarèl said no
more about it; it was a thing resolved on and done
with; his sunny temper threw off its momentary
shadow, and he gave himself up, as his habit was, to
the easy, light-hearted, debonair enjoyment of the
present.

All that day we enjoyed Berlingancio, and the next

he sauntered about Florence with me, whilst Brunótta
stayed in to mend her torn kirtle. He was bent upon
making me happy, and he succeeded. That day lives
now, golden, and long, and clear, in my remembrance
—a very king of days.

The weather was so radiant with the coming of
the spring that even in those deepest shadows of the
walls it was bright with the sweet youth of the year.

There were great masses of violets and of the
snow-white wood anemoli selling at all the corners of
the streets. The people sat out before their doorways, working and talking, laughing and chaffering,
glad of heart because the winter was gone for nine
good months, in which they would be free to live at
pleasure in their heaven of the open air.

Between the grey grim piles of the war-worn stone,
looking up, one saw the smile of the blue blue skies;
beyond the gates there was the silver gleam of the
loosened waters, of the budding fields, of the fruitful
olives, of the far-off hills.

All the day long we sauntered there, he talking
often of the city's past, with phrase so teeming with
the colour of language and the poetry of history, that
one listened in enchanted breathlessness as to some
sorcerer's tale.

Lelio Pascarèllo, whom one and all called Pascarèl,
was artist in every fibre of his temperament. Passionate, sensitive to external influences as any woman,
full of poetic thoughts and impulses, he joined to
this the vivid Florentine energy and the gay Florentine
ardour.

There was much in him of the bright vivacious
humour which was in Buffulmaco and Bramante; of

16*

that love of sport and of ready jest which laughs like so much sunlight over the great memories of Giorgione and Da Vinci.

Linked to an incapable companion he would have rid himself of the burden with the same witty skill as Brunelleschi, and locked in his study by an exacting patron, he would have escaped by the window to enjoy his pleasures in the streets, in the same ardent and amorous determination as Fra Lippi's.

He seemed to have just left those wise, fearless, gay, tumultuous times when the great sculptors went laughing to buy their eggs and cheese in the market; when the great painters challenged each other to gay duello with pencil and with chisel; when the great artists held their rapiers no less ready than their brushes; when men worked and loved, and fought and jested, and swept all the Arts within the one magic circle of their universal genius in that easy strength which looks the miracle of saints to this weakling world.

He loved light, and air, and indolence, and mirth; the mere sense of living sufficed for him with a voluptuous content which those of northern lands can never know; to lie and dream on a grassy slope, and watch the lithe brown arms of a girl as she washed linen in the brook below; to go singing through the luminous moonlight with a dozen comrades, waking the echoes of old, dim, marble streets; to laugh and jest round the charcoal fires in the winter *veglie*, or lying in the deep corn on the moonlit threshing-floors at harvest time; to toss a draught of wine behind the thick screen of a pergola foliage, whilst bright eyes laughed at him and bright sunbeams darted on him through the leaves, and made his year as one long holiday, from the Beffano to the feast of Ognissanti— these were enough for Pascarèl.

Sometimes, as we went that day, he stopped before some cobbler's stall or some stove where the last chestnuts of the year were toasting, and exchanged with the Florentines presiding over them fantastic passages of drollery and wit. Sometimes he encountered some barrow rolling on its way with woollen stuffs and silken handkerchiefs, or some truckful of oranges and lemons, and took the sale of these out of the hands and the mouths of their vendors, and made the crowd around them split their sides with his quaint and subtle Tuscan humour. Sometimes he would enter some old dusky church where some world-famous picture made a glory in the darkness, and, standing before it, would let his thoughts and his words roam dreamily over the deepest meanings of art and the remotest mysteries of history in all that abstract meditation which is the most precious indulgence of the scholar.

Half a hundred times a day his mood and his manner altered with that ardent vitality in every phase of their countless changes which was the life and soul of the man himself. Not for one whole half hour together was he the same throughout; and yet, grave or gay, riotously laughing with the crowd, or dreamily questioning the lost secrets of the old masters, selling a yellow bandana to a housewife at a fair with buoyant raillery, or straying through the dim arcades of the old academies tenderly recalling the heroism and the learning of their earliest ages, he was always, in all his contrasts, Pascarèl.

He was like the child's toy of the kaleidoscope, with every moment his moods changed their shapes with unpremeditated caprice; but the hues which made them did not alter.

"Were you truly a tinker's son?" I asked him, late in that day, when we were stretched again upon the grass of the Cascine woods.

"Che diamine!" he cried, in the expressive Tuscan affirmative. "Utterly and simply a tinker's son. But, to console you, though tinkers we had become, we were of a race that yielded in ancientness of blood to none. I think old Malispini even accounts for us as amongst those who, on coming out of the Ark after the Deluge, bestirred themselves in the building of Fiesole. In the old, old days, my people were of that territorial nobility beside which the Medici are mere rubbish of yesterday. We were Ghibellines, and in their ruin fell, of course. Our utter destruction came when one of us would have a palace fashioned by Orcagna, to pay for which his descendants in the third generation had to sell nearly all their worldly goods and lands, like that hapless fool Luca dei Pitti. Jews of the Oltrarno got the little there was left in time. Old races die hard with the load of long debt round their necks; but——they die. For two centuries we had been poor, poor, poor. Poor as the devil. At last we worked for our daily bread. Old races have done worse. My grandfather toiled to and fro as a facchino in the country where his forefathers had scowled defiance on Carlo di Valois, and mowed down the burghers round the red Carroccio on that terrible day, 'che fece l'Arbia colorata in rosso.' From a facchino to a tinker is hardly a fall; perhaps it is even a rise, for a tinker must own some little stock in trade of tools, whereas the facchino only toils underneath the goods of other people. At any rate, a tinker my father was, God save his soul! and a man of most infinite humour. I know he scratched a prince's coronet on his smelting pot. Coronets have been in worse places. He was weak enough, I am ashamed to say, to be ever proud of his lineage, and fed me when I was a little fellow on all sorts of dead glories out of Dino Compagni and Villani. But I ran about with bare legs over Tuscany, and cared nothing that I ran over the graves of my ancestors. At any rate it was more harmless than to run about with a bare sword as those Pascarèl princes did. It was queer, perhaps, to blunder into some old church in some little hill-town or city of the plain, and see a great white statue, and read the record of some mighty Pascarèllo; and all the while one was a Pascarèllo too, though only a little mischievous dog, ragged and hungry, scouring the country for saucepans to mend. It set one thinking, no doubt. But, after all, what did it matter?"

"It would have broken my heart!" I cried, where I sat beside him amongst the crocuses.

Pascarèl laughed.

"It was likelier to break my head. For, being a little fool, and strong for my years, I would get fighting for that coronet on the smelting-pot times out of number with half the boys of half the villages we entered. They thought a coronet on an old iron pot ridiculous, and they surely were right; but I was resolute to have both pot and coronet respected, being my father's; and perhaps I was right also. At any rate, I had the courage of my opinions, and got half killed

for them over and over again, as all people rash
enough to keep such ticklish possessions as opinions
invariably do.   A princely couronne and a travelling
tinker! Supremely ridiculous, that is certain; but
would they have been less so if I had whimpered and
had not fought? It is stupid to have a bad cause, no
doubt; but after all, as far as we ourselves go, perhaps
it is not the cause that matters so much as it is one's
way of upholding it.   The Carroccio was a sorry childish emblem in itself enough; but does that take from
the grandeur of the deaths of the Tornaquinci round
it? My Carroccio was my father's old tin pot; but I
am glad even now to think how many sucking Tuscans I in my babyhood thrashed for sheer love and
honour of that sacred household god. Not love of the
coronet, mind you, but love for what he had put there;
if he had scratched a cat's head on the pot, and they
had laughed at it, it would have been the same to
me, and I, Pascarèl, should have been bound to fight
for it."
    "Did you ever work with him?" I asked, glancing
at those long, slender, brown hands of his which were
weaving some rushes together.
    "Altro! of course I did. Tinkered many an old
woman's copper kettle all along the country, east and
west, from Livorno to Venice. But I never took to
the work. I had a natural genius for making holes,
not for mending them. The people used to call me the
Marchesino, in derision of the leaves and balls on the
tin pot. But they dropped that after they found by
frequent experience that I could make holes in their
sons' skulls past all power of apothecary's soldering.
Not that I was a bully, believe me; but when they

shouted their 'Marchesino' in derision I thought of
the marble Pascarèlli in the churches, and hit out—a
little too straight home sometimes.   I was a little lad
at that time, trotting on bare legs after my father's
barrow from house to house all over the land.   It is
all forgotten now.   I buried his tin pot in his coffin
with him, as his forefathers were buried with their
golden crowns, and I have buried all the old follies
with it.   I was fifteen years old when he died."

"And you are the last Pascarèllo?"

"The very last.   Much good may it do me.   The
people, God bless them! have forgiven me all the
broken heads of my boyish time, and have learnt to
love me—well.   I am afraid the Ghibelline Pascarèlli
who live in marble in the churches could never say as
much."

"And you are content with that love?"

"Eh, Dio! I should blush for myself if I were not."

A great darkness stole over his face as he spoke
—that melancholy of an Italian face which is as intense as is the sunlight of its happiness.

"Oh, cara mia, when one has run about in one's
time with a tinker's tools, and seen the lives of the
poor, and the woe of them, and the wretchedness of
it all, and the utter uselessness of everything, and the
horrible, intolerable, unending pain of all the things
that breathe, one comes to think that in this meaning-
less mystery which men call life a little laughter and
a little love are the only things which save us all from
madness—the madness that would curse God and
die."

A little laughter and a little love!   Across the
brilliant fancies of my supreme ignorance the words

fell with a pathetic meaning. Was this all, indeed, that the wide world could offer? And was it worth while to wander so far to reach so little?

"Yes, cara mia," he said, with his quick divination of another's thoughts. "Yes. They are all that are really worth the having in this world; and they lie so close to us sometimes, and we flee away from them, not knowing, and perhaps we never meet them face to face or have them in our reach again. For neither of them will come for the mere asking."

"How, then, shall we gain either?" I asked.

He smiled.

"There was once a youth who was a shepherd. He was all alone in the world, and sorrowful. No man tarried with him, and no woman found him comely.

"A fairy took pity on him, and gathered a yellow blossom of celandine, and put it in his hand. 'Breathe on the flower, and wish thrice,' she said. 'Three times you shall have your desire.'

"He breathed once on the golden flower, scarcely believing in his own good fortune. 'Let me laugh as other men do,' he wished. Immediately he laughed on and on, not pausing, over a flagon of wine that was never emptied; but there was no joy in his mirth, and he grew sick of it.

"He breathed a second time on the flower. 'Let me love as other men do,' he wished. Instantly a young maiden kissed him on the mouth, and he toyed with her, and yet was not content; it seemed to him that her lips were cold and her eyes without any light.

"Then he breathed the third time on the flower

and cast it down weeping, and crying, 'Let others laugh and others love. Joy is not for me, I see.'

"Then, strange to say, all at once his heart grew light, and he was glad, and sang aloud with rapture, and the maiden rejoiced beside him, and the kisses of her lips were warm and sweet as the suns of summer.

"The fairy took from him the golden flower. 'Now laughter is yours and love,' she said. 'For the wish that you wished was for others, and pure of the greeds of self.'

"Do you know what the story means? No; you have only just got your yellow celandine, and have scarcely breathed upon it."

But I knew what it meant enough to know that he himself used his golden flower for the gladness of others—always.

CHAPTER IV.
Beside dead Fires.

UNDER the financial government of Pascarèl my florins seemed endlessly to expand. As yet I did not appear upon the stage with any of them, though he trained me for it sedulously with all the skill and subtlety that were given to him by the unerring instincts and the long practice of his art.

We were completely happy; Brunótta was a little humble merry soul, quick as a mouse, bright as a bird, honest, I thought, as the day. Cocomero and Toccò worshipped the ground that their chief even trod on, and would have laid their lives down willingly to do his bidding in the merest trifle. Whilst Pascarèl himself, the life and soul, the alpha and omega, of the small community, governed it with that gentle sway which lends to obedience as sweet a charm as lies in liberty.

He inquired everywhere, as best he could, for tidings of my father and of Florio. But either the people knew nothing, or those who knew anything had been bidden not to reveal it; we learned no intelligence of any sort, and at the post in the Uffizi he heard that letters from Verona had been addressed to the name of Tempesta, and were still lying there unclaimed. Doubtless, these neglected things were those which old Maso Sasso had penned for Mariuccia in the den of his loggia.

Pascarèl sought, honestly and unweariedly, on my behalf; but he did not affect to be sorry for the result.

"No one who has once caught hold of destiny likes to lose that slippery sovereign," he would say, with a laugh; and so I remained with him and his, through the cool weeks of the Quaresima.

At times, indeed, he spoke to me — like one who does an unwelcome duty — of seeking shelter for me in some convent's safety and stillness; but my passionate terror of the captivity disarmed his wiser resolves; and, indeed, to have won the money necessary to secure such a refuge was as impossible to me as to draw down the moon; and to take it from him, as he sometimes hinted,—for he said he had a few hundreds of lire laid by in the hands of a goldsmith of Florence, lest any evil should befall him and leave his troop adrift,—would have been a debt from which, child though I was, all the instincts in me revolted.

Before we left Florence on the springtide wanderings, he betook himself to Verona, to see, for his own satisfaction, what could be learned of my father. I heard long afterwards that he went at great peril to himself, and in disguise, from the hatred of the Austriaci against him; but of this he said nothing to me at that time. Of danger to himself he never spoke. This was only a week or so after I had first fallen in with the merry little party in the ilex woods, and I was vaguely startled to feel how deadly a blank his absence caused to me. The skies lost all their light, and the city all her golden and transfigured beauty.

He placed me, whilst he went, at a house on the other side of the river, where a good friend of his, Orfeo Orlanduccio, a master worker in mosaic, dwelt.

Orlanduccio was a widower, with one little, pretty, merry child called Bicè. They were very good to me in the dusky ancient house, through whose grated casements one looked out, like prisoners, on the world, and whose massive chambers were all rich with carving, and scented with that curious old world incense-like aromatic odour of which the Florence streets are full.

It was in the Via de la Pergola, not far off the house that the Duke gave to Cellini; and as I leaned against the barred windows I used to think of the bronze-workers in that little garden, and of the fierce molten metal seething out under the flame from the oak timbers; and of the stream, hot and red, like blood from a murdered man's throat, crushing in to fill the beautiful mask of the Perseus, and of the artist—breathless, agonised, torn betwixt hope and fear, rent by the noble rashness of genius and the feebler human dread of accident—coming out under the dark hanging fig-leaves with armsful of his household gods of silver and pewter and copper and gold, and casting them all into the furnace, as children were cast to Moloch, so that his Thought might arise from the fires and live for all time in men's light.

Orfeo Orlanduccio was a grave, melancholy, stern, good man; he had been lamed in the wars of Carl-Alberto, and was subject to suspicion for his advanced political creeds; he had a noble grey head like Luca della Robbia's, and it was a picture to see him in his dark workshop piecing the tiny fragments so deftly into all manner of delicate arabesques and dainty flowers with his lithe slender fingers that had used to grasp a sabre to hard purpose, they said, in earlier days.

I stayed with him and the little, saucy, smiling rosebud of a Bicè whilst Pascarèl went northward. Brunótta did not come with me there; indeed the mosaic maker seemed to me to know little or nothing of her existence.

On the fourth day of my stay with them, the good Orfeo, coming from the market-place, was arrested and borne to the Bargello under some accusation of conspiracy. I know not what, but all liberal thinkers were under suspicion in those days.

His apprentices brought word of his misfortunes, and little Bicè, a merry babyish thing, of nine or ten, cried her pretty eyes red with weeping for her father, and in the evening time her foster-mother, a peasant of the Casentino, came in and bore her off to dwell in the country till her parent should be set free, which might not be for many months, they said.

I remember the sense of desolation, of belonging to no earthly soul or thing, that shivered over me that night as the little heedless child went, laughing through her tears to hear the mule bells ring, and the apprentices took down their caps and stared at me stupidly, and the woman who did the housework there in the daytime, having cleaned her pots and pans and swept up the kitchen, came and looked at me with her arm in her side, and asked me, meditatively:—

"The signorina will betake herself to her friends? the lads sleep out, and then I will bar the place up safe. Orfeo has been in this sort of trouble before. Men are such fools;—they will craze their heads for things that have no concern for them. Will the signorina go; I want to bar the doors; it is dark now."

I begged her to let me stay a little. I had promised Pascarèl not to leave this house until he came for me, and no force in Florence, I think, would have availed to make me disobey him.

A rebel to all other authority since my babyhood, I took a passionate delight in obeying this stranger's mere glance and gesture.

The donna di fatìca, moved by my loneliness and my supplications, lit me a lamp and left me, promising to return in an hour, when go I must, she said, for she had served Maestro Orfeo twenty years and more, and was not going to leave his bottega open to thieves for all the yellow-haired signorini in Christendom.

Her heavy steps trod slowly out of the stone
passages, and the massive nail-studded door closed
behind her. My heart sank as I was left alone in
the empty house with its unfinished mosaics strewn
over the floor, and its dreamy aroma from the millions of pine cones and oak logs that had burned on
those old hearths in the fires of five hundred centuries.

It was one of the oldest dwellings in Florence.
Its massive stones and iron stanchions had stood
against sack and siege, flame and mob. It was only
antique and strange with the 'prentices' merry feet on
the stairs and Bicè's rosy round face at the grated
casements, but when one was alone in it, at night,
there seemed dim clouds of ghosts in every dusky
chamber.

My heart leaped with the sweetest gladness it had
ever known as I heard a light swift footstep on the
stairs, and the clear sweet ring of a Tuscan voice.

"My donzella!" it called, in the gloom, "are you
all alone here?"

I sprang to him in joyous welcome, and did not
notice till he had sat down beside me on the oaken
settle by the fireless hearth that his face looked worn
and weary.

"Yes, Orfeo is imprisoned," he said, impatiently.
"There is nothing to be done. He is known to be in
the confidence of Mazzini, and papers have been
found—do not let us talk of it. His child is safe,
and he will come back to his old place in a year or
less. He is a good man and true. We must have
patience."

He was silent. The lamp burned dully. The old
house was silent around us.

"I am vexed for him—and for you," he said, after a long pause. "I thought, dear signorina, that it would be better for you to stay with little Bicè than to roam with us. Orfeo is the only man whom I can trust. My friends lie amongst poor people—very poor—or men honest, indeed, but reckless and given over to wild work, who can be of no sort of good to you. Orfeo, indeed, I could have trusted. He would have given you a safe home, though a poor one. But it seems willed otherwise."

"But I am to go with *you!*" I cried, aghast at this disposal of me.

He smiled gently, but a darkness and impatience passed like a mist over his face. He was silent, trimming the wick of the oil-lamp.

"Well, so it seems, dear donzella," he said, after awhile, with a certain hesitation not natural to his frank, free, rapid modes of speech. "Well, I will do my best by you—God help me, and forgive us sinners! Nevertheless, if Orfeo had not fallen on this evil chance, it had been better."

"If I be any trouble to you," I began——

He stopped me with a tender gesture.

"Never say that—it is not that I mean. It is—a safe and quiet home were better for you. But since fate wills it otherwise, oh, cara mia! credit me, you shall be as sacred to me as though my dead mother lived to care for you."

I looked up at him in wonder at the emotion in his voice; his thoughts were in nowise clear to me.

There was a long silence in the dark old house.

He leaned against the wall, lost in meditations that my imagination failed to follow.

He looked down suddenly, and spoke:

"I have learned nothing at Verona," he said, with a certain tone of sadness that wounded me, for it seemed as though he were regretful not to be rid of me. "No one has seen your father, nor could anyone give me any news of him. Nor do they appear to know any more of who or what he really is than you do. But there is one sad story that I heard for you, and that is of your old master."

"Ambrogiò?" I cried, and all my heart went back to the poor old lonely man whom I had forsaken in a child's eager desires for fresh fields and pastures new.

"Yes, dear donzella," answered Pascarèl.

I sprang to my feet eagerly; he answered me with a slight, hopeless gesture of the hands that chilled me into a great awe.

"He died the night you left Verona. They found him dead over his empty brazier in his garret—all alone. The children saw him first; going to take their lesson in the morning. He is buried by now."

The simple words seemed to pierce my heart as I heard them.

My poor dead master!

I saw the place — the still lone garret, the uncurtained lattice, the robin singing on the sill, the dreary roofs, and the snow mountains far beyond; the miserable home, with the grey ashes of cold fires in the earthen brazier; the children at the half-opened door, peeping with pale scared faces, and whispering together, and pointing at the figure on the hearth—all the sad, dreary, colourless picture, drawn in the black and white of Age and Death, arose before me as I listened.

I sank down on a bench, and cried bitterly, as for a woe all my own.

Was this the end—the only bitter end — of all those years of wrong and want? One other nameless grave in the snow under the bleak blasts in old Verona!

Pascarèl let me sob on, and did not seek to console me; but I poured out all the history to him in my sorrow, and he listened gravely, there, in the old, dim, lonely room, heavy with the scent of the long-died-out fires that had warmed so many faces and forms that were now dust in the crypts and sepulchres of the city.

"You must never tell the tale but to me, my child," he said, at length. "The secret belongs to the dead. He chose to keep it in his life; you must keep it for him in his death. Rothwald is rich and famous? Yes; why not? Justice is not of this world."

"But why does God permit such things?" I cried, in the despair of my poor lost master's wrongs.

Pascarèl gave an impatient sigh.

"Oh child! Has the human race solved that problem in all these many thousand years since the first men dwelt in the first lake-cities? We shall never know that till our souls leave our bodies——"

"But for no punishment to fall!" I cried, and sobbed afresh, weighed down with the burden of all those long, lone fruitless years, whose end was a beggar's grave in sad Verona.

"Ay! if the bolts would smite, and the heavens

17*

would open, life would be so much easier, and hope
so much easier too," said Pascarèl; "but, perhaps, even
in this world, there may be more punishment than we
can know.

"Listen, donzella," he pursued. "Did never you
hear the story of Andreä dal Castagno, who lived here
in the street hard by? No? Well, then—

"He and the bright Venetian Domenico dwelt
together in great and close friendship; so much so,
that they shared the same chambers, painted in the
same studio, were inseparable in pursuits and pleasures, and aims and endeavours, and were cited all
through the city as the very symbol of faithful comradeship.

"Well, one night, the Venetian went forth as
usual, with his lute under his cloak, to serenade his
mistress in the moonlight; and there, in the dark
archway of the street, a dark figure lay unseen in
wait for him, and he was stabbed through and through,
and his love-song was stifled in his throat, and he was
slain.

"Who had killed him?

"The city could not tell.

"Andreä was found painting quietly by lamplight when they bore the dying man home; and he
tore his hair and rent his garments in agonised
lamentation over the bleeding body of his dear dead
friend.

"Yet Andreä was the murderer.

"For greed of the secret of the oils and varnishes,
some say; some say for envy of the woman's love.
Which no one ever rightly knew.

"Andreä lived in honour all his days. He was a

great artist, and all men spoke well of him. Suspicion never fell on him. Had not Domenico breathed his death-sigh in his arms, blessing him to the last? Nay, the State even employed him to paint the traitors hung on the city walls by their heels—and his brush did not falter.

"He had long life, I say, and everything to make it good and even glorious. Yet, though he had riches, and fame, and, as men call it, happiness, he never once in all that time could ever quite forget. He never once forgot; he never ceased to see the kindly faithful face dead there in the lustre of the summer night; he never ceased to hear the familiar voice in the last love-song ere he had stifled it in its death-struggle; he never ceased to be pursued night and day by the remembrance of his guilt; never, that we are sure; for, though he kept his secret close all his life long, he could not keep it to the very end. On his death bed he confessed his crime, and Florence, though at the tenth hour, despoiled him, and dishonoured him, and gave him a felon's grave."

I shuddered as I heard.

The tale told in that old dark Florentine room, within a stone's throw of the place of murder, had a terrible ghastly awe in it. I shrank closer to Pascarèl, and he stretched his hand out and took mine.

"Did I tell you too frightful a story?" he said, caressingly.

"No, no," I murmured, "it is not that. But my poor old master! And see here: if Andreä were

chastised, what did that compensate Domenico? It
could not give him back his life and love——"

"Of compensation to Domenico there was none,"
said Pascarèl, sadly. "But of chastisement to Andreä I think there was enough. I told you the tale
to show you that, where we think glory and gain are
most abundant, there sometimes burns the fire that
quenches not, which men call remorse. Your master
left his vengeance with his God. We must so leave
it likewise. And now, donzella mia, you shiver in
this cold dark room. Come out, and let us get to
the light and warmth again, and forget all these
weary meditations. You must wander with us; those
Fates on the onyx so will it. Well, I swear to you,
carina, that you shall never repent your trust in me."

He touched my hands lightly with his lips, and we
went down the stone staircase, and out of the dark
and lonely house of the mosaic-worker.

I clung close to him as we went through the now
gloomy streets, and I was glad when we reached the
little bright archway of the locandà in Oltrano, where
Brunótta met us with many exclamations, and with
the ruddy flame of a wood fire she had lighted glowing on her little plump figure and her gorgeous silver
ear-rings.

The Arte was shut that night, for it was the Domenica
di Passione.

She had a little supper ready for us of shining
brown alardi, crisply fried, and stewed rice with
pears. She, like Pulci's Margutte, was given to swear-
ing "neither by black nor blue, but only by a good
capon, whether roast or boiled," and had no notion of
starving even on the gravest fast of the Church.

It was all quiet in the quarter of the Silver Dove.

Bells were sounding for the vespers, that was all; and as we sat at our little meal people streamed by the open door, going in flocks to pray in the great white vaulted stillness of the Santo Spirito.

Pascarèl and I were silent that night.

He thought of his friend Orfeo; and I of my old dead master.

Nevertheless, we were both glad, I think, that the morrow was not going to part us; and whilst Brunótta and the boys played together at taròc, I sat and looked every now and then at the delicate profile of Pascarèl against the shadows from the oil-lamp, and felt no trouble or fear for the future.

CHAPTER V.
Giudentu dell' Anno.

WE stayed in Florence through the long, cool, sunny weeks of the Quaresima, broken here and there with the mad frolic of the Mi-Carême, and the fun of the Fairs of the Innamorati and the Curiosi and the Gelosie at the Gates of the City.

The great lilies, white, and azure, and purple, were just beginning to bloom everywhere round the city, and the streets and the woods seemed to shine as snow with the clusters of the stainless anemoli.

There is nothing upon earth, I think, like the smile of Italy as she awakes when the winter has dozed itself away in the odours of its oakwood fires.

The whole land seems to laugh.

The springtide of the north is green and beautiful, but it has nothing of the radiance, the dream-fulness, the ecstasy of spring in the southern countries. The springtide of the north is pale with the gentle colourless sweetness of its world of primroses; the springtide of Italy is rainbow-hued, like the profusion of anemones that laugh with it in every hue of glory under every ancient wall and beside every hill-fed stream.

Spring in the north is a child that wakes from dreams of death; spring in the south is a child that wakes from dreams of love. One is rescued and welcomed from the grave; but the other comes smiling on a sunbeam from heaven.

All the Quaresima we abode in Florence; and he made glad and perfect to me each lenten hour as it glided by; and when the sun set, it left me always tired, happy, thoughtful, full of peace.

CHAPTER VI.

The old Star Tower.

ONE day, I remember, we strolled slowly out by the Romano gate towards the hills as the day drew to its close.

The old frescoes on the house wall were bright in the afternoon light; there was a group of soldiers drinking; there were some asses laden with straw for the plaiters' market on the morrow; a bare-foot, brown-frocked monk went by amongst the soldiery; the cypress and ilex road stretched up into the distance; coming down the Stradone was an old white horse with a pile of fruit upon his back, and a lad in a yellow shirt at his bridle; about the base of the old broken statues of Petrarca some children played.

"How very little that is!" said Pascarèl. "And yet it is all a picture. It is a pity ever to do anything in Italy; the country is made just to lie still in and dream in, with the body half asleep and the mind wide awake, but lost in fancies. Italy soothes us as a mother's arms lull a wayward child, if only we will let her do it: but if we struggle from her natural influences, and try to spend our lives in strife, then her sun stings, and her dust blinds us, and all her charm is gone."

So, talking whilst we passed the people, and followed closely by the three dogs, he took me up to the Star Tower of Galileo amongst the winding paths of the hills, with the grey walls overtopped by white fruit blossom, and ever and again, at some break in their ramparts of stone, the gleam of the yellow Arno water, or the glisten of the marbles of the City shining on us far beneath, through the silvery veil of the olive leaves.

It was just in that loveliest moment when winter melts into spring.

Everywhere under the vines the young corn was springing in that tender vivid greenness that is never seen twice in a year. The sods between the furrows were scarlet with the bright flame of wild tulips, with here and there a fleck of gold where a knot of daffodils nodded. The roots of the olives were blue with nestling pimpernels and hyacinths, and along the old grey walls the long, soft, thick leaf of the arums grew, shading their yet unborn lilies.

The air was full of a dreamy fragrance; the bullocks went on their slow ways with flowers in their leathern frontlets; the contadini had flowers stuck be-

hind their ears or in their waistbands; women sat by
the wayside, singing as they plaited their yellow curling
lengths of straw; children frisked and tumbled like
young rabbits under the budding maples; the plum-
trees strewed the green landscape with flashes of white
like newly fallen snow on alpine grass slopes; again
and again amongst the tender pallor of the olive
woods there rose the beautiful flush of a rosy almond-
tree; at every step the passer-by trod ancle deep in
violets.

The air was cool, but so exquisitely still, and soft,
and radiant, that as the old people came out of their
dark, arched, stone chambers, and sat a little in the
sun, and made up into bunches for selling the blossoms which their children gathered by the million,
without seeming to make the earth the poorer, one felt
as if the sun shining on them as it did must make
them young again—as if no one could very long be
very old or very sad in Italy.

It was the thought of a child, and of a happy
child. When one is old it must surely be better to
creep away under the mists, into the darkness of some
chimney-corner, in the chill, short twilight of the love-
less and bitter North, than to behold this divine light,
cloudless and endless, which seems to beat with all
the pulses of passion, and to laugh with all the sweet,
soft, foolish ecstasies of love.

Who was it that called Italy the country of the
dead? Not they surely who have beheld her in the
days of spring.

About the feet of the Tower of Galileo, ivy and
vervain, and the Madonna's herb, and the white sexagons
of the stars of Bethlehem grew amongst the grasses,

pigeons paced to and fro with pretty pride of plumage; a dog slept on the flags; the cool, moist, deep-veined creepers climbed about the stones; there were peach trees in all the beauty of their blossoms, and everywhere about them were close-set olive trees, with the ground between them scarlet with the tulips and the wild rose bushes.

From a window a girl leaned out and hung a cage amongst the ivy leaves, that her bird might sing his vespers to the sun.

Who will may see the scene to-day.

So little changed—so little, if at all, from the time when the feet of the great student wore the timber of the tower stairs, and the fair-haired scholar, who had travelled from the isles in the northern sea, came up between the olive stems to gaze thence on Vallom brosa.

The world has spoiled most of its places of pilgrimage, but the old Star Tower is not harmed as yet, where it stands amongst its quiet garden ways, and grass-grown slopes, up high amongst the hills, with sounds of dripping water on its court, and wild wood-flowers thrusting their bright heads through its stones.

Generations have come and gone: tyrannies have risen and fallen: full many a time the plain below has been red with the invader's fire, and the curling flame has burned the fruitful land to blackened barrenness; full many a time the silence of the olive thickets has been broken by the tumult of war and revolution, and the dead bodies of men have drifted thick as leaves in the blood-stained current of the river.

But nothing has been changed here, where the old square pile stands out amongst the flowering vines.

It is as peaceful, as simple, as homely, as closely girt with blossoming boughs and with tulip-crimsoned grasses, now as then, when from its roof, in the still midnights of a far-off time, its master read the secrets of the stars.

You can see it to-day—any day that you will—this quiet shadowy hill-side place amongst the fields.

But come up softly between the old gnarled olive stems; tread noiselessly the winding pathway where the wild hyacinth shakes its blue bells on the wind; be reverent a little—if reverence in this age be possible—as you climb the narrow wooden stair, and through the unglazed arches of the walls look westward where the sea lies, and southward towards Rome.

Be reverent a little, for a little space at least: for here Galileo learned the story of the sun; and here Milton, looking on Valdarno, dreamed of Paradise.

CHAPTER VII.
Due Amori.

WE scattered the pigeons that day as they picked their way amongst the rose trees, and we went across the sombre quiet court, and up the wooden stairs, on to the square roof where the great Tuscan had sat so many and many a night with his listening pupils round him, and, beneath, the dark stillness of the sleeping plains.

"How fair she looks down there!" said Pascarèl, resting his eyes fondly on the City. "I have seen pretty well all the world, but I have never seen any-

thing that can make one forget her. I am of the same
way of thinking as was Visino;—better a flask of
Tribbiano and a berlingozzo of Florence than all the
kings and queens and courts and camps in Christendom. Look at her now; she lies like a golden galley
of old upon a silver moon-lightened sea."

Very fair indeed she was, the Lily Queen, that
evening.

There had been shadows all day, and in the west
there were masses of cloud, purple and blue-black,
spreading away into a million of soft scarlet cirri that
drifted before a low wind from the southward, tender
and yet rich in tone as any scattered shower of carnation leaves.

Through that vast pomp of dusky splendour and
that radiance of rose, the sun itself still shone; shone
full upon the City.

Leaning on the broken edge of the watch-tower
and gazing down below, all Florence seemed like the
seer's dream of the New Jerusalem; every stone of her
seemed transmuted; she was as though paven and
built with gold; straightway across the whole valley
stretched the alchemy of that wondrous fireglow, and
all the broad level lands of the Valdigreve were transfigured likewise into one vast sheet of gold, on which
the silver olives and the dim white villages and villas
floated like frail white sails upon a sunlit sea.

Farther—still farther yet, beyond that burnished
ocean—the mountains and the clouds met and mingled,
golden likewise, broken here and there into some
tenderest rose-leaf flush, miraculously lovely, as a poet's
dreams of nameless things of God.

We stayed long, and watched it high above on the

wooden roof of the tower; watched it until the sun had set, and the glow had died, and the stillness of evening had fallen over the hills and plain, and past our faces flew a little grey downy owl.

"Your fathers saw Galileo?" said Pascarèl to the bird as it went, "and thought what a fool he was, no doubt, to sit mooning there with his face turned to the stars instead of hunting moths in the night air and slaughtering mice under the olive stems as they did. To be sure:—the owls and the world, no doubt, were quite of one mind concerning him. When there is a nice, plump, black mouse to be killed down on the clay, what greater folly can there be than to stay on high staring at stars? Who would not be an owl ten times sooner than a Galileo?"

"Are you serious?" I asked him, when we leaned against the wooden rail. I had not then learned to disentangle his thoughts from his language.

"Altro!" he cried, sending a pebble down into the olive foliage beneath. "Who would not be an owl? To escape all the toil and moil of the day, asleep in a cosy ivy hole; to doze all the hours away, and only awake to kill and eat; to be able to swear there is no such thing as a sun, because we are too blind to see it—what can be finer than that? It is such a popular type, too; ten thousand times more popular than a Galileo!"

I looked at him where he leaned with his arms on the parapet of the roof, and his profile, clear and dark, against the delicate silvery greys that had followed the rose glow in the heavens.

He had more interest for me than Galileo or the owls; in no way could I reconcile the grace of him, the wit of him, and the look of his face with the mode of his life, which was scarcely above the grade of vagrants and of mountebanks.

It seemed to me so strange that any man of such various learning and such ironical perception should thus willingly pass away his years in the homely and grotesque career of a strolling player.

*　　　*　　　*　　　*

"What could ever first make you take this life you lead?" I asked him, incredulously, when we stood together on the top of the star tower.

"I fell in love," said Pascarèl, promptly, leaning over the roof-wall to watch the shadows steal over the long cypress stradone, and come slowly upward and upward to the heights whereon we stood, "not for the first nor the fifth time, of course, but truly enough for that matter. A set of French comedians came to stir the stately silence of old Pisa. They were merry, poor, happy-go-lucky people who played their way all along the Riviera. Clever people, too—French players always are.

"Amongst them there was a girl whom we called the Zinzara, because of her pungent tongue. I am not sure that she was handsome, but she had a *diable au corps*, you know—no, you don't know—no matter!

"To see the Zinzara play Phædre in the first, and dance the cancan in the afterpiece, was a revelation. I had always maintained that women could not possess genius, but I gave in before her. Her renderings of Racine were miracles, and so were her soups and salads.

"She would scare your very soul out of you with her whirlwinds of passion, and her whisper was like the hiss of a snake, and her eyes seemed a blaze of fire and passion, and then half-an-hour after you would see her in her one poor little room, with her cuffs turned back from her long white hands, and she would mix you oil, and lettuces, and beet-root, or toss you a herb omelette over her stove with a skill that half the cooks of Paris could not have equalled. She was a true Frenchwoman, the Zinzara. I have never seen her like since.

"It was she who made me an actor. I had always had a taste for it, but when I saw this Paris mosquito the die was cast. I had finished all my course in Pisa. For that matter I had swept all before me, and won all there was to win. Indeed, they actually offered me a professorship of mathematics. Never say that I have not rejected greatness.

"I was two-and-twenty; I was an Italian; I was Pascarèl; and they imagined that I should settle down to lead all my life in old Pisa like an owl in a belfry till I grew as old, and as grey, and as silent, and as forgotten of God and man as Pisa is herself! But they meant well; only they knew nothing of the fitness of things. Academies never do.

"If I had meant to stay, the Zinzara would have swept my intentions to the winds. I had a room I was very fond of, high up in a tower, with the river washing against the walls far away down below. There were scores of cobwebs, and legends, and ghosts attached to it, but I slept too soundly in those days to take heed of any one of them. I had hundreds of books there, and my tubes, and prisms, and telescope, and I had passed seven years there after the fashion of Faust, only that I had all my life before me, and being young broke up my learning and science with nights of nonsense and days of pleasure that needed no devil's cordial.

"I loved my room, and was loth to quit it, and almost it tempted me to stay in Pisa; but one fine morning, as I read my Plato for the thousandth time, I heard a merry noise and laughter in the street at the foot of the tower; and looking out I saw a little set of people all ready for long travel, and going gaily on their way. It was the Zinzara and her brethren going back towards their France.

"They had the sun all about them; they had great clusters of cherries in their hands; they were eating, and laughing, and singing; they were dusty already, but what of that? they were going to the green country, to the blue sea, to the charm of change, to the tumult and merriment and variety of life.

"The spell of the Wanderjahre was cast on me, to say nothing that I was really in love with that poor Zinzara.

"An hour after I had made over my room and my books and my instruments to my best friend, Ezio Luccone, and I had caught up the mosquito and her friends on the high road for Livorno, just as the sun reached to noon. From that day I was a player.

"I stayed about two years with that troop, all that time on the Riviera or among the little mountain towns of Savoy.

"The Zinzara taught me all she knew. For the matter of that I had found my vocation, which assuredly did not lie in a professorial tribune.

"I used to write comedies and 'revues' for them.

No! I have not a scrap of what I wrote left. What does that matter? If one have any *orð sodð* about one at all, either mental or moral, one never counts what shreds of the good metal one drops along the roads. If others pick it up, let them. To be of ever so little use is all one can hope for in this world.

"At the end of two years the troop broke up; it is a miracle amongst actors when any set of them holds together half as long, and I went by myself to Paris, where, too, I played.

"But I never cared much for Paris. One cannot open one's mouth when one talks that language; and amongst those shining zinc roofs, and that blaze of white paint and of gilding, I grew thirsty for my own great dark palaces, and still historic garden-ways, and moonlit plains song-haunted, and measureless distances only swept by clouds and wind. Do you not know? Oh, yes; anyone who has once breathed in Italy knows. And to anyone who had not, there would be no use in talking."

"What of the Zinzara?

"Oh, the usual thing of the Zinzara. She loved me very dearly for a time, and then she picked up a Marquis out of Monaco—only a Marchese di Truffaldino I am afraid, poor thing—and flung the salad-bowl at my head.

"Women always fling something at you when they are angry with themselves for having been in love with you; a great genius flings a stinging 'Elle et Lui;' a poor actress can only fling a kitchen missile that comes handy. Perhaps the latter is the better. It is not so disagreeable to be forcibly reminded of the radishes and endive of the past, as it is to see all one's old follies and passions served up with pepper and mustard.

"The poor Zinzara! I have not a notion what became of her. She had genius of a sort indisputably, both for tragedy and cookery. But she never fastened her mark on the world, though she had the making both of a Rachel and a Vatel in her.

"Peace be with her wherever she be; she enlivened two bright summers for me; she taught me the tricks of the stage; and she only broke her wooden supper-bowl, and not either my head or my heart."

I was silent as he ceased speaking; I had only the most vaguely innocent notions of what this his passion for the Zinzara might mean; but I had a vague and restless impatience at hearing him speak of any love for any creature at all.

His gaze went westward as he spoke.

Close at hand, on its own quiet hill-side, stood the little convent-church of Sta. Margheritá, the highest point of all, bowered close amongst olive and fruit-tree foliage, with the village slanting away from it in a dusky line of roofs downward to where the Pazzi tyrannicide was planned amongst the villa gardens.

Pascarèl looked across to it. It is not changed since its beautiful novice left its saintly peace and stole down through the amorous olive shadows to the lawless love of Fra Lippi.

"Do you not see Fra Filippo," said he, "gathering his monk's frock about him, and speeding up there to steal a glance at Lucrezia through the convent grating, if chance favoured? What grace was there in that scamp of the Carmelites, that Rabelais of painting, that Falstaff of the fine arts, that a woman, young

18*

and rich and beautiful, should leave all for him, and
cleave to him so faithfully? Some heart and soul
there must have been. The city saw in him a wild,
frolicsome, mad monk, fitter to worship Silenus than
Christ. But there must have been some soul in him
—some soul tender, pitiful, spiritual, profound,—or he
had never painted his S. Stefano of Prato till it made
the fierce men of his own day weep, and he would
never have loved those green, wide, laughing countries
which made him greater than Masaccio, and the first
of the Florence painters of landscape. Perhaps that
soul in him the young nun saw. Are we ever truly
read, save by the one that loves us best? Love is
blind, the phrase runs; nay, I would rather say Love
sees as God sees, and with infinite wisdom has infinite
pardon."

His voice grew very sweet and still, and the
dreamy look came into his eyes as he leaned there
gazing across at the little red roof of Sta. Margheritá,
whose solitary bell was tolling the Ave Maria over its
silent woods.

His thoughts were far beyond me; I was but a
heedless child, and of where his mind had wandered
I knew nothing; and of the greatness of such a love
as he was wishful for, doubtless, in his heart even
then, I had no more conception or measurement than
I had of that baser passion such as he had been lured
with by the Zinzara.

*   *   *   *   *

He spoke no more; the night had fallen quickly
and completely, as it does in Valdarno when once
the sun's disc has dropped behind Carrara.

We went slowly together down the stairs and

across the court and through the olive downward to the City, and we passed within the gates again as the stars began to burn, and the sheets of moonlight to lie white and wide on river and piazza. The world, so tired though it be with fruitless pain, so dull in drowsy apathy, so weary of for ever giving birth to what for ever perishes when touching on its prime, the world is once more young again when the moon shines on Italy.

"To my fancy," said he, softly, as we paused a moment on the bridge of the Graces to see the silver width of the stream shine away on either side into the sweet tremulous darkness of the hills, "to my fancy, when the gods of the golden age were driven from earth and walked no more amongst men, they looked back once, and said, 'that we may be remembered a little in this land—we, the old banished gods of the old, fair, dead faiths,—let Paradise return to earth when the moon wakes above Italy.' Her nights are gifts of the gods that she has, this Italy of ours; it is so trite to say so—ay, because it is so true."

Florence was very still that night as we went through her streets from the old Star Tower.

It was the Holy week.

Here and there, from some low open door, a Miserere was pealing. Here and there the shadow of a monk fell across the broad white stones. Here and there a lamp burned before some street shrine hung with those scentless flowers that are the joyless Christian symbol of immortality.

But Florence never can be very sad. Her tears and smiles lie close together. If she draw the saintly cowl about her, her fair eyes laugh from beneath the folds, so that you half shall swear the robe of penance is a masker's domino.

She tells her beads with one hand, but she touches her lute with the other.

Even this night as we went, though it was the season of the saintly Quaresima, there was a mandoline trilling from some high casement in a palace tower; in an old dusky doorway there was the glisten of a girl's white dress and a cuirassier's flashing breastplate; from a fretted balcony of stone fashioned with lilies and fawns' heads a beautiful dark woman, gathering about her a mantle of black and gold, dropped a single rosebud to a lover who waited below for the pretty symbol; far, far away, across the great white luminous piazza, there came the sound of voices, in chorus, laughing to light scorn the lenten lamentations; some men and maidens had been in the meadows and were bringing home sheaves of the lilies, they danced as they came in the moonlight, and a young boy played a viol before them.

Pascarèl looked and listened, then went onward with a smile.

"Is not my Florence perfect?" he murmured. "Some say I talk of her as though she were a city of fairie. Well, a fairy city she is to every poet and every lover. Was she not builded in a night by Hercules as a pleasure toy for Venus and Flora, made with the stones from the golden Arno water, and set up in a meadow of lilies? Hercules gave her his strength as a birthright, and Flora being content, touched the soil and said, 'All the year long flowers shall blossom here, and their smile shall not cease in any season;' and Venus, being well pleased likewise, called her son to her, and said, 'When you dart your arrows hither wreathe them with roses, and wing them from the eagle and the dove.'"

CHAPTER VIII.

The Lily-queen.

HE did indeed love Florence with a tender passion.

Paris is the Aspasia of cities, but Florence is the Heloïse; upon the brilliancy of her genius and her beauty there lie always the shadow of the cloister, and always the divinity of a great sacrifice.

Men, with any soul in them, love Florence reverently; for tuneful and thoughtless though her laughter be now, and although now the strangers of northern isles and western worlds coarsely intrigue in her pleasure-places, and basely cheapen her treasures in her streets, Florence cannot be changed or lowered, for in her day she suffered much and failed often, and aspired greatly, and set her seal with a pure hand on much of the noblest work of the world.

To Pascarèl she was as a living thing.

Not a stone of her but had a tongue for him. Not a dark nook in her quietest ways but for him was filled with some figure of the past standing out in the gold and colours of idealised tradition, like some form that a monk had drawn upon his missal vellum.

Gay and idle, and buoyant and amorous indeed had been the tenour of all his days in Florence; laughed away to the tinkle of mandolines, the chink of wine-glasses, the riot of carnival mirth, the twittering love chirp of women quickly won and lightly lost.

But beneath this life of his there ran another vein, deeper and truer, and filled with the strong heroical blood of the past; and he would go through the Florence ways many and many a time, lost to all the daily stir around him, and seeing nothing but the wistful spiritual eyes of Angelico, or the white bare feet of Ginevra, or the flicker of the torch in the hand of the Black Giàn, or the dread of destiny on the face of Luisa Strozzi.

He would laugh at himself for his joy in it, for he would say that he was a citizen of the world, and entered no narrower classification; but at heart the love of Florence was always warm with him, continual wanderer from her olive valleys though he was.

He knew the story of her every stone and spandril; he would trace the steps of all her heroes and prophets inch by inch along the narrow ways; for him her paven courts were eloquent with a thousand tongues; and all the curling leaves and shining traceries of her sculptures had a million whispers of the great workshops where great men had wrought at them amidst the eager reverent eyes of pupils who, in their turn, took up the glorious tale, and told it to the nations.

And now and then, coming out of the Bargello into the broad silvery sunlight, or leaning on the old Rubaconte parapet, looking far, far away, to the snows of Vallombrosa, now and then he would bestir himself and speak of Florence, with that swift rush of that mellow Tuscan which has the war clang of the clarion and the love-note of the lute together in it.

"Her riches?" said he, in one of those moments, answering some thoughtless word of mine.. "No. It was not the riches of Florence that made her power—it was her way of spending her riches; a totally different thing, cara mia.

"Amidst all her commerce, her wars, her hard work, her money-making, Florence was always dominated and spiritualised, at her noisiest and worst, by a poetic and picturesque imagination.

"Florentine life had always an ideal side to it; and an idealism, pure and lofty, runs through her darkest histories and busiest times like a thread of gold through a coat of armour and a vest of frieze.

"The Florentine was a citizen, a banker, a workman, a carder of wool, a weaver of silk, indeed; but he was also always a lover, and always a soldier; that is, always half a poet. He had his Caroccio and his Ginevra as well as his tools and his sacks of florins. He had his sword as well as his shuttle. His scarlet giglio was the flower of love no less than the blazonry of battle on his standard, and the mint stamp of the commonwealth on his coinage.

"Herein lay the secret of the influence of Florence: the secret which rendered the little city, stretched by her river's side, amongst her quiet meadows white with arums, a sacred name to all generations of men for all she dared and all she did.

"'She amassed wealth,' they say: no doubt she did—and why?

"To pour it with both hands to melt in the foundries of Ghiberti—to bring it in floods to cement the mortar that joined the marbles of Brunelleschi! She always spent to great ends, and to mighty uses.

"When she called a shepherd from his flocks in the green valley to build for her a bell-tower so that she might hear, night and morning, the call to the altar, the shepherd built for her in such fashion that the belfry has been the Pharos of Art for five centuries.

"Here is the secret of Florence—supreme aspiration.

"The aspiration which gave her citizens force to live in poverty, and clothe themselves in simplicity, so as to be able to give up their millions of florins to bequeath miracles in stone and metal and colour to the Future. The aspiration which so purified her soil, red with carnage, black with smoke of war, trodden continuously by hurrying feet of labourers, rioters, mercenaries, and murderers, that from that soil there could spring, in all its purity and perfection, the paradise-blossom of the Vita Nuova.

"Venice perished for her pride and carnal lust; Rome perished for her tyrannies and her blood-thirst; but Florence,—though many a time nearly strangled under the heel of the Empire and the hand of the Church—Florence was never slain utterly either in body or soul; Florence still crowned herself with flowers even in her throes of agony, because she kept always within her that love—impersonal, consecrate, void of greed—which is the purification of the individual life and the regeneration of the body politic. 'We labour for the ideal,' said the Florentines of old, lifting to heaven their red flower de luce—and to this day Europe bows before what they did, and cannot equal it."

"But she had so many great men, so many mighty masters!" I would urge, whereon Pascarèl would glance on me with his lightest and yet uttermost scorn.

"Oh wise female thing, who always traces the root to the branch and deduces the cause from the effect! Did her great men spring up full-armed like Athene, or was it the pure, elastic atmosphere of her that made her mere mortals strong as immortals? The supreme success of modern government is to flatten down all men into one uniform likeness, so that it is only by most frightful, and often destructive, effort that any originality can contrive to get loose in its own shape for a moment's breathing space; but in the Commonwealth of Florence a man, being born with any genius in him, drew in strength to do and dare greatly with the very air he breathed.

"Moreover, it was not only the great men that made her what she was.

"It was, above all, the men who knew they were not great, but yet had the patience and unselfishness to do their appointed work for her zealously, and with every possible perfection in the doing of it.

"It was not only Orcagna planning the Loggia, but every workman who chiselled out a piece of its stone, that put all his head and heart into the doing thereof. It was not only Michaelangelo in his studio, but every poor painter who taught the mere a, b, c, d of the craft to a crowd of pupils out of the streets, who did whatsoever came before them to do mightily and with reverence.

"In those days all the servants as well as the sovereigns of Art were penetrated with the sense of her holiness.

"It was the mass of patient, intelligent, poetic, and sincere servitors of art, who, instead of wildly consuming their souls in envy and desire, cultured their

one talent to the uttermost, so that the mediocrity of
that age would have been the excellence of any other.

"Not alone from the great workshops of the great
masters did the light shine on the people. From
every scaffold where a palace ceiling was being deco-
rated with its fresco, from every bottega where the
children of the poor learned to grind and to mingle
the colours, from every cell where some solitary monk
studied to produce an offering to the glory of his
God, from every nook and corner where the youths
gathered in the streets to see some Nunziata or Ecce
Homo lifted to its niche in the city wall, from every
smallest and most hidden home of art—from the nest
under the eaves as well as from the cloud-reaching
temples,—there went out amidst the multitudes an
ever-flowing, ever-pellucid stream of light, from that
Aspiration which is in itself Inspiration.

"So that even to this day the people of Italy have
not forgotten the supreme excellence of all beauty,
but are, by the sheer instinct of inherited faith, incapable of infidelity to those traditions; so that the
commonest craftsman of them all will sweep his curves
and shade his hues upon a plaster cornice with a perfection that is the despair of the maestri of other nations."

So he would talk on at divers times, as we paced
the twisting lines of the streets, or paused on some
white olive slope to look backward on the tumult of
the roofs, with the battlements of the Vecchio tower
rising out like some old sea-galley from the waves of
the rippling sunshine. And I grew quickly to share
this tender, fantastic, filial affection of his for the City
of the Lilies.

Nay, who could do otherwise who has once dwelt within the magic circles of her storied walls?

Say some day at noontide you feel a little weary of it all.

Say it is midsummer, and the strong Leone sun is white on every stone; and the very cicale have hushed their chatter, and have gone to sleep.

Arno is nearly dry; grass grows between its pebbles, and straw is laid to bleach on its deserted bed. The buildings are scorched and colourless; the olives are pallid in the heat; the cypresses strain thirstily upward against the sky, as though seeking a rain-cloud and finding none in all the shadowless wide blue.

Say for once you are almost a renegade to her. The zinzari have been troublesome, and the sun beats against the blinds, and will not be denied. Your eyes ache with the radiance as they do when you throw off your mask after the opera ball.

You, for once in a way, are tired of the city, and think you will arise and go to that old, cool marble court in the villa amongst the hills, where the vine shadows play all the day long, and the waters drip in the deep acanthus shadows. Or else you dream a little in remembrance of clear green alpine rivers, shining in greenest meadows; of Tirol pine-slopes, rising to the snow with deep blue shadows asleep on bluer lakes; of Swabian woods or of Thuringian forests, wet, still, and full of song of birds, into whose leafy darkness no daylight ever comes.

Perhaps in the blazing Tuscan noon you think of these or such as these that you have known, and that are all lying there across the dreamy flush of the rosy Apennines.

Say in the daytime you are thus, for once perhaps,

faithless,—yet with the nightfall she will take up afresh her supremacy.

The long bright day draws to a close. The west is in a blaze of gold, against which the ilex and the acacia are black as funeral plumes. The innumerable scents of fruits and flowers and spices, and tropical seeds, and sweet essences, that fill the streets at every step from shops and stalls, and monks' pharmacies, she fanned out in a thousand delicious odours on the cooling air. The wind has risen, blowing softly from mountain and from sea across the plains through the pines of Pisa, across to the oak-forests of green Casentino.

Whilst the sun still glows in the intense amber of his own dying glory, away in the tender violet hues of the east the young moon rises.

Rosy clouds drift against the azure of the zenith, and are reflected as in a mirror in the shallow river waters.

A little white cloud of doves flies homeward against the sky.

All the bells chime for the Ave Maria.

The evening falls.

Wonderful hues, creamy, and golden, and purple, and soft as the colours of a dove's throat, spread themselves slowly over the sky; the bell tower rises like a shaft of porcelain clear against the intense azure; amongst the tall canes by the river the fire-flies sparkle; the shores are mirrored in the stream with every line and curve, and roof and cupola, drawn in sharp deep shadow; every lamp glows again thrice its size in the glass of the current, and the arches of the bridges meet their own image there; the boats glide down the water that is now white under the moon, now amber under the lights, now black under the walls, forever changing; night draws on, then closes quite.

But it is night as radiant as day, and ethereal as day can never be; on the hills the cypresses still stand out against the faint gold that lingers in the west; there is the odour of carnations and of acacias everywhere.

Noiseless footsteps come and go.

People pass softly in shadow, like a dream.

You lean down and bask in this sweet air that is like a breath of paradise.

Against your hand there are great clusters of the red oleander, that burn against the gleaming snowy globes of the half-opened magnolia flowers. The voice that is dearest to you on earth is low upon your ear.

From some other casement open like yours there comes the distant cadence of a mandoline. A sheaf of lilies is flung from a balcony with a laugh. A woman goes by with a knot of pomegranate in her dark hair. A break of song floats down the silence.

"Addio, gioja mia, addio!" drops tenderly down the wind like leaves shaken from a rose.

On the parapet of the river two lovers lean and watch the stream as it glides to its grave in the grey sea-sand, as their own passion glides to its grave of dead desire.

You smile, and know there is no grave for yours; he says so at the least, and you believe.

It is night in Italy.

It is night in Florence.

In all the width of the world is there aught so perfect elsewhere? With a glad heart you will answer, nothing so perfect anywhere.

In such a night why cannot the lips we love kiss us forever—forever—forever—into the dreams of death?

BOOK IV.

THE WANDERING ARTE.

CHAPTER I.

Il bianco Aspetto.

Do you know the delicate delights of a summer morning in Italy?—morning I mean between four and five of the clock, and not the full hot mid-day that means morning to the languid associations of this weary century.

The nights, perfect as they are, have scarcely more loveliness than the birth of light, the first rippling laughter of the early day.

The air is cool, almost cold, and clear as glass. There is an endless murmur from birds' throats and wings, and from far away there will ring from village or city the chimes of the first mass. The deep broad shadows lie so fresh, so grave, so calm, that by them the very dust is stilled and spiritualized.

Softly the sun comes, striking first the loftier trees and then the blossoming magnolias, and lastly the green lowliness of the gentle vines; until all above is in a glow of new-born radiance, whilst all beneath the leaves still is dreamily dusk and cool.

The sky is of a soft sea-blue; great vapours will float here and there, iris coloured and snow-white. The stone parapets of bridge and tower shine against the purple of the mountains, which are low in tone, and look like hovering storm-clouds. Across the fields dun oxen pass to their labour; through the shadows peasants go their way to mass; down the river a raft drifts slowly with the pearly water swaying against the canes; all is clear, tranquil, fresh as roses washed with rain.

In such a daybreak in the soft spring weather we left Florence by the gate that was once in the old days broken down for the mule of the Vicar of Christ to pass through into the city.

Pascarèl was too inveterate a wanderer by instinct and habit to remain long in one place, even when that place was circled by the hills so dear to him; and he was looked for eagerly with the spring and summer in all the towns and villages through Tuscany and Umbria, and the flowering Romagna and the drear sea-washèd Maremma.

The Arte, which was light and cleverly constructed, was at such times sent onwards on the back of mules, on the flat cart of a contadino, on the top of a hay-waggon, on the shoulders of sturdy hill peasants, or any manner of conveyance which best served the moment, and the sight of the red and white flag fluttering from the pile of canvas and wood was a signal for a headlong rush and a shout of joy from the whole population over the face of all the country.

As for ourselves we walked always where there was any beauty, whether along the river-shores, or through the fields and vineyards, or along the brown sides of the hills, or beside the play of the tideless sea, on the hot yellow sands, or across the plain from one little old walled town to another.

Pascarèl and his little troop had never been extravagant enough to take any other mode of travel than

that which their own limbs afforded, except when they
needed to get quickly from one province to another.

They always sauntered on from town to town, from
village to village, staying on the road as fancy moved
them. They had gone on in this way all across Italy,
and half across Europe; and as for me I liked nothing
better than to do as they had done.

As soon as the sun showed his red disc where he
rose above the southern seas and the eastern deserts
far away, we used to rise ourselves and set out upon
our pilgrimage for the day, so that each portion of it
was accomplished before the heats of noon. Or at
other times, if they had not played anywhere that night,
we set forth when the moon showed herself, and went
on our way through the wonderful lustre of her, which
seemed to throb everywhere like so much conscious
life.

In these wanderings I learned for the first time how
beautiful is the beauty of Italy.

In the old town of Verona, I had been nothing but
a passionate little rebel, hating my poor, pale prison-
house for its poverty and monotony, whilst the people
with whom I had dwelt had seen no wonder in that
which had been about them from their birth, and had
found their vital interests lie in the scantiness of the
oil for their lucernate, and the uncertainty of the
measure of the soup for their morrow.

With Pascarèl, and wandering thus through the
length and breadth of the Romagna and of Tuscany,
a surer and higher perception awakened in me, and
my heart and my mind alike stirred into sympathy
with that ethereal loveliness of air, of distance, and of

light, which is, as it were, the very soul of all Italian scenery.

Green plains have a certain likeness, whether in Belgium, or Bavaria, or Britain. A row of poplars quivering in the light looks much alike in Flanders or in Normandy. A rich wood all aglow with red and gold in autumn sunsets is the same thing after all in Rhineland as in Devon.

But Italy has a physiognomy that is all her own; that is like nothing else, which to some minds is sad, and strange, and desolate, and painful, and which to others is beautiful, and full of consolation and delicious as a dream; but which, be it what else it may, is always wholly and solely Italian, can never be met with elsewhere, and has a smile on it, and a sigh in it, that make other lands beside it seem as though they were soulless and were dumb.

It is not the intensity but the ethereality of its colour which is its charm; for it reflects every colour this wonderful "bianco aspetto" of Dante.

Colourless itself it takes by turn every hue, and returns every gift of the sun's rays so exquisitely, that there is no single tone which is not by it purified and spiritualised.

At sunrise and at sunset most especially, but more or less throughout the entire day, this wondrous whiteness beams and blushes into the million hues of the flame opal.

Watch it from one year to another and you shall never find it twice the same.

When the blue mists of daybreak drift across it; when the clouds duskily cast their violet shadows on it; when the tremulous wood smoke curls up in the rosy air; when the whole mountain side is flushed like apple-blossoms, darkening here and there where the pines grow into softest amethyst; here and there lightened where the sun strikes into such glow, that like love it becomes "tanta rossa che appena fora dentro al fuoco nata," in all these changes and in a thousand others that sweep each other away again and again in endless succession throughout each hour of the twenty-four, this "bianco aspetto" is the love-liest thing that the world holds.

It is the loveliness of a dream world; it is the loveliness which all other poets as well as Dante have beheld in their imparadised vision of a life eternal; and compared with it the denser colours and the stronger contrasts of more northern lands are almost coarse, and seem to have no soul in them, and speak no message from the gods to man.

Indeed all lands are soulless where the olive does not lift its consecrated boughs to heaven.

Noble and fruitful though the face of them may be, a certain pathos and poetic meaning will be lack-ing in them, if on their hills and in their valleys the olive do not hover like a soft rain-cloud shimmering to silver with the light.

For the olive is always mournful; it is amidst trees as the opal amidst jewels; its foliage, and its flowers, and its fruits, are all colourless; it shivers softly as though it were cold even on those sun-bathed hills; it seems for ever to say "peace, peace," when there is no peace; and to be weary be-cause that whereof it is the emblem has been banished from earth because men's souls delight in war.

The landscape that has the olive is spiritual as no landscape can ever be from which the olive is absent; for where is there spirituality without some hue of sadness?

But this spiritual loveliness is one for which the human creature that is set amidst it needs a certain education as for the power of Euripides, for the dreams of Phædrus, for the strength of Michelangelo, for the symphonies of Mozart or Beethoven.

The mind must itself be in a measure spiritualised ere aright it can receive it.

It is too pure, too impalpable, too nearly divine, to be grasped by those for whom all beauty centres in strong heats of colour and great breadths of effect; it floats over the senses like a string of perfect cadences in music; it has a breath of heaven in it; though on the earth it is not of the earth; when the world was young, ere men had sinned on it, and gods forsaken it, it must have had the smile of this light that lingers here.

This beauty, the beauty of perfect outline, of faint transparent hues, of immeasurable horizons, of wondrous silvery effulgence in which the eyes seem to range and reach until the mere sense of sight grows into a voluptuous rapture, all this became known to me as I wandered through those old old lands by the side of Pascarèl.

Some instinct towards it had been with me always; but through him I learned to know what it was that I felt; and lesser things than this became through him also eloquent to me and beautiful.

The fruitful soil where flowers rose at every step, as though the sods still felt the touch of the divine thyrsus. The sad cypress rising straight against the sky's pale gold with stars of cyclamen white about its feet.

The vast, dim, cavernous churches, dark as night, save where the lamps of the high altars burned. The lonely aisles where tired feet of peasants wore their way across the marble pavement where great men were laid forgotten in their tombs.

The radiant glad dawns when through the air came ringing the clear sounds of countless bells across the fields to wake the sleeping world. The old bruised shrine set at the dusky corner of some populous streets, so that men looking upwards saw, and remembered, and went the better for a fleeting thought of God on to the daily labours of their humble lives.

The moonlight, magical, mystical, unutterable with the dense ebon shadows making but the more lustrous the wondrous silver world on which they slept. All these he gave me eyes to see, and, whilst I saw, taught me why they filled me with such soft delight.

CHAPTER II.

Étoile qui file.

WE wandered all over the hills and the plains, along the course of the rivers and through the wide and rich champaign of the Valdarno; pausing here, pausing there, as the whim of the moment served, now setting up the wooden theatre on the hillside, amongst the olive woods, now letting it find its momentary resting-place amidst the fortresses and monasteries of some old God-forgotten city.

Sometimes up amongst the mountains we had need to make our home with the peasants, for there was no inn to go to, and no fare but onions and black bread. Sometimes in the cities the harsh laws which still prevailed at that time in some districts swooped down like vultures on the free discourse of Pascarèl, and drove him forth from the gates, leaving his gains behind him.

Sometimes it happened to us to lose our way, or to have night down on us ere we knew where we were, and we had to camp there where we found ourselves, on some hillside, under the chestnut trees, and raise a bonfire with the dead leaves, and sleep around it as best we could until the sun rose.

But all this was little hardship in that gracious weather of the springtime, and above us there was always the brilliance of the deep blue sky, and around us there was always the gay good humour of the hardy and gentle people.

The life was quite beautiful to me, and would have been so, I think, to any one with anything of the child or anything of the poet in them. The people were so fond of us, or, at least, of him, that all the way we roamed was strewed with endless little acts of tenderness and of goodwill that blossomed like the cyclamen along our path.

Quaint old women in huge straw hats and with smiling, brown, shrivelled faces, would bring us little cheeses or golden honeycombs wrapped up in vine leaves. Girls, with lovely dreaming eyes like the San Sisto Madonnas, would come out from the sun-baked, flat-roofed houses with gifts of eggs packed cosily in rose leaves, or strewn over, for luck's sake, with Our Lady's herb.

Sometimes from the white villages with their watch towers in their midst, there would ring out for us alone, in the golden silence the sweetest melody of chiming bells that seemed to ripple like so much laughter over the low-lying roofs amongst the vines.

We were always amongst the people. Pascarèl played for no one else.

The opera-houses, where the sweet notes of men's throats were hired with gold and diamonds, were for the rich and well-to-do, for the dainty masked dames in the carnival time, and for the noble lovers who wove their intrigues under the shelter of roulade and fioritura.

Pascarèl's little theatre was for the populace alone; for the bronzed vine-dressers, who laughed herculean laughter in their broad bare chests; for the tanners and coopers and smiths, who came with the heat and the smirch of their labours upon them; for the peasant women who had worked weeding in the fields all day, and sat in the tent with their big brown children sleeping at their breasts; for any and all whose lives were hard, and whose bodies were bruised by toil, and who were glad to forget with him a little while the tax that emptied their bread-pot, and the hunger that gnawed at their vitals.

Give an Italian a copper coin, and though it be the sole thing that he owns in the world, he will spend four-fifths of it on the playhouse.

Pascarèl knew his countrymen's fable; and he loved best of all to play for those who had not even the copper piece, and who must have stood all night outside the longed-for paradise had it not been for the joyous summons which rang out to them from his voice crying,

"Come in—come in; you can pay me with a laugh f I prove worth it. Not a soldo in any one of your pockets?—oh, my friend, you must be either the utterest fool or the honestest man in all the universe. Well, never mind. Come in—come in; laugh or hiss as you like, but come."

And they did come by thousands; it was the audience that he preferred—he who surely by his gifts and graces might have done with the world almost whatever he might have chosen.

"You have no ambition!" I said to him one day.

He answered me, with his bright laugh, "None—absolutely none!"

We were resting on the slope of a hill in the Casentino in the sweet maytime.

It was late in the day. The land beneath us was white with the delicate, sad pallor of the endless olive woods. Above, the west was all one soft flame-radiance of that miraculous rose which is to all the other hues of heaven as the ethereal grace of Petrarca is beside all other odes of love.

"But that is very strange?" I reasoned to him. "Where would the world be if all men thought as you do?"

"Much where it is, no doubt," he answered me, "and unstained, moreover, by the bloodshed of war. Do you think that the world owes anything that is worth keeping in its Arts to so personal a passion as ambition? You are very wrong.

"No true artist ever worked yet for ambition. He does the thing which is in him to do by a force far stronger than himself.

"The first fruits of a man's genius are always pure of greed.

"In time, indeed, the world gets at him and tempts him, and if he be not strong, will bribe and weaken him. That is one reason why the creations of an artist's maturity seldom realise the promise of his youth.

"But no mere ambition ever raised the piles of Brunelleschi, shaped the gates of Ghiberti, created the Inferno and the Hamlet, or gave us the Concerto in C minor of Felix Mendelssohn.

"In these days men are governed by personal ambitions, and, as a consequence, they have ceased to produce greatly. In these days no man will be content to chisel humbly, but to his very best, a corbel or a spandril for another man's St. Peter's; not a whit; every one will have his own building all to himself, be it only a gaze-a-bo or a magnified cucumber-frame.

"After all, it was not only that Michelangelo and Lionardo were greater men than we, it was also because their pupils were content to grind the colours and prepare the earths with uttermost perfectness in their simple share of the great work. Now-a-days, did you ask a young artist to grind your colours, he would tell you with scorn that he was not a shopboy.

"When we can get back that single-hearted absorption into Art which characterised the mediæval

schools of Italy, then we shall get back with it greatness of execution in Art.

"You remember Il Parmeggiano, who never heard
the tumult of the sack of Rome go on in the streets
around him because he was so engrossed with painting
at the time? The soldiers broke into his studio and
found him, brush in hand, and ignorant that the city
had been stormed.

"Well, nothing less than that makes a great artist,
and it is just that vital absolute absorption of all
personality of which there is nothing — absolutely
nothing—in the modern mind. It is always outside
its own creations; vainly or coldly always outside
them.

"The modern priest of art does not believe in his
own God—and in art, above all other religions, who
that has not faith can work miracles? Art is the
divining rod that will blossom like the almond-tree;
but it will be bare and barren if the magician himself
half scoff and wholly doubt."

"But, surely," I reasoned with him, wistfully, "surely
those men dreamed that they were doing what would
keep their memories fresh in the thoughts of men for
many ages?"

"I doubt it," said Pascarèl. "I doubt very much
that they ever thought at all about it in that light.
The true artist does his work because he loves it—
because he cannot choose but do it. Do you suppose
the architect of Cologne Cathedral would have torn
his plans up if he had foreseen his name would have
been forgotten?"

"But surely an immortality of remembrance——"

"Fine immortality!" quoted Pascarèl. "Napoleon

was right in his scoff at our Tiziano. Immortality!
Bah! the brief noonday that carrion flies take to suck
at a dead eagle. Immortality—be so good as to tell me,
donzella mia, if you can, who were Eugœan of Samos,
Bion and Diœchus, Eudemus of Paras, Lampsacus,
Damastes, Xanthus of Sardis, or Phericydes of Leros!"

"I never heard of any one of them."

"No! And plenty of people, more learned than
you, are in the same plight. And yet they were all
authors of Asiatic Greece who, in their day, looked
for as much 'immortality' as Herodotus. To come
into our own country—tell me who Trissino was, and
what he did?"

I confessed that the name of Trissino said no
more to me than the name of any one of the little
flowers that sprang up by millions underneath the
vines.

"Do you know who Trissino was?" he repeated.

"No."

"There again!—why, he believed that he had restored the epic to Italian verse in all its most heroic
proportions, and sneered at his contemporary, Ariosto,
as only good for the vulgar. Did never you hear,
then, of Tito and Ercole Strozzi?"

"No."

"Heavens! And yet they were, or were thought,
famous poets; but the world is like you, and only remembers Luisa Strozzi because men were mad for
her face, and she made a picturesque figure coming
down the hill by San Miniato that night of the fair at
the Feast of the Pardon. But to descend a century
or so;—what, pray, were Chauvelin, Daunou, Riouffe,
Ganilh, Ginguéne, Larromiguière?"

I confessed my ignorance, looking across at the sapphire lights on the Carrara mountains.

"No, again! And yet those men, with the rest of the hundred Frenchmen of the Tribunal of Ninety-Nine, dreamed, surely, of imperishable renown. 'A line in an universal history!' as my wise Napoleon said again after Cairo. True, he arrived later on at getting a whole page for himself; but to print such a page, you must distil seas of human blood to make the only ink that will not rub out with the wear of the ages: and even then, as soon as a greater conqueror comes, you will have your page blotted and turned into a palimpsest. You remember how, in your old Verona, there is a rude, dusky, nameless grave in the mausoleum of the Scala, and above it a superb equestrian in marble, with three stages of sculptured saints and prophets all to himself in might and glory; the first, the tomb of the assassinated; the second, the tomb of the assassin! Believe me, Fame in the world allots things very much like the Scala's sculptor."

I was silent; I thought of poor old wronged Ambrogiò dying by his fireless and childless hearth, whilst as we had passed through Florence the names of Rothwald and Alkestis had loomed large upon the walls.

"Besides—ambition for a player!" laughed Pascarèl, not waiting for my answer, "you might as well say let the dog-grass blowing there try to root itself and grow like that stone-pine. 'Ci-gît le bruit du vent' is our only fit epitaph.

"Thistle-down, smoke, soap-bubbles, 'les étoiles qui

filent, qui filent, qui filent et disparaissent,' those are all our emblems.

"They reproach us that we only live to laugh and to love, and take no thought for the morrow. Why not? There is no morrow for us.

"The player can leave nothing behind him; not even a memory. 'You should have heard him,' say the old people to the young of the dead actor. 'You should have heard him; he was great, indeed, if you like.' But what do the young believe of that? There is no proof.

"Such greatness as the dead man had, went out with his breath like a lamp that was spent.

"We live in the present; we live for the present. Why not, I say?

"We are straws on the wind of the hour, too frail and too brittle to float into the future. Our little day of greatness is a mere child's puff-ball, inflated by men's laughter, floated by women's tears; what breeze so changeful as the one, what waters so shallow as the other?—the bladder dances a little while; then sinks: and who remembers?

"Ambition for such a thing as that?

"Grow oaks from the thistle-down; weave ships' cables from the smoke; change the soap-bubble into a prism for astronomers; arrest the falling star as a fixed planet in the spheres; and then, if you will, talk of ambition for a player!"

He had risen as he spoke, and walked to and fro, brushing the tall foliage of the undergrowth of acacia and cane; he spoke with passionate scorn, and though he laughed, there was for once some undertone of bitterness in his easy mirth.

He jeered at the thing he himself was; no man's heart is wholly free of care and doubt when he trenches on the semi-suicide of any self-contempt.

"But players have been great," I said to him, not knowing well what to say. "Great in their lives at least? And rich?"

"Rich, oh yes!" he echoed, breaking down with one hand a head of iris. "A million francs a week you mean, and diamond snuff-boxes from a prince's hand—oh yes—if that be greatness. Good heavens! before you have fairly entered on a woman's years, how thoroughly a woman's heart beats in you!"

"What do you count greatness, then?" I asked, gathering, as I rested on my arms, face downward on the grass, the clusters of the white anemoni, and all the bright spring flowers of the hills.

Pascarèl, standing beside me, looked away to the rose-radiance of the west with that strange introspective musing look in his eyes which comes so suddenly into Italian eyes, and has so intense a melancholy in it, and also so much of that spiritual beauty which their country has.

"There is an old legend," he made answer to me, "an old monkish tale, which tells how, in the days of King Clovis, a woman, old and miserable, forsaken of all, and at the point of death, strayed into the Merovingian woods, and lingering there, and harkening to the birds, and loving them, and so learning from them of God, regained, by no effort of her own, her youth; and lived, always young and always beautiful, a hundred years; through all which time she never failed to seek the forests when the sun rose and hear the first song of the creatures to whom she owed her joy.

Whoever to the human soul can be, in ever so faint a sense, that which the birds were to the woman in the Merovingian woods, he, I think, has a true greatness. But I am but an outcast, you know; and my wisdom is not of the world."

Yet it seemed the true wisdom, there, at least, with the rose light shining across half the heavens, and the bells ringing far away in the plains below over the white waves of the sea of olives.

CHAPTER III.
The Riband and the Mandoline.

Not many weeks after, whilst the year was still young, the old city of Pisa came in our way in our wanderings; and Pascarèl would fain turn aside from the bright sea-road, and stay within its walls a little.

I saw the ruined rival of Florence, the city "senza fede," once the mart of the world and now a desert. I saw, too, the scholar Luceone, a gentle, meek-eyed man, with the brow of Ghiberti and the mouth of Fra Giovanni. I saw the old Faustus-like room in the tower, with the owls in its broken masonry, and with the Arno washing its base at one side, and on the other the narrow darkling street that the comedians had gone through with jest and song on that Easter morning which had decided the fortunes of Pascarèl.

The old city was sad and sombre with Orcagna's Death reigning over its solitudes as the only sovereign left to it out of all the arrogance and plenitude of its years of power.

So still it was, so unbroken the shadows slept upon its grass-grown stones, so dully the yellow water

dragged its way through the yellow sand, one might
have thought that it was only that very day that the
deathblow had fallen on it away there where the
wanton sea abandoned it to kiss and serve Genoa.

"Do you not see Margharità of France?" said
Pascarèl to me in Pisa one evening, as we strayed
along, "leaning there out of the old palace window in
just such a stormy red and gold night as this, perhaps,
sick to despair of the gilded captivity, and planning
with the gipsies to escape? I wonder no one has
ever painted that scene; the delicate wanton royal
head stretching out in the crimson dusk to hold
council with the black-browed vagabonds. Can you
not fancy the fret of her, and the fever and the revolt,
that made a barefoot liberty seem sweeter than all the
Medicean pomp?"

But I shook my head, and told him no, which
saddened him a little as we went. A barefoot liberty
was well in its way, no doubt, but to be a princess,
was not that better?

It seemed to me that Marguerite must have been
but jesting with the gipsies when she schemed thus
with them here in dead old Pisa.

So thankless are we to Fate when it is fair for us.

I had all for which the heart of Margaret had
hungered, beating itself like a caged bird under its
jewelled bodice; I had it all as I went along the sad,
windless, unpeopled streets, which his voice filled with
sweetest music for me, and the red sun burnished
into ancient pomp and panoply; I had it all and but
half valued it—alas! alas!

At Pisa, as I say, I saw that old college friend of
Pascarèl, the scholar Luceone. He was a gentle,

meek-eyed man, with pensive eyes, and a tender sad face, like the face of Masaccio.

He lived up in the Faustus chambers, with the owls outside his casement, and the river water washing below, and on the other the narrow pent-up street that led away to. the gate for Leghorn, and was very content in them, and grateful to his fate, asking nothing better of the gods and men than to dwell there in the heart of the academic city, in the midst of the dreary sand plains, with the zanzari hooting and hissing all night amongst the ancient walls.

He touched the self-drawn portrait of Pascarèl with many beautiful and tender lights, so that I saw that the painter had done himself but sorry justice.

"I am so happy here—so happy," said the gentle philosopher to me one day, as I leaned out of the high arched grated window from which Pascarèl had watched the Zinzara and her troop go by on their seaward way, "and I owe it all to him. He was a greater scholar than I. I was his second in mathematics, but only second, never his equal. Ah! you would not think it, you, who only see him smoking over his little comedies, or gathering beans with a pretty peasant in an inn garden.

"But it is true. There was never a greater scholar born than Pascarèl. So great that though he had been very wild in many of its pranks, and in that manner a constant terror to the academy, they wanted sorely to keep him always for the glory of Pisa, and they offered him the vacant Chair of Mathematics when our poor old Dottore died of apoplexy.

"Now, let Pascarèl tell you what he will, it is a fact that the professorship would have been very wel-

come to him for awhile at least. He would have
tired of it and gone on his own ways in time, no
doubt, but he would have liked to have had it, for he
loved these rooms of his, and at that time, for all he
was so gay and even riotous, he had a passion for
science, and for all manners of abstruse study, which
he could pursue at his ease and leisure here.

"But he knew that I was very poor, he knew that
I had an old mother and a sister to keep, he knew
that I pinched myself of bread and oil, and that I was
glad to pick up the leavings off the dishes of the
younger students, so what does he do?

"He goes straightway to the authorities, and he
says to them in his careless fashion, 'Illustrissimi, I
thank you for your offer, and the honour you would
do me, but do not take my meaning ill if I tell you
that you have made a great error. I am only a reckless good-for-nothing, a scamp at heart, a riotous free
liver, who, as your excellencies know, have had the
gates shut against me scores of times, and black
marks against my name always. Do not give your
empty Chair to me; but give it to one who is as good
a mathematician as I am, as sound a scholar as I am,
and who, unlike me, will furthermore do you credit
by the simple and blameless life that he leads. Give
it to Ezio Luceone, and I, Pascarèl, will hold myself
as beholden to your Signoria, as though I filled the
Chair myself.'

"That is what Pascarèl said to them, and they
were so struck that they gave it to me, and I have
held it ever since that time.

"He told you he surrendered it to follow that
Frenchwoman and her comedians. Oh! no doubt.

That is just like him. But he relinquished the professorship in the month of March, and the Zinzara and her people only came into the town at Easter time, which fell, as I well remember, towards the middle of April in that year.

"It has been a wonderful thing for me, most wonderful. The stipend is quite enough to keep my mother in perfect comfort; and my heart and soul are in my work; and the college lads love me and I love them; and I ask no better life of God or man.

"But it is Pascarèl I owe it to most surely; only I pray of you do not tell him that I have told you, or he will never forgive me, never. I came to know it through one of the Signoria, which vexed him sorely; he had always tried to make me believe that it was only just the reward of my own merit. But it was all his own doing—all.

"I was the gainer, you see; but nevertheless my heart ached when I saw him go for ever out of the sea-gate with his pack on his back and his mandoline slung from his shoulder; the mandoline he has now! yes. The Frenchwoman put a scarlet riband to it, I remember, sitting just there down in the street in the sun as they ate pomegranates one warm Easter day.

"He does not know what has become of her, so he says; but he was wild about her then; a handsome woman, I remember, with great burning black eyes and beautiful feet.

"She did with Pascarèl what she liked; if it had not been for her I think the world would have heard of him. For he had some ambition in those days; and he is the last of the Pascarelli, you know. And they were really princes once? oh, yes! you may read it in Malespini and Villani."

So the gentle scholar would murmur on, and I would listen, leaning my body over the grated sill, and watching the narrow street far down below, where in other days the Frenchwoman had sat, and wound the scarlet riband about the stem of the mandoline, with the lights of the sun and of Pascarèl's eyes shining on her.

I hated to think of it; I hated to think of that far-away love-lightened past of his, in which I had no memory and no share.

Every woman, at all young and innocent of life, has felt the feeling that I mean when she has loved.

Pascarèl came behind me that day, having heard the latest words of his old friend.

"Ah, yes, cara mia," he murmured, softly, while sadly. "So many hands have tied so many ribbons to the mandoline—yes, I shame to say so—and the ribbons have all fluttered away God knows where, some to the dust-hole, some to the carnival-ball, some to deck other men's guitars, some to lie amongst the cinders in the ragpicker's basket. But after all what does that matter? the ribands never touched the chords of the mandoline; the ribands were only for fairs and feast-days and follies; it takes something stronger and better than a riband to get music from the strings."

I understood him a little though not wholly, and was comforted, leaning there out of the grated window as Marguerite had leaned when she had communed with the gipsies, and thought their liberties and love lore better than the gilded palle of the Medici.

CHAPTER IV.
The Poets' Country.

WE did not wait very long in Pisa.

The laughter of the Arte wakened its hollow echoes, and the Florentine pennon fluttered amongst its haunted ways for a brief space only. And whilst it was still springtime—late spring—we left its gates and went over the ghostly plain that had been soaked through and through with the blood of so many centuries of warfare, and so back into the Val di Greve and between the mountains along Arno's side.

Only to one place was he always constant amidst his inconstancy; wander away from it perpetually as he would, no less surely would he ever again come back to where the Vecchio battlements were set sharp as lion's teeth against the sky.

He would always come back thither; and Saint John's Day, and the Beffana, and the Pasquâ, and the Berlingancio, and the Ceppò, and the Capo d'Anno, and the Anna feast, when the flags of the Trades were set round the church, and all the other *giorni festivi* that are as many as the golden eyes in a child's string of daisies, would have been robbed of much mirth and life to the populace of Florence, if they had failed to bring through the gates Pascarèl.

All that lovely May time we were afoot through Tuscany.

Is there anything in all the world so beautiful as the springtide greenery of Italy?

The gold of her sunsets, the wonder of her orange groves, the rose of her evening skies, the grandeur of her sterile mountains, on these and on their like words of adoration have been lavished by the million; but who has stayed to bethink themselves of her homelier and humbler charms?

And yet, of these also, she has so many—so many.

Come out here in the young months of summer and leave, as we left, the highways that grim walls fence in, and stray, as we strayed, through the field-paths and the bridle-roads in the steps of the contadini, and you will find this green world about your feet touched with the May-day suns to tenderest and most lavish wealth of nature.

The green corn uncurling underneath the blossoming vines. The vine foliage that tosses and climbs and coils in league on league of verdure. The breast-high grasses full of gold and red and purple from the countless flowers growing with it.

The millet filled with crimson gladioli and great scarlet poppies. The hill-sides that look a sheet of rose-colour where the lupinelli are in bloom. The tall plumes of the canes, new born, by the side of every stream and rivulet.

The sheaves of arum leaves that thrust themselves out from every joint of masonry or spout of broken fountain. The flame of roses that burns on every handsbreadth of untilled ground and springs like a rainbow above the cloud of every darkling roof or wall. The ocean spray of arbutus and acacia shedding its snow against the cypress darkness. The sea-green of the young ilex leaves scattered like light over the bronze and purple of the older growth. The dreamy blue of the iris lilies rising underneath the olives and along the edges of the fields.

The soft, pretty, quiet pictures where mowers sweep down with their scythes the reedy grasses on the river banks; where the gates of the villas stand wide open with the sun aslant upon the grassy paths beneath the vines; where in the gloom of the house archways the women sit plaiting their straw, the broad shining fields before them all alive with the song of the grilli; where the grey savage walls of a fortress tower on the spur of the mountains, above the delicate green of young oaks and the wind-stirred fans of the fig-trees; where the frate, in broad-leaved hat of straw, brushes with bare sandalled feet through the bright acanthus, beaming a Rabelaisian smile on the contadina who goes by him with her brown water-jar upon her head: where deep in that fresh, glad tumult of leaf and blossom and bough the children and the goats lie together, while the wild thyme and the tre-foil are in flower, and the little dog-rose is white amongst the maize; where the sharp beak of the gal-ley-like boats cuts dark against the yellow current, and the great filmy square nets are cast outward where the poplar shadows tremble in the stream; all these, and a thousand like them, are yours in the sweet May season amongst the Tuscan hills and vines.

The earth can be no greener even away yonder in the pine valleys of the Alps; and for the air,— what air can be like this that wanders from Adriatic to Mediterranean across a land of flowers bearing lightly on its every breath and breeze the burden of love songs, the sighs of nightingales, the odours of budding fruits, the warmth of amorous suns?

Poets of every nation have celebrated the great and the gorgeous scenery of this land that is the

native land of every artist; its magnificence of outline, its riot of hue on sky and earth, its voluptuous
delights and violet seas, its classic ruins, and its dryad-
haunted groves; these have been over-painted and
over-hymned till half the world is weary; but of its
sweet, lowly, simple loveliness that lies broadcast on
every hillside and under every olive orchard, amongst
the iris lilies in the meadows, and along the loose
lush grasses where the sleepy oxen slowly tread their
fragrant path—of these, I say, not one in a thousand
wanderers thinks, perhaps not one in ten thousand
even knows.

All that time we wandered about according to
our whim and will, from the blue waters of Spezzia
to the green fields of the Casentino, and from the
spires of Milan to the shadows of St. Mark.

We never tarried long in any place; the true
nomadic temper was in Pascarèl.

The flag of our wooden Arte seldom fluttered
longer than two or three evenings under the same
knot of chestnut trees, or on the same hillside. A
certain restlessness always impelled its owner to frequent change and movement, and though he would
lie and dream for hours together in the sun, he preferred that the sun when it rose should seldom find
him in the same spot where it had shone on him at
its last setting.

We went through all the historic country that the
Apennines girdle with their broad belt of vine leaves
and marble; the country of the poets that has heard
their "sweet singing" through so many centuries, from
the love-notes of Catullus to the death-sigh of Tasso.

Beneath Peschiera, that still "sits a fortress" as

in Dante's time, to denote the old Teutonic Tyrol ways.

On the stones of the sad City of the Lake, builded above the bones of that "cruel virgin" who wandered from far Thebes to lay her down to rest amidst the "thousand fountains."

Through the Reggio district at the mountains' foot where Boiardo had sung, and laughed, and loved, and fought his graceful life away.

By sad Ferrara, repenting in widowed loneliness the crimes of her lord of Este against the poet who dared to plead in the teeth of pride "per amor mio."

Far northward as Cremona, where the seeding grass and the wild barley grew above that dreadful ditch, once filled up with the bleeding and stifled peasants thrust into a living death that the knights might spur their horses in safety over the chasm whilst Carlo Malatesta's golden mantle fluttered in all the pride of war.

Southward within the sound of Santa Lucia's bell, in saintly Assisi, when the morning dews were wet on the ivy-grown bridge of the Clausura, and the linnets sang in the same old boughs that had sheltered the birds that once had chaunted their Easter litanies to S. Francis.

To strange San Leo, mighty watch-tower of nature, towering over the wide wild waste of up-tossed rocks and barren mountains.

Along the treacherous moonlit waters of the Pô, where the bridal barge had floated to the moat tower, whilst Lucrezia in her albernia of woven gold bent before her lord, and the torches glowed on the plumes

of the Moorish dancers, and the Bacchides was played
to the sound of Mantuan music.

On the high hills, once the eyrie of the Eagle of
the Montefeltro, where Dante dwelt with the great
Ghibelline chieftain, and the hazel eyes of the baby
Sanzio opened to the light.

In the green gay country where merry-hearted
Pulci strung together his "heaps of sonnets big as the
clubs they make of cherry blossoms for May-day."

Amidst the Lombard fields and garden where
Ariosto, " 'twixt the April and the May" of his life,
had loves as many and as roseate as pomegranate
blossoms in a July noon.

By old Urbino, in whose gaunt silence the silvery
echoes seemed to come of Raffael's laugh, and Tiziano's
wooing, and Bembo's wit, and the voices of Vittoria
and Veronica, and the applause of that gay and
gracious court as it listened to the cantos of the
"Furioso" and the pages of Il Cortegiano, in the
mosaic-chamber, whilst the sea-winds blew over Monte
Carpegna, and the stars rose above the iron-stone of
Nero's mountain.

"If I had been any famous personage at all, I
think I should have chosen to be Boiardo," said he
one day as we sat under the shadow of a fig-tree in a
little village of the plains, whilst the white oxen trod
slowly under the blossoming vines, and the shallow
threads of water were all blue with hyacinth and iris.

"Boiardo's life," said he, "must have been worth
the living from first to last in that pleasant and thrice-
famous Reggio country, green with the vines as this
is. A beautiful life—bold, free, gracious, loving, and
well loved; a life full of the deeds of a soldier and

the dreams of a poet, a life made sweet and fresh by the open air, heightened by passion and battle, but chiefly absorbed in the ideal, for did he not set the bells of Scandiano all a-ringing until the people all thought a new saint had been canonised, when it was only his joy at having found a fit name for his hero! Boiardo was to be envied, I admit: much maybe for having begun the 'Orlando,' but much more for having his name pass into a proverb for a fair fortune. 'Heaven send Boiardo to your house!' So the country folk of all the Reggio district say still when they wish you well. How a man must have been adored by his countryside to be transmitted *so* down the stream of tradition!"

He spoke thus of Boiardo, nothing arrogating to himself; yet it was hardly less love that was won by him through all his birth country.

The fame of him was not indeed spread like that of the courtly rhymester of the "Orlando Innamorato" amidst nobles' palaces and in kings' circles, but there was not a lowly capanna betwixt the two seas that was not the lighter and the gladder for the fall of his footstep on its threshold, and not a peasant from Alp to Abruzzi that would not bring forth to honour his coming the last shred of the goat's flesh and the last drop of the rough red wine.

Money he had not to give them, but he gave them all the riches he had—mirth and music and goodwill, and a strong hand to part them in their quarrels, and a tender patience to aid them in their wants, and a sunny wit to beguile them in their sorrows.

There was, indeed, always that about him which

made one think of Ariosto and of Gabriello's lines on that great Lombard:—

"Credere uti posses natum felicibus horis
Felici fulgente astro Jovis atque Dionis."

At his coming the people trooped out from all their villages and towns in wildest welcome. The shout of "Pascarèl, il Pascarello!" from some shepherd in the fields or some lads playing pallone on the outskirts, brought the whole population of any place which he approached rushing helter-skelter towards him, running and singing before his footsteps, and almost fighting for the coveted honour of giving him shelter for the night.

He might have drunk a hundred stoups of wine, he might have kissed a hundred women, he might have supped at a hundred tables within any gates he entered.

The poorest hamlet got together some little show of riches in his honour, and the best of everything, if poor that best might be, was dragged forth and spread out in delighted homage before him under the fig-trees or the cork-trees in the mellow evening light.

I grew to understand how and why he was so happy with his life, and how and why he would have been loth to leave it for any other. There were in it such perfect liberty, such continual change; and what touched him most, I think, so great a love for him everywhere.

It was perhaps only a sunshiny form of selfishness, the laughing and indolent life that this man of fine powers and of fine culture led from village to village over the face of his native land.

Yet it had a great influence over me that purified and ennobled my faults and my follies, and I think it had often the same over the populace amongst whom he dwelt.

For once in a hamlet on the plains, when cholera raged, I saw Pascarèl welcomed as though he had been an angel who had brought them healing on his wings; and once in a turbulent street riot in Vicenza, he controlled a furious and death-dealing mob with the mere charm of perfect courage and trick of timely and skilful wit.

I think the earnestness that lies in the Italian character is altogether overlooked.

Its indolence, its gaiety, its love of pleasure, lie on the surface, and are steadily measured; but the depths of it are graver—very grave indeed--grave even to a profound melancholy.

The Italian character is made up of contrasts, more strongly marked and vividly opposed than that of any other nation; and these contrasts are welded not seldom into as perfect harmony as is possible to human nature; for an Italian is melodious even in his discord, and is symmetrical even in his contrariety.

See the country in a time of flood, of pestilence, of fire—she is heroic, and the woe of one is the woe of all, with an unanimity of action and a strength of emotion that can alone arise out of a national character at once tender and full of force. Northern nations have nothing, for example, comparable for self-sacrifice to the Misericordia. For consolidation, for devotion to duty, for all the deepest and purest forms of charity, the Order has no equal in Europe.

Where else will you see, as you can see all through

Tuscany, the nobleman leaving his masked ball, the lover his mistress, the craftsman his labour, the foeman his vengeance, to go at the sound of the tocsin, and aid the poor and the sick and the dying?

Superficial commentators wonder that the disciples of Savonarola could come from the same people as the debauchees of the Decamerone, but the wonder is very idle.

A passionate sadness underlies in silence the gay and amorous temperament of the Italian; and not only in metaphor, but in fact, will the hair shirt of a silent sorrow be worn by him under the ribboned domino that he carries so airily in his life of intrigue.

No one will ever see it except one woman out of his many loves who is near enough to him to touch his heart as well as stir his passions;—no one else will ever see it, but there it is—and his sword is there too.

This earnestness was in Pascarèl beneath all the vivacity and lightness of his temperament; and it produced in him that mingled strength and tenderness which endeared him to the people.

Often when we have been in the city he has left my side as we laughed at some winestall in the market or played dominoes before some sunshiny trattorià, and has vanished in obedience to the bell of the Misericordia.

Often when we have gone through some village in which pestilence was raging, or where some sudden flood of water had washed away the little wealth of the contadini, he has taken his place by the sick beds or beside the bereaved and homeless peasantry, with a skilful gentleness and brotherliness that was more balm to the sufferer than herbs or gold.

I think that his laughter was all the richer over the cards and the wines in the little vine-hung loggia of the bettolini, because his eyes were dim many a time over a suffering and penniless stranger who would have died unaided and unshriven but for the pity of the player of the Arte. And I am sure that the salterello and the stornello were all the gayer and the sweeter on his mandoline, because he could touch the strings of it into melody that would soothe the death-bed of a child with visions of the angels.

CHAPTER V.

Fumo di Gloria.

THIS wandering life was to me perfect. I wished for nothing better than all that laughter at the wine fairs; than all that merriment at the village festivals; than all those stories told in the great threshing barns; than all that gay chit-chat with the women laying their straw to bleach on the shores, or the men spreading their river nets where the leaves thrilled in the wind; it was all perfect to me, as it would have been to any other creature young and of healthy body, and a soul not spoiled by the world and its ways.

And as for the people;—the dear people!—the more I dwelt amongst them the more I loved them. There is no other people on the face of the earth so entirely loveable even with their many faults as the Italians. But what is known of them by other nations?—hardly anything at all.

That the Italian patrician may be little understood outside the pale of his own immediate associates, it is not difficult to conceive. His confidence is rarely bestowed: and the pride which fences him in is at once the most delicate and the most impenetrable that a man can place betwixt himself and the outer world.

But it is passing strange that the Italian popolano, open to whosoever will to study him at their leisure, the Italian of the people, as seen in his streets and fields, by his hearth, and his market stall, is as little understood and as invariably misrepresented.

French vivacity and ease have passed into a proverb; yet, in reality, the French people are studied and conscious compared to the Italian, who is the most absolutely unstudied and unself-conscious of all God's creatures.

True, the Italian, even in the lowest strata of social life, has a repose and a dignity in him which befit his physiognomy and evince themselves in his calm and poetical attitudes. See a stone-breaker, or a mason, or a boatman asleep in the noonday sun, and you will surely see attitudes which no sculptor could wish bettered for his marble.

True, too, you will do ill to make a mock of him; high or low, it is the one unpardonable sin which no Italian will pardon; he is given also to the immoveable obstinacy of that animal which he will never name save under the delicate euphuism of "the little black gentleman;" and he has a lightning-like passion in him which may smite his neighbour to the earth in a trice about a cherry-stone, or a broken broom, or any other *casus belli* of the hour.

But, then, lo! how bright he is, how gregarious, how neighbourly, how instant and graceful in courtesy, how eager and kindly in willingness; how poetic his glee in song and dance, and holy day and pageant; how absolute his content upon the most meagre fare that ever held body and soul together; how certain his invariable selection of a pleasure for the eye and the ear rather than one for the mouth and the stomach.

See the gay, elastic grace of him; the mirth that ripples all day long about him like the sunlight, the laughter that shows his white teeth, the tumultuous shouts in which his lungs delight, the cheery sociability that brings him with a knot of his own kind at the street corners and under the house archways to talk the hours away with tireless tongue and shrewdest wit, and say, is there a creature kindlier or more mirthful anywhere in the width of the world?

And he will always have some delicate touch of the artist in him too, and always some fine instinct of the gentleman—let him be poor as he will, ill clad, half-starved, and ignorant even of the letters that make his name, let him feel the summer dust with bare feet, and the mountain wind through a ragged shirt, nay, let him be the veriest scamp and sinner, in the world —but he will wear his tatters with a grace; he will bring a flower to a woman with the bow of a king; and he will resent an insolence with an air to which no purples and fine linen could lend dignity.

With the people I was happy all through that sweet season of the spring and the summer; and to pleasure Pascarèl, there was nothing they would not do to smooth the hardness of their modes of life to the donzella.

Not that such hardships counted for much with me.

From my infancy I had known what hunger meant to the full as well as any beggar child, and my years in old Verona had been bare of all save the sternest necessities of existence.

Pascarèl was true to his word.

It was always well with me. I never saw or heard anything that dear old dead Mariuccia would have deemed unfit for me had she been living then to shield me. Full of mirth indeed we were; mirth, endless and unstrained, babbling like a brook amongst the flowers and weeds of daily acts and words; but amongst it all there was not so much as a coarse word which could have harmed me; and when we were with the populace, who were apt to be coarse enough themselves in their jests and songs, Brunótta, at a sign from him, would slide her hand in mine and draw me gently away up to some little attic in the roof, or aside under some leafy pergola, and keep me there talking, always, as my habit was, of the miracles and the perfections of the life and ways of Pascarèl.

I was always to her the donzella; she was always a little shy with me and a little humble.

"Tanta bellina, tanta bellina!" she would murmur often, looking at me with a soft puzzled wistfulness in her bird-like eyes: and all that I could do availed nothing to induce her to set herself upon an equality with me. Day by day, instead of growing more familiar with me, she seemed to feel the difference that was between us with a clearer perception, and treated me with a wondering homage, of which my natural vanity was well contented to avail itself.

Nothing in the way of worship came much amiss to me at that time.

I had ceased to be troubled about the tinker's pot; I was consoled by the memories of the great race whence he came.

21*

I had got in my mind a little picture of him as he must needs have been in those days: a slender, lithe brown child with beautiful eyes; full of mischief and of tenderness; of odd fancies and of loyal impulses; running along the white sun-baked roads of his beloved country with a little clattering burden of kettles, and flagons, and stewpans slung behind his shoulders.

And his father, too; I pictured him also, a man of much humour, as he said, telling strange, marvellous stories as he sat in the dust of the wayside tinkering his pots; a man who never could utterly forget that his people in old remote times had been great in the land, and who was always a little grave, with a little touch of the old arrogance, though a good kindly soul and a boon companion when the wine went round after the village games.

For those vanished grandeurs and powers of his race, which were almost mythical to him, Pascarèl himself never once cast a sigh down the wind. What his father had told him in childhood many an evening sitting under a wayside crucifix mending the copper pots and pans of the countryfolk might be true or might not.

The perished nobility of his forefathers woke no envy from him.

"It had bean certainly a great race once; yes," he was wont to say, while half sceptical of the fact himself, "at least, so my father would have it; and Malespini, if that old liar may be believed about anything, which is doubtful. Traces of it crop up here and there in quaint old places; here a tomb, there a fortress, here a bronze knight that the children aim at in their games; there a manuscript, that some old monk unearths from his chapter rolls for want of something to do.

"Oh, I believe it was all true enough.

"There were mighty Pascarèlli in the olden days. But I am very glad that I was not of them; except, indeed, that I should have liked to strike a blow or two for Guido Calvacanti and have hindered the merry-making of those precious rascals who sent him out to die of the marsh fever.

"Great?

"No; certainly I would not be great. To be a great man is endlessly to crave something that you have not; to kiss the hands of monarchs and lick the feet of peoples. To be great? Who was ever more great than Dante, and what was his experience?—the bitterness of begged bread, and the steepness of palace stairs.

"Besides, given the genius to deserve it, the up-shot of a life spent for greatness is absolutely uncertain. Look at Machiavelli.

"After having laid infallible rules for social and public success with such unapproachable astuteness that his name has become a synonym for unerring policy, Machiavelli passed his existence in obedience and submission to Rome, to Florence, to Charles, to Cosmo, to Leo, to Clement.

"He was born into a time favourable beyond every other to sudden changes of fortune—a time in which any fearless audacity might easily become the step-ping-stone to a supreme authority; and yet Machiavelli, whom the world still holds as its ablest statesman—in principle—never, in practice, rose above the level of a servant of civil and papal tyrannies, and, when his end came, died in obscurity and almost in penury.

"'Theoretically, Machiavelli could rule the universe; but practically he never attained to anything finer than a more or less advantageous change of masters. To reign doctrinally may be all very well, but when it only results in serving actually, it seems very much better to be obscure and content without any trouble.

'Fumo di gloria non vale fumo di pipa."

"I, for one, at any rate, am thoroughly convinced of that truth of truths."

I hearkened to him sorrowful; for to my ignorant eyes the witch candle of fame seemed a pure and perfect planet; and I felt that the planet might have ruled his horoscope had he chosen.

"Is there no glory at all worth having, then?" I murmured.

He stretched himself where he rested amongst the arum-whitened grass, and took his cigaretto from his mouth:

"Well, there is one, perhaps. But it is to be had about once in five centuries.

"You know Or San Michele? It would have been a world's wonder had it stood alone, and not been companioned with such wondrous rivals that its own exceeding beauty scarce ever receives full justice.

"Where the jasper of Giotto and the marble of Brunelleschi, where the bronze of Ghiberti and the granite of Arnolfo rise everywhere in the sunlit air to challenge vision and adoration, Or San Michele fails of its full meed from men. Yet, perchance, in all the width of Florence there is not a nobler thing.

"It is like some massive casket of silver oxydised by time; such a casket as might have been made to hold the Tables of the Law by men to whose faith Sinai was a holy and imperishable truth.

"I know nothing of the rule or phrase of Architecture, but it seems to me surely that that square set strength, as of a fortress, towering against the clouds, and catching the last light always on its fretted parapet, and everywhere embossed and enriched with foliage, and tracery, and the figures of saints, and the shadows of vast arches, and the light of niches goldstarred and filled with divine forms, is a gift so perfect to the whole world, that, passing it, one should need say a prayer for great Taddeo's soul.

"Surely, nowhere is the rugged, changeless, mountain force of hewn stone piled against the sky, and the luxuriant, dreamlike, poetic delicacy of stone carven and shaped into leafage and loveliness more perfectly blended and made one than where Or San Michele rises out of the dim, many-coloured, twisting streets, in its mass of ebon darkness and of silvery light.

"Well, the other day, under the walls of it I stood, and looked at its Saint George where he leans upon his shield, so calm, so young, with his bared head and his quiet eyes.

"'That is our Donatello's,' said a Floréntine beside me—a man of the people, who drove a horse for hire in the public ways, and who paused, cracking his whip, to tell this tale to me. 'Donatello did that, and it killed him. Do you not know? When he had done that Saint George, he showed it to his master. And the master said, "It wants one thing only." Now this saying our Donatello took gravely to heart, chiefly of all because his master would never explain where the fault lay; and so much did it hurt him, that he fell ill of it, and came nigh to death. Then he called his master to him. "Dear and great one, do tell me before I die," he said, "what is the one thing my statue lacks." The master smiled, and said, "Only—speech."

"Then I die happy," said our Donatello. And he—died—indeed, that hour.'

"Now, I cannot say that the pretty story is true; it is not in the least true; Donato died when he was eighty-three, in the Street of the Melon; and it was he himself who cried, 'Speak then—speak!' to his statue, as it was carried through the city. But whether true or false the tale, this fact is surely true, that it is well—nobly and purely well—with a people when the men amongst it who ply for hire on its public ways think caressingly of a sculptor dead five hundred years ago, and tell such a tale standing idly in the noon-day sun, feeling the beauty and the pathos of it all.

"'Our Donatello' still to the people of Florence. 'Our own little Donato' still, our pet and pride, even as though he were living and working in their midst to-day, here in the shadows of the Stocking-maker's Street, where his Saint George keeps watch and ward.

"'Our little Donato' still, though dead so many hundred years ago.

"That is glory, if you will. And something more beautiful than any glory—Love."

He was silent a long while, gathering lazily with his left hand the arum lilies to bind them together for me.

Perhaps the wish for the moment passed over him that he had chosen to set his life up in stone, like to Donato's, in the face of Florence, rather than to weave its light and tangled skein out from the breaths of the wandering winds and the sands of the shifting shore.

END OF VOL. I.

PRINTING OFFICE OF THE PUBLISHER.

COLLECTION

OF .

BRITISH AUTHORS

TAUCHNITZ EDITION.

VOL. 1317.

PASCAREL BY OUIDA.

IN TWO VOLUMES.
VOL. II.

PASCARÈL.

ONLY A STORY.

BY

OUIDA,

AUTHOR OF "TRICOTRIN," "CHANDOS," ETC.

COPYRIGHT EDITION.

IN TWO VOLUMES.

VOL. II.

LEIPZIG

BERNHARD TAUCHNITZ

1873.

1875, March 20.
Gift of
hur St. John N.
of Cleveland, O
(H. U. 1876.)

CONTENTS

OF VOLUME II.

BOOK IV.
(CONTINUED.)
THE WANDERING ARTE.

BOOK V.

THE FEAST OF THE DEAD.

PASCARÈL.

BOOK IV. *(Continued.)*

THE WANDERING ARTE.

CHAPTER VI.

Gwyn Araun.

"What life then would you really like?" I asked him once, in bewilderment at his utter scorn for all manner and degree of aggrandisement, and the touch of impatience at his own mode of existence which now and then escaped him.

"Gwyn Araun's!" he responded, promptly; "I think that is the only perfect one that ever was known upon earth."

"Gwyn Araun?" I asked, in amaze. "He was not a Florentine."

"No; he was not a Florentine. He comes of a race called Fable. We have never been famous for harbouring his kind. They loved shade; and we are all light. Gwyn Araun and his race are ferns that grow where it is moist and dark. They belong to the primæval ages of the world. Gwyn Araun, to begin with, had a horse that could transport him anywhere in an instant — to the moon if he wished. He could converse with the stars and the flowers, the clouds and

the trees, the gods and the butterflies, turn by turn.
He could wander invisible, and take any shape that
he desired. He had absolute omniscience, and he
used his power always to save and to soothe and to
pleasure mankind. Finally he had an ivory horn, at
whose note of enchantment all melancholy fled. That
is the only perfect existence I ever heard of, and he
lived in the golden age of Myth, in the depths of the
Scandinavian woods or Teuton forests, I do not quite
remember which."

"And what became of him?"

"He disappeared. That is another perfection of
Gwyn Araun's species. They never die, they disappear.
If we did the same it would be much more agreeable;
it is difficult to retain much idealism, when one knows
one must end in a wooden box, and have the flies
buzzing about one as about a sheep's trotters on a
butcher's stall. Gwyn Araun vanished because he fell
in with a sage of prosaic mind, who, being bidden by
him to a feast of spiced meats and ambrosial draughts
in jewelled dishes and cups of gold, saw with the eyes
of the flesh only, and stubbornly maintained that there
was no food or drink at all in all the place, but only
dead forest-leaves and brook-water. Which so dis-
gusted Gwyn Araun that he fled from earth for evermore. But he comes back sometimes even still in the
shape of a poet, invisible to men, and riding on his
winged horse that can circle the sun in five seconds;
and then he spreads the divine feast again; and again
the prosaic sage which calls himself the World repeats
the same scoff at it; and, again, Gwyn Araun flies
away in sorrow and disdain. That is, as the World
phrases it—the poet perishes broken-hearted."

This was the manner in which Pascarèl would talk to me when the mood was on him, lying under the vines in the noon heats, lazily touching a chord of his mandoline, or wandering down some hill-side when the moon was high amongst the trembling stalks of maize.

And the charm of the quaint, fantastic, half-spiritual, sportive, pathetic, whimsical discourse of his so grew upon me, little by little, that it acted like a spell. All my rebellion against my fate, my desires for riches, my feverish dreams of strange fortunes and of high estate, sank away into an absolute contentment. Beside a dreamer who only thought a life like the Genius Gwyn Araun's worth the envying, all mere ambition looked meretricious and empty; and beside a philosopher who broke his dry bread contentedly under a peasant's house-vine, after a half day's march along the mountains, one becomes ashamed to yearn after such pitiful things as pearls and rubies and fine raiment.

CHAPTER VII.

Olivet.

Pascarèl believed in genius. It was his religion. For mediocrity his contempt was boundless.

Genius he had himself, and of the rarest sort. The countless trifles which he flung away with such lavishness amongst the populace were gems of the utmost perfection in their kind.

The brightest wit, the subtlest philosophy, the most gracious charms of poetry and symmetry characterised these ephemeral creations which he composed one after another, without effort, almost, one could have said, without thought, and which, when they had served their turn for a few nights, he remembered no longer, and which would have been thrown away and lost for ever had not little Toccò, who worshipped him, been wont tenderly to collect the scattered scraps and ends of paper on which Pascarèl wrote down these fancies in a careless stenography which served him and baffled all others.

My own dreams that I might have any touch of genius in me he dismissed with unutterable contempt, half gay, half tender.

"Genius!" he cried. "Cara mia, when you sang in the Market-place of Verona, you were a perfect picture, that I grant. But a dog leapt on you with muddy paws, and you paused in your singing to brush the snow off your yellow skirts. If you had had any genius, singing as you sang, what would you have known though fifty dogs should have soiled your gown! You have no genius. Be thankful. What do women want with it when they have as fair a face as you! At your best you will never be more than a mandoline, which will answer in true chords to the touch of a fine player. You will never originate a cadence one whit more than the mandoline ever does."

"And what shall I be at my worst?" I cried, not well pleased at his verdict.

"Oh, at your worst, of course, you will be the mandoline with every string broken, like everything else at its worst. But what is more probable is, that you will fall into the hands of some musician who will just get out of you all the vile flourishes and ornate fioriture which go down as good music in this world, you all the while believing the bungler who runs his roulades on you to be a great maestro.

"It is women's way. They always love colour better than form, rhetoric better than logic, priestcraft better than philosophy, and flourishes better than fugues. It has been said scores of times before I said it.

"Nay," he pursued, thinking he had pained me, "you have a bright wit enough, and a beautiful voice, though you sing without knowing very well what you do sing. But genius you have not, look you; say your thanksgiving to the Madonna at the next shrine we come to; genius you have not."

"What is it?"

"Well, it is hard to tell; but this is certain, that it puts peas unboiled into the shoes of every pilgrim who really gets up to its Olivet.

"Genius has all manner of dead dreams and sorrowful lost loves for its scallop-shells; and the palm that it carries is the bundle of rods wherewith fools have beaten it for calling them blind.

"Genius has eyes so clear that it sees straight down into the hearts of others through all their veils of sophistry and simulation; and its own heart is pierced often to the quick for shame of what it reads there.

"It has such long and faithful remembrance of other worlds and other lives which most mortals have forgotten, that beside the beauty of those memories all things of earth seem poor and valueless.

"Men call this imagination or idealism; the name does not matter much; whether it be desire or remembrance it comes to the same issue; so that genius, going ever beyond the thing it sees in infinite longing for some higher greatness which it has either lost or otherwise cannot reach, finds the art, and the humanity, and the creations, and the affections which seem to others so exquisite most imperfect and scarcely to be endured.

"The heaven of Phædrus is the world which haunts Genius—where there shall not be women but Woman, not friends but Friendship, not poems but Poetry; everything in its uttermost wholeness and perfection; so that there shall be no possibility of regret nor any place for desire.

"For in this present world there is only one thing which can content it, and that thing is music; because music has nothing to do with earth, but sighs always for the lands beyond the sun.

"And yet all this while genius, though sick at heart, and alone, and finding little in man or in woman, in human art or in human nature, that can equal what it remembers—or, as men choose to say, it imagines—is half a child too, always: for something of the eternal light which streams from the throne of God is always shed about it, though sadly dimmed and broken by the clouds and vapours that men call their atmosphere.

"Half a child always, taking a delight in the frolic of the kids, the dancing of the daffodils, the playtime of the children, the romp of the winds with the waters, the loves of the birds in the blossoms. Half a child always, but always with tears lying close to its laughter, and always with desires that are death in its dreams.

"No; you have not genius, cara mia. Say your grazie at the next shrine we pass." ●

I heard him with humiliation and a sense of my own littleness.

Though he had never cared to make gold or fame with it, there was in everything that this man did or said the indefinable charm of that originality and that poetry which are called for want of a better definition by the name of genius.

And I had dared to think my poor little trick of song, which I shared with the blackbird on the cherry bough, had been genius likewise!

I felt ashamed of my presumption. I had only talent—a facile and delicate talent enough, but nothing that was higher. My song was pure and flexile, and could reach with wonderful ease high and far, as the stroke of a bell sounded on high over a sunny, still country.

But it was no more than the bird's gift as it sings under the pink cherry-blossom.

CHAPTER VIII.

École Buissonnière.

It won me much love, however, amongst the people.

Amongst the people and the little troop of Pascarèl I was most often spoken of by my old Veronese name of L'Uccello.

Although he would never let me act, he now and then permitted me to sing to his audiences.

Whenever he did give his consent, which was but rarely, I used to run on to the little stage with rapture, and look down on the multitude of swarthy, eager, admiring faces with a delight that was half childishness and half vanity.

They were good teachers, too, in this careless école buissonnière, those little knots of the Italian populace, unerring in their censure of any imperfection, enthusiastic in their welcome of any excellence.

They gave me stimulus' and strength; it stung me to be hissed for a false half-note by some black-browed pewterer or some open-eyed taverner's boy. In much these people were my masters, by accuracy of ear and facility of execution; and the roughness of their inexorable criticism, joined with the sincerity of their hard-won homage, completed for me the musical education which Ambrogiò had so well commenced.

Now and then it so happened that I pleased them so well, that when the little curtain dropped they would break in gay riot on to the stage, and bear me off in the midst of them, covering me with flowers, and shouting vivas through the quiet of the scattered village and the moonlit fields.

Poor old Uccello! I thought of him often as his country people hailed me by his name.

Of all the poetic figures of the Cinque Cento there is surely none more pathetic than his; going so timidly about in the midst of the great, gorgeous, busy, passionate Florentine life, absorbed in the one vast conception, with which scarce any man ever credits him; painting on the walls of his humble home the likenesses of the animals which he loved so well and was too poor to keep; living with his birds that fluttered for ever round his patient head, as he sat and worked out the immeasurable gifts which the world takes at his hands without once thinking of the giver.

"Ah, mia cara! Si voi sapevete quanto la Prospettiva m'è dolce!"

How one hears the gentle words sighed out in the long nights, of whose cold and sleeplessness the old man felt nothing, as he dreamed over his one priceless discovery.

And in his life Florence knew him not; Florence laughed at him; Florence only saw in him a meek, quaint, fanciful, timid soul, good for very little in the victorious city.

There were only his birds that knew, his birds that talked with him and solaced him, we may be sure, even as their brethren did St. Francis.

The good and sad old Uccello!—I used to think of him often, very often, when the people shouted his name about me after I had pleased them with my voice, as we went homeward from the theatre in the summer nights with the olive shadows all alive with fireflies, and the stretching plains of millet white as the waves of a starlit sea.

The adoration of me under my old Veronese name that the villagers gave me far and wide, inspired me with many strong desires to show myself upon his stage in the towns and in the cities to a hushed many-coloured crowd as I had done in the Cathedral Square at Verona.

But to this wish Pascarèl showed himself inexorable.

It was all very well to sing in some little homely paese amongst the hills, or amidst the fields in Tuscany, or the Adrian Romagna, in my amber and purple

skirts, when there was no one there to hear but the
contadini off the farms, or the straw-plaiters, and
stone-cutters of the village. These were my nights of
triumph.

But all the same, I aspired to some wider sphere.
I wanted to be heard in the cities. I wanted to take
my share in amusing the larger crowds, when we
paused in the alpine shadows of Milano, or amidst the
Romanesque wonders of Ravenna, or beneath the
aërial and gorgeous pinnacles of S. Marco.

But of this Pascarèl would not hear.

"No, donzella, it is not for you," he would answer;
and I found it of no avail to urge my cause; for
Pascarèl was too Italian not to have a woollen thread
of obstinacy running here and there through the soft
bright-coloured velvets of his temperament.

"Why is it not for me?" I said, one day, as we
came down from San Marcello and went on our way
towards the little town of Pistoia.

We were that day at Gavinana, I remember; having gone up under the chestnut trees, over the rocky
road, in the bright coolness of early morning.

The heavy June rains had swelled the mountain
streams that were tumbling and foaming with delicious
sound far below in the Rio Gonfio. The broad green
lawn of the Vecchetto under its deep chestnut shade
was lonely and wet and fragrant, as though it had
never been steeped red in the blood of the last Republic, and in the grove of the Doccio the thrushes
were singing where once there had shivered the lances
of Florence.

We had been talking of those times when the
tower chimes of the little castello had all rung loudly

a stormo, and where the shady grass-grown market-place, that now only echoed with the tinkle of a mule's bell and the splash of its quiet fountain, had heard the savage shouts of Spain, as great Ferruccio fell pierced with a thousand wounds from pike and arquebuse, and thinking to the last of Florence.

We had been talking of all these times as we sat at our simple meal of bread and wine and melons, under the ancient chestnuts, and Pascarèl had been sighing, as was his wont, that his lot had not been in those vivid and virile days.

"There was so much more colour in those days," he had said, rolling a big green papone before him with his foot. "If, indeed, it were laid on sometimes too roughly. And then there was so much more play for character. Nowadays, if a man dare go out of the common ways to seek a manner of life suited to him and unlike others, he is voted a vagabond, or, at least, a lunatic, supposing he is rich enough to get the sentence so softened. In those days the impossible was possible—a paradox? oh, of course. The perfection of those days was, that they were full of paradoxes. No democracy will ever compass the immensity of Hope, the vastness of Possibility, with which the Church of those ages filled the lives of the poorest poor. Not hope spiritual only, but hope terrestrial, hope material and substantial. A swineherd, glad to gnaw the husks that his pigs left, might become the Viceregent of Christ, and spurn emperors prostrate before his throne. The most famished student who girt his lean loins to pass the gates of Pavia or Ravenna, knew that if he bowed his head for the tonsure he might live to lift it in a pontiff's arrogance in the mighty reality and the yet mightier metaphor of a Canosa. The abuses of the mediæval Church have been gibbeted in every language; but I doubt if the wonderful absolute *equality* which that Church actually contained and caused has ever been sufficiently remembered. Then only think how great it was to be great in those years, when men were fresh enough of heart to feel emotion and not ashamed to show it. Think of Petrarca's entry into Rome; think of the superb life of Raffael; think of the crowds that hung on the lips of the Improvisatori; think of the influence of S. Bruno, of S. Bernard, of S. Francis; think of the enormous power on his generation of Fra Girolamo! And if one were not great at all, but only a sort of brute with stronger sinews than most men, what a fearless and happy brute one might be, riding with Hawkwood's Lances, or fighting with the Black Bands! Whilst, if one were a peaceable, gentle soul, with a turn for art and grace, what a calm, tender life one might lead in little, old, quiet cities, painting praying saints on their tiptoes, or moulding marriage-plates in majolica! It must have been such a great thing to live when the world was still all open-eyed with wonder at itself, like a child on its sixth birthday. Nowadays, science makes a great discovery; the tired world yawns, feels its pockets, and only asks, 'Will it pay?' Galileo ran the risk of the stake, and Giordano Bruno suffered at it; but I think that chance of the faggots must have been better to bear than the languid apathy and the absorbed avarice of the present age, which is chiefly tolerant because it has no interest except in new invented ways for getting money and for spending it."

Then, moralising thus, he had sliced the papone, and we had made our morning feast before the matins bell had rung over the little ancient deserted town.

The birds had been singing under the broad green leaves above our heads, the sunshine was sweet and clear upon the old towers and the worn grey stones; in the stillness the little torrents made sad rushing sounds; across the piazza went an old monk and a little barefoot child with her arms round a golden pumpkin.

That was all—all—where once the last battle of free Florence had been fought out and lost.

It was one of those tranquil, innocent, joyous days, · which had so little in them, and yet so much, days of bright weather, of tireless feet, of innocent dreams, of unspeakable gladness, days when the whole land was before us to stray at fancy, and the people made us welcome from the one sea-shore to the other.

When our morning meal was over, and the wrinkled rinds of the melons flung to the black pig that had strayed out of a house by the church and borne us company, sniffing for chestnuts where the last javelin had pierced Ferruccio, we left the little town upon its spur of wooded rock, and sauntered out by the Porta Piavana down the leafy ways to Pistoia, whither the Arte had gone on backs of mules before us, and where Pascarèl intended to act that night.

Pistoia was but a small place, but it was in a humble way a city, and the people a month or two before had made a fus with me there, and had gathered under the casement of the locanda to listen to me

2*

singing within, and had cheered and applauded me
half through the night.

I begged to be seen on the stage there, but Pascarèl
was, as on all other occasions, inexorable.

"Why is not for me?" I argued with him. "Surely
it is good enough for your sister, why is it not good
enough for me?"

His face flushed, and as we walked along the
road, by the foaming water, he cut impatiently at the
tall canes that grew by the side of the stones.

"What has that to do with it?" he answered me.
"Brunótta is a silly little thing, whose feet are the
cleverest part about her; she cannot read, she cannot
be harmed, she is happy in her humble estate. But
you—in time to come—be a great singer, if you will.
There will be nothing to hinder you. But you shall
not do your future such an ill-turn as to be seen on
my stage whilst you are too young to know all the
risk you would run, and all the tarnish you would
gain. Besides, your father lives, no doubt, though we
find no tidings of him. I do not choose to take the
chance of one day being upbraided by him for having
allowed his daughter to show herself in a booth
amongst strolling players, whilst she was too much of
a baby to dream of the life-long injury that she wrought
herself."

I walked silently beside him with a swelling heart,
and a pride sorely wounded.

A baby!

I consumed my soul in muteness and bitterness,
while watching the canes bend and break under his
petulant strokes, whilst the Gonfio flashed brownly
amidst the pebbles of its precipitous bed.

Then with that instinct of coquetry which comes untaught to every woman in whose face men ever care to look, I turned my head over my shoulder, and glanced at him full in the eyes.

"A baby!" echoed I; "I am a head taller than Brunótta, and you—you seem to think me woman enough sometimes!"

His eyes flashed into mine a regard so sudden, so subtle, so ardent, that the languor and the fire of it seemed to sweep over me like a sirocco.

He stood still a moment, and caught my hands and kissed them; his own were burning.

We went on by the curving course of the torrent, quite silent till our travel of that day was done.

Oh, glad and gracious days!

I love to linger on them, for they were lightened with the sweetest sunlight of my life. Never since for me have flowers blossomed, and fruits ripened, and waters murmured, and grasshoppers and grilli sung, as in the spring and summer of that wondrous time.

To rise when all the world was flushed with the soft red of the earliest dawn; to go through the breast-high corn at speed, with scarlet poppies clasping the gliding feet; to see the purple wraith of rain haunting the silvery fairness of the hills; to watch the shadows chase the sunrays on the dusky purple of the mountain-sides; to feel the living light of the cloudless day beat as with a million pulses all around; to go out into the lustre of the night aflame with lucciole, until the dark still plains blazed like a phosphorescent sea; to breathe the wondrous air, soft as the first kisses of men's love, and rich as wine with the strong odours of a world of

flowers; these were my joys, joys at once of the senses
and the soul.

CHAPTER IX.
The Feast of St. John.

LITTLE BRUNÓTTA had always seemed to me as
innocent as mindless, and as happy a thing as any
firefly that danced away its little life amongst the
boughs of the magnolias and over the fields of maize.

She was supremely ignorant, infinitely good-natured,
and always content, humming on her heedless way
with all the light-heartedness of youth; and all that
buoyancy of nature, which seems to go in exact proportion to the poverty and ignorance of every creature. Brunótta, with nothing in the world but a pretty
face and two twinkling feet that could dance her every
night into as much money as would pay for her bread
on the morrow, was happy always—as it is not given
to any to be happy when once they have become the
owners of either mind or gold.

Brunótta, indeed, when she saw her brother and
myself lingering to watch the sunset fires pale into the
ethereal luminance of the night, would shrug her
shoulders and go in to see that there were enough
onions put in the soup, or that the donna di facienda
did not get at our leathern flask of wine and weaken
it with water.

Brunótta, when he and I were as she called it,
stargazing in some old monastic church where, neglected
or forgotten by the world, some painting of Rozzi or
Girolano was slowly dropping to pieces in the damp
and darkness, Brunótta would be busy in the tavern

kitchen ironing out her dancing skirts, or standing chattering over all the gossip of the town at the well in the market place with the young men and the old mothers.

Brunótta, with all her homage for Pascarèl, was not as averse as might have been wished to the coarse compliments of the youngsters of the places we passed through, and on more than one occasion at our coming unexpectedly upon her had shot round the corner of a garden wall, or through the portals of a public building with suspicious swiftness and shyness, leaving to confront us some sturdy contadino in his brown cloak and red shirt sleeves, cracking his whip over his mule's head with a sheepish look of conscious guiltiness.

Brunótta was certainly only a little plump brown earthen pipkin of commonest clay, and had nothing in common with the fine porcelain of her brother's nature, but she was a little cheery tender soul, full of good-will to all living creatures; and if Pascarèl saw any faults in her he never chid them, but treated her with the habitual indulgence and good-humoured oblivion that he might have shown to a child too much a favourite ever to be rebuked, but too ignorant to be ever consulted or considered.

I held her in sincere affection: she was very good to me, and observed with me always that wondering, deferential homage which she had from the first blended with her cordial familiarity.

"You are a donzella, and Pascarèl says you are not as we are," was her formula always in answer to my expostulations against the services she rendered me and the distance which she would occasionally remember to set between herself and me.

She would trot to and fro untiringly in my service. She would always take care that some daintier fare than their own was prepared for me. And whenever any of her many adorers brought her offerings from the village fairs or fruits off their own little bits of land, she would always bring me the best of it all, and urge me to take it:—"It is worth nothing, signorina, nothing at all; but just to please me!" she would say.

And then I used to pretend to be charmed with the thing—perhaps some hideous paste necklace or some gaudy-flowered handkerchief, which was of no more use to me than the statues in the piazza; and it was all done so honestly and with such good-will that I got to love the little dancer out of sheerest gratitude.

One day she pressed one of these gifts upon me, a choicer one than common, a band for the hair, of the Sicilian fashion, and of real silver. I took it and fastened back my own hair with it as I had seen Sicilian women do; it was really pretty, and I said so.

"Oh, do keep it, signorina!" she urged on me for the twentieth time. "Pray keep it. Look! I have got all these corals for myself—real corals. They suit me very much better. That silver fillet is made too delicate for me. My great coarse black braids would break it; and it looks so pretty just holding-in all that loose gold of your hair."

It was San Giovanni's day; the great feast of the Saint of Florence, a beautiful smiling Midsummer day, with the pleasant breath of a sea-wind blowing through the radiance of its warmth and light.

At sunrise all the chimes were pealing, and all the

high altars were dressed with masses of roses and lilies, and all the city was waking up to one of those days of mingled masses and mirth which are the delight of the Italian popolani.

Our Arte stood brave on the green meadow, where the grass was high along the little stream where Calandrino once searched for the magical stone of invisibility, and that day the theatre had many rivals for the popular favour.

All the lines of the buildings were threaded with gay coloured lamps, to be lit when the night should fall, and all down the cascine woods, under the oaks and the ilex, the canvas of mountebanks' booths, and the bright colours of itinerant shows, and the little dainty bell-tents of the vendors of bibiti and berlingozzi were ranged one on another in a pretty pleasure camp.

All the day long the people were threading the streets and the woods with that pleasure in the simple sense of sunshine and of sociability which is characteristic of the Tuscan temperament.

All the day long we wandered and laughed, and chattered and sang songs, and ate and drank under the trees, and watched the humours of the crowds.

Now big Brindellone rolled on his old historic way; now a squadron of cavalry swept through the sunlight; now a bespangled acrobat turned somersaults above the pines; now the athletes raced each other round the circle; now a negro climbed into the highest foliage to set the lamps amongst the boughs; now a troop of children danced, with great bouquets in their hands, to the music of some piping flute and fluttering lute that heralded some saltimbank's performance.

And everywhere the grass blew, and the ilex shadows flickered, and the magnolias opened pale and cool in the heat, and the lovers wandered away down the dim green aisles, and the mountains were dreamily blue, like the iris in Maytime.

San Giovanni's day—old as the walls of Florence, dear to her since the earliest time that she ceased to be a pagan, and was baptised a Christian queen in the old basilica that is still sacred to the seer of the Syrian Desert.

San Giovanni's day,—it was the very heart and core of Florence life,—the very pearl of the people's traditions.

Its lines of fire trace the battlements no more, and no more glitter on the moonlit water; it is dying slowly away, and the city instead is bidden to the Feast of the Statute. But the Feast of the Statute is not the same thing to the people, and the heart of Florence is not in it as it was in the old glories of their own St. John.

But on this day when the Arte stood beneath the Apennines, and we laughed and sang under the ilex shade, San Giovanni's day was in the height of its power, and had no rival, save in old King Carnival, whose kingdom lay buried in the winter snows, and never clashed with the rose garlands and summer sovereignty of St. John.

It was a pagan way of deifying her patron saint, no doubt; but Florence is always half a pagan at heart—she, the daughter of Hercules, who saw the flying feet of Atalanta shine upon her silvery hills, and heard the arrows of Apollo cleave her rosy air.

She cannot ever altogether forget the old cultus, that laughter of hers is still heathen, an echo of the joyous ages when the symbol of immortality was the butterfly on the brow of Psyche.

Pascarèl, who was all pagan, laughed his glad way through the day, enjoying and scattering enjoyment broadcast; telling fortunes, selling wares in the fair, pelting the children with confetti and ciambellini; playing dance tunes on his mandoline; leading the songs over the barrel of chiante broached in the shade of the ilex, whilst half a kid smoked by a gipsy fire, and purple plums and cherries of Prato tumbled out of dusky rush baskets, and the great Cavolo, who is a titular divinity in Italy, slept in rotundity and benignity in the smoking soup-pot with his court of garlic and of beans around him.

Italy has three kings—Cavolo, Carnivale, and Cocomero,—and between them the reign of the seasons is joyous all over the land.

But Pascarèl would not have been Italian soul and body as he was if, with all his gay good-humour, and his sunny elasticity of temper, passion, fierce and swift as the lightning's play, had not slumbered in him to be roused when occasion served.

Though I had wandered with him these four months and more, I had seldom seen him out of temper — never seen him fairly angered. But St. Giovanni's day showed me a little what his wrath could be.

Little Brunótta excited it early in the morning, when she tripped like a little sparrow down the green glades of the woods in her brightest holyday gear, with heavy silver ornaments about her, and the glories of a new rose-coloured kirtle flashing in the sun.

"One loves the very name of the day," said Pascarèl, as we walked along under the limes that were all in flower, with here and there shining a white rose-laurel, and here and there glowing a red pomegranate-tree all in blossom. "One loves the very name of the day, if it were only for Ariosto. It was on a St. John's day that he saw Alessandra Benucci, with the vine-leaves on her robes, and the laurel on her golden hair, coming through these very streets of Florence with the strong June sun bright upon her, as the town went mad with joy because Leo and the Palle had won the triple crown. The dear Ariosto was a swift lover, no doubt, and a bold, and a most inconstant; we have his own word for it. How could a man be otherwise who saw in fancy that face of Angelica asleep under her bower of wild roses? She must have paled all living women — that perfect creature who brought Sacripant from the Circassian hills, and Agrican from the Caspian seas, and made a fool of even the great Paladin himself."

"What is the good of talking so about a creature in a poem that never existed at all?" said Brunòtta, who had so little imagination in her that it was hard at times to believe in her nationality. "*We*, too, met on St. John's day; you remember that night, Pascarèl?"

"Do you remember this day three years?" she cried to Pascarèl, who had remained silent. "What weather it was! — and all that press of people on the bridge—and how frightened I was because the fire-

works hissed—and how you came behind and took
me by the waist and lifted me down into your boat—
and I took you for some great lord, Pascarèl; do you
remember, because you spoke so softly, and your
white coat was so fresh and clean——."

"I remember!" said Pascarèl, with petulance, cutting the leaves with his cane as he went.

"Took him for a lord!" I cried. "What, did you
not know him, then?—did you not recognise him?—
how was that?"

Brunótta laughed gleefully.

"Why, it was the first time I saw him!" she cried,
and then stopped short in the middle path of the green
stradone, and stood blinking at him and me with
half-shut, frightened, shy, cunning, pretty brown eyes.

Pascarèl stifled a half-dozen oaths under the droop
of his moustaches.

"I had been a wanderer so long," he said, coldly,
"and Brunótta had never left her foster-mother and
her village away there in the Casentino, and knew
nothing except the names of her goats and the trick
of her straw-plaiting. Come on quicker, donzella, or
we shall miss the start of the Barberi."

I hurried on at his desire, and Brunótta followed,
penitently murmuring into the ear of Cocomero. I felt
that there was some secret connected with this day of
St. John.

The little scarlet-mantled, brown, saucy thing followed us, sulkily, like a scolded child; and by the
glance of her, restless and cunning, I saw that she had
done something amiss of which she was conscious;
but I was too happy to weary myself much with con-
jecture; what did anything really matter after all?—

the sun of Florence was shining above head, and
Pascarèl laughed beside me.

Now, as we went along, her silver and corals
glimmered bravely on her brown throat and arms, and
the band that she had given me caught the sunlight
in the avenue as it glistened beneath the lace veil,
which, to pleasure Pascarèl, was always cast about my
head in Genoese fashion, in preference to any other
head-dress.

Pascarèl's eyes flashing uneasily from her to me as
we hurried to see the riderless horses start from the
gates, caught for the first time the perception of some
new ornament upon us both.

He paused suddenly in the midst of the green
walk, whilst the other pleasure-seekers streamed on
unnoticed.

"Where did that trinket come from, donzella?"
he asked me, the swift Italian anger lighting up his
eyes.

"Brunótta gave it me this morning," I answered
him, attaching no import to the answer.

But he apparently attached much, for he turned
sharply round upon her as she followed us with the
two lads.

"And who gave it to you, Brunótta?" he asked.
"And how came you by those silver and coral gew-
gaws that are all new on you I see?"

Brunótta flushed under her sun-burnt skin, and
shifted herself uneasily on to one foot like a little
ruffled duck ill at ease.

"Rossello Brùn gave them to me," she muttered.

"Rossello Brùn! And who, pray, may that be?"
asked Pascarèl, pausing there under the ilex shadows,

with the angry light increasing in his eyes, and a restless impatience betraying itself on all his flexile features.

"Annunziatà Brùn's brother, the sailor. He is with his people a little while, in the Sdrucciolò," murmured Brunótta, with her heart fluttering in her mouth. "I had a bit and drop with 'Nunziata yesterday when you were in the botteza with the signorina over all that ugly pottery; and Rossello is a fair-spoken, honest man, and he had just come from Sicily and brought the things; and he had seen the donzélla in the street with you, and thought her handsome, and he has been friends with me for ever and ever so long. And the corals and things were for me, and that silver fillet for the signorina. And where is the harm? I am sure there is no harm. Other women take all they can lay their hands on————"

"And since when have you been in the practice of imitating them?" asked Pascarèl.

I should not have thought that his voice could have sounded so sternly, or that his eyes could have had so fierce a flame in them as they had now where he stood before the palpitating and frightened Brunótta.

"Have you taken gifts before?" he asked at length, when he had waited some time for her to speak.

Brunótta shifted herself on to the other foot, and put one little plump finger in her rosy mouth like a chidden baby.

"Not often," she muttered at last; but it was easy to see the denial was a lie, and a lie not easy to tell,

with that full sunlight and those searching eyes falling
relentlessly upon her.

Her glances were roving restlessly from place to
place, going in every direction, rather than encounter
the gaze of Pascarèl; and suddenly the sullen, embarrassed trouble on her face cleared; a look of eager
relief lightened it; she espied an object upon which to
divert the anger of the moment from herself.

"There is poor Rossello!" she said, with the coolest
treachery in the world. "Go and scold him—his is
the fault; not mine!"

With a true woman's justice she surrendered her
accomplice to cause a diversion in her own favour.

She pointed out as she spoke a brown, loftily-built
man in a sailor's dress, who stood amongst a troop of
people round a pole, on which a spangled acrobat
was climbing; the sailor affected to be absorbed in the
gymnastics, but his restless, glittering eyes roved ever
and again from the meadow where he stood to the
avenue in which we were pausing.

Pascarèl, without a word, lightly loosened the
trinkets off Brunótta's throat and wrists, and invited
me, by a gesture, to unfasten the band from my hair;
with all the ornaments in his hands, he swept out of
the stradone and across the pasture on which the
tumblers and climbers were performing hard against
the old pozzo of Narcissus.

We stood motionless, and following him with our
eyes; a vague fear fell upon us all, and Brunótta, who
always wept easily, began to shake her little shoulders
and sob.

"He will kill him, as like as not," whispered Cocomero, to whom it seemed the passions of his chief

were not unknown terrors and tragedies. "Do you not remember, Brunótta, that day two years ago when he was angry at Ravenna?—he as good as murdered the count for kissing you in the fair, and throwing him a gold piece for payment?"

Brunótta sobbed aloud that she remembered only too well, and that the count had meant nothing but courtesy, and that it was terrible to have to deal with a man all lightning and gunpowder as Pascarèl was if only a word went wrong.

Meanwhile, across the sunny green meadow, strode Pascarèl, with that habitual action of his, which was as swift as a bird's, and as light as a woman's.

We stood and watched, powerless and breathless. There was the lofty pole of the acrobat, the climber aloft in a blaze of spangles, a particoloured crowd staring upward, a belt of green boughs, and in the midst of it all the figure of the marinaro.

Pascarèl cut through the throng as a sickle through wheat, and went straight to where the sailor was, and tossed the trinkets into his face.

The chattering of the eager crowd drowned every word he spoke, but a space between the gymnast and his spectators left the forms of Pascarèl and of Rossello Brùn plain before us in the sunlight.

The Sicilian stood like one stupefied for a moment, bewildered, no doubt, by the sudden flash of the ornaments in his eyes; then the silver and the coral fell together in a little heap on the turf, and the sailor snatched a long knife from his girdle.

We saw the naked blade of it, like a snake's tongue, glitter in the hot keen air.

The people did not see; they were staring upward

at the acrobat, and discussing furiously with one another the chances there were that the pole would break beneath him, and the pole was at that instant bending like a reed, and the poor clown was in jeopardy; and the Florentines had neither eyes nor ears for any other thing than that reeling mast against the trees, and the gambling that they were rejoicing their hearts with on its hazards.

We alone, left in the stradone, saw that deadly flash of the southern steel.

Brunótta screamed, and hid her eyes, and fell upon her knees, crying to the Virgin; but I said nothing.

I stood and gazed with wide-opened eyes, unblenching, like one turned to stone.

Before the dagger could sheath itself in his breast Pascarèl, with one of his lithe and subtle movements, sprang and caught the sailor's arm in the air, and held it there fixed as in a vice. Then, throwing his other arm round Rossello, he wrestled with him and flung him backwards on the turf with a dull, hollow crush that resounded above all the glad tumult of the people's wagers.

He twisted the knife out of the Sicilian's hand, snapped it across his own knee, and tossed the fragments across the meadow.

Then he walked back to us through the sunshine, calm and colourless, and with no trace of anger on his face, singing half aloud to himself as he came the burden of one of my songs.

"Do not take things again, Brunótta," he said, gently. "It is bad for those who give them to you. That pole there will not break, though the people would give their souls it should. Let us go and see the Barberi."

"But you might have killed him!" I murmured breathlessly, clinging to his arm in terror still.

He smiled down into my face.

"Altro! Of course I might have done, and I shall probably be very sorry that I did not before the sands of life are run out with me. But you see, signorina mia," laughed Pascarèl, "Florentines were always magnanimous, that is well known. Don't you remember the great Asses Bell that tolled day and night for a month before we went to war 'for greatness of mind, that the foe might have full time and warning to prepare himself.' To be sure, Semifonte, and the Ambona, and a few other little trifles are to be set up against our generosity; but what would you?— even Florentines are human."

No one had interfered.

To an Italian combat seems the natural issue of any quarrel, and a murmur went through the crowd of "jealousy!" which explained the action to the satis‑ faction of all.

Rossello Brùn accepted his beating quietly, if he resolved in himself to take vengeance some dark night in a lonely passage-way; and Pascarèl's passion, as transient as it was violent, left no trace on him to mar his sunny and good-humoured enjoyment of the day.

Jealousy?

As I heard the whispered word pass from mouth to mouth in the laughing sightseers, I felt my cheek burn and my heart beat high. No man is jealous of his sister; so then his wrath had been for me?

It was pleasant for me to think so; pleasant with a sweet, tumultuous, unrestful wonder that I could not altogether understand, but that made the rest of San Giovanni's feast hours burn brighter than any that had gone before.

I remember in the fair under the trees Pascarèl that afternoon bought Brunótta, to console her, a gorgeous necklace of silver and great amber beads, with a medallion of the Madonna, gleaming in many colours, suspended from the chain. But for me he only bought a beautiful ivory-white magnolia, just opened, with all the spices of Asia in its breath.

"It is a cup fit for the King of Thule," said he, as he handed it to me.

The necklace cost several lire, and the flower but a copper piece; but I would not have changed my magnolia for all the jewels that ever gleamed in Golconda.

CHAPTER X.

On the Hills.

SOMETIMES there would be brought a message to Pascarèl from some old rambling white castello set on a hill slope, with all its treeless mountain side bare and brown as a man's hand—a message bidding him come up thither and amuse its duca or cavaliere, where he yawned through the listless day, in the old, vast stone chambers, with no sound to break the monotony of the hot hours, except the shrill saw of the cicala and the fall of the water in the fountain in the court.

But Pascarèl never would obey that sort of summons.

"The signore can come to me," he would answer to the messenger, and send him back as he had come, along the blinding bleak ascent to the old villa where it stood with blistered walls in the midday sun.

"Dio! Not I, if I know it!" he would say to Brunótta, who always would fain have gone up to the great house, as she urged that there was sure to be good chiante and savoury messes steaming and stewing somewhere towards three o'clock in the day; and Brunótta was of opinion with the Giant Morgante that dinner at least was no dream.

"Toil up that hill in the sun," he would reply, "to make a bow to Don Antonio or Ser Lorenzo, as he stirs out of his siesta after a surfeit of quails?—what! heat and fuss oneself before sunset over French drolleries and Florentine oddities in the face of his Illus trissimo, to be rewarded with a yawn and a concession that one is not so very poor, after all, for a strolling player, and a little pitiful wonder that one has never tried one's fortunes at the Logge theatre? Not I, if I know it. If illustrissimi want to crack their sides with laughter, let them come down into the valley to my little wooden house, and see if I can make them do it there. I shall never go to them, that is certain."

And he never did: having a good infusion of obstinacy in his disposition, and, along with his Florentine republicanism, some lingering reluctance, no doubt, more or less strong in him, for the last of the once mighty Pascarèlli to bend his body as a comedian, and tune his mandoline in old houses in which his fathers had feasted as equals or harried as conquerors.

The Pascarèlli had been cut down, root and branch, stem and twig, centuries before, in one of those ruthless and complete destructions by massacre, and exile, and confiscation with which so many of the histories of the old territorial races end abruptly, like great hardy oaks uprooted and smitten through and through, and blackened to the youngest crown of leaf by a thunderbolt.

It was all a thing of the past—such a far, far away past, too; it was all emptiness, rubbish, weakness—anything contemptible and absurd that you might choose to call it. So he said.

But all the same, Pascarèl, who had fought for the coronet on the smelting-pot when he was a little bare-legged rogue, ,scouring the country from fair to fair, Pascarèl had something of the pride of race in him; and he would not go up to villa or castello, no, not if it were ever so, to pleasure the noble yawning there among the vine shadows on the marble floors, in the long, hot days when the very lizards seemed to pant in the cracks of the earth, and the very stones seemed to shiver in their whiteness and their nakedness because no moss would cover and no dew would cool them.

Sometimes the "illustrissimi," nothing daunted nor offended, did come down from their hill fastnesses or their olive thickets to the fair or the festa, where their peasant folk were laughing their hearts out in the little wooden house of Pascarèl, and they would pay their money and enter and laugh too, which they were welcome to do, as far as he was concerned, though the populace would as soon have been rid of them.

Life was very dull, no doubt, in those long summers to those noble people in those vast dusky, silent dwellings up there on the bare-swept side of some spur of the Apennines or the loneliness of some Friulian or Emilian hollow, lined grey with olives, as a bird's nest with sheep's wool.

Life was very dull, no doubt, to them, watching the waste amongst their vines, or chronicling the cones of their silkworms, there in the old places where their fathers had rioted with Ezzelino as the slaughter went on in the cells of St. George, and had ridden love-raids in Sicida with the Biandrati.

Life was very dull, no doubt; and now and then some one of them would find his way into the little theatre glimmering brightly with its oil lights under the silvery moonlit leaves on the edge of some mountain village or hamlet of the marches, and there amongst the stone-cutters, and the vine-dressers, and the goat-herds, would sit and smile at the pasquinades of Pascarèl, and call for him as vociferously as the rest, "Fuori! fuori!" when the curtain fell.

Amongst those now and then there would be some obscure lordling with a face like an Attavante miniature, or some young Sordello, fretting his soul in the monotony of his war-wasted and tax-shaven fief; and these would surely find their way behind the little stage to us, and offer to Brunòtta many gay compliments, and to me very graceful phrases, backed most likely on the morrow with flasks of montepulciano and great clusters of camellias or magnolia flowers.

Pascarèl was wont to break the necks of the good wine with an angry twist of his wrist, and pour it out in a headlong fashion to all the country folk of the place, touching none of it himself. He always dealt in this mode with any gifts from the villas.

"Let them leave us alone," he would say, impatiently. "They paid their coin at the door, I suppose: there is nothing more needed of them. The wine I want to drink I can buy; and when I can afford to buy it no longer, there is always a public well in every square for any ass to drink at, heaven be praised!"

"Che—e—e—e!" murmured Brunótta, wonderingly, at such outbursts. "That is odd indeed. You were not like that in the old times, Pascarèl. When the like of those noble lads came, they were welcome, and you would laugh and drink with them just as well as with the others. What is your quarrel now?"

Pascarèl would toss a wrinkled pomegranate up into the sunshine.

"What does it signify? None that I know of: the good townsfolk of Bergamo yonder cut the throats of a hundred odd Calabrians, as you may have heard, because they carved the wings of the fowls in a wrong fashion at supper. We Italians are an unaccountable people. We take our likes and our dislikes hot and strong, and neither gods nor devils can change us."

After which profanity he would slake his thirst with the pomegranate.

One day only he broke through this rule.

At one time, when we were wandering through the hills that lie round the plain in which the little brave walled city of Lucca stands, there came to him many urgent messages from a villa on the mountains praying him to go up thither, because the heir and only son of the house was a child and a cripple, and could not stir from his threshold to gain any amusement or distraction of his pain.

Pascarèl resisted long, then gave way to the impulse of compassion, which was always stronger with him than any prudential or personal consideration.

So as the sun went down, we left our village where the wooden Arte had been set up under a clump of chestnut-trees, and we took our way along the face of the hills to where the great villa had stood long before in the old days when Lucca had hung upon her tower the chains of her freed Castracani.

Pascarèl had been inclined to leave me in the contadina's cottage which served us for an inn; but I had begged and besought him to let me go with them so eagerly, that he who seldom found the force to refuse me let me have my way, and I walked beside him through the thick, rough herbage full of blue borage, and the white stars of Bethlem, and the many-coloured cups of wild anemones, Brunótta and the two lads following in our wake, along the side of the hills, where the little, brown, bare mule track wound up, and up, and up into the heights.

Pascarèl had the lute slung across him; and as we went, we sang to it staves of contadini choruses, of love songs, and the like, such as the peasants sang as they guided the oxen through the fields or searched for the aphis in the vine leaves.

Now and then the kids scampered from our path; now and then a puff of blue wood-smoke rose through the branches from some charcoal-burner's cabin; now and then, some great magnolia flower shivered its rosy needles at our feet; far away down below, we could hear the Ave Maria chiming from the church towers in the plain; above, low rain clouds, fretted and edged with amber, floated near the sun; over all the sky was that wondrous evening hue which is like the soft violet-blue of the iris, and is so clear and yet so mystical, as children's eyes are when they wake from dreams of angels.

We looked up at it through the traceries of the boughs of the cistus, and the ilex, and the fig-tree, and we thought of the skies of Raffael; and we changed the gay allegro of the popular songs to choric thoughts of great Palestrina and antique symphonies of Lasso; and so went along the hill-path in the delicate light, and were glad of heart because the earth was beautiful like this, and we were free to move hither and thither in its soft air as we would.

No northern landscape can ever have such interchange of colour as the Italian fields and hills in summer. Here the fresh vine foliage, hanging, curling, climbing, in all intricacies and graces that ever entered the fancies of green leaves. There the tall millet, towering like the plumes of warriors, whilst among their stalks the golden lizard glitters. Here broad swathes of new-mown hay, starred over with butterflies of every hue. There a thread of water sown thick with waving canes. Here the shadowy amber of ripe wheat, rustled by wind and darkened by passing clouds. There the gnarled olives silver in the sun. And everywhere along the edges of the corn and underneath the maples little grassy paths running, and wild rose bushes growing, and acacia thickets tossing, and white convolvulus glistening like snow, and across all this confusion of foliage and herbage always the tender dreamy swell of the far mountains.

It is only the common country where the oil and wine and corn are pressed and reaped; it goes for leagues and leagues and leagues, over many a perished city and unrecorded battle field, everywhere where the soil is tilled between the mountains and the sea; it is simple and lowly enough, and no poet that I know of has sung it; but it is beautiful exceedingly, and its hues would be the despair of any painter.

The villa was high upon the mountain side—vast, dusky, crumbling, desolate without, as all such places are, and within full of that nameless charm of freedom, space, antiquity, and stillness, that does no less perpetually belong to them.

Where these old villas stand on their pale olive slopes, those who are strange to them see only the peeling plaster, the discoloured stone, the desolate courts, the grass-grown flags, the broken statues, the straying vines, the look of loneliness and of decay.

But those who know them well love them and learn otherwise; learn the infinite charm of those vast silent halls, of those endless echoing corridors and cloisters, of those wide wind-swept, sun-bathed chambers, of those shadowy logge, where the rose glow of the oleander burns in the dimness of the arches; of those immense windows wreathed with sculpture and filled with the glistening silver of olive woods, and mountain snows, and limitless horizons; of those great breadths of sunlight, of those white wide courts, of those tangled gardens, of those breezy open doors, of those wild rose trees climbing high about the Ætrurian torso, of those clear waters falling through acanthus leaves, into their huge red conche; of that sense of infinite freedom, of infinite solitude, of infinite light, and stillness and calm.

A stranger will see but the nakedness of the place, and the sadness thereof, by reason of its impoverishment and of its age; but let him wait a little in that marble silence where the cicala rings from dawn to eve, let him wander a little in those peaceful ways where the lemon boughs are golden against the monastic walls, let him live a little in that liberty of air and sunshine where the vines uncurl in the drowsy warmth and the tulips spread a thousand colours to the sun, let him rest a little in it all, and after awhile all other places will seem surely to him dark and narrow, and gaudy and full of noise, and in their hues and substances soulless and meagre, and a little coarse, beside the old white villa on the silent olive hills.

It belonged to a great family, and the old chambers were still full of ancient and costly treasures; though the outside walls had long been peeled bare by the sun and the winds, and weeds might grow as they would amongst the oleanders and camellia trees on the stone terraces.

Italy cannot be trim and smirk in modern wise and modern gear; half muse, half mænad as she is, with the thyrsus and the calliope in her hands, and her feet scorched by the smoke of war, she can neither deck herself with theatric paint and power, nor gird herself with a housewifely care and prudence.

The wild vine on her blown hair, the old Etruscan gold on her bare breast, the tangle of knotted ivy cast about her loins, the snow of the field-lilies wreathing

her beautiful bruised arms,—these are her only ornaments.

Let her alone with them.

She is best so.

CHAPTER XI.
The Hobble of Lead.

WE went into the great open court of the villa
just as the last sun rays died away behind the hills;
Pascarèl flicking his mandoline into harmony with the
lazzarone song which he was humming to himself.

They brought us wines and meats in the great
breezy loggia, where the fig leaves curled around the
dull tawny gold of the traventine cornice.

The moon rose; all ate and laughed and jested;
the old servants stood and looked on and gossiped
and laughed too; great puffs of odour were blown, by
a light breeze, from the magnolias.

This is how one lives in Italy, sauntering, talking,
idling, dreaming, always in the open air, always
amongst the flowers, always finding the people ready
to lean their arms on an old wall and exchange some
good-humoured chit-chat while the lizards run in and
out the stones and the nightingale sings in the ilex
leaves.

Then we went within to the central hall, where
the raised platform built for musicians was to serve
us as a stage. When all was ready we saw that
though the lad of the house was a cripple, indeed,
who was carried in on his couch by a servant, the
villa was at that moment full of gay people strayed

over from the baths in the hills above Lucca and from the sea places of Spezzia and Livorno.

As Pascarèl watched the hall fill with them from behind the screen that was drawn across our stage, a dark displeasure flushed his face; he saw that he had been tricked into coming thither to arouse a set of idlers. But there was no help for it; he had agreed to play, and play he did in two of his own briefest, wittiest, gayest, most sparkling and most satirical pieces.

"But you shall not sing for them, donzella," he said with an oath in his throat. "You shall not sing a note for them, that I swear."

I who was proud of my talent in that way, and had set my heart on displaying it to those brilliant looking persons, was sorely chagrined at his decision, and had I loved him less I should have rebelled against it.

As it was, I sat in mute unwilling submission on a stool behind the screen, through the chinks of which I could see the great dim hall, the oil-lamps, the group of noble people at the farther end, the door-ways filled with the eager faces of the household, the high windows open to the night, and the pale flood of moonlight that poured through them across the marble floor.

Perhaps in the solitude of those chestnut woods idlers ceased to be critical; or perhaps the genius of Pascarèl and the mirth of him swept languor and apathy before it, as fogs are swept away by sea winds.

Whichever it was, as he played to them, they were stirred to almost as much enthusiasm as though they were his general audience of vine-dressers and pewterers and cobblers and shepherds; first in his comedïetta, where the irony bit as sharply as aquafortis, and then in a bright, airy, satirical grotesque, graceful sort of masque, in which all his little troop were concerned and in which he was wont to improvise the most stinging verses that would suit the humour of the moment, with all the skill and all the salt that ever Lorenzo Cavelli himself could have displayed when he lampooned the Tedeschi from under the old three-cornered hat of Tuscan Stenterello.

And yet very bitter were his rhymes that night; showered in profusion from his flexile lips like almond blossoms shaken downward in an April breeze.

Very bitter;—I was not sure why;—perhaps because he had been thus entrapped into beguiling the lazy hours of a few rich people, or perhaps because it struck him a little hardly that he should come as a strolling player into old feudal places where the Pascarèlli Princes would have only come with a herald's note 'of defiance and a flutter of the Red Lily on a white standard in the sun.

Whichever it was, or whether both in one, it gave an additional burnish to the gold coinage of his wit that night; he had never been keener, subtler, swifter, and he strung his glittering pasquinades together on the finest silken chord of decorous derision.

"A clever rogue," I heard one of the villa people say, when they leaned on their couches in the shadow of the great vine-canopied windows, and another assenting, murmured back:

"Beaumarchais and Lemaître in one; what does

he do here strolling with a wooden booth? The fool might make his hundred francs a night in Paris."

Then, the thing being over, they called him again and again upon the platform before the screen which had served for all his scenery, and yet again, not satisfied, summoned him by a servant to go up the hall and speak to them in person.

But thereto Pascarèl gave point blank refusal.

"Go and tell your illustrissimi," said he, "that I bow to them upon the stage because I belong to my public whilst I am in my art; but the moment that I cease to play I cease to be an artist; and with me personally they have no more to do than with his holiest Holiness the Pope."

And when the servant having delivered this message, or more probably having translated it into some politer guise, they sent again and yet again with no happier result; and in the end the illustrious persons themselves being curious as to who could thus so well amuse them without any adjuncts of scenery or decoration, came down the hall to visit this contumacious stroller who deliberately refused to obey the invitation which he should have construed humbly into a command.

Pascarèl received them with the frank nonchalance of his habitual manner, which never varied at any time for prince or peasant. Being a Florentine, he was a little curter, a little cooler with the first than with the last; that was all.

The great persons essayed in all ingenious ways to discover his history and his reasons for straying across the country like a mountebank when he had a talent that would make him welcome on the most famous boards of Europe. But Pascarèl was too truly Italian not to be as impenetrable at some moments as he was transparent at other.

"Tuscan eyes can say everything, or can say nothing," and Pascarèl's eyes as well as his lips and his gestures and his inflections of voice were truly Tuscan in this sense.

Had he cared, he could have been as fine and as subtle a master of craft as ever was he who studied men and their motives under the boughs of the Rucellai gardens. But it would have been too much trouble for him, and the rule of his temper was frankness.

Whilst they talked with him they gazed at me while I leaned against the screen.

As I had come to a great house my vanity had led me, careless of the heat, to take out my old gorgeous dress of amber satin and purple velvet, which I kept for feast days and high holyday, loving its richness, its weight, its very incongruousness; treasuring it too a little because I had worn it that day when he had given me the ring of the Fates.

One of the villa guests, a man young and handsome, with a look that was familiar to me in his eyes, paid me many graceful compliments, and gleaned from me much more about the life we led than his friends could gather from Pascarèl. Hearing that I sometimes sang in our theatre, and was called l'Uccello by the people, he brought the mandoline from a corner where it had been cast down, and eagerly entreated me for one song at least.

I glanced at Pascarèl; his face grew very dark.

"You sing to villagers, why not to us?" urged the

foreigner with that look on his face which startled me
with some vague remembrance. "It seems to me that
your impresario keeps the fairest constellation in his
histrionic heaven for his own especial pleasure; that
is scarcely just to his audience;—or to the star herself."

The boldness of his eyes and the insolence of his
accent gave more meaning to his words than shone
upon their surface. Pascarèl listening keenly, though
affecting to be in converse with the seigneur of the
place, Pascarèl swung round, his changeful eyes flashing
and stormy in his wrath; and took the answer from
me in hot haste.

"My histrionic heaven does not open its gates for
gold. I came to-night thinking to pleasure a sick lad.
I find that I was tricked into whiling the empty hours
of a herd of idlers. I have given you what I choose,
and you shall have nothing that I do not choose. Put
the money you would pay me in the poorbox of your
chapel, and learn for once, oh, most illustrious, that
we of Florence never were docile to dictation yet."

With that sole sudden outbreak of the anger which
had been gathering in him all the evening through
since he had first seen that he had been decoyed
thither on an exaggerated pretext, he swept the mandoline from my lap, signed to the two lads to follow
him, and with a salutation to the owner of the villa,
took my hand with his gravest grace and led me from
the hall.

The people he had thus suddenly abandoned were
too amazed or too incensed to follow him. We went
out unmolested into the moonlight.

Their servant indeed was sent after him with a

profuse present in money, and even a silver box embossed with the count's own arms; but Pascarèl tossed
them all back again with so impetuous a disdain and
so headlong a torrent of fiery words, that the bearer
fled in terror, crying aloud that he never had thought
to have lived to see the day when a Florentine would
have refused a payment.

After that we went on in silence down the white
terrace steps and under the avenues of ilex and cypress,
Brunótta in the rear, and shaking her little plump
shoulders in pitiful sobs, because she would have had
so good a supper if only Pascarèl had not been so
impetuous; she had seen it all laid out on the table
in the loggia, and she had even smelt it too; for the
ideas of Brunótta found their paradise in

{ "Un' oca beurica piu che burre," }

and similar juicy dainties, and she had all Pulci's
disdain for

{"Qualche fratta frutta,"}

and the like poor stuff for supper; being hardly
Italian at all in her tastes, except so far as her love
of idling and of dancing may be counted to her
credit.

Pascarèl for once did not attempt to console her,
but strode on apace through the gardens. He did
not slacken his steps nor speak until he was out of
the gates of their vineyards, and once more on the
mule path along the side of the hills.

Then he turned to me, for him a little roughly.

"What made you look so much, donzella, at that
insolent fool who bade you sing? You were half inclined to do his bidding—too!"

4*

"He had a look of my father in his eyes," I answered him dreamily, still haunted by the vague and shadowy resemblance.

"Ah! what, was that all?" laughed Pascarèl, with a contented sound in his voice.

All! it seemed to me that it was very much.

I was always pursued by the fancy that perchance some day or another those very great people to whom my father undoubtedly belonged would somewhere arise and claim me.

In the old time I had wished it fervently, and spent upon the vision of it many golden hours of fancy, but now it made me shudder a little. No life could seem more perfect to me than the one I led. Even my father himself I had some fear rather than much strong desire of meeting.

"Why were you so angered against them?" I asked him in counter question. "They meant well, I think; and I heard one of them say that with your genius you would make a hundred francs a night in Paris?"

In the moonlight, as he walked beside me, I saw the quick disdain smile on his mobile lips.

"If I could make a thousand—still I should lose my liberty."

"But you would be famous?"

"Famous? Oh yes! About as much so as the bull they decorate for Mardi Gras, and lead about with music, and eat afterwards in stews and steaks. A day's carnival of flowers, and then the chopping-block of the critical butchers, and then annihilation in the teeth of the world's oblivion;—a player's fame lasts just as long as the bull's. But perhaps—if you wish it, donzella,—perhaps——"

"Perhaps what?"

"Perhaps—one day I will go up for my Mardi Gras and risk my murder afterwards, if you have a fancy to handle my paper laurels in those soft little fingers of yours. Perhaps?—Who knows?"

So we went on along the rough hill-side, and Pascarèl recovered the serenity of his temper, and again strains of Pergolesi and of Lasso were heard in the moonlight as we went down through the glistening herbage with the smell of the flowering vines rising up to us from the plains below.

It was midnight when we reached the little village in a cleft amongst the rocks and chestnut woods where our temporary home had been made.

All its small world was asleep. There was no light except where a knot of fireflies burned under the great leaves of the gourds and the pumpkins in the contadina's gardens.

Where our wooden Arte was planted, its red and white flag drooped in the moonlight and the clear drowsy air, as though it were sad to think how in other times its scarlet giglio had been borne in victory aloft over clumps of spears along that plain beneath where Lucca lay.

Pascarèl glanced up at his flag as he passed his theatre.

"I told you truly, donzella," he said, with a certain sadness in his voice, "truly, the night I saw you first, that Art, being once weighed by the gold it brings, changes the Hermes' wings it lent you for an ass's hobble of leather and lead. Like the ass, you can graze so shackled, but it is all that you can do. Unhappily women always prefer grazing to flying. Sarto's wife has many sisters."

With that he bade me go within, for we had to rise with the sun on the morrow; and as I undressed by the light from the gleaming skies I could hear the little shrill voice of Brunótta still piping its lamentations over the savoury meats she had lost, and through the casement screen of the vine leaves I could see the shadow of Pascarèl passing slowly to and fro along the slip of turf in front of the porch, thinking his own thoughts, no doubt, of the paper laurels and the hobble of lead.

And all the while the living fires of the lùcciole burned above the green seas of flax and maize, and shone like clusters of fallen stars along the side of Shelley's Serchio.

CHAPTER XII.

The Legend of the Lùcciole.

"The pretty lùcciole; one cannot wonder that the poets love them, and that the children believe them to be fairies carrying their little lanterns on their road to dance in the magic circle under the leaves in the woods.

"But you know what the lùcciole really are? No! Oh, for shame!

"I heard it when I was a boy from a dark-eyed woman, with a mouth like a rose, who leaned down from her loggia in the summer-time, and gleaned them from the acanthus coils to set them in her hair.

"The lùcciole are just this: they are all the love words that are spoken in Italy.

"For these are so eager and tender and burning that no other land hears their like, as they fall from the lovers' lips in the lustrous moonlit midnights, when the mask is thrown down with the knots of roses, and the ball is left far away and forgotten, and the hands are folded fast in one another, and the soft sighs tremble to silence in the softer warmth of caresses.

"Now, long, long ago, the god Eros, who has always reigned supreme in this land, the god Eros, floating one summer night, as is his wont, from balcony to balcony, from breast to breast, breathing through mortal mouths those amorous ardours, bethought himself that it was sad that things so beautiful should perish with a breath, and to himself, thus musing, said:—

"'These murmuring and burning words,—surely they should be deathless, for they are so old, so old, and yet they are so new, and no man's mouth is weary of them, and no woman's ear is tired. They ought surely to live for ever. They are too perfect to die with a breath. See—I whom men call Love—I will give these sweet words wings, and let their fire burn in them like the stars, and fling them out upon the summer nights, and let them live their lives in glory there amongst the dewy darkness of the myrtle and the blush flowers of the wild pomegranate. And so no love word shall be ever lost, but shine amidst the flowers as a lùcciola.'

"As Eros said so did he; wherefore the lùcciole gleam in millions all through the months of summer

whilst the magnolias shed their rose-flushed arrows on
the balconies, and the vine shadows dreamily darken
the logge wherever the lovers lean.

"Year after year they burn, tender and fitful fires,
along the green garden ways and under the women's
casements—deep in a lily's white heart, or high where
the rose-laurels climb.

"Some say they die in a day; some say they live
on for ages. Who shall tell? They look always the
same.

"For are they not winged words of passion—the
same yesterday, to-day, and for ever?

"And this is the truth of the lùcciole.

"Let him who doubts, walk abroad in the gorgeous
nights of the midsummer, when they make pale the
red oleander, and light to flame the magnolia whiteness, while the notes of the lute thrill the stillness,
and under the shade of the ilex two shadows lean one
on the other.

"He will doubt no more then—if he love."

*   *   *   *   *

I heard Pascarèl tell this legend a few nights later
on in the sultry June weather, when the lùcciole were
bright over all the land; sparkling in the grasses,
dancing in the boughs, clustering around the corn-
stalks, and lighting the chestnut forests.

We were in a little village in the mountains, a
little beautiful green nook in a deep gorge with one
of the many hill-torrents bubbling and foaming headlong down its rocks. The people had clustered round
him at sunset, and had caressed him, and clamoured
for a song, a story, a personation, anything; and he,
with a touch or two of the mandoline, and leaning his

back against a great castagno tree, had rhymed for
them, in the quick improvisation that was at once
nature and habit with him, and strung together for
this knot of charcoal burners and of quarry workers
strings of golden fancies and pearls of wit and wisdom.

All kinds of poetic imaginations and of quaint
conceits fell lightly into rhythm off his lips with all
the tender, gay, sympathetic humour of Puléi and of
Berni in them. He had refused to pleasure the noble
idlers in the white villa above the Serchiò, but he
begrudged nothing to this little community of rough
foresters as they gathered about him under the
shadow of the chestnuts with the warmth of the after-
glow and the dreamy obscurity of the descending
night upon their upturned faces.

Many things that he said may have been obscure
to them, for when the mood for speech was on him
he forgot all except the thoughts which thronged upon
his fertile and lavish fancy. Yet they in a manner
understood it all, for the Italian peasant is quickly
touched to "fine issues," and has a poetic pathos in
him which utters itself in his rhymed rispetti and
ritornelli.

He had chosen the better part, no doubt, since he
was so content; in wandering thus amongst his country
people he was free as any swallow on the wing. But
he had said truly, Sarto's wife has many sisters; to
women the crowns of Francis seem ever better than
peace of conscience and immunity from care. As I
looked at him where he stood under the broad green
·shadows of the chestnut, with the starlight of the early
night upon his face, and the musical, sonorous Tuscan

rhythm coursing off his tongue, I could not but wish that the world knew him as I knew him; that the great people of the great cities should be his auditors rather than these labourers of the mountains and the forests.

I wanted to fasten the gilded string round the foot and draw the broidered hood over the eyes of my free and fearless hawk, in lieu of leaving him to lean on the wild west wind and spread his wings to the sun in full liberty: that is to say, child though I was, I was a woman.

A little later, when he had shaken himself loose from the people, and we were sitting under the chestnuts alone on the edge of the hillside with the lucciole-lightened plain before us, far, far down below, I returned to the old story with which in those days I must sadly and often have teazed him. I tried so hard, I know, to persuade him that the hobble of lead was a golden band that fastened only more firmly the pinion of Hermes. But he shook his head and laughed, and would not be convinced.

"What would you?" he said, almost impatient at the last. "I am not the great genius you think me. I am only a wandering idler with a trick of my tongue, that half the peasants in the country share with me, and a whole knapsack of droll, quaint, out-of-the-way fancies as jumbled and, perhaps, as worthless as the odds and ends of a curiosity dealer's barrow.

"I promised you last night to go up for the paper laurels? Nay, 'promise' I never did. I said I might, to please you. But not even to please you, I think, shall I ever bring myself to go into harness. The nomadic life is what suits me.

"Women do not see the beauty of it—no! They are for ever breaking bounds and roaming in imagination, but it is always into some land flowing with milk and honey, and abounding in creature comforts. Even my divine Angelica never forgot a banquet. Now I do not care for banquets, and I care very much for liberty.

"You cannot alter me, my donzella. Nature cast me in her gipsy mould so many years before ever you were born. It may sound very shocking to say so, but between ourselves I have very little doubt, I assure you, that Menighella's life was a great deal happier than Michelangelo's.

"You know that cheery, simple, merry wanderer whom Michelangelo loved so well? straying over the country with his sketches that the contadini bought at fair and market; his S. Francesco, that the peasants would have frocked in gay colours in utter defiance of fact and the frate; his quaint little saints in pasteboard, and his waxen Christs, for which his illustrious friend gave the models.

"Think of the fanciful pleasant days he had in all the little towns and castella, with his light load of apostles in terracotta and martyrs in millboard; welcome for all the baptisms and weddings and feasts and fairs; and bidden to sup here, drink there, laugh with this one, sorrow with that, according as the people bought a S. Anna to bless a baby's birth, or a S. Petrus to guard a mother's grave.

"Oh, take my word for it, roving, humble, merry Menighella must have been much happier than his mighty friend, badgered by Pope and council, and hunted by patrons from city to city; besides, the ambulant artist can have been no fool, and must have had a soul in him, or he had never been so dear to Michelangelo."

I listened to him, glad as I was ever of hearkening to the swift sweet music of his voice. It was a perfect night: the forests were still as death; the great moon hung yellow and lustrous as gold above the dark edge of the high mountains.

"But men you honour did not disdain fame?" I said, a little timidly, to him, for I had always of him that soft sweet fear—which yet is not fear—without which no woman's or girl's love is worth a fallen chestnut husk. "Look at your Ariosto! and I think you are as great a poet as he, only you never will write down a word."

He laughed gently.

"As great a poet as Ariosto, because I can string the terza rima at times as an old woman reels thread off her distaff? Oh, my child, you would make me as vain, if I believed you, as the dauber Niccolò Soggè when he dared to challenge Del Sarto.

"It is national in us, that is all, that knack of verse. Jules Janin says somewhere, 'to say an Italian poet, is needless; say an Italian, and the poet is a matter of course.' Now I would not go as far as that, but there is a certain truth in his pretty compliment. We are always poets at heart and Romeos when the moon rises.

"It always seems as if that well-spring of poetry and art which arose in Italy, to feed and fertilize the world when it was half dead and wholly barren under the tyrannies of the Church and the lusts of Feudalism; it would always seem, I say, as though that water of life had so saturated the Italian soil, that the lowliest hut upon its hills and plains will ever nourish and put forth some flower of fancy.

"The people cannot read, but they can rhyme. They cannot reason, but they can keep perfect rhythm. They cannot write their own names, but written on their hearts are the names of those who made their country's greatness. They believe in the virtues of a red rag tied to a stick amidst their fields, but they treasure tenderly the heroes and the prophets of an unforgotten time. They are ignorant of all laws of science or of sound, but when they go home by moonlight through the maize yonder alight with lucciole, they will never falsify a note, or overload a harmony, in their love songs.

"The poetry, the art, in them is sheer instinct; it is not the genius of isolated accident, but the genius of inalienable heritage.

"It is universal. It is an Easter egg that lies alike in the hands of gentle and simple; not a Roc's egg, that falls from the skies once in a thousand years. Being thus diffused it has ceased to produce individual and conspicuous achievement: but it is this diffusion which—bringing with it a perpetual ideality and an eternal youth—will render possible for us our Italia Rediviva."

As he ceased to speak, as though in answer to him, there came from the distance the sound of a man's singing. Down below, through the maize, there was going a little knot of peasants; they carried great bundles of green canes on their shoulders; the

mighty friend, badgered by Pope and co
hunted by patrons from city to city;
ambulant artist can have been no fool,
had a soul in him, or he had never
Michelangelo."

I listened to him, glad as I wa
ing to the swift sweet music of
perfect night: the forests were st
moon hung yellow and lustro
dark edge of the high mountai

"But men you honour di
said, a little timidly, to him
that soft sweet fear—which
which no woman's or gi
chestnut husk. "Look a
you are as great a poe
write down a word."

He laughed gently,

"As great a poet
the terza rima at tir
off her distaff? O
as vain, if I bel
Soggè when he

"It is natio
verse. Jules J
poet, is need
matter of co
but there is
We are al
moon rise

"It
and a
world

vivid
.ain whe
longer than

said, with a sigh
say. I am afraid so
life in these days; ri
py; even success, if one
o the roots of it, is moderat

was never at any

... ever any kind of life so
... the improvisatore in the
Accolti's for example.
... the sun can never

... of the Church and the lusts of flesh
would always seem, I say, as though the
had so saturated the Italian soil, that the
... its hills ... lights all over which
... flower of ...
... read, but ...
... they can keep perh...
... own names, but written ...
... of those who made them
... eve in the virtues of a
... their fields, but they
... the prophets, but they
... of all laws, of an
... home by
... with her
...

... the land, the
... and most
... arl...ded
... the
... in
... ned
... at fell

... the genius,
... a wondrous
... r him to tread
... and the poetry of
flowers to be woven
as he would. All the
its contadini, like so
to that the breath of
an harp, ...inds of the summer.
like the winds
...ord, the brigand chief, the fierce
...egging friar, the weaver and the
...prince-bishop and the page... the Ghetto Jew, the
... lattice, and the page in his satin hose,
... mistress above in her silk-hung balcony,
... trooper's leman below with a wound in her
...d breast—all the vast motley... of the century his
...paint and to sing as... great sun-
...t piazza, with... swallows wheeling against the

lùcciole flashed from their feet as they passed away into the darkness where their little homes were gathered round a campanile; the voices, softly sighing, died away in the wild sweet love songs that echo all over the land unwritten by any human hand, only passed from mouth to mouth, from age to age, telling the one eternal story.

We listened till all was silent.

He turned to me and smiled.

"Does all poetry want to be written to live? Ah, no! cara mia—not so long as men love."

A soft strange trouble, that yet was infinitely peaceful, stole on me. I sat quiet in the white moonlight and put my hand into my breast and felt for the stone Fates. They were quite warm where they rested against the beating of my heart.

The tears filled my eyes suddenly; sweet tears, and glad; I could not have told whence nor why they came.

"Ah! you are right, you are right," I murmured. "What does fame matter? your life is so beautiful as it is!"

He stretched his hand out and held mine closely, and sighed a little as he answered. His moods were so swift in variation; his fancy was so vivid and so fast; one could never quite be certain whether any mood would last with him much longer than a butterfly may rest upon a flower.

"Ah, dear donzella!" he said, with a sigh, "perhaps, that is too much to say. I am afraid so. It is hard to find a beautiful life in these days; riches are not hard to come by; even success, if one is not too particular as to the roots of it, is moderately easy likewise; luxury, there is no doubt, was never at any time so general.   But beauty——

"Perhaps there was never any kind of life so really beautiful as that of the improvisatore in the middle ages; such as Bernardo Accolti's for example. What a life that must have been: the sun can never have set on it.

"Roaming the length and breadth of the land, the guest of all that that was most brilliant and most graceful in each city; everywhere the streets garlanded and the shops closed at his coming; everywhere the whole people, from princes to beggars, gathered in the vast squares, in the breathless sunlight, hushed like little listening children at the first words that fell from his lips.

"All the pageantry, all the warfare, all the genius, all the tumult of the age, spread like a wondrous gold-threaded tapestry before him for him to tread on it as he chose.   All the passion and the poetry of the era close to his hand like flowers to be woven into his own myrtle wreath as he would.   All the nation, from its cardinals to its contadini, like so many chords of an æolian harp, that the breath of his mouth could thrill like the winds of the summer.

"The mountain lord, the brigand chief, the fierce free lance, the begging friar, the weaver and the armourer, the prince-bishop and the Ghetto Jew, the damsel at her lattice, and the page in his satin hose, the ▮▮▮▮ mistress above in her silk-hung balcony, and the trooper's leman below with a wound in her ragged breast—all the vast motley of the century his to paint and to sing as he would in the great sun-burnt piazza, with the swallows wheeling against the

blue sky, and on the edge of the listening crowd—
who knows?—perhaps the angel face of Raffaelle.

"And then always for rest, Urbino, with the
breath of the Adrian sea and the breeze of the Apennine hills blowing through its palace chambers, and
the night waning on Bembo's tireless wit, and the
morning breaking above the Monte del Cavallo before the Court of Love had solved one half its
problems. A beautiful life that, a beautiful life that,
if you will.

"I am not sure that I do not envy Bernardo even
more than Boiardo, though the fire of his words was
quenched with the ashes of his body, and when we
read him now, we find him dull as dust, and wonder
what the spell was that once held all Rome speechless
as he spoke.

"Well, there is a compensation in all things. Bernardo *had* his life: a perfect life surely, if a whole
people's applause, and years that were as one long
feast day, count for anything. But Bernardo's is an
empty name now to all save a few scholars who only
hold him as a poor stilted sterile fool; and where is
the child that has not heard of One who died war-
worn, and heartsick, and exiled, alone in Gothic Ravenna?"

His voice sank dreamily into silence.

We stayed there both silent a little while under the
chestnut shadows; the wind from the south blew over
us on its way to wander over the country of the poets.
Then, silently still, we arose and went homeward; the
moonlight white about our lingering feet.

I leaned long at my little lattice that night, watching the lucciole where they shone amidst the waves of

millet and amongst the tendrils of the vines; rocking on the bough of a rose, or glancing in clusters where the leaves of the arum grew thickest.

I stretched my hands out and caught one as it went by my casement, and held it, half gladly and half timidly, as a child holds a ladybird that it deems a fairy.

Had it been a love word once on any woman's ear? Had Romeo breathed it, or Paolo? Had it died of its own sweetness, as love will? Had it life et as he said, amongst the roses?

It told me nothing, but burned there; a little captured in the hollow of my hand.

I looked at it a little while, then let it go and dance upon the wind.

"What do I want with you?" I murmured to it; "if you be living fires, yet you are dead words. And I have his—all his—for me alone."

Then half ashamed that even the lùcciole should hear me, I shut the lattice, and, whilst my face grew warm as with some noonday fervour of the sun, I stole into my bed and slept and dreamed.

CHAPTER XIII.

The Tomb of the King.

From the date of St. John's Day, Brunótta treated me with coldness and with something that was almost like aversion. Her gifts and goodness to me ceased, and nothing that I could do or say would win a smile from her.

I had noticed sometimes before that when we were with Brunótta he treated me differently, with more

deference, but with far less tenderness.   Before Brunótta he never kissed my hands, nor let his eyes dwell
on me fondly, nor called me all the pretty caressing
names that he lavished on me when we were alone.

Sometimes, too, I noticed the bright merry eyes of
the little Tuscan watch me with a keen, hard suspicion, and at times she would turn away from us with
some little sullen, petulant phrase that was only not
satirical because her powers were not equal to more
than a childish sulkiness.

But the only result of this change of manner in
her was to send her more to the companionship of
her favourite Cocomero, who was a good, silly, laughter-
loving lad, always comically afraid of the flail of her
tongue; and to leave Pascarèl and me more free to
wander by ourselves through the vine-shadows of the
country sides and the dim arcades of the ancient cities.
And I was too glad of this to give the cause more
thought.

Cocomero and Brunótta were so well suited to one
another, they loved to wrangle for a lean poulet, to
gossip at a village well, to cheapen trumpery at the
fairs, to tussle with the tavern keepers, to cheat the
guards at the town gates by bringing in a smuggled
snipe or water melon.

These were their daily joys; whilst to them Pascarèl
and I seemed utter fools, dreaming through the fields
content with a bird's song, or wandering for hours in
some old silent grass-grown place abandoned by the
world, but to us memorable for the sake of some great
life that there had opened to the light in the dead ages.

"If it were not for me you would all go without
bit or drop from dawn to moonrise," Brunótta would

cry, displaying some booty from the farms that she
had borne into the town under the very noses of the
unsuspecting guards at the gateway, and which was
made tenfold more sweet to her by the falsehoods and
perils which she had incurred in its transit. "A beautiful plump peahen—eating for a prince—and spinach
and herbs to garnish it—all for three soldi—worth
walking out four miles for any day—things are so dear
in the markets. Spinello lived and died here?—and
you two have been dreaming over him and Petrarca
all day? The Saints help us! What fools are clever
folk! And who was he when all is said? A dauber in
colour? Oh, I know; his paintings are in the little church
—whitewash would look as well, and it kills insects
too. A Madonna one must have, of course, but Our
Lady I know is quite content with a wax figure of her,
and those pretty paper flowers and some coloured
tapers—they look much better than the frescoes—Che-
che! how fat the hen is!—and all for three soldi, Pascarèl!"

Pascarèl would shrug his shoulders with silent ineffable disdain, and go out into the archway of the house
and stand under the vine-leaves, sending smoke into
the air with a troubled and impatient contempt upon
his face.

They were as far asunder as the poles these two
who travelled together, played together, lived and
laughed together, and yet never caught sight one moment of each other's souls.

That day he and I let the fat peahen stew on
neglected amongst its herbs over the little charcoal
pan, and wandered about the old, old streets of Arezzo,
talking of Mæcenas and Petrarca and the merry Bacco

5*

in Toscana and thinking wistfully of that noble old cathedral that was levelled with the dust for the war lust of the Medici.

He was sad at heart thàt day; the contact of Brunótta's low little soul seemed to have jarred on him; his hours of melancholy were not frequent, but the gloom, when once it settled there, was deep.   Sometimes he was curt and full of scorn in it; this day he was gentle, and his eyes dwelt on me with a soft pain in them.

We searched, and vainly, for Spinello's tomb; like the cathedral, it was lost in the summer dust.

There was a tired looking, humble olive, that by its look had grown there beneath the walls five hundred years if one; but all the pomp and beauty of the pagan temple had dissolved like a dream of the night. We sat in the shadow of the olive, and in our fancies rebuilded the temple.

It was full midsummer.

The Tuscan sun was burning in a cloudless heaven. A cloud of swallows were silver in the light.   The mountains were soft in hue as rose-leaves.   Everywhere in the plains of maize the shrill cicale were loudly singing their rude love odes.   Above the grey walls there was a flush of pomegranate flowers, and amongst them there hummed the yellow porselline that the people so prettily say bring happiness wheresoever they rest.

The city so great in Etruscan, in Latin, and in Renaissance days, was very quiet in cloudless sunshine.

It was all bright and hot, northward over the Tuscan olive valleys, and southward, where tawny Tiber dragged his way, deep bosomed in the Umbrian oakwoods.

"It is just the same country," said Pascarèl, glancing down north and south. "Just the same scene as when Mæcenas was born here, and Pliny pondered beneath the garden-trees upon the hills yonder.

"The city has crumbled to dust twice, and been rebuilded in new fashions, though the new is now so old that we cannot find Spinello's tomb, but I doubt if the district has changed a whit since Livy wrote of it.

"What a great book a great student might write upon Arezzo! What an epitome in this single town of the Etruscan, of the Roman, and of the Mediæval life! And of the Renaissance alone what countless and various types!

"Fighting ecclesiastical Tarlati; shrewd, gay, merry Redi; our idealic Petrarca; good heavens! one could string great Arezzan names until the sunset!

"The history of this one town might be the history of Italy, and of all its wonderful complexities and contrarieties of character and of circumstance.

"By-the-bye I hear they have found a new Etruscan tomb in that olive orchard where you see the little cloud of people. The tomb of a king they say by his ornaments. Myself I should like to know something of the ornament-makers.

"What manner of men were they those earliest gold-workers whose art is the despair of modern goldsmiths?

"Did they sit in the sun as we do now and hear the cicale chatter? Did they labour for love of the art or greed of the shining metal? Did their hearts go down to the grave with those chains on those fair dead women?

"What a sad tender grace there is about that old Etruria! A whole nation swept off the face of the soil, and leaving only a few placid dead that melt to dust as the air touches them, and a handful or two of golden chains that neither rust nor time can alter.

"Their temples, their palaces, their laws, their armies, their very history, all have perished; and only these golden toys of theirs live and shine in the modern daylight.

"Ah, Dio mio! how full the world is of wonder! Only its wonders are all the children of Death, and chill us when we touch them."

So he spoke his fanciful thoughts aloud, lying stretched on the hillside, under the walls of the city. His meditations often clothed themselves in that facile and picture-like speech which is national with the Italian; for amongst these people who have all more or less in them of the improvisatore abundant detail and fluent expression are natural as the breath of the lungs and the lips is to others.

"We will go and look when the shadows lengthen at that Etruscan tomb," he said, taking a little lizard in the hollow of his hand. "We shall not find old Spinello's if we hunt all the week.

'Appena i segni
De l'alte sue ruine il lido serba.
Muoiono le città; muoiono i regni:
Copre i fasti e le pompe arena ed erba :
El 'uom d'esser mortal par che si sdegni.
Oh nostra mente cupida e superba!'

"His tomb is gone," he pursued, and his voice sounded hushed and sad in the dreaming silence of the sunny plains. "And that great Latin inscription is trodden somewhere underneath those clods that the bullocks are treading. What does it matter? He had a good life here for ninety years.

"It must have been such a good life—a painter's —in those days; those early days of art. Fancy the gladness of it then—modern painters can know nothing of it.

"When all the delicate delights of distance were only half perceived; when the treatment of light and shadow was barely dreamed of; when aerial perspective was just breaking on the mind in all its wonder and power; when it was still regarded as a marvellous boldness to draw from the natural form in a natural fashion;—in those early days only fancy the delights of a painter!

"Something fresh to be won at each step; something new to be penetrated at each moment; something beautiful and rash to be ventured on with each touch of colour,—the painter in those days had all the breathless pleasure of an explorer; without leaving his birthplace he knew the joys of Columbus.

"And then the reverence that waited on him.

"He was a man who glorified God amongst a people that believed in God.

"What he did was a reality to himself and those around him. Spinello fainted before the Satanas he portrayed, and Angelico deemed it blasphemy to alter a feature of the angels who visited him that they might live visibly for men in his colours in the cloister.

"Of all men the artist was nearest to heaven; therefore of all men was he held most blessed.

"When Francis of Valois stooped for the brush he only represented the spirit of the age he lived in. It is what all wise kings do. It is their only form of genius.

"Now-a-days what can men do in the Arts? Nothing.

"All has been painted—all sung—all said.

"All is twice told—in verse, in stone, in colour. There is no untraversed ocean to tempt the Columbus of any Art.

"It is dreary—very dreary—that. All has been said and done so much better than we can ever say or do it again. One envies those men who gathered all the paradise flowers half opened, and could watch them bloom.

"Art can only live by Faith: and what faith have we?

"Instead of Art we have indeed Science; but Science is very sad, for she doubts all things and would prove all things, and doubt is endless, and proof is a quagmire that looks like solid earth, and is but shifting waters."

His voice was sad as it fell on the stillness of Arezzo—Arezzo who had seen the dead gods come and go, and the old faiths rise and fall, there where the mule trod its patient way and the cicala sang its summer song above the place where the temple of the Bona Dea and the Church of Christ had alike passed away, so that no man could tell their place.

It was all quiet around.

The black and gold demoizelle hummed above in the red pomegranate flowers. The long curling leaves and auburn feathers of the maize were motionless in the windless air. Beneath the vines great pumpkins shone like gold, and little lizards glanced like emeralds in the light.

It was all so bright, so quiet, so full of sweet summer life, here, where a whole nation had passed away from the face of the earth, leaving but a few crumbled stones as the sum of its story.

"I would rather have been Spinello than Petrarca," he pursued, after awhile. "Yes; though the sonnets will live as long as men love: and the old man's work has almost every line of it crumbled away.

"But one can fancy nothing better than a life such as Spinello led for nigh a century up on the hill here, painting, because he loved it, till death took him. Of all lives, perhaps, that this world has ever seen, the lives of painters, I say, in those days were the most perfect.

"Not only the magnificent pageants of Leonardo's, of Raffaelle's, of Giorgone's: but the lowlier lives—the lives of men such as Santi, and Ridolfi, and Benozzo, and Francia, and Timoteo, and many lesser men than they, painters in fresco, and grisaille, painters of miniatures, painters of majolica and montelupo, painters who were never great, but who attained infinite peacefulness and beauty in their native towns and cities all over the face of Italy.

"In quiet places, such as Arezzo and Volterra, and Modena and Urbino, and Cortona and Perugia, there would grow up a gentle lad who from infancy most loved to stand and gaze at the missal paintings in his mother's house, and the cœna in the monk's refectory, and when he had fulfilled some twelve or fifteen years, his people would give in to his wish and send him to some bottega to learn the management of colours.

"Then he would grow to be a man; and his town would be proud of him, and find him the choicest of all work in its churches and its convents, so that all his days were filled without his ever wandering out of reach of his native vesper bells.

"He would make his dwelling in the heart of his birthplace, close under its cathedral, with the tender sadness of the olive hills stretching above and around; in the basiliche or the monasteries his labour would daily lie; he would have a docile band of hopeful boyish pupils with innocent eyes of wonder for all he did or said; he would paint his wife's face for the Madonna's, and his little son's for the child Angel's; he would go out into the fields and gather the olive bough, and the feathery corn, and the golden fruits, and paint them tenderly on grounds of gold or blue, in symbol of those heavenly things of which the bells were for ever telling all those who chose to hear; he would sit in the lustrous nights in the shade of his own vines and pity those who were not as he was; now and then horsemen would come spurring in across the hills and bring news with them of battles fought, of cities lost and won; and he would listen with the rest in the market-place, and go home through the moonlight thinking that it was well to create the holy things before which the fiercest reiter and the rudest free lance would drop the point of the sword and make the sign of the cross.

"It must have been a good life—good to its close in the cathedral crypt—and so common too; there were scores such lived out in these little towns of Italy, half monastery and half fortress, that were scattered over hill and plain, by sea and river, on marsh and mountain, from the daydawn of Cimabue to the after-glow of the Carracci.

"And their work lives after them; the little towns are all grey and still and half-peopled now; the iris grows on the ramparts, the canes wave in the moats, the shadows sleep in the silent market-place, the great convents shelter half a dozen monks, the dim majestic churches are damp and desolate, and have the scent of the sepulchre.

"But there, above the altars, the wife lives in the Madonna and the child smiles in the Angel, and the olive and the wheat are fadeless on their ground of gold and blue; and by the tomb in the crypt the sacristan will shade his lantern and murmur with a sacred tenderness:

"'Here he sleeps.'

"'He,' even now, so long, long after, to the people of his birthplace. Who can want more of life—or death?"

So he talked on in that dreamy, wistful manner that was as natural with him in some moments as his buoyant and ironical gaiety at others.

Then he rose as the shadows grew longer and pulled down a knot of pomegranate blossom for me, and we went together under the old walls, across the maize fields, down the slope of the hills to the olive orchard, where a peasant, digging deep his trenches against the autumn rains, had struck his mattock on the sepulchre of the Etruscan king.

There was only a little heap of fine dust when we reach the spot.

When they uncover the dead faces — the faces dead two thousand years—they are always perfect in these Etruscan tombs; but at the first touch of light they seem to shiver; they cannot bear the day; in a moment they dissolve like a snow flower that the sunrays strike; there are only left the golden chains lying in the grey soft dust.

The violated grave yawned under the olive tree; the coffin had been broken open; the peasant had eagerly rifled its jewels; a little throng of people from Arezzo were standing looking at the mound of ashes; the sad silvery olives were all around; above, in the city, there were bells ringing.

We looked too: then went away in silence along the edge of the ripening maize.

The dead king had reigned here on the hills ages ere Rome had been; ages ere Horace had sung of Soracte; ages ere the chariots of Augustus had rolled through the broad amber seas of the Umbrian harvests; ages ere the marshes by Trasinone southward, yonder across the fields, had been red with the slaughter of consul and cohort, and strewn with the fasces and eagles.

The dead king had reigned here; and after two thousand years his nameless dust was rifled for the greed of peasants, and lay friendless in the sun there beneath the olive branches.

We went through the gates in silence.

At our resting-place in the Via dell' Orto, where the eyes of Petrarca had opened to the light, Brunótta met us in the arched entrance, in the rosy evening stillness, with shrill rebuke for her peahen overstewed and spoilt by waiting.

CHAPTER XIV.

The Gold of Etruria.

PASCARÈL played that night in Arezzo. But a strange fancy came to him.

At the last moment, as his turn came for the stage, he flung off his gay dress and abandoned the jesting little piece he was prepared for, and flung the grave Florentine lucco about him, and went before the lamps with only his mandoline.

He struck a few chords of it, tender and far-reaching, that made silence fall on the little crowd of Tuscans and Umbrians that filled the Arte, which was unroofed that night to the breathless summer skies.

Then he began to speak to them, quite quietly at first, with his luminous eyes drooped and full of retrospection, his voice as clear as a bell on the great stillness.

A certain fire of improvisation fell on him, and his words dropped naturally into the swing and measure of the terza rima. Verse to the Italian is natural as laughter to the child or as tears to the woman.

The dust of the dead king under the olive trees outside their gates was his key-note; a note grave and tender, on which his redundant fancy strung every variety of meditation and of metaphor.

All the life of the dead ages revived in his words and gestures.

The lost people of unknown Etruria lived again in his passionate fancy.

"There was a gold worker in Etruscan Arezzo; the delicate metal bent to his hand finedrawn as the thread of a spider's web; he was poor and alone, but quite happy; an old olive grew by his door and he worked in its shade all the day; the gold was in his hands like a maiden's hair, and he talked to it, and wove it, and loved it.

"One day the king's daughter went by, and her horse sought a drink at his well. She rode on and took no thought of him; but his olive was no more the tree of peace by his threshold.

"He haunted the steps of her temples and palaces until the king's people beat him away with rods. He could work no more for his masters, and he fell into great wretchedness, and the olive tree pined for him and withered away grey and useless as the silver beard of an old dead man.

"Now it came to pass that there was a famine in the land — in these broad plains of Tuscany and Umbria, where the yellow waves of the wheat spread so far and wide: and all the people besought the Bona Dea whose curse was on the black and barren land.

"And the oracle of the temple spake and said, 'Let a sheaf of corn be made of gold and bound up with twelve thousand gossamer threads in gold, finer than the web of the spider, and the lands shall blossom and bear full harvest.'

"Etruria was full of gold workers, and hundreds on hundreds essayed the task, but all failed; for who should work gold so that the spider's spinning should be less fine and less frail?

"Then he who had loved the king's daughter rose

from his wretchedness, and remembered his ancient learning, and said, 'Give me gold, I will try.'

"At first they mocked him; a poor naked out-cast, crawling feebly in the sun. But the famine in-creased; all the city was full of lamentation by day and night; mothers slew their children not to hear their piercing cries.

"The king came down from his weary throne and said, 'Let the beggar have gold, and try; it can be no worse with us if he fail, since thus we perish.'

"So they gave him gold, and he shut himself alone for six days, and on the seventh he opened the door and came out into the sunshine amongst the multitude of the breathless people, and in his hands were the golden webs of twelve thousand threads, so fine that the spider's gauze beside them seemed coarse.

"The people were silent; the passion of a great joy and fear was on them; by tens of thousands they dragged their fleshless limbs after him, always in silence, to the temple of the Bona Dea.

"There was a great blight everywhere; the black earth sickened under it; the famished people watched with bloodshot ravenous eyes; was the weaving fine enough? Would the goddess accept the offering?

"There was silence in the temple; the strong sun shone on the web of twelve thousand threads.

"Then the oracle spoke, and said, 'By gold shall Etruria live. Let the earth rejoice and bear.'

"And in one moment, on all the earth whereon Etruria held dominion, the green blades broke through the parching soil, and grew and ripened in a second's space in every valley and on every hill.

"Then the multitude cried with one voice, 'Bear

him to the palace, crown him on the king's right hand. Let him have his will in all the land. From the bonds of death he has set us free!'

"But he, still on his knees on the threshold of the temple, looked up, and said, 'Nay, I want nothing;—has it made *her* smile?'

"And with that he stretched his hands gently outwards to the sun and died.

"The king's daughter never knew that it was for her the golden web was woven.

"But the gods knew, and said, 'By its gold-workers let Etruria live. For this man's love was great, and its witness shall endure when the nation has perished from the earth and its very records have passed away as the clouds dissolve before daylight.'

"So to this hour, through all the Etrurian land, the vanished people are ever to be traced by the golden links that shine through the dust of the tombs; and the Etrurian gold is without speck or flaw, or equal anywhere, but rises from its burial ever and again where the olives shiver in the summer winds and the maize feathers blow above the buried cities."

It is nothing as I say it now, this tale of his, that fell from his lips that night instead of jest and laughter: but as he spoke it, with the deep blue skies over our heads, with the sweet, cool, acacia-scented air streaming in from the open doors, with the rise and fall of his wonderful voice that could sigh like a sea-shell and sound defiance like a clarion, with that old Etrurian land around lying white beneath the moon, with the mighty Tiber rolling there away beyond the oak-woods, with the dust of the dead king

so near, under the olive-tree on the side of the hill;—
with all these—with the shadows on the Florentine
robes and the Florentine face of Pascarèl, in the
tawny half-lights of the dim Arte, the tale had a
strange poetry and pathos that moved the passionate
people as they heard it to tears.

And when, as it drew to a close, the swift facile
words came faster and faster from his lips, falling
without strain or visible consciousness into the
sonorous rhythm of the Petrarcan sonnets;—when he
passed from the past to the present and spoke of
the living Italy which had become the inheritrix of
Etruscan grace and Latin power, and was the daughter
of such mighty dead, that her descended nobility became a divine obligation;—when, with all his soul
kindling at the fire of his thoughts into a poet's faith
and a prophet's inspiration, he stood, with outstretched
arms and flashing eyes, calling on the treasures of
the past to become the weapons of the future, and the
divided children of the nation to bind themselves into
one bond of brotherhood by the chain of a perfect
purpose woven fine and indestructible as the gold
chain of Etruria by the force of love;—when his impetuous and impassioned improvisation swept like a
storm-wind over the listening people, the moonlight
from the cloudless skies shining full upon his face,—
then a greater force than that of the player fell upon
him, and he who held them thus silent in Arezzo,
ruled them by the strength of the patriot and the
spell of the poet.

The people streamed out quite quiet when his
voice had ceased, and went quietly along their various
ways through the haunted streets of Petrarca's city.

In many eyes there was the gleam of tears.

They did not dare to cluster round him with shout and song that night, and bear him off as was their wont to some wine feast within the walls. They left him alone, as one who was their master and apart from them.

Only some lads, quite young, whose fathers had died with Carlo Alberto and with Ugo Bassi, drew near him timidly, and gently kissed his garments as in homage.

These were all his thanks in grey Arezzo. But could any greed of pomp or storm of plaudit have been greater?

He himself said never a word, but left us to go indoors to our rest in the street of Orto, and went away outward through the gates into the shining country where the moon was white upon the fields of olive.

CHAPTER XV.
The Sceptre of Feathers.

I REMEMBER that night, that sweet hot August night, I sat sleepless at the open window, watching down the moon-lightened street for the sheer sake of seeing Pascarèl pass through its shadows when he should come homeward.

The hours went slowly by, and he did not come. The old street was silent as a grave; beneath me, before the entrance of an old palace, two Italians stood talking together. They looked gentle people, and their accent was pure and scholarly.

"What genius has that stroller Pascarèl!" said one of

them; "and what a sway over the people, and what a rush of words, and what a choice of powers! In the Trecento he would have been at the head of Tuscany!"

"Oh, altro!" assented the other, heartily. "But in our modern days it is not the men of genius who are eminent; it is the men of talent. All the earth over, it is careful and cautious combination which now succeeds; and it is exactly this of which the nervousness, the impetuosity, the impressionability, the force and the weakness of men of genius, are incapable. This man Pascarèl might have led High Italy when she was a group of art-cities, that could be grasped together like a bundle of divining rods or firebrands, and hurled at church or empire by a hand that was fearless enough and able enough not to let them scorch it. But what place is there for a man of his sort of capricious inspiration, and poetic temper, in any part of modern Europe? What Europe crowns now are—drill-sergeants and accountants."

And the Tuscan having said so much, sauntered on with his friend through the high, dark archway where the acanthus was clinging about the old sculptured bosses of some race whose very name had perished in Arezzo.

As they disappeared, there came into the street the figure of Pascarèl; his white dress caught the gleam of the moonbeams, and he passed thoughtfully down the grey stones, through the cool brown shadows.

The church clocks of Arezzo were tolling four o'clock; in the east there was the first tremulous lighting of the skies that heralds daybreak.

6*

He came slowly down the street, very slowly, under the leaning antique walls that had heard the first frail wail of Petrarch's opening life.

Looking up, he saw me where I leaned above. There was a trecento stone gallery to my casement, and in it was growing, set in a great red conca, a gum-cistus, all white with flower.

I looked down to him through the leaves.

"Ah, donzella! up so very early?" he said to me. "That is not wise when we are not upon the road. What! not been to bed? Oh, that is very wilful."

"You have not been to bed yourself," I said to him. "What did you find in those fields? I thought you would never come back."

"You have been watching for that? I shall be very angry if you ruin your health in such nonsense."

He did not look very angered. There was a smile on his mouth, and the beautiful sudden light in his eyes that I loved so well.

"But what did you find in the fields?" I cried to him. "Have you been to the king's tomb again!"

He paused a moment, then glanced down the street to see that it was empty.

"Well, no, donzella," he said, hesitatingly, with a little flush on his face. "I may as well tell you—it will give you pleasure. You were sad to-day for that poor contadino, with his old sick people and his seven children, who had had nothing to eat all the summer, the worm being at his wheat, and his padrone a hard man? Well, I went to take him half the Arte's receipts. It was so full I could easily spare him that

without begrudging ourselves another fat peahen.
And I went to-night—well, because walking at night
is pleasanter than by day in this time of the year, and
I thought I should meet the poor heart-stricken wretch
just going out across his fruitless fields—as I did.
Besides, the old woman, without food, would not have
lived long past noon. It is no use talking to people
about a chain of gold for Italy, unless one does one
little miserable mite towards forging a lilliputian link
of it."

"Oh, I am so glad, so glad!" I cried, in my
thoughtless delight in him, leaning down through
the cistus flowers of silver. "It is so good of you, so
like you. What did the contadino say? Was he not
happy?"

"Ah, we will not talk about what he said," murmured Pascarèl, lightly. "When you have seven children and an old father and mother all wailing for
bread, and a hard padrone who will screw you down
to the letter of the Mezzadrià, and, if the soil be
empty, lets your mouth be empty too,—of which hardness there is very little in this Tuscany of ours, God
be praised,—when you are in this sort of plight, of
course any little gift brings gladness to you, and you
are apt to talk a very great deal too much about
gratitude, as this poor fellow did, until I was fain to
run away from him, and leave him weeping over his
two lean bullocks, who look the worse for no pro-
vender themselves, poor beasts! But get to bed,
bambina mia; these old streets are not too healthy
in the moonlight. Good night, and dream of Petrarca."

But I dreamed, instead, of Pascarèl.

He might have ruled Tuscany in the old days of Gian della Bella, or the Uberti—so they said. Well, like enough. But was it not better as it was?

I thought nothing could be freer or gladder than this life he led.

It was like the old sceptre of peacock's plumes that Mariuccia had set on high, with the blessed palm-sheaf; in emblem of so many simple joys, of laughter in a garret, of a bowl of field-born violets, of jests over a pan of chestnuts, of a dusty brocade brought down from high estate to embellish a child's masking.

The world would have contemned, like my father, the sceptre of feathers.

But could the world have given aught better in exchange?

I thought not,—sinking to sleep, while the day-break stole over the dusky stillness of Arezzo.

And I was sure that the poor contadino, hurrying homeward at sunrise to his capanna, in the midst of his barren fields, bearing food and oil to his famished children, and wine to his old dying people, would have thought not likewise could one have asked him.

The gold was rare and costly that had been found in the tomb of the king that day; but it seemed to me that all the gold in Etruria could not have outweighed that impulse which had sent the feet of Pascarèl on their errand through the moonlit olives.

We wandered awhile about old Umbria. The mighty oak woods were welcome in the hot suns of

August, and there was no sweeter place for a Mid-summer dream than where the birds were singing in the flower-sown shadows about S. Francis's quiet Carceri.

We loitered in Gubbio, thinking of Maestro Georgio and of his wondrous rainbow hues; and we sat on the stony slopes where Pliny's villa once stood by the thread of hill-fed water; and we watched the sunset colour burn on the Spoleto mountains, with great rainclouds waiting the fall of night to break above the marshes; and we sauntered in the clear elastic dawns, over the sites of the buried cities, where the goat cropped herbage above the sunken altars, and the smoke of the charcoal-burners curled up amongst the oak boughs where the incense had once risen to Jupiter Feretrius, or Venus Pandemos.

And thence we strayed into Tuscany for the vintage month, and laughed to our heart's content amongst the vines, and saw the wines pressed in the old, wasteful, classic fashion, and the children tumble half-drunk amongst the reddening leaves, and the dogs gorge themselves on grapes unstinted, and the great wains roll homeward laden with purple wealth through the narrow paths where the crocuses were all alive again in millions, till the earth was like one great amethyst with them, and across the vast, still, sleeping valleys, where the sun was still hot, and the white homesteads were all hung with the golden ropes of that year's millet.

We worked and laughed and feasted on grapes with the rest all the shining days through, and at evening the Arte was thronged with the lusty Con-tadini, their mirth the readier for a plenteous vintage, and their strong brown limbs grape-stained like the limbs of Bacchus.

The recoltà, which was of abundance, except in some few places, as about Arezzo, where the fly and worm had ravaged, made Tuscany all glad and gay, gladdest and gayest of all the Val di Grève, and the Mugellino, and the Val di Chiana, and the other Pianurè lying close about Florence.

We paused in all the little towns one by one, and October passed away, golden and sultry, and ruddy with jest and song about the great wine vats; and the gardens full of the strong sweet smell of damask autumn roses and the waxen tuberosa, and the grass filled at every step with the vari-coloured cups of the wild anemones.

On the first day of the new month, which is dedicated to all the saints—in imitation of the old great Latin feast of all the gods in the times of "gli dei falsi e bugiardi," we came down from the heights where we had been amongst the forest farms of the Casentino and of Vallambrosa.

For the weather had grown chill there on the mountains, and we had come slowly downward with intent to go into Florence and rest there through the winter frosts, until the time of Carnival should have come round again, and have again passed away, killed with the cannonade of the Confettè.

Before he should enter the town, however, Pascarèl had taken a fancy to set the Arte a little while under Fiesole, so that the scattered people in the little paesi along the hill sides should have their hour's mirth under the Red Lily without being driven to take a long tramp for it down the stony slopes. And the place he chose for the Arte, and got permission to use from the owner, whom he knew, was a narrow piece of grassland amongst the stripped vineyards, with the grey bleak slopes rising above, and making sunrise late and sunset very early to the few who dwelt in that ravine of the mountain-shed Mugnone.

The Feast of the Saints rose a cloudless and radiant day, in which the scent and the warmth of the summer were sure to prevail, so soon as the first chill crispness of the early morning on the heights should have disappeared before the sunrays.

I remember how we came over the mountain side in the clear cold of the early day.

How we heard the matins bells ringing in the dusky depth where Florence was lying.

How we watched the white mists lighting little by little as the sun came over the edges of the hills.

How the libeccio was blowing keenly as we crossed the square of Fiesole, but fell into a mere soft breeze as we went down the winding road between the grey stone walls and the wild green hedges, with ever and again some scarlet glimpse of roses burning above a villa gate.

It was only cold enough to make the air free and elastic and inspiriting as a sea air.

All the hillside was in a pomp of scarlet and purple, and gold and bronze, with great masses of deep green where the ilex and acanthus grew, and soft pale greys where the olives were. Everywhere there were clouds of autumn flowers. At times, as we passed some wine-presses under the trees, the people shouted us a gay good-day. At times a kid, browsing amongst the stripped vines, bleated a tender little note upon the silence.

I remember how we went down the shelving zig-zag ways, the mules having passed before us at daybreak with the Arte in charge of a peasant lad. Pascarèl and I were foremost; he had his mandoline slung about him, and struck it now and then so that a sound, sweet and fine as the call of a thrush, came from it, and seemed to drift away down amongst the wreaths of the mist.

At some little distance Brunótta followed, talking eagerly with Cocomero of a quarrel she had had with a contadina about some duck's eggs in the place where we had slept. Little Toccò ran hither and thither at his fancy, now chasing a lizard, now plucking a rose that nodded over a wall, now stopping to chatter with the women plaiting the straw.

I remember how we went down the hill light-hearted in the morning air, pausing reverently as a priest passed by with the Santissimo for some sick creature, a white-frocked chorister going before him ringing the little bell along the peaceful ways.

I remember how we strolled on silenced for a moment or two, and then talked of the winter in Florence, and fell softly, as people will who have learned to love one another, into recollection of the first day we had met in the City of Lilies; and so, with the west wind in our faces, came down above the bridge of the Badià, where the old brown monastery stood, russet with age, amongst the olive and the mist.

I remember how we broke our fast whilst the sun was still low in the east, at a little dwelling-house a mile above the village, where Pizzichiria was scrawled in chalk along the wall, and the green bough above the doorway told that the tenant of the house sold wine as well.

I remember how we sat out under the pergola where some grapes still hung, and brake our bread and drank sweet foaming draughts of milk, the cow meanwhile, in her shed hard by, gazing at us with her eyes of Hèrè over a great green dew-wet mound of trefoil; and below, amongst the olives, the sacred Solitudine, rising gaunt and bare, and brown and sombre with innumerable memories.

I remember how we sat there, and laughed and clattered gaily, and then took up the mandoline afresh and sang all sorts of follies and of fancies, and then rose and strolled away down the hills to see where they would set up the Arte, and soon found a broad field a few roods above the Badià itself, where the fattore, knowing us, had given eager acquiescence for the throne of our hedgerow Thespia to be erected.

Ah, yes; I remember it all so well—so well—that last day of that glad, poetic, fanciful, careless life which was fated to be broken off suddenly and for ever, as the pomegranate flower is snapped from its stalk by the mistral.

BOOK V.

THE FEAST OF THE DEAD.

CHAPTER I.

The Fountain of the Pine.

It had been all summer—endless, cloudless summer—from the time of the carnival violets to the time
of the autumn cyclamen.   And there was no foreboding of storm or of winter in the air that day of All
Saints, though, whilst I knew it not, I heard for the
last time the soft low laughter of Pascarèl—of my
lover;—my lover surely, though he spoke never directly
of love but only uttered it in those million ways and
words and charms of touch and eloquence of glance
which are love's truest, subtlest, and most perilous
language.

He and I stayed in the field behind the Solitudine
and threw ourselves down there beside a little thread-
like brook whose water was all red and purple with
anemones.   Little Toccò wandered away as his habit
was under the stripped vines; Cocomero had stayed
with Brunótta to help her, as they said, beat some
linen in the shallow course of the Mugnone.

It was yet quite early in the morning, and the
gentle coolness of daybreak had not left the air.

It is quite wild up there; the hills rise steep and
sombre, their sides dark with the cypress; the stream
runs through a deep gorge, and a bridge with a pointed

arch rises over it quaint and grey; at this time, before the floods of winter had come down, it was still shallow, and a man was wading it with a fishing-net upon his back.

Southward, above us, rose the old Etrurian slopes, and the walls and towers of the city that perished for daring to aspire to be rival of the Scarlet Lily.

Westward towered the great Salviati pile amongst its vines and olives: and lower down was the smaller, humbler villa set in a sea of roses, and girt with willow and lemon and magnolia, whither the great nobles were wont to come down in the hush of the fruit-scented nights to their love trysts; directly at our feet was the gloom of the Solitudine; away there in the far centre, betwixt the lines of hills, Florence was stretched as a white swan may spread her wings to sleep upon her river nest. Yet not so far but what we heard each note of her warning chimes; for it was the feast-day of the saints, as I have said, and the bells of her countless churches were calling to one another.

All about us were the vine lands and the olive woods, the rich rank vegetation sown thick with wild anemones. And so we resolved that there the theatre should stand, and then we threw ourselves down amidst the thick grass and the trefoil with the delicate heads of the cyclamens about us in tens of thousands.

"No theatre was ever better placed," said Pascarèl, lying at my feet amongst the olives. "Not even where ankle deep in thyme the Latins laughed over the roaring fun of Plautus. It is a little profane, I fear, to set a playhouse so near the Badià?

"When one thinks how often those great sad eyes

of Dante's have gazed through this same mist of olive leaves away to the dome of the Duomo yonder. It is very profane, I am afraid.

"When one thinks of all those monks, too, of San Marco-in-Urbe, who used to come up here to their mountain Badià to rest their eyes and souls a little out of hearing of the city riot:—Savonarola who, in all his life of storm and prayer, and triumph and torment, had time to cherish a damask rose-tree:—and that bravest of brave souls, Domenico, whom one loves, I think, almost better than any other saint or hero of them all:—Fra Bartolommèo must have worked here too; though there is not his mark upon the walls: —and the divine Angelico sometimes left the dim old convent down in Florence to come hither and paint for the Solitudine.

"They must have been amongst his most blessed days—alone here with his pure thoughts and visions; and the precious colours waiting on his hand; and about him the solitude of the cloisters, and the country silence of the hill sides. How wise he was,—how very wise,—to put away from him the proffered mitre and the possible tiara!

"Yes; this is every inch of it haunted ground, sacred ground, though the bullocks tread it with the ploughshare and the reapers strip the vines.

"Do you ever think of those artist-monks who have strewed Italy with altar-pieces and missal miniatures till there is not any little lonely dusky town of hers that is not rich by art? Do you often think of them! I do.

"There must have been a beauty in their lives—a great beauty—though they missed of much, of more than they ever knew or dreamed of, let us hope. In visions of the Madonna they grew blind to the meaning of a woman's smile, and illuminating the golden olive wreath above the heads of saints they lost the laughter of the children under the homely olive trees without.

"But they did a noble work in their day; and leisure for meditation is no mean treasure, though the modern world does not number it amongst its joys.

"One can understand how men born with nervous frames and spiritual fancies into the world when it was one vast battle-ground, where its thrones were won by steel and poison, and its religion enforced by torch and faggot, grew so weary of the never-ending turmoil, and of the riotous life which was always either a pageant or a slaughter-house, that it seemed beautiful to them to withdraw themselves into some peaceful place like this Badià and spend their years in study and in recommendation of their souls to God, with the green and fruitful fields before their cloister windows, and no intruders on the summer stillness as they painted their dreams of a worthier and fairer world except the blue butterflies that strayed in on a sunbeam, or the gold porsellini that hummed at the lilies in the Virgin's chalice."

His voice dropped in its dreamy melody down the tranquil air joining the hum of the insects, the chimes of the distant bells, and the splash in the shallow Mugnone as the fisher waded over its stones. Stones which were now so dry that a rabbit could have hopped from one to another of them without wetting its white feet; although in winter time the little mountain stream so often rages in tempest and wrecks the homesteads, and deluges stalls and byres.

He shifted his attitude a little, and his hand played amongst the anemones; the lights and the shadows changed on his face as the boughs above were blown to and fro by the fresh sea wind.

"I am not sure," he went on, "that if I had been born then I should not have been a monkish painter myself; though I fear I should have worn a cuirass like fighting Fra Benedetto, and scaled the walls like libertine Fra Lippi. The Angel Mónk would have found no fraternity, I fear, with me.

"Will he be angered, think you, that we set the Arte so near to his altar-piece?—and Savonarola, who said to all gaieties Retro Satanas?—or Dante, who had small patience with any puppets or pleasure-seekers? He was so much here, or so they say, when he would withdraw from Guelph and Ghibelline, and be at peace a little while. One can believe he wrote better here, in the quiet of the hills and with sad Fiesole so near, than down in the street by San Martino where it was all so cramped and dark.

"Yes;—I am troubled about that;—it is irreverent to set the little lily flag of the Arte flying here. And the villagers of Marco Vecchio are lusty of lung, and will laugh loud and trouble the stillness of the old Solitudine. Yet it must have heard worse in its time: many a shriek as the Salviati steel went through a peasant's breast for daring to breathe against seigneur-ial rights; many a crash and clamour of crossed arms down there in the defile as the lances of Hawkwood swept from the mountains; many a groan stifled there in the waters as the Imperial reiters clattered with devil's joy through the curse and the smoke of the burning hill sides. Do you not see it all?

"And Dante, with his crimson lucco trailing, coming up wearily there through Marco Vecchio, and glancing at the dead horses on the bridge, and the empty casques, and the broken lance heads amongst the grass under the vines, and then going on his way into the quiet of the Badià, sick at heart?

"Yes: certainly Dante must have seen and heard worse things than Toto's little cap and plume and the villagers' harmless laughter before our stage to-night. And though I have spoken evil and light things to you, donzella, of players, yet I am not sure that we have not done more good if we could sum it up than half the preachers and the poets. With the poets indeed we have gone hand in hand from all time; and without us Shakespeare and Racine, Calderon, and Goldoni, would have been dumb to their nations; and as for the preachers, Savonarola was a good man and true, and Francesco d'Assissi was blessed of all peoples, and the name of San Bruno is great for all time; but on the whole I doubt if any of them did more to blow a health-giving breeze through the world's lazar houses than have done in another fashion our much slandered Pantomimè."

Pascarèl was silent awhile; when he spoke it was with some impatience.

"The great Austrian diamond, the Lemon Stone, was picked up for two soldi in our Mercato Vecchio off a pedlar's stall. If I chanced on such luck as that, donzella!"

He stopped abruptly; his thoughts seemed to me

irrelevant and oddly strung together—Dante and the ducal diamond?

"If you did?" I echoed.   "Well?—what if you did?   Tell me?"

He laughed a little.

"Nay, the face of the world would be changed for me.   That is all."

"Changed!   And can you want that?   Are you not happy?"

"Six months—and all my life before—I was. Yes."

My eyes filled with a sudden rush of tears that blotted out the sight of Florence.   For the first time I thought him cruel.

"That means—before you found me!   If I torment you, let me go?   And yet sometimes you seem so glad to have me!—"

I was but a child, and I spoke as a child: but the fire that swept over me from the momentarily uplifted eyes of Pascarèl, scorched the word to silence on my trembling mouth.

He caught my hands and kissed them with eager and tremulous tenderness, as his habit often was with me.

"Do not jest about that.   You are the life of my life," he murmured, holding my hands against his lips the while.   Then he was silent too.

"But," I whispered to him, wistfully, perplexed strangely, and vaguely touched to apprehension— "but, if I gave you pleasure indeed, why should you be so much less gay than when you knew me first! Then, all things contented you; you laughed, and were never troubled.   And now you seem to be forever wistful for some fate you have not; you, who were used to say that you would hardly change with Boiardo or Bernardo!"

His face was turned from me as he listened, and he moved a little restlessly.

"Cara mia," he said, endeavouring, I thought, to speak more jestingly, with but little success, for he was too frank of nature to counterfeit well the gaiety that in happy moments was so natural to him—"oh, cara mia, you have read—or I have recited to you—the Orlando Innamorato many and many a time. Do you not remember how, when Rinaldo found himself in Arden, the single garden-lily struck him to earth—all Paladin though he was—and the blows of the white and red roses left him more dead than alive, and made the sharp edge of his good sword Fusberta of no more strength or worth than a straw? Every man comes, soon or late, to that unequal flower-combat in the enchanted forest; and the armour that has been proof against the dragons, and the shield that has been undinted by the giants, are of no avail to help him, once by the Fountain of the Pine."

My cheeks grew warm and my heart throbbed quickly in wild tumult as I heard; I said nothing; I felt a sweet dreamy happiness steal over me.

For was not the garden-lily that struck down Rinaldo the weapon of the youth who was called Love?

And was not the Fountain of the Pine the one from which Rinaldo, drinking after the wounds of the lily, grew blind to both the worlds of truth and magic, and saw only "la dolce vista del viso sereno" of the Sister of the Lion, of the Rose of Pentecost?

If he said so much, why not yet a little more? the dim wonder of it drifted vaguely over me, but it was only vaguely, for I was happy in the knowledge that I was dear to him, and I was too young to question of what sort or of what strength this half silent and half eloquent love might be.

"Let us talk of what we would do if we found another Lemon Stone in the market," he said gaily, with a certain impatience in his voice. "Ah, you are ashamed of me for hankering after riches at the last like this? Well, I am ashamed of myself, but if I found it I doubt if I should keep it. Whatever I own in the evening is always gone before the next day's sunset. But only think how odd it must be, to go through the market poor as Job; hungry perhaps, and with the hot pavement scorching your feet through the holes in your boots; and then to see a queer-shaped bit of glass, and give a copper-piece for it because you are sorry for that poor old wretch, whose only stock in trade is that stall of miserable *Roba*, and then to go home to your garret with it, and be struck by some strange look in it as the sun's rays catch it so, that you take it over the way to your friend at the little pharmacy, who is a man of science in his small way, under his bunches of herbs and his glass retorts: and then all at once to know that by that shining thing no bigger than a walnut, you are become all in a minute the master of a kingdom—only think of it all; I could almost talk myself mad with the very fancy of it. But in those stories of diamonds they never tell us what becomes of that first buyer of it, who has all the real sorcery and music of its history. One would like to know if he ever went back to the market-stall and shared his gains. One would *hope* he always did; but human nature being what it is, that is doubtful, very doubtful, I am afraid."

I listened to him in some wonder; Pascarèl, the man of all the world to whom riches were most indifferent and who had resisted all manner of temptations and refused to turn his genius into gold—to dream thus of the treasures locked in a cube of carbon! I struck him on the lips with a scourge of seeding grasses, and scolded him for his new-born avarice.

"Dear donzella," he made answer in his caressing voice, and with more warmth on the darkness of his face than the sun brought there, "you must have read a thousand and one eastern tales in your time. Did never you read of the shepherd who was quite happy guarding his flocks in the wide Persian plains, and roaming at will with no thought but where to find a fresh watercourse when his beasts were athirst, or a cool grove of palm and date wherein to lay him down when the stars arose—quite happy all his years, until one day the king's daughter rode by and her shadow fell betwixt him and the sun? And he was never again content; never, never again. Have you not read of him?"

"But I am not a king's daughter!" I cried, and then was silent; there on the hillside that was sown with cyclamen, close above the Badià.

He laughed a little; a low, soft, sad laugh that had more tenderness in it than tears have:—doubtless at the unconscious ingenuousness with which I took to myself the Persian tale.

He drew me down close to him where he leaned at my feet amongst the grass.

"You come of great people, I suppose; people who would scarcely care to see you on a strolling player's booth. And you have a higher kingdom than any; the kingdom of innocence;—wherein I have no right to trespass."

He was silent a long while, whilst the chimes rung slowly from above, where Fiesole was calling her scattered flock to the fold:

"You have heard of Alaran," he said, abruptly. "Alaran, of Acqui, who bore off the daughter of Emperor Otho, and having nothing in the world but two horses, kept one to convey her away with, and sold the other to buy a hut in the forest, where he turned charcoal-burner. Legend says that the imperial Alaxia was happy as the birds in the woods in this humble estate, and that one day great Otho going hunting in all his pomp, after he was summoned to the Roman crown, called for a cup of water to a peasant-girl, and looking down on the face of the woman who brought it, saw the face of Alaxia gladder, and not a whit less proud than it had been in his own palace. What do you say to the story? do you wonder that the princess was content with the hut in the oak glades?"

His eyes sought mine with eager wistfulness. I laughed a little happily, and thought I knew why she had been so glad there in the charcoal-burner's cabin.

"No; I do not wonder," I said, softly, more to myself than him. "Once I should have wondered, but now—I understand."

He did not ask me why, but his hand closed fast and warm on mine.

"Ah! my donzella," he said softly and very sadly, after a little time. "So you think—so you think, being a child. But you might repent. See here,—I am content with my life—it is good enough in its way, though nameless and fruitless also perhaps. But I cannot disguise from myself that it is not a fit life for you.

"You are truly a 'donzella'; you have the hands, and the feet, and the voice and the ways, and all the pretty imperious graces that belong to those gentle born.

"You were reared hardly? Yes, I know.

"But you have the instincts of a baby princess for all that.

"Could you be content always to go a-foot in all weathers, to sleep in little humble places, to eat homely fare as we do, to live with the people—the Italian people, it is true, but still the people only?

"And that is why I wish for the Lemon Stone.

"Do you understand now?"

I half laughed and half cried as I heard him, with the glad golden morning all around, and my hand folded close in his.

It was only a sceptre of peacock's plumes that we had.

I knew that; but it seemed to me better than the winged sceptre of gold and ivory that symbolled the empire of the world.

I tossed a shower of anemone cups above our heads as I cried to him,—

"I do not understand! I do not want to understand! I shall be content anyhow, anywhere, any time—always—with you!"

He let go my hands—for him almost roughly—and rose quickly to his feet, and paced to and fro quickly under the trees silently, with the broad flap of his hat drawn down over his eyes. He brushed and trampled the anemones ruthlessly as he went; I could not tell what moved him, whether anger or pain.

I loved him well—indeed,—loved him with all the ardour and simplicity of a child who had never before had any great affection for any living thing; but I missed that subtle sympathy, that perfect passion and patience which alone enable one heart to feel each pang or each joy that makes another beat.

His moods were as changeful as the winds, and at times there was a restless impatience and depression on him which was far beyond my understanding.

I did not comprehend now what I had said amiss; the idea had occurred to me that he was growing tired of me, and it made me sad; in the early days he had never been capricious thus. I did not go to him therefore, but sat still amongst the grasses and the fruitless boughs of the vines.

Ah, Dio mio! if I had gone to him and asked him why he was so grave, he might have spoken—who knows?—and the face of the world would have been changed for us. For what would I not have pardoned had he asked me?

After a little while, he mastered whatever emotion had moved him, and came to me again. He spoke in his old gentle, caressing way, a little colder, perhaps, if anything, and less gay.

"Dear donzella, you are very good to care to

wander with me," he said softly. "But I fear it is but
a sorry mode of existence for you; and I fear your
horoscope contained something better for your future
than a strolling player's homeless career.   The clear
planet that presided over your birth cannot have been
the tinsel star on the painted foreheads of the Pantomimi. But, altro! we have had enough, and too much,
of such serious chatter.   Some day we must talk
seriously indeed, and I must—but never mind now.
It is All Saints Day, and, perhaps the last day of
summer.   There was frost at sunrise.   Let us be happy
while we can, carina.   Such a morning as this," he
said, after a pause, laughing himself back into that
gaiety of soul which lived side by side in his nature
with a certain passionate and poetic sadness: "and all
this red gold of autumn ours, and a whole long sunny
day in which to wander as we like, it is infamous to
be melancholy, or to be athirst for lemon stones, or
for anything more than the good that we have got.
Lean backward to be in the shade of that tree; and
let your hand lie quiet in mine—so; and now I will
tell you a story."

I loved his stories; I had the insatiable delight in
them of a young mind to which romances were unknown; and his skill in telling them was marvellous.

The heroical absurdities of the Morgante Maggiore,
and the Furioso, the grotesque fairyland, and miraculous
adventures of Basile; the feuds and love-tales of the
populace, as Cortese sang them fresh from the market-
place of Masaniello; the narratives of Boccaccio; the
jests of Berni; the comedies of Goldoni—all these and
their like were stripped of all coarseness and harmful-
ness which they might possess, and served to me de-

corated by all the grace and playfulness of his own fancy added to them.

I was readily consoled: when he was gay and good to me, no shadows had power to rest on me.

No lemon stone could have added anything to my perfect peace and gladness as I lay there under the golden-fruited pear-tree amongst the cyclamens, with my hand in his, listening to the sweet, sonorous cadence of his voice, while the Lily of Florence floated on the flag of the wooden theatre, and the robins chirped amongst the many-coloured autumn blossoms, and the sun was high, and the radiance was cloudless above the Solitudine.

I was a child; I needed nothing more than the joy of the moment; and whatever darkness he might see in the future it was all light to me; for did it not lie in the sweet sunshine of his smile?

It was All Saints Day; we could hear the bells ringing in the city all the morning long; we leaned there on the hillside, and took no thought for the morrow—the morrow that was the Feast of the Dead.

CHAPTER II.
The Night of All Saints.

THAT evening he did not play at his Arte, and we strolled down the hillside into Florence as the sun set.

Brunótta elected to stay behind; she had some shirts to iron, as she said, and wished to sup afterwards with a blacksmith's wife in Marco Vecchio. Coco was missing when we left the hills, and little Toccò alone ran beside us, throwing his ruzzolà as gleefully as though he had been six years instead of sixteen.

It was a beautiful warm red and gold evening, promising to be stormy on the morrow, but splendid then, as the sun set, and full of odour from the full wine-presses where they stood beneath the trees, and the glow of roses that burned over every villa wall.

We went into the city on the carretta of a contadino piled with fresh hay; for we cut hay all the year round in Italy.

The old mule stumbled down the stony ways; I sat amidst the flower-sown grasses, and drew the dead daisies in it through my fingers; Pascarèl walked beside me; the boy ran on before; the contadino told us stories of his crops and vines, and of the prices he had made by his wife's home-woven linen; sometimes we had to draw up against the wall and wait to let a waggon-load of grapes go by; all along the road the people were sitting out at their doors.

It had been a good vintage time, and all the world was content; at the gates even the soldiers who took the custom dues were in good humour, laughing over flasks of new red wine.

The city was all life and light. It was a beloved feast of the people, and the streets were full.

All the bells were pealing; there was music everywhere. Women leaned from the casements with roses in their hands. Over all the place there was a curious dreamy golden hue, deepened here and there into deep bronze shadows, at times broken by a flush of scarlet, as a wood fire glowed through an open doorway, at times paled into a pearly coolness when the last daylight gleamed upon the marble of a statue or a tomb.

The Florentines were all out, flocking to the churches, to the theatres, to the bands of music, to the coffee houses, playing dominoes in the street, chaunting praises at the vespers, wandering by the river side, or gambling at morra at the corners of the streets.

We ate black figs and drank black coffee hard by the old palace of the Strozzi, with the cornice of Cronaca still catching the sunrays, whilst the walls below were black as night, and the passers-by were illumined by lantern and lamplight shed from doorway and casement, and little bright specks of flame like glowworms sparkled as the stands of the chestnut-sellers wandered from place to place, and the vendors of amaretti and brigidini shouted from corner to corner.

Then having long before lost little Toccò, where some street-tombola for toys and fruits had attracted him, we too wandered away, and strayed with others up the stairs of the little Loggè theatre, above the old mediæval granary, and laughed our hearts out over the merry melodies of Don Bucefalo, and then came out again into the streets into the starlight.

"To-morrow will be the Feast of the Dead," said Pascarèl, his voice dropping softly, as we went through the Street of the Dead. "There will be only the sound of the Miserere all over Florence to-morrow.

"Well, no city has so true a cause to pray for her dead, for none other has dead so great.

"Will any pray for Ginevra, I wonder? I think

you will, gioja mia. Do you not see her, on just such
a night as this, flying down this very place?

"There is no story so perfect as the Ginevra tale.

"The dreadful loneliness of the great dome as she
awoke beneath it; the vast haunted stillness, with here
and there the whiteness of a moonbeam; these quiet
gloomy streets at midnight; the black shadows; these
yawning archways, like the gates of tombs; the trembling, hunted, heart-sick thing, with her bare feet
wounded on the stones, and the grave-clothes falling
from her shivering limbs; everywhere denial, incredulity, horror, superstition; everywhere the closed wicket
and the cry of terror as at some unearthly appari-
tion.

"Then at last the lover's threshold, the timid summons of despair, the open door, the instant welcome;
not a doubt, not a question, not a fear—What matter
whether living or dead, of heaven or of hell?

"What matter whence she came?

"What matter what she brought?

"Welcome, thrice welcome, as flowers in the Maytime.

"Welcome and precious—since the face was *hers!*"

His voice had a thrill of passion in it that seemed
upon my ear, in the silence of the deserted street,
sweet as the song of the nightingales in the ilex
forests in the nights of Midsummer. I felt—without
well knowing what I felt—that it was not of Ginevra
only he was thinking.

"And it was all true too, here in this Via della
Morte," he said, very softly and sadly, after awhile,
drawing me closer against him as we went under the
solemn shadow of the leaning walls; and he uncovered

his head reverently in the moonlight, as though there had passed by him all those dead, for whom his Florence on the morrow would beseech her God.

We went on in silence until we had passed through the Gate of San Gallo to go homewards towards the hills.

"That cost us in all just four soldi," laughed Pascarèl, as the city barriers closed behind us. "Figs and coffee and music, and all for the price a rich man gives for one cigar, or one peach, away in Paris. What do we want with a Lemon Stone? Our coffee would be in eggshell china, to be sure, and we should have red velvet arm chairs at the Pergola; but should we be any the happier really? tell me, donzella, should we?"

"How could we be any happier?" I answered him dreamily.

It had only cost four soldi, that sweet starlight evening, amongst the laughter of the people and the ringing cadence of the Bucefalo; but what of that?

The gladness was with us that never comes twice in a lifetime, and our hearts had an echo for the music that made it sweet as the voices of angels.

He did not answer.

As I glanced at his face, there was a certain vague disquietude upon it that stole there all suddenly, while his eyes beamed on mine in the shadows, with the look that had made silence fall between us that day beside the Rio Gonfio.

"Ah, carina, you do not know, you do not know," he murmured softly.

What was it that I did not know? That look in

his eyes made my heart beat in a strange tumult, and I did not ask him.

We went in silence up the hilly road, with the stars shining overhead. He passed his arm around me to aid me in the toilsome way, and drew my hand in his.

No palace floor strewn with roses was ever softer to the sandalled feet of an eastern queen than seemed that stony dreary way to me.

The road was quite deserted at that hour. The moonrays made it white and calm.

The dust of it was changed to silver, and its jagged walls seemed like ivory where the light touched them, and like malachite and porphyry where the green ivy and the golden vine leaves crossed each other.

From the wine-presses full of juice of the grapes there came strong fruitlike odours.

In the stillness we could hear the goats browsing off the grass under the stripped vines. There were sweet scents of roses, of pasture, of grazing cattle, as we passed the villa gates. Away in the city below there was a sound of men singing to the chords of a lute. Above, against the lustre of the skies, rose the white outlines of sad Fiesole.

We paused a moment to rest within the garden walls of a villino. Cypresses were swaying plume-like in the wind; wild roses were blowing, half-closed, with the dews shut in their hearts; a stream of water dropped slowly into a marble shell; clusters of yellow grapes hung about a broken statue of dead Hyacinthus.

We stood there close together, with the stars above us, and on the cool night air the scent of the crushed grapes and fallen leaves.

In the soft gloom, his eyes burned into mine; his arms drew me closer; his lips touched my hands, my cheeks, my throat.

Are there any who have not known these hours?— they have heard but half the language, have seen but half the sun.

We spoke but little. What need were there for words.

We went slowly, after awhile, homeward up the road, which at another time would have seemed steep and dreary enough, but to me was beautiful as the earth can only be once in the length of any life.

There were no lights in Marco Vecchio, nor in the little humble place where we had made our dwelling. There was only the moonlight glistening on the convent walls above upon the heights, and a falling star that ran swift and bright until it dropped in the sea of the olive woods.

I went up to my little bare chamber, where the brick floor was white from the rays of the moon.

He stayed without, walking to and fro beneath the bronzed leaves of the walnuts.

I was sleepless and full of those dreams born of memory, which are sweeter than all the dreams of fancy.

The small square casement of my chamber was hung round with thick acanthus coils; beyond them the stars of Orion gleamed in the deep blue of the skies.

All the hillside sloped away dimly towards Florence, pale under the moon, and only black where the cypress grew. The worn marbles and dulled frescoes of the old historic villas gleamed like silver, and below in the valley the lights of the city glowed as a cluster of lùcciole glows in the harvest amidst the blowing maize.

The roof of the house was low; the upper chambers were underneath the eaves, some broken blocks of macigno, grown over by a fig-tree, were beneath my window. He, looking upward, saw me leaning there.

He paused a moment; then, lithe as a deer, swung himself by the boughs of the fig until he could touch me where he stood.

The great dark leaves were all round him; the moonlight was upon his face. He drew my hands about his neck, and murmured the sweetest words of passion that lie in the tongue of Tasso, of Romeo, of Francesca.

The perfect night was all around us. We were alone beneath the throbbing stars, amidst the burning roses.

There, in the old Badià, men, dreaming of heaven, had missed the heaven that we entered by a touch, a look, a breath.

CHAPTER III.

Sunrise.

I LAY awake for very happiness that night, and rose so soon as the sun came over the hills and through the broad screen of the fig foliage.

It was a beautiful wet, cool dewy world into which I ran joyous and bare-headed from out the little lowly capanna on to the misty side of the hills.

I was a child in my joy; I was full of the present;

I had no thought beyond; I reasoned on nothing; I reflected on nothing; I only wanted to hear him say once more he loved me.

Life was not more real to me than if we had been genii, like the Gwyn Araun he envied; it was a wonderful perfect flowerlike thing that I held in eagerness and ecstasy, doubting not that it came from God.

I ran into the sweet, cold, rosy, misty morning, with the bronze of the reddened vine leaves about my feet, and looked up at the blue sky and laughed a little gladly and low, and then felt my eyes fill with delicious tears, and stood still, wondering if ever any creature had been so blessed as I.

About me was all the gold and crimson of the autumn foliage; the whole hill-side seemed to burn with it up to the brown walls of the old Badià; but away in the valley there was a dense white fog in which Florence was hidden from sight; even the golden cross of her cathedral was no longer visible.

I dropped on to a stone bench in the olive orchard of the cottage, and sat and dreamed, and listened for the footfall of Pascarèl. But all was quite silent round me.

My heart fell a little. I had thought that he would have been watching as eagerly for the dawn as I was.

After a while bells began to ring in the city under the pale shadows of the fog. I could hear them where I sat on the hill-side; but they sounded muffled and sad.

A woman came through the olives to cross the bridge of San Marco. She passed me closely; she was weeping quietly.

I looked at her in a sort of wonder; in this world

—my beautiful, wonderful fairy world—how was any sorrow possible?

"I go to pray for my lost children," she said, gently, in answer to the look upon my face. "It is the Feast of the Dead. May you never know grief, my pretty signorina."

She went on under the olives. I shivered a little where I sat, with the red vine coils bright about my feet: the mists dense as clouds in the valley.

Florence was veiled in her white shroud; she was mourning her dead.

I had forgotten what the day was.

I gave a swift thought to the lonely nameless graves in cold Verona.

What had happened? Nothing.

And yet in the stead of my perfect joy there stole on me a vague fear.

CHAPTER IV.

Sunset.

ALL was quite still on the hill-side.

A few peasants went through the trees to matins in the old monastery church.

The bells rang on wearily and mournfully, echoing through the fog.

Little Toccò ran down to me with a ruzzolà in his hand.

"He went into the town before the sun was up; he left me this for you."

On it Pascarèl had written, "I must go into Florence, but will be back ere sunset."

8*

A great darkness fell on me. The bells seemed to be wailing for the dead.

It was only a day, indeed; but then I had dreamed such perfect dreams of this single little day amongst the red autumn leaves, hearing of his love forever and forever and forever, and yet never enough. Alone with him on these haunted sacred hills.

A lattice was thrown sharply open; a shrill voice called—

"He is gone into the town, and never let me know; and I want coffee, and pins, and a shoestring, and the saints know what not! and nothing is to be had in this beastly place, be it ever so. Toccò, run in the village and see if you can buy aught worth the eating. HE would never care if he lived on acorns!"

It was Brunótta making her daily lamentation.

I rose, and wandered away out of hearing; that little sharp voluble voice jarred upon me.

Little Toccò passed me, running with a few scudi to do her errand.

I stayed him a moment on the hill.

"Do you know why he is gone?" I asked him, wistfully.

Toccò shook his curly head.

"Not I. But I think—at least the cowherd said so—that he seemed troubled as he left the house at day-dawn. Perhaps he is gone to pray for someone dead. It is the day of the dead, you know. But I must make haste, signorina, or Brunótta will box my ears, surely."

The lad flew down the slope and across the bridge to the village. I strayed away amongst the olives, choosing hunger in that peace and stillness rather than encounter the perpetually ringing chimes of Brunótta's chatter.

Under the wall of the Villa of Mario a dairy-woman gave me a draught of milk and a crust, and I wandered by myself all the morning, dreaming, dreaming, dreaming always of him. Of him alone.

Had he gone to pray for any dead that he loved?

My heart for a moment was heavy at the thought. I was jealous even of a memory that might be dear to him; but not for very long. He loved me now.

What matter the rest?

So·many hands had touched the mandoline—yes, no doubt. But I had a sweet, vague sure instinct that one chord had been reached by me alone.

When the day had passed the meridian, all my spirits rose again. He had said that he would be back before sunset. I might hope for him every moment.

I returned through the fields and orchards lingeringly and happily; the mists had all lifted by noon.

It was another clear summer-like day. The golden cross of the duomo glittered in the hollow where the city lay.

In the village, the people, having prayed for their dead, were out in their holiday gear; they were talking cheerfully of the abundant vintage, and some of them were dancing under the red vine foliage to the sound of a flute and a fiddle.

I saw, afar off, Brunótta, brave in a scarlet kirtle and white bodice, with the amber beads of St. John's Day round her throat, merrily footing the salterrello with a brawny blacksmith of San Marco. Her white

teeth shone, her little rosy face laughed, her small
plump feet twinkled ceaselessly, the sunshine fell
about her, the gold and bronze of the dying vine
leaves hung above her head; she was as happy as a
grillo in the grasses.

I went into the garden of the capanna we had
lodged at and sat down in a green nook of it, whence
I could see the bridge and the white road beyond as
it shelved down towards Florence.

I lost sight of the dancers under the vines, but I
could watch him come up from the city, or fly to meet
him if no one looked.

The little garden was gay with all kinds of autumn
flowers; for the daughter of the house was one of the
flowersellers of Florence.　There were great bands of
scarlet salvia blossoming, and many yellow heads of
gourds and pumpkins.

A pergola stretched from the threshold to the garden wicket; grapes still hung on it, and the leafage
was a brilliant tangle of red and green and gold. I
sat on a bench in one corner of this, whence I could
see the shallow sunlit river; children were wading in
it with many joyous cries, and a grey mule was drinking
at the ford.

I was shut in by the green leaves.

Now and then a great lustrous bee or moth went
humming through the bean blossoms.　I could see
through the vine foliage the white wall of the house
and the open window of the kitchen; the padrona
went to and fro past the window in a white coif and
a red petticoat, with copper vessels in her hands.

Lazily, every now and then, I lifted my arm over
my head, and drew down one of the grapes off the

clusters that hung above there. A grey cat was walking slowly through the maze of the pumpkins on the ground. Beyond the garden walls there were the fields and the vineyards, and beyond all these again, Fiesole and the mountains.

Ave Maria bells were ringing dreamily down in the valdarno.

It was five of the clock in the afternoon; there was no light on the sun-dial on the wall, but a tawny glow like molten gold was shed over every thing from the western skies above the hills.

The rabbits were scudding with bustle and glee amongst the cabbages. Far away at the other end of the garden two little children were gathering great yellow pears off the side of a shed, eating and laughing as they filled the rush baskets with the fruit.

A white pigeon spread silver wings against the deep cloudless blue of the sky. The houseleek on the red sloping roof turned to vivid gold. The woman of the house hummed to herself fragments of song as she went to and fro past her open window; and I could hear the merry music of the flute where the villagers were still dancing.

Why do I think of all these things? I do not know: only the leaves and the flowers, and the beasts and the unconscious people that have all been about one in any great misery seem to become a portion of it, and burn themselves into one's brain—forever.

The sadness of the daybreak had passed away from me with the vanished mists. My future seemed to glow before me — golden, beautiful, indistinct, sacred, as the cross of the cathedral glowed down in the valley.

I sat and dreamed over the tender music of his voice, which could lend to the simplest phrase or commonest greeting all the eloquence of a caress.

For the last time in my life I was happy with that perfect happiness only possible in extreme youth, which is only half conscious of itself, and does not awaken to question either its wisdom or its hereafter.

After a while there was a rustle and a step, and Brunótta, hot and tired, pushed her way through the leaves.

She stopped short as she saw me.

"I thought you were on the hills, signorina," she said, sullenly, and stood posed on one foot, like a little sulky bird, as her habit was when not quite at her ease.

I looked up and smiled on her. I loved every living thing that day, and though she had been capricious and out of temper with me recently, I had never forgotten all the goodness she had shown me in the early days of my wanderings with the Arte.

"Have you had a good dance, Brunótta?" I asked her. "I saw you in the village with that big black Domenico."

"There is no harm in stretching one's limbs awhile," said Brunótta, sulkily, as though I had accused her of some fault. "I went to mass in the morning, of course. Of course one always prays for the dead. They never haunt you if you do. Though, for the matter of that, I knew a good soul in Casentino who paid a dozen masses every Quaresima to keep her husband quiet in his grave, and it was all not one bit of use; he was a pedlar, and was thought murdered for good and all by brigands, but just when she was married to a rich poulterer, and comfortable, he came to life again, and all the church money was wasted that she had paid for six years and more;—if that was not enough to try a woman!—still, I always say prayers for them, for they can do one a great deal of hurt if they like. And I am always afraid my old father may come any night, for there was a matter of fifteen soldi for goat's milk that we quarrelled about the very day he fell down in a fit; and his very last words were, 'If I get out of my grave, I will have those soldi, you wicked wench.' He said that even with L'Olio Santo upon him."

And Brunótta paused, overcome with her recollections, looking vaguely and still sulkily at me, as she rested one foot on the other.

I listened with a little wonder; it was the first time she had ever spoken of her father, though she had often told me of the cruelties of her foster-mother in Casentino; and this dying thought of the soldi seemed to me wholly unlike the gay, ironical, humorous and whimsically proud man whom Pascarèl had so often described to me as the graver of the prince's coronet upon the old tin tinker's pot.

Moreover, if Pascarèl had been fifteen when his father had died, how could Brunótta, who was so many many years younger than he, remember the dead man at all?

"You mean your foster-mother's husband?" I said, looking away down the white road and thinking little of her, only eagerly watching for the shadow so familiar and so dear to me to fall across the sunny bridge.

"I mean my father," said Brunótta, stubbornly, and was silent, with the guilty, conscious, cunning look upon her face that she had worn on the day of the San Giovanni.

I did not think much of her.

My eyes went across the bridge to that little white glimpse of road on which with every second I hoped to see the elastic slender figure, the white dress, the dark oval face, like an old picture, that I had so often watched for in such happy hours, but never watched for with such a beating, eager, tremulous heart as now.

When at last I looked at her she was still in the same position, looking like an angered chidden child, but with a certain apprehensive cunning on her ruddy face.

"Why, Brunótta, how you stare at me!" I cried, growing a little tired of her gaze. "Is there anything strange in me to-day?"

In answer, her lip fell, her plump shoulders heaved, and she began to sob aloud.

My heart stood still with terror. My fancy flew to every kind of evil that might have befallen him.

"What is it?" I cried, breathless with fear. "Any accident—any sorrow—to him?"

Brunótta dropped at my feet in the dust, a little ruffled heap, like a gay-plumaged bird that is beaten down by the rain.

"*He* is well enough! Or I daresay he is," she muttered, sitting there upon the sand.

She caught hold of my skirts with both hands, and hid her face, and began to sob aloud.

"No, no, he is well enough. It is you, signorina.

Will you go away, and let us be happy once more?
We were so happy before you came. I have been
telling him so, ever so many days past, but it is all
no use. You have bewitched him, and he cares nothing for me. Will you be generous and go away?
You are so handsome, and men care so much for you.
It will be sure to be well with you anywhere."

"Go away!" I echoed, stupidly. I thought I could
not fairly be awake.

"I was so sorry for you in the wood that day," she
went on, pushing my skirts aside, and speaking in
petulant passion, while her round black eyes swam in
tears. "Ah, Holy Gèsu! It is always one's good deeds
that turn round and sting us like wasps. It is very
hard to do right in this world. It costs one so much.
And I was fond of you, donzella; oh yes! I am fond
of you still, if only you will go right away. I will
pray for you night and morning to our own black
Madonna of Impruneta, and she will look after you,
and see you want for nothing. I am sure she will if
I ask her; for I never miss mass on her feasts—not
once; and whenever I have owed her a candle for any
good that she did me I always have paid it, in the
very finest wax, too. She will care for you, that I
am sure; and, besides, what will you want for, anywhere? You can do as you will with men. There
is no strength like that strength. It comes to one
here and there, in tens of millions, they say; and you
have it. I do not grudge you it. Oh no. I would
not have you think that——"

"Think what?" I cried to her, still amazed and bewildered, and not dreaming the truth.

"That I am jealous of you. Oh no, I am not jealous,

But if you would just go away. We were so well till you came. That first night he was wise and I the fool. He said to me, 'Why bind up with our hedgerow flowers this beautiful stray hot-house rose?' And I, like a fool, only laughed at him, and saw no harm. Though, of course, I might have known full well what the end would be. He will kill me, I daresay, for speaking to you. So he must. I would rather die."

I rose and drew away the hem of my dress with which her hands were nervously playing. I looked down on her in incredulous amaze.

"Are you mad, Brunótta? What is it you mean! How can I hurt you? Cannot you speak simply and straightly, and say what it is that you want?"

She cast a scared glance down the long green aisle of the pergola to make herself sure she was not overheard: there was only at the farther end the white wall of the house and the open casement, with the woman still moving to and fro and still singing.

"I mean you to go away," she muttered, under her breath, with a certain sound almost of fierceness in her voice. "To leave him. Cannot you understand?"

"No, I do not understand. Why should you want me away? You were the first who asked me to stay. You mean something more, Brunótta. Speak out——"

"I know I was the first to ask you to wait with us," she cried, with a great sob, half of pain, half of passion. "Have I not said it is always what we do best that most hurts us. It is always so. I speak as plainly as I can. I tell you to go.

"He will kill me, no doubt; so he must. From the very first you bewitched him.

"I might have known a man as poor as Pascarèl does not give away twelve gold florins, making believe they were got back from a thief, without love having something to say in it. He worked very hard to make up those florins; he did all kinds of coopers' and coppersmiths' work ever so long, and you never knew.

"You were so glad to get back your florins you believed any follies he told you.

"He has loved you from the first, that I am sure. That day when he half killed the Sicilian it was out of rage for you, not for me. And only look at him now!

"Before he saw you, there was not such a gay-hearted, mischief-loving, careless creature in all the country. He loved his wine, and his wit, and his comrades, and his nonsense, and he had kisses and jests for every woman he met. I was never jealous of *them*.

"And now not once in ten times will he sup with the men when they ask him: as for the women, he never looks at one; and when he is alone—I mean when you are not there—he just sits dreaming, dreaming, dreaming, and never a word to throw at a dog!"

She paused, breathless from the rapidity and vehemence of her words, and I stood as breathless before her. My face burned; my heart beat; my brain whirled. All wonder, all offence, all amazement, were drowned in me under the flood of my own delicious happiness—he loved me.

I did not think to answer her. I was thinking only of that perfect sympathy, this unutterable gladness, which bound my life to his with silver cords.

A strolling player! I could have laughed aloud in delicious mockery of my old dead pride. A tinker's son! What matter? I cried in my heart; I knew him a king amongst men.

The little shrill, petulant voice of Brunótta came strangely on my ears, as though from far, very far away.

"He will kill me if ever he know!" she was crying. "For he said to me that first night when we had found you in the wood, 'Not a word, Brunótta, never a word —as you value my love and your life.' And I promised him; nay, I swore by all the saints that I would never tell.

"No doubt they will burn me below, sometime, for that; though if they put women in hell for just breaking their word, I cannot think how they find room in the place.

"It is bad to break a promise, I know. But I have begged Pascarèl to send you away from us, and he will not. And so at last I must speak, and I will. It is three years ago last San Giovanni's day since he said to me, 'Piccinina, will you wander with me?'

"We were at the fireworks on the Carraia bridge, you know, and I was frightened and screamed because a rocket fell near me; and he lifted me down into a boat he had got on the river; and there were young men with him, and coloured lanthorns, and wines and sweetmeats, and they sang; and it was all so merry and good, that when he asked me I thought the life would be one big feast day always.

"And I was so sick of the casentino, and the goats and the straw-plaiting; and one had to tell a thousand lies to get a scudo for oneself, the old people were so sharp and so mean; and then all one's savings went in absolution, of course; and such a fuss to get leave to go off to a fair as never was, and such a rage if a youngster kissed one! I remember being beaten black and blue by the old woman after this very fair up here at Fiesole because I went to have my fortune told at the Buda, and there was a brave-looking boy from Prato who was full of money, and——"

She stopped and coloured all over to the brown rings of her pretty hair, and glanced at me with cunning eyes, whilst I listened, comprehending nothing that she said, and waiting in astonished silence to hear the purport of her words.

"So you see, signorina," she went on, breathlessly, "I thought to myself, when Pascarèl in his boat, said to me, half joking, 'Pretty bird, will you fly away with us?' I thought to myself I would jump at it, and get away once and for all from the goats and the plaiting; and then, you know, Pascarèl looks like a marquis; and I knew I should dance as much as ever I liked; and who could tell that he had it in him to be such a tyrant, and would make such a fuss about taking a trinket?

"Ever since that Giovanni's night I have been true to him, quite true to him, that I vow; and if I have had a neckkerchief here and an earring there from a man or two, what does it signify?

"I have never given anything back for it, that I swear by all the saints—scarce a fair word even, for Pascarèl is so fierce. And how can one live in a playhouse as if one were in a convent? It is ridiculous to say such things; and if one may not laugh and gossip, whatever is life worth having?

"And I have put up with all that, though at my age one does not like to be cooped up like an abbess; and I have borne with his temper—and it can be a horrid one, as you might see that day with poor Rosello Brùn—and I have always had a care that he should have a good supper, though for himself he never knows whether he is eating a capon or a crow.

"And then all in a minute it is the donzella this, the donzella that, and one is set aside in everything —a stranger, who has not even so much as a silver bodkin for her hair that she can call her own.

"But if you will go away it will be well again.

"It is your face bewitches him; and that pretty, proud, saucy way you have with you. But if you will go away he will think nothing about you in a month. He forgets very soon, does Pascarèl."

I heard her in perfect bewilderment, my thoughts too astray in their own sweet confusion for me to be able fairly to seize the sense of her words.

"But, Brunòtta, I cannot understand," I murmured. "Why should you not have come with your brother when you found him on Giovanni's night? and why should I be asked to go away now that he——"

I stopped abruptly. My face burned, and I turned a little away from her. I remembered that the affection between us was his secret, and must not be given to the winds by me.

Brunòtta's hands clutched nervously at the scarlet fringes of her dancing skirt; her face paled a little under its ruddy brown; her eyes glanced slyly through the leaves; she strained her throat to see that there was no hearer in the little garden or at the wicket in the acacia hedge; then she dropped her head sullenly,

and, with a little cunning laugh, like a child when it
has broken some precious toy, muttered beneath her
breath—

"Signorina, he is not my brother!"

"Not your brother?" I echoed, vaguely.

Her meaning did not dawn on me. I had never
been deceived by any creature; so far as I knew, no
one had ever told me an untruth; to give and receive
good faith had always seemed to me a law of life as
natural as to draw the breath.

And of any evil I had but the most shadowy con‑
ception. There were women in the world who were
wicked; so much I knew; but of what shape or mean‑
ing their wickedness took I had but the vaguest im‑
agining.

"No! Nobody but a baby like you would ever
have believed that folly," said Brunótta, still crouched
at my feet in the dust, her fingers plucking at her
scarlet fringe. "How you should ever have believed
it I cannot think. There have been thousands and
thousands of things that ought to have told you if you
had not been as blind as an owl in the daylight. But
if you will just go away, it will be as if it never had
been. You must never say that I told you; he would
murder me. Go away quietly. You will come to no
harm. You have a face that is your friend anywhere.
And I will pray to our Lady for you, I will, honestly,
and she will have a care of you. Whenever I have
promised her anything I have always paid it faithfully.
We fell in with a horrible storm off Catania once, and
I vowed her three pounds of candles if we got out of
it safe, and I bought them in the very finest wax and

offered them up at San Frediano the moment I set foot in Florence——"

"Not your brother?" I echoed, dreamily watching the grey cat straying amongst the pumpkins. "You mean you were only his foster-sister. I am not astonished at that."

"He is no brother of mine at all," she retorted, sullenly. "I tell you he is no kith nor kin of mine. I only saw him for the first time that San Giovanni's day three years and more ago. I had never set eyes upon him before. You might have guessed at once— only you are such a baby. And I never would have told you, only I know you love him yourself, and he loves you."

I listened with a strange sound like rushing waters beating at my brain. I did not understand, and yet the green fields, the red vine-leaves, the evening sky, that had grown grey as the sun had sunk behind the hills—all eddied round me in a dizzy maze.

A man—any man, however base, I think—would have had pity on my innocence and bewilderment. But a woman who is jealous has no pity, and Brunótta had none.

She laughed, a forced little laugh, hard, cunning, and cruel—a laugh of envy and vengeance together.

"How strange you look, signorina! I am sure I never dreamt you half believed that story. Who that had eyes in their heads *could* think he was my brother?"

"Not your brother?" I echoed the words mechanically.

That falsehoods were daily human food, that a lie was the small brass coinage in which the interchange

of the world was carried on to the equal convenience
of all, was a truth of which I had no suspicion.

"Not your brother!" I repeated again. "What do
you mean? What is he, then?"

A deadly coldness clutched at my heart as I spoke.
I did not know what I feared or what I thought, but
a great woe seemed suddenly to gather close about me.

Brunótta threw herself on her knees at my feet in
the chequered shadows from the foliage overhead. She
sobbed convulsively in a passion of repentance and
of tears.

"I had sworn to him never to tell you. And now
I have told; and he will kill me if ever he know.

"When we met you in the wood that miserable
day, and I, like a fool, asked you to join your life with
ours, he took me aside, and he said to me, 'What does
the donzella think that we are to each other?' And I
answered him that you had taken it into your head
that I was his sister, and that I had not contradicted
you—that was all.

"Then he said to me, 'So let it rest, then. Mark
my word; I will not have her ears soiled with the
truth. She is innocence itself. If she go with us she
must never know. It is a sorry sort of protection, but
she might fall under worse.' And that night he made
me solemnly promise him—nay, I swore to the saints
—that I would never tell you the truth of my relation
with him.

"I meant to keep my word; I did, indeed. I never
was tempted to break it till that storm about Rosello
Brún. That made me feel mad against you.

"At first I had thought, 'She is a donzella; she
will find her own great people; it will only be for a

little space.' And I felt a sort of love for you; I did indeed. You were so different to me.

"But after that my eyes were opened, and I have watched him, and I have seen that it was you whom he loved, and not me any longer; and then I have thought and thought, 'If I let her stay with him, soon he will not so much as cast a look at me,' and that made me mad; and I said to myself, 'Why should I be so coy with her, and not tell her the truth, when it is easy to see she would ask nothing better than to be in my place.'

"The people do nought but talk of him and you. They know what such *amicizia* means, if you do not; and very nice it is for me to hear their jokes at my expense.

"And then to hearken to him, always—the donzella this and that, and such care had of you as if you were a princess born, when all the while you are a lesser thing than I, for what, pray, do you ever do to get your bread? But I wash, and bake, and stew, and mend his linen, and do all manner of things—to say nothing of my bringing in money for him by my dancing; while you lead a life like any cockered-up peacock on a villa terrace, though all the time, as everyone knows, it costs Pascarèl half the theatre's receipts to keep you and to pay your lodgings.

"And yesterday I saw him look at you—just with that look in his eyes that it is like a sorcery for one; and I would not wait any longer. I said, 'She shall know to-day, and I will see if she will go, or if she will wait and oust me and take my place. It is best to know the worst straight at once.'"

I stood and heard.

CHAPTER V.
Nightfall.

I REMEMBER staring at the russet leaves and the blue sky, at the children under the pear-tree and the grey cat that walked amongst the yellow pumpkins. And that it could be the same world, that it could be going on in the same light and laughter, seemed to me horrible, hideous, incredible.

For me the world was dead.

I did not speak; I did not move.

Brunótta grovelled, frightened and sobbing, at my feet. The beautiful vine foliage, the drooping grapes, the shimmering of sunrays through the darkness of the leaves, the blaze of sunset light on the white wall beyond, the gleam of scarlet from the woman's kerchief moving to and fro in the window, the silver glisten of the earrings in the bowed head at my feet—they went giddily round, and round, and round in a sickening whirl of colour before my blinded eyes.

For many and many a month afterwards, whenever I closed my eyes at night, I saw them still.

"You will not tell him, donzella?" whispered the poor, little, treacherous, cowardly creature on the earth before me, clutching closer the hem of my skirts. "You do not know what his passion can be. He would kill me. He would kill me surely. If you do not care for him, go away; go straight away, and I shall be happy again; he so soon forgets. But if you love him, as I think, best say so to me straight out. I will make an end of my life some way; it does not hurt much. And I could not live to stand by and see you take my place——"

"Your place!"

The outrage broke the spell that held me paralysed. Poor, little, foolish, ignorant, coarse-fibred soul! How could she know the shame she did me? How could she tell the unbearable torture to me of that level with herself to which all ignorantly she dragged me.

But in the pain and desperation of my wound I was incapable of excuse or justice for her.

I was stunned and maddened by the shock of the first sense of falsehood, the first perception of evil, the first horror of treachery that had ever touched me.

Some indescribable unknown guilt seemed to rise around me, like noxious fumes of baleful fires, and stifle all the young life in me. Of the sin of the world I knew nothing; of the treason of it I knew as little.

That I had been betrayed, insulted, outraged, was rather an instinct with me than any reasoned knowledge. He had deceived me; that was all I knew, and all I cared to know.

She grovelled in the sand before me, clutching my skirts, bathing my feet with her tears, beseeching me not to reveal her broken troth to him.

When I thought that he had loved her, and then loved me—oh God! how wretched, base, and poor a thing I grew in my own sight!

I loathed myself as much as I loathed her; and yet, great heavens! how I hated her, because his lips had touched hers; because she, too, had known that touch, that smile, that kiss which, child as I was, I would have given my life away to win one hour!

And *he* loved *her!* this timorous, treacherous, base-born, base-bred fool, who was not even true to him, who had not even such poor, simple, natural virtue in her as lies in loyalty and in good faith.

All the blood in me burned like a flame. I drew my skirts from her grasp, and thrust her away with my foot. Looking back on the unutterable passion and horror of that time, I wonder now I did not strike her.

I understand how men strike women—men who are not cowards either.

"You will not tell him?" she moaned, dragging herself upon her knees again to me. "You will not tell him? You do not know how violent he can be in his rage. You will not tell him? He would kill me."

I thrust her again from me with an unutterable loathing. He had loved her! loved this craven thing which could dare betray him, and yet not dare to brave his vengeance.

"No; I will not tell him," I answered her; the words seemed to suffocate me as I spoke.

She had been good to me once; in her way she had shown me hospitality and good will; she was safe from any revenge of mine.

A sudden fear seemed to fall on her with my answer; not fear for herself, but fear of me. No doubt my face looked strange to her—there, where I stood in the vine shadows, with the golden sunset world reeling around me, and all the beauty of my young life struck dead in me at one blow.

"Are you going away?" she muttered, under her breath. "How you look! I wish now I had not told you. If you love him indeed so much——"

I seized and shook her, mute.

"Oh fool, fool, fool!" I cried to her. "Have you no fear that *I* may kill you?"

I thrust her away once again with such violence that she was driven from me, like a spurned dog, under the shadows of the leaves; and she shivered a little and crouched, and then rose slowly on her feet and stood shivering and sore afraid. But I had taught her silence.

I left her there, and went down the green length of the pergola, out of the gold of the sunny garden, across the archway of the threshold, and so on into the darkness and the coldness of the house.

At every step I dreaded to hear the voice of Pascarèl.

I went up to my own little room, and barred the door, and flung myself on my bed in a stupor of misery.

All my faith in God and man seemed killed in me.

CHAPTER VI.

Along the Mountains.

AGAINST the little square of the open window the breeze gently blew the clusters of roses that had climbed there; the chirp of the birds was shrill on the silence; there was a soft splash of water below as some one filled and refilled the metal pail at the well. All these things were distinct to me and horrible. My love was dead; why were not all other things dead too?

I did not cry aloud, and my eyes were dry; what

I had heard, and the shame of it, seemed to have scorched and shrivelled all the life in me. I was little more than a child. I was all instinct; I had no reason. I abandoned myself without meditation or analysis to any impulse of the moment.

My love for him had been one of the noblest, sweetest, purest impulses of my life. It had been better than myself. All love, if it be worth anything, is higher than the nature that begets it.

My love had subjugated all weaker and vainer things in me; it had vanquished my pride, and my selfishness had been subdued and destroyed by it.

It had been passionless because quite childlike; it had been quite happy only to see him come and go, to have the clasp of his hand, to listen to his fancies and his dreams; it had possibly irritated him often by its unconsciousness and its contentment in so little; and yet it had been intense with all its innocence, and, in its way, perfect.

Had I been older I should have paused and weighed awhile these cruel doubts that had fallen on me, like drops of scalding lead upon an open wound.

Had I been truer and more faithful I should have known that the love of a woman to be worth aught must be dog-like, and take good and evil alike in implicit faith, and kiss the cherished hand that deals the blow.

Had I been wiser in the world's wisdom I should have been able to measure the emptiness and the weariness of these mindless ties, of the soulless bondage woven that fatal night, when, for sake of a rosy face and a smiling mouth, he had said, "will you

wander with me?" as the boat shot away in the moonlight.

But I was only a child, and I loved him with a
child's ignorance and a woman's narrowness, and I
was only alive to the one intolerable unutterable
shame which seemed to fall on me with the coarse
invective of this creature, who begrudged her place
to me.

And with it all, a nobler despair, a deadlier woe,
smote me in the sense—so slow to dawn on me, so
blasphemous, as it still seemed to me—that he could
have told a falsehood to me, that he could have let
me live on and on and on, unthinking and unsuspecting, in the tainted sunshine, in the plague-smitten
beauty, of a paradise of lies.

Since then I have known passions that beside it
were as the rushing stream of lava beside the limpid
mountain burn; yet I doubt if I have ever known a
love, more purely and perfectly love, than this I then
bore to Pascarèl.

And it was all dead—worse than dead; struck in
the eyes, as it were, with all the insult of a blinding
blow. At a stroke, the words of this poor false fool,
had dragged it down from the heaven of its innocent
exaltation, and levelled it with all that was poorest,
basest, meanest, coarsest, in the acrid jealousies of
women and the amorous infidelities of men.

Her jealousy degraded me in my own sight.

Beyond every other thing I was proud. The
evil had been subdued by his influence, but never
uprooted; beneath the sting of torture it rose up in
tenfold strength.

"Take her place—take her place!"

I said the words that had outraged me a thousand times over and over again between my locked teeth. There were times when the ferocity of a beast awoke in me, and I was on fire to spring at her throat and kill her.

For he had loved her once: so I believed, at least; I who knew nothing of men or women either.

Nothing of the brevity of the mere desire of the senses. Nothing of the leaden weight of a sensual bondage. Nothing of the languid reluctance of a sated fancy to strike and free itself. Nothing of the indolent impulses and mindless passions with which the heart of a man may be drawn hither and thither without once touching or sighting the goal of its ideal. Nothing of all which might have given pardon to him, to her, to myself.

The innocence of youth is cruel, because it is of necessity also ignorance, and ignorance is cruelty always.

I did not stir, my eyes were never wet, no cry escaped me; but where I lay, face downward, as I had flung myself, I bit through and through, like a wild animal that is trapped, the woollen coverture of my little pallet bed.

The time went on; the robins ceased to sing, the roses blew against the window frame; when I looked up it was quite dark, and there were stars shining.

I heard the pressure of a foot upon the woodwork of the old, ricketty, worm-eaten door, a feeble, little, sobbing voice began to mutter through it to me of a thousand selfish terrors. The sound of it stung me to blind fury; he would be home at sunset; home to

her and me; one at the least I vowed to heaven he
should not find there.

I had no space for hesitance, no time for thought;
there was but one way—I was young and supple as
a willow bough, and mad with pain—I sprang on
the stone coping of the casement, turned and grasped
the network of the rose-stems, and the boughs of the
fig, knotted and tough from half a century of sun and
storm.

Then holding by that hazardous support, I let my
body drop along the surface of the leaf-covered wall,
dragging a ruin of rose leaves as I fell. The house
was very old and low: I touched the grass beneath
with a dull shock, but without violence; as I reached
the earth I heard above the crash and splinter of
the panels forced and driven in before the blows
of some one whom Brunótta had summoned in her
affright.

It was quite dark; the garden was deserted; I
paused an instant to draw my breath; with the soft
shower of the rose leaves still like tears upon my
face.

I felt bodily pain, but that only served to madden
me, as the lash maddens a beast already bruised; I
leaped the low stone wall of the garden and flew like
a lapwing into the dusky shadows.

Little Toccò leaned over the wall that parted
the garden from the olive orchards. He was singing
clearly a sweet merry melody, and gazing down
through the gloom to try and see who passed across
the bridge. I crept up to him and slid into his hand
the onyx with the Fates.

"Give it to him when he comes," I murmured.

The boy started and stared, no doubt at the changed sound of my voice; but dreading lest he should detain me, I thrust the stone into his hold and fled away through the shadows before he well knew who had spoken to him.

Behind me I heard a noise of many voices, and as the household of the little place roused itself to its Padrona's summons. Turning my head once I saw lights flash in its windows and underneath the trellis of its pergola. I held straight onward, running with winged feet where the grass lands allowed my passage, stumbling and slipping where the maples and the vines woven together opposed my progress.

At times I fell into the trenches cut in the hard soil against the hill floods of winter. At times I bruised myself on the tangled sticks of dying vines.

At times I lost myself amongst the thickets of olive, shining white as the winding-sheets of ghostly apparitions. At times I sank over my feet in shallow brooks that rippled from the mountains, and went on with my garments heavy-weighted with the moisture.

At times I crouched in some shed or under some sheaves of maize to get my breath, and then I saw scattered over the country, close about the little wine-shops, the lights of lanterns that flickered fitfully in and out amongst the foliage; and then I gave myself no rest, but gathered my skirts close and ran again.

At length—it may have been one hour, it may have been three or four, by the look of the stars it was quite night—one of the vineyards that I crossed opened abruptly and without fence upon a highway on which I heard the sound of a horse's feet.

Looking behind I saw no lights; there was only the great brooding darkness of the deserted country, with here and there a silvery gleam as some ray of the young moon caught a belt of olives, or a breadth of water.

I went into the road and waited there. To be beyond their reach I knew I must not pause to rest amidst my flight. I knew, too, that I was nearly at the end of all my force.

Through the gloom there came towards me a white horse, with a red woollen covering spread over it in the Tuscan fashion, dragging slowly a contadino's cart.

As it drew near me I saw, by the light of the lantern which hung at the shafts, that the peasant was an old man of seventy or eighty years.

His cart swayed heavily backward on its wheels; it was filled with straw and earthenware; he dozed as he went, and the horse picked its own way amongst the stones at will.

I called to him and stopped him; he awoke, thinking of roadside robbers, and began to mutter incoherent prayers to a leaden saint in the band of his hat.

I made him, with difficulty, understand that I was harmless and alone and tired, and that if he would give me a lift for a league or two I would pay him well. When he had recovered his alarm, he told me that he was going with his pottery to a fair at Settignano; that to get a good place amongst the stalls it behoved traders to be there whilst the dawn was grey; that he never hurried or harassed his beast, and so had started at nightfall to make his journey by easy stages.

He hesitated some time over my offer, then yielded.

The cart was a light one, he said, and my weight was light too; it would not harm the horse; I might get in amongst the straw if first he saw my money.

I gave him the little gold piece that my father had given me on the stairs in Verona; it had been slung round my neck with the onyx. He let me climb up amidst the rough pottery of his trade stock, and the patient beast set forward again upon its road; the old man settled himself again to doze at ease; the cart creaked onward down the steepness of the slopes, the lantern glimmering redly in the gloom.

He paused a long time in the desolate grey piazza of Fiesole.

All the town was asleep upon its high hills, but there was some friend he knew dwelling by the church who at his rap hung out a lantern on a hook in the wall, and brought him a flask of wine, over which they talked long together in the darkness.

Then the horse jogged on again along the stony gloomy roads, on and on and on into the oak woods of Borgunto, where the great masses of wooded hills sloped away, above and below, in an intense stillness, only broken by the cry of an owl.

It is a winding and difficult road that passes along the side of the mountain from the town of Fiesole to the old fortress of Poggibonzi, and the agony of the slow and weary way seemed endless.

After awhile the clouds broke and the moon shone out; through the oak leaves one could see the vast

silent valley stretched far, far below, and the amphitheatre of the endless hills encircling it. Even in my
stupor and misery I had some vague sense of its wonderful, solemn, mystical shadowy beauty.

Only a week or two before we had gone up that
road on our way from Casentino to the annual fair of
S. Francis at Fiesole, and we had talked of Masaccio
and Desiderio as we saw their little white town on
the slopes, and had gathered the wild anemones that
covered the ground with bloom, and had sung songs
to the mandoline, passing under the acacias by the
fortress walls, and mounting higher and higher and
higher with a gay good-morrow to the smith at the
mountain forge.

Only a week or two before! And now!

The hours passed in a horrible nightmare for me.
The cart shook, jolted, rattled on the stones; my
body was bruised and lacerated by the thickets and
the vines; the palms of my hands were bleeding from
the thorns of the rose-trees; the night was very cold,
as autumn nights are, north of the Abruzzi. But the
misery of my thoughts killed in me all sense of bodily
pain.

All I heard was the sweet music of his voice. The
music·lost to me for evermore.

The night seemed endless.

The horse often paused to rest and crop a little
of the wayside grass or drink at some stone tank in a
monastery wall.

The old contadino awoke now and then to say a
word to it, or to trim his lantern, then slept again,
while the rope of the reins dropped idly from his
wrists.

The road seemed interminable, going down, down, down, along the face of the hills, always with the same stretches of olives and vines on either side, always with the dark vapours of the plain spread like a sea beneath. Now and then an owl flew by with a low croak; now and then there shone a little gleam from some lamp at a roadside shrine—that was all the change there was.

The cart crawled on under the boughs and past the dusky stone walls, still down, down, down into the lower wood, where the oak is changed for the fir tree, and the path becomes sharp and sheer and bent into curves that make the stoutest mule stumble.

The first grey of daybreak had scarcely lightened in the skies when the horse paused at a turn in the descent. The old pottery dealer woke for the first time with eyes wide opened, shook himself, and descended from his seat.

The old man roused me roughly.

"Signorina, you had best get out here if you want Florence. I go to Settignano, and that will be out of your road. Keep straight on, and go down, down, always, and you cannot miss to come to the Croce Gate."

The cart jolted on its way to Masaccio's birthplace, and I staggered, blind, and sick down under the stone-pines.

I felt feeble, broken, aged by ten years. My head was giddy, and the sunshine swam around me in bright rings of amber. I felt numb, and, when I moved, the earth seemed hollow and tremulous beneath my feet.

So, like one blindfolded, I stumbled down into the City that is called Beautiful.

CHAPTER VII.
The Church of the Cross.

It was full sunrise.

The light was streaming from the east, golden and glistening as it came gleaming across the desert. In the streets deep shadows still slept. Lithe brown hands were unloosening the wooden lattices, and flowers pent in casements thrust their heads out to the air.

All was very quiet.

There was only the sound of the bells tolling for the first mass of the churches, tolling everywhere, north and south, east and west, over the wide val-darno. Here and there a priest passed to some holy office; here and there a sun-belated reveller went gaily home touching a mandoline; here and there a woman with brown bare arms swept down her steps or hung her linen out of window, gossiping the while to neighbours across the passage-way.

It all went giddily and dimly round before my sight. I was faint, and my limbs shook as I dragged them over the stones.

There was a sound of footsteps and of outcries behind me.

On the sheer instinct of the hunted deer, I paused and shrank into the shade, and gazed around for shelter. Close against me the doors of the S. Croce stood open. The vast, dark, solemn church yawned like a grave. I crept into the shadow of its porch.

At its altars they were saying the first mass.

A lady, all lace and jewels, as she had come from some palace ball, was on her knees in the dusk and the solitude praying, while the voices of the priests echoed dully under the vast vaulted roof that shelters the dust of Michelangelo and Giotto.

Behind me were the darkness, the coldness, the peace of the great church, the lights burning dimly far away, the sepulchral undertones thrilling the stillness.

Before me, in the open air, there came, swift as the wind, a rush of feet, a clamour of angered voices, a shower of weapons, a tramp of horses, a cloud of dust, a flash of daylight, and, in the midst, a gleam of beautiful bold eyes that last had looked at me in the white moonshine underneath the leaves away on the hill-side by Dante's Solitude.

The crowd went by like a whirl of dust and of leaves on a day of scirocco. I sprang and caught the arm of an old man who had uncovered his head reverently as it went by the church.

"What is it? Oh, nothing," he said, with a shadowy smile. "Nothing. They broke on the wheel in *my* time. How scared you look, you pretty child. It is only the ducal guard who are taking Pascarèl to the Bargello; and the people want to rescue him, that is all. Done? No, he has done nothing that I know of; but the town cares for him, and he tells awkward truths, and it has been easy to seize the salt in his speech and tax it. There was a sort of riot yesterday, and he quelled it; but they made that an offence against him. A player and a populano! What right has he to power?—to such power as Love gives and gets? So they arrested him last night, and they take him now to the Podestà for judgment. I daresay they will give him three months in prison. For the Bargello is strong and the people are weak as yet."

The old man, still with that subtle wintry smile upon his face, shook my hold off him, and went feebly along the street.

The crowd in its cloud of dust had passed from sight. I lost all sense of where I was, and fell, like one dead, upon the stones of Florence.

———

BOOK VI.

THE QUARTER OF THE DOVE.

CHAPTER I.

Oltrarno.

You know the old old quarter, whose emblem on the banners that were borne in war around the red Carroccio, was the Silver Dove? The church is there, though flame has ravaged it thrice; but the standard that bore the bird of the Holy Spirit over the reek and carnage of the plains has crumbled away none know whither in some closet or crypt of the city.

Yet the quarter is barely changed at all, since in the days of the Republic the men of San Lorenzo and of San Giovanni crossed the river to sack it from end to end under the storm of arrows and the rain of fire.

It is dark, and dull, and noisy, and noisome there in the old historic quarter of the Silver Dove: and yet it is so full of story, so sacred, with so many names and memories, that there is a charm about its twisting gloomy streets, its high walls shutting out the sun, its dungeon-like chambers, its iron-bound palaces, grim and firm set as sea-washed cliffs, its huge archways dark as Erebus, its narrow passage-ways where two mules can scarce pass one another over the slippery and uneven stones.

It is all haunted ground in old Oltrarno. Come

to it in a summer morning. There is no sun in it,
except in some square-walled garden behind the
frowning front of some antique, coronetted house,
where stray sunbeams make a glory on shining lemon-
boughs and broken water-cisterns. It is all dark, for
the houses are so high, and the walls lean so close.
It is full of the strange, dreamy old-world Florentine
odour, that smells always as though some king's coffin
had been freshly opened, and the spices and the per-
fumes of the cere-clothes lately loosened on the air.
The people are walking, leaning, gossiping, laughing,
quarrelling, all in the open street, and at the open
threshold. The cobbler is at his stall; the tinker at
his barrow; the huckster at his board of cloths and
linens; the melon-seller at his truck of green paponi.
In every one of the great dusky interiors there is an
etching worthy of Rembrandt. In every one of the
sculptured, unglazed windows, there is a study of
colour fit for Velasquez. It is all dark, and dusty,
and noisy, and noisome, I say, and yet in its way it is
beautiful—the place is so gruesome, and the people
are so gay.

And then—so many steps are echoing after yours,
so many faces look at you from the grated windows.

See—in that dim street there is old Toscanelli's
white head bending over the charts busy with vague
dreams of the unknown world across the seas;—yonder
enters a saucy, airy, ribboned, plumed cavaliere, who
sings a stornello as he goes, and fingers the sprig of
box with which he is playing the Lenten love game,
begun in Carnival with the original of Madama Pam-
pinet;—away behind the Carmine church, where gentle
Masaccio came and painted in his title-deeds to im-

mortality, runs a little barefoot, ragged imp, his mouth full of stolen convent cherries, whom poor old Mona Lapaccia tries to catch and lead to the good friars to be fed and clothed, and made in his due time into Fra Lippì;—under the deep shadows of the walls there goes to his sombre and frugal home the finest wit and keenest logician of the Rucellai Gardens, musing on sore straits of personal poverty, and foreseeing, perhaps, with a certain delicate, cynical sadness, that he who lives with clean hands the honestest of men in Florence will so pass down to posterity that the name of Machiavelli will be used, to all time, as synonym for Prince of Rogues.

See there—who comes down hither in the gloaming of the last night of Carnival? by the corner that is called of the Lion, under the shade of the Carmelite's church? Handsome and reckless still, as when he, Benvenuto, hurled defiance at Diane de Poitiers from the Tour de Nesle,—prince of craftsmen and king of egotists—since his eyes opened to the light in the little house in the Chiara street, full of its flutes and clavecins and harpsichords, its mirrors of silver and its viols of ivory, wherein, in the winter nights, the old father sat "singing all to himself" by his brave oak fires for pride and gladness of heart, because a son was born to him and to the city. He is come to seek the recreant Tonino,—he has left his workshop in the Mercato strewn with grotesques in gold and acanthus leaves in silver, and blazonries in enamel, and lilies in diamonds, and poniards in damascened metal;—the sword that hangs by his belt was red a little while ago in the sack of Rome;—the gold crowns in his pouch are payments for Fontainebleau from King Francis—he is in anger and in haste, yet going thus through the darkness to the ingrate monk he thinks a little wistfully, great artist and reckless liver though he be, of the old days when he and Michelangelo, and Piloto, the goldsmith, used to saunter hither on summer eves to listen to the madrigals when all the dim night world was dewy with the scent of roses.

See there, yet again,—through the gloaming, goes a white-frocked Dominican, with bent head and meditative eyes; of all the many thousand monks in Florence, he is "Il Frate" to the people. When he scourges himself in the crypt, and sees the pictures and the sculptures feed the flames, does he ever sigh for that old bright vine-hung bottega where he woke with the sunrise and worked till the evening bells, when he was only Baccio della Porta, the painter, dwelling just outside the gate here, where the cypresses guard the entrance of that glad green country whose smiling beauty gained it its gentle name of Verzajà even in the dry grim records of the city's rolls?

Down the old street of the Augustines there comes a group of merry-makers fresh from the laughter and the wine-cups of the supper at the tavern by the Tower of the Amidei away by the Jewellers' Bridge. They loiter in the moonlight to hearken to the sweet singing of the street-choristers, and note with painters' eyes one beautiful, gentle, golden curled youth, to whom many a white hand undoes a casement, or lets drop a lovescroll tied with a tress of hair. They are men who are called Michelangiolo, and Cellini, and Bugiardini, and Albertinelli, and Manzuolini

A little while, and Michelangiolo paces the stones alone, with his cloak wrapped about him and his hand ready to his sword-hilt, and his heart heavy for the fate of free Florence; for the bell of the people has long rung a stormo, and his cannon bristle and his bastions rise on the old monastic heights, and the fire has burnt black the shady gardens of Gicciardini, and above them, on the hills where Corsini built the cloisters for the Augustines to dwell in all their days in peace, there the fierce Spaniards are crying, "Lady Fiorenza, bring out your brocades, and we will measure them at the pike's length;" and there, too, floats that banner which has been for ever the malediction of Italy, on whose yellow folds there is blazoned black,

> "l'Aquila grifagna
> Che per più divorar due becchi porta:"

In the morning when the birds are singing in the old grey gardens behind the old grey palaces, and the walls lean together and frown against the sun, you, thinking of all these who have trodden the stones before you, shall stray slowly down the Via Maggiò— the Street of the Maytime—the street named from the sweet season of the lilies and the lovers in the old amorous days of free Florence, when, with the first morning of May, the youths of the city went forth from the gates by the sunrise, and came back with the spoils of the woods and the fields to the sound of the lute and the viol, and at every grated casement hung up the branch of hawthorn, and the knot of ribbon, and the scroll of love words, each wooer for his own innamorata, so that under the green wreath of leaf and blossom the dark iron-bound walls looked

like the helmet and hauberk of Rinaldo flower-decked
by the rose trails of Armida on the amorous banks of
Orontes.   And so musing, you shall pass out by the
gates and feel the sweet winds blowing fresh again
over the vine-lands of the Vald'ema, and you shall
meet a woman carrying white roses with her to lay
upon some tomb upon the hill there; and you shall
think of the night feast of Pardon, when all Florence
was wont to flock up hither under the stars to wash
their souls clear before the fall of Pentecost; and so
quiet of heart, and yet glad for the beauty of dead
days, and of the living summer time, you will go up
and up higher and higher till you reach the stillness
of the olive-woods upon Arcetri.

Shall you be dull and weary in dark Oltrarno—
now?

Nay, not if you have eyes that see, and ears that
hear.

But the world is full of deaf and blind.

CHAPTER II.

At Boccaccio's Window.

I was both blind and deaf in that horrible time.

I think a flower, when they break it off its stalk
and throw it down to sicken in the sun, must feel as
I did all those weeks and months. Only the flower
faints and dies, and is so far at peace; but I lived on,
though all my youth, and heart, and soul, and hope
were killed in me.

It seems so long ago; so very, very long ago; and
yet at times near, as though it were only yesterday,

that I saw the people sweep past the great gaunt pallor of the Santa Croce, his face in their midst within the reddening light of dawn.　The vast yawning dark—the woman with her jewels at her prayers —the gleam of the silver at the altars—the sweet shrill voices of the singing children—the rush of the crowd—the ghostly gleam of day—how near they all are, and yet so far.　Sometimes I fancy they were only dreams—dreams, too, all that one glad summer year of wandering—and then I go slowly over the links that bind me to the time, as other women in their pain tell beads.

The links are clear enough, but I can say no prayer to them.　My beads are full of thorns, and hurt me—still.

There must be good people, though one doubts it so.　A woman saw me fall thrice on the stones before the Florentine Pantheon, and had me borne upstairs to her little chamber before the Misericordia bell could boom for me.　She was an old woman, and quite poor; she got her living darning the silken hose of dancers and of ladies; she lived in that little crooked passage-way under the shadow of the Pitti, where old Toscanelli dreamed his way across the unknown waters to the unknown land, and gay Boccaccio, with his cynical fine smile, loitered to see the dames of Florence pass in their gold-fringed litters and their gemmed zibellinè to the feasts in the Palaces of Bardi and Frescobaldi.

She was a little brown, crisp, clean woman, seventy years old; she had a wide, bare, stone chamber under the unceiled roof; all day long she darned at the stockings, looking now and then out of the window, as Boccaccio had done before her, but seeing no gold-fringed litters and jewelled dames, but only the weary mules, and the pushing people, and the pedlar's stall of cloth and linen, and the cobbler at his work over the way.

In that barren chamber I lay sick unto death for weeks, talking in so strange a confusion of cities and villages and flowers and singing birds, and the notes of lutes and the shine of the moon on the maize fields, that none who heard could make sense of the medley. There she kept me; there I slowly got my hold again on life as youth will even when most re-luctantly; there I recovered in a dull, hopeless, sullen, stupid way; and there the dreamy days would roll away with gleams of the beautiful rose-flecked sky just left to madden one above the frowning palace pile.

The old creature would sit in her garret window sewing on at the silken hose; there was delicate carv-ing all about the window, and a great shield with a marquis's crown above; it had been a palace in the old days when the San Lorenzo men had set all Ol-trarno ablaze from the Niccolò gate to the Frediano. There she would sit and sew; chirping to my dull deaf ears in her Tuscan; she had stories for all the stockings that used to lie in a great mixed heap in a rush basket—the needy duchessa's with the gay bal-lerina's.

"See!" she would say, holding one after another up to the strong light. "See! what a little atom that is—just worn in the ball of the foot with dancing,—a fairy might put it on, and for certain a lover has been glad to stroke it, many and many an hour when the dance was over and done with, and the fire-flies put their lamps out ere the sun rose, and in the balcony where those little feet were, it was all so still—so still."

"And then again," she would go on, diving down for a stocking thrice the size, "a big one this, no beauty in it; broad as a pumpkin leaf and thick as any melon—worn in the toes—you know what that means. Pirouettes by the dozen on the Pagliano boards; standing strained on tip-toe as a Lotus Lily or a Queen of Night. No story in it that is pretty like the lover's to the little fairy feet. And yet, perhaps, you know, some poem after all; some homely thing sung to a baby's cradle and a shuttle's swing, in some weaver's bare garret where the meal-pot would be empty and the stove be empty too, if the young, fresh, brown mother did not run out into the cold and strip her kirtle and dress herself in clouds and flowers to dance for a silver coin before the gay theatre lights? Ay—who knows? A big, square, ugly pair of hose, no doubt, but worth the better darning maybe than those dainty ones of the pretty marchesina's, after all."

So she would chirp to herself, driving her long needle deftly all the day; a poet who could not read, but only feel, like many millions of her country people.

Pascarèl would have talked with her for the hour and found her histories for all the stockings tumbled in the rush basket on her feet. But I—her chirping made my heart more sick, my brain more dull, my life more desolate. I was thankless, so utterly and cruelly and unremorsefully thankless, as only very early youth can be.

For in later years we throb all over with so many wounds, that we have learned to value the hand that plucks a dockleaf for our nettle sting, though we know well no balm can heal the jagged rent in the breast that no man sees.

Old Giùdettà darned her hose under the sculptured shield, and trotted to and fro between the lattice and my bed of sacking in the corner where she had laid me, and prayed for me every chilly morning in the great white silence of the Sta. Spirito, and begged her own brass-framed red and blue picture of the Madonna to have a care for me, though I seemed but a sad little pagan to her, where I lay and sobbed and moaned wearily through all the sickly hours.

How good she must have been, a woman so old as that, and so poor that she sewed stockings from the first peep of the sun to the last flare of the oil-wick. Yes; she must have been good indeed. She died after one day of sickness only, a year later, so I heard; her needle in her old worn, tired hand, smiling, they say, and wondering if the Madonna would ever let her darn a little there in heaven for mere old remembrance sake.

I told them, when I heard that, to set her up the whitest, fairest cross that ever shimmered in the light above there under the cypresses on the dusky Miniato slopes. Cold gratitude, you say?—but am I worse than nations when I measure my debt by a stone's height and breadth?

There is nothing so ingrate as a great grief; and mine was bitterly thankless, utterly apathetic. I took what she did for me indifferently as a right; I had no thought of her; all the thought I had was with that sweet dead hour when the vintage moon had shone above Fiesole.

She would sit and chirp all day in her sonorous Tuscan; she had darned stockings all her life, she said, drawing her threads so fine no one could tell where the silk once had gaped.

She was most good to me, and I most thankless.

She was very poor; but she pinched herself in her measure of oil and her handful of meal to tempt my sickening indifference with the rosy heart of some prickly southern fig, or fresh pomegranate. She was childless and cheery, and loved by her neighbours, and had no need of me: yet hardly could a mother have been more patient with my ingratitude and fierce despair than she was. I was so young, and friendless, and unhappy, it was plain to see. That touched her, and she kept me. Ah, you who say there is no honest fruit of love and grace beneath that sweet wide-opened sun-swept flower, of an Italian smile—how little way you see, and how you lie!

Did ever you hear of Signa Rosa? Nay—not you.

She lived forty years in widowhood on the sea-shore by Nizza; a small, slender, beautiful old woman, very beautiful, they say,—I never saw her, for she died in my babyhood, but I have heard this from many tongues,—well, she bound the peasant's coif about her head, and did her homely service daily for herself, and never stirred across her threshold except when early mass was ringing over the orange thickets; but her country folk sought her from far and near for consolation and for counsel; in her the dove's gentleness and serpent's wisdom were blended; peace-making was her office; and none sought her who did not leave her simpler, purer, better for her words of solace; so she dwelt for near half a century, the sanctity of the cloister about her, yet in her the warmth of human sympathy, the sweetness of widowed fidelity, and the passion of maternal love; so she dwelt where the palms of the riviera rise against the blue sea skies, and when she died ten thousand Italians followed her to the grave, and to this day the country numbers her with its holiest names.

For Signa Rosa was the mother of Garibaldi.

Without such women, think you that Italy would ever have such sons?

Indifferent to, insensible of, anything that moved around me, I listened and answered with no sense of what I heard or said. I used to lie and watch the figure of Giùdettà, brown against the golden sunset lightened panes; and wonder feebly why I could not die—that was all.

It was the winter season of pleasure and pomp.

One morning lying there face downward on my mattress of grass, I heard gay, tumultuous shouts and bursts of music, and the shrill pipe of eager voices, and the sun was shining yellow and broad across the floor.

Another little old woman, a gossip of Giùdettà's, came and stood by me awhile; she had a new dark kirtle, and a scarlet ribbon in her white hair, and some brave silver rings in her ears.

"I wish you could get up and come, poverina," she said kindly. "You are so young to lie and die like a motherless kid there; and they are bringing in the Carnival, and it is good to see. I have never missed once for seventy-two years!"

I shivered and turned farther from her sight, and buried my face in darkness.

The familiar merry welcome name of the old Catholic king struck like a knife into my aching heart.

All the day long I lay there shrinking from the sun rays, and striving to hide from the sounds and the shouts of the streets. The chiming bells, the laughing voices, the furious fun, the blaring trumpets, all came in a dull echo across the river into the chamber where I lay; and I shuddered and cowered down as those do who, in the dead of night, believe that they behold the risen ghosts of their lost and buried loves.

Mercifully for me, Carnival reigned and rioted on the other side of Arno, and in the old still dusky quarter of the Silver Dove silence and solitude only had dominion as the people flocked across the bridges and left it to the coming of the chilly twilight.

Giùdettà stayed with me, and sat at her work in the casement.

"We are always dull in old Oltrarno," she said.

I was thankful. I shivered where I lay, when on the nights of Dominica across the river from the arches by the Vecchio Bridge there floated to us the distant tumult of the Midnight Fairs.

The Carnival went by, and all the coolness of Quaresima, and the bright brevity of Pasquà, followed it, and in their turn passed by and dropped into the things that were.

I heard the shrill gala shouts and the clamour of the Berlingaccio; I heard the Lenten bells swing in monotonous measure from dawn to eve; I heard the joyous cries of the lovers and the children tossing their Easter eggs into each other's breasts, or bearing home their sheaves of palm. I heard it all telling the passage of the feasts and seasons as chiming clocks ring away the dying hours. I heard it all sitting against the empty stone hearth, heart-sick, and weaving the threads to and fro, to and fro, to and fro.

For me, every one of those fasts and feasts had voice, and the dead days lived in them, as a dead child lives for its mother in the tones and the glance of every laughing yearling that creeps out to catch her black skirts in rosy fingers. She shudders from the tender touch;—so I shuddered from the sunny hours.

CHAPTER III.

By the Mouth of the Lion.

THE cold had gone; it was the balmy, cool, spring weather united with the golden Tuscan noons and the roseate Tuscan twilights that had welcomed me when I had first passed the gates of Florence. I had been three months with Giùdettà, and had not left my bed. I was a wan, shrunken, tired thing, with immense startled eyes and short clipped curls; few would have recognised in me the child that had wandered in the wake of the Arte through all the blossoms of the year from the bright crocus to the tremulous cyclamen.

One day I was lying listless and feeble in my dark room, where no ray of light could come from the narrow grated casement, when suddenly there arose upon the noonday quiet a rush of many feet, and a wide echo of deep voices that seemed to rend asunder the old walls.

She sitting by the window, thrust her stocking off her arm, and leaned as far out as the grating would allow her; a little, bent, eager, curious figure with the glow of the noon light catching the silver rings in her ears.

"Che, che!" she cried. "What a clamour and clatter,—all the town is out,—they have those free three-coloured flags, too, that the lads got shot so often for, years ago, and that the priests say will always bring on us poison in the wells and pestilence. There is little Tista, the baker's son, amongst them; he is always a bit of tinder. Ah, Tista, Tista, tell me what it is all about. Are the people mad?—or is Giotto's gold cap put atop the campanile?—or is the Pope come? Che, che! Stop a bit, Tista, and say a word, boy."

There was a shrill boy's voice, clear as a silver trumpet upon Easter day, that pierced above the din and joyous uproar and came through the darkness of the chamber to me.

"It is Pascarèl set free of the Bargello, and we make high holiday. Dress your casement, good mother, and at sunset bring a light there, or we will break it sure to-night."

I sprang from my bed—I whose wasted, fever-stricken limbs for three long months had never known me upright,—I bruised my bare arms and my hollow cheek against the iron grating; I beat my aching breast against the bars like any fresh caged bird. But all I saw was the gay glad tumult of the crowd heaving and gathering under the broad sunshine, with the three colours of free Italy tossing high against the scarlet cross of Florence. Then, too weak to stand, my feet

11*

gave way beneath me, my hands loosed their hold upon the stancheons, the bright multitude in the narrow, dusky street was blotted into utter darkness; I fell moaning and bruised upon the garret floor.

At night she hung her light within her window, as Tista, the baker's son, had bidden her; and went quietly herself to vespers, as was her wont. Ever since I had heard the one name ring down the street, I had leaned there, pressed against the grating, to watch the return of the people through Oltrarno.

I loved him so—dear Heaven! and yet almost I hated him. He had deceived me! He had deceived me!

This was the iron in my soul. It is an error so common! Men lie to women out of mistaken tenderness or ill-judged compassion, or that curious fear of recrimination from which the highest courage is not exempt. A man deceives a woman with untruth, not because he is base, but because he fears to hurt her with the truth; fears her reproaches, fears a painful scene; and even when she is quite worthless, is reluctant to wound her weakness. It is an error so common! But it is an error fatal always.

Night fell quiet; the oil-lamp glimmered in the casement. I forgot the light it shed upon my face, but crouched there, watching with wide beaming eyes the coming of the crowd.

The eighth hour echoed from the Vecchio as there rolled in on the silence—the deep sea-like sound of a rejoicing people. The tramp of many feet came distinctly over the bridges. The swell of song vibrated against the massive walls.

Strained against the grating, I watched and listened.

Then, after a little space, they poured through

the narrow passage by the Lion's Mouth, they came, the people of Oltrarno — artizans, painters, mosaic-sellers, wood-cutters, cobblers, traders, all in a confused moonlight struggle, with banners above them and shouts rising from them; and in their midst my darling, with the white moonlight on his dark straight poetic brows and on his dreamful eyes.

Breathless I pressed against the iron bars — breathless I gazed, as only any creature can who, for months of silence and of absence has never once looked upon the face it loves.

I forgot the light shed on me — he looking up at the eager people that filled every illumined casement, saw me where I leaned, and with one great cry, like the cry of a drowning man, he sprang down from the height on which they bore him aloft upon their shoulders, and forced his way up the ink-black slope of the steep stairs, and thrust his foot against the fastened door, and broke into the room.

Then with a great cry he caught me in his arms, and held me close there in the great darkness, as a man will hold some dear thing dead. How many moments went I know not; as there are years in which one does not live a moment, so there are moments, I think, in which one lives a lifetime.

The moonlight went whirling by; the darkling shadows swam round me like eddying waters; the floors trembled; then my eyes closed beneath his kisses, my sense grew faint, the world was dark — all dark. But it was the sweet, hot darkness of a summer night; and even then I know I prayed, so far as I could pray, that I might die in it.

The trance of passion passed.

After a while, whether the time was short or long I cannot tell, the cloud upon my senses seemed suddenly to lift; the deathlike trance of passion passed. I lifted my head, and strained myself backward from his hold, and shivered where I stood.

For I remembered.

He, with a quick vague fear awakening in his eyes, held me against him.

"Why look at me like that?" he cried, and then was still.

What I answered I cannot tell. All madness of reproach that ever any tongue could frame, I know left my own lips in that blind, cruel hour. All excuse for him and all goodness in him I forgot: ah, God forgive me, I forgot! He had deceived me; that was all I knew or cared to know.

I had longed for his touch, his look, his word, as prisoners for liberty, as dying youths for life; and yet, now that he was there, all the pride in me flamed afresh, and burned up love. All that I poured on him were hot upbraiding, and broken bitter scorn.

"You shall not touch me, you shall not touch me!" I cried to him, wrenching myself from his hold as we stood there, in the paleness of the moonlight, with the shouting of the baffled and impatient crew filling the air with its strange tumult; in the noise, in the flashing light, in the sudden passion of joy and. terror, of love and hate, my brain was gone. I had only this one memory left, and with it the instinct to wither him with his shame.

I do not know either what he said in answer. I knew he kneeled there in the moonshine, kissing my hands, my dress, my feet, pouring out to me in all the eager fervid eloquence of his nature the rapture, the woe, the wonder, the sorrow, the shame, and the remorse that turn by turn had their sway over him.

"Loved her!" he cried, as I flung the word back on him again and again and again in the fury of my solitary instinct. "Loved her! Oh, God! do not profane the word—oh, child! how should you know? Love? What has love to do with the mindless follies and the soulless vagaries of men? One catches the rotten pear that falls with golden skin across one's summer path; but what fruit of thought, what flower of fancy, what fragrance of heart or soul can there be there? Another passer-by had had it, coming first. Oh, gioja mia! oh, anima mia! listen, listen, listen, and believe! If you love me, be jealous as you will of the wind that touches me, of the sun that shines on me, of the air I breathe, or of the earth I tread, but never be jealous of a soulless love. There is no dead thing in its cold corruption that a man can ever loathe as he loathes that!"

I shut my ears to the sweet pleading of his heart. I wrenched my hands from him. I struggled from his arms.

"Ah! so you say, ah! so you say," I said to him. "But why should I believe you? You deceived me once!"

His head bowed itself down upon my feet; he was silent a moment, then he raised his face quite bloodless as the dead are in the chill moonrays.

"Oh, my darling! I know, I know!" he murmured softly. "But be gentle, have patience; what else then could I do? I was frank with you—as frank as I could be; not to lay evil bare beneath your guileless eyes. I told you from the first we were unfit for you; only you pleaded so to stay, and my heart pleaded for you. You were so young, so helpless, so utterly lonely in your defenceless ignorance; and I tried to get better shelter for you, and I failed. And you were happy, and you heard no harm. It was a shame to love you, and let one's-self be loved. Ah, yes! I know, but it was all so natural, so innocent, so unforeseen; ah, light of my eyes! I sinned to you, indeed. But all the while I strove so hard to do my duty to you,—such poor and feeble duty as I could. Can you not forgive me that I erred in weakness?"

Almost I yielded as I heard; the crowd, astonished and impatient, surged with loud outcry through the narrow street below; but all that I had ears for was that sweet, sonorous, passionate voice that had made its music for me in the old dead days in the moonlightened fields, whilst the maize was all ablaze with the love fires of the lucciolei. Almost I yielded: all the life in me was yearning for his life; for the softness of silent kisses; for the warmth of folded hands, for the gladness of summer hours spent side by side in the ilex shadow, for the passion and the peace of mutual love that smiles at the sun, and knows that heaven holds no fairer joys than those which are its own, at the mere magic of a single touch!

Almost I yielded, held there by his close-clasped arms, his face looking upward as he kneeled there where the moonrays fell.

A moment—a word—and it was mine again; mine for evermore; mine a thousandfold more strong in sweetness, and more sweet in strength than I had known it whilst the wild libeccio blew the fragrance from the trampled grasses and the trodden grapes and the tossing roses on the hillside on the night of the saints beneath Fiesole. A moment, and it was mine. And I, oh fool! oh poor, vain, proud, half-hearted little fool! I shut my heart to him, and shuddered in scorn from the deep dreamful delight that stole upon me like a trance.

Should the lips that had touched hers seek mine again? should the man who could sink to that baseness of a sensual bondage kneel at my feet and pray to me for union of my soul with his?

I dared not trust myself to look on him; I flung my head back, and strained against the all-compelling force of his embrace.

"You talk—you talk—you talk—as poets do!" I cried to him, in my vain, bitter, childish rage. "It is your art, your trade! You string the terza rima for a brazierfull of contadini's pence—any night they ask you—at a village fair. A poet—you, who for three years could find companionship in such as she; who, for all those seasons could stay unshamed and show yourself upon your stage beside her like your own dancing dog beside its chained and collared mate! I will not hear you—no! It is too late. Go to her— go! Since once you found your level with her, keep it. It is too late, I say:—words?—oh, yes! They are your art; I know. You can make men weep, and laugh at them in your sleeve. You can make children laugh; and you all the while as weary and sad as death. That is your trade, to lie. A little lie or two —one more or less—what does it signify? You dupe a woman—what of that? It is your art to fool the world with the sham artifice of every counterfeit emo-

tion.   Practise on every fool that loves you—her or
me, or any other—what does it matter? you are still
upon your stage!"

He loosed his arms from round me and rose
slowly, staggering a little in the dusky shimmer of the
shadows and the moonbeams. There was a look upon
his face that I had never seen there. God forgive me!
So, I think, must a man surely look who gets his
death-blow straight through flesh and bone, and lives
a second's space to look death in the face.

"You say that—you?" he murmured; and then
was still, resting his eyes upon my own in an un-
spoken reproach, that pierced me like a knife thrust
through my heart.

"Yes, I say it—I—why not?" I cried to him, stung
by remorse at the pain I dealt, and yet driven on by
what I deemed my wrongs. "Have I not seen you,
heard you, watched you a hundred times if once,
playing at any passion that you would?   Of course it
was so easy to cheat me, a child that trusted you,
and took your every word as a fixed law of God's!
From first to last you know that you deceived me;
from the day you gave me the gold florins, to the
night you said you loved me. If you had loved me,
would you have let me live in that paradise of falsehoods for one single hour? Would you not rather
have sought for me my father and my kindred! I
come of a great race; I told you so; somewhere in
the world live people who would own and shelter me,
people who would lift me up into some light of fair
repute and of known dignity. If you had loved me,
that is the thing you would have done; I being too
young, and poor, and simple, and ignorant to be ever

able to do it for myself: you boast of honour; you say you are the last of a once mighty line, though only now a wandering player; if it were so, if you were worthy of the loyalty and love those people in the streets give to you for their country's sake, would you have let your feet rest or your eyes close until you should have given me some firm, straight place in life, some hold upon my kith and kin, some knowledge of my heritage? For me it is impossible; but for you to have done that, how easy! *Then*, indeed, I might have said you loved me."

He was quite quiet as he listened. Men are so generous—oh, heaven, yes, how generous—for only think how rare it is that ever a man will strike a woman? And they, themselves, daily, hourly, incessantly stung, and bit, and galled, and chained by scorpion words and adder kisses! Men are so generous; he was so. He never once lifted up his voice and said, as he might have said so justly: "And what title had I to serve and save you? Why did I not leave you as I found you, a beggar in the ilex wood that day?"

He was quite quiet. All the glow and eagerness and fervour of passion had died off his face; it grew cold, and colourless, and still, with the impenetrable stillness of an Italian face that masks all pain.

"No doubt you are right," he said, gravely. "It would have been better had I done so. But,—you doubt I loved you,—I?"

In lieu of such a gentle word as that, why did he not throw me down under his feet, and cast on me his goodness and his grace, his tender thoughtfulness and patient care of me, like coals of fire on my vain,

foolish cruel head? If men set their heel more often
on what is weak and worthless, I think women might
be better than they are; God knows.

All my old perfect love for him, all my old perfect
faith in him, welled up in my faint heart and almost
broke the forces of my bitter vanity and greed. Almost, but not quite; for what I knew, might he not
have come to me fresh that very night from the babbling lips and the brown hands of his old toy?

I was passionate with woman's passion; I was
cruel with children's cruelty.

"Why should I believe you?" I cried to him.
"You have let me believe a lie--once!"

His face flushed crimson, then grew very pale
under its olive darkness. I think he looked as a dead
man must do. He shrank a little as though one had
struck him a blow, a blow that he could not return.

"You have a right to reproach me as you will,"
he said very gently. "And how should you know,
how should you know?"

A heavy sigh ran through the words and made
them barely audible. He looked at me very long,
very wistfully, with no passion in his eyes, only a
despair, that was so great that it chilled me into
speechless terror. For it was so unlike himself, or at
least I thought so in my ignorance. He paused a
moment, looking so.

A convulsion of longing seized me to throw myself
into his arms and cling to him for ever, for ever, for
ever, forgetting all and all forgiving. But I was a
child; I was fierce, I was ignorant, I was wayward,
and I had been wounded in the one sweet, sacred,
perfect faith of my short life. I stood there silent and

unyielding; my burning eyes were tearless, my scornful mouth was mute.

There must have been that in my attitude, or in my look, or in my silence, that stung him like some insult, for the blood flashed back into his face, and he raised himself with his old dauntless and grand gesture.

"Even *you* shall not say that twice," he murmured. "I will serve you in other ways, God willing, but you shall not see my face again. Farewell."

Before I had measured the force of what he had said he had gone; turned away and passed from sight.

A single step, a single cry would have called him back. But I stood motionless and silent still; and let him go: O God!

The clamorous people thronging the staircase and the stairs, filled the night with their loud outcries. I called him back, but all in vain; my voice was drowned in the tumult as a child's death-cry in a storm at sea.

CHAPTER IV.

Dead Roses.

THIS was in the week that followed upon Pasquà.

The summer months went by, and I neither counted them nor knew what they were bringing.

The days and nights passed by in an agony, at times fierce and at others dull, but always agony like that of a gunshot wound which burns like a flame one hour and aches like a bruise another.

The face of Pascarèl I never saw; and once when

little Tista went by and Giùdettà asked him what was become of the wild fellow for whom he had made her burn her lamp all night, Tista called up to her sadly, "He is out of the city, mother; and we are flat as ditch water—all of us."

I never stirred out;—never once.

I thought that it would make me mad to see the sun shine upon his Florence—and I did not fear death, but I feared madness.

I had seen it once, in a beautiful dark woman in old Ferrara, whose lover had been swept down in the winter floods and drowned before her eyes, and she was forever walking to and fro along the water's edge and calling to it to give up her 'Dino; I had seen her pacing there crying forever the one name when the sun was up, as when the moon was high; she was sacred in Ferrara; the rudest ruffian of the streets would not have touched dead 'Dino's "Pazza." And sometimes I feared—in the hush of the night I often feared—that I should be just like her. For all I said, ever, and ever, and ever, was just one name, as she did,—only I said it in my heart,—and no one heard.

I never stirred out—as I say.

Often Giùdettà strove to take me with her to Sta. Spirito, and draw me out to see the humour of the streets; but week by week, and month by month dragged on, and I stayed there by the cold hearth and saw the hand's breadth of blue sky burn above the palace roof, and prayed—as far as I ever prayed —to have an end made to my pain in death.

But death, like other gifts, comes not for our asking.

One morning, as I lay there upon my bed, old

Giùdettà drew her stocking off her arm, put down her spectacles, and looked at me with her brown Tuscan eyes.

"Do you know that it is the Ascension week, and we are now in June?" she asked me suddenly.

I shook my head wearily; what to me was the flight of time, or the advent of summer?

"I have seen sixty-eight summers come and go," she said, after a pause.

I did not answer.

"Sixty-eight summers," she said again. "There was a time with me when the sight of the sun and the smell of the flowers made me sick—soul and body—as you are."

I heard her, but her words were nothing to me. I should not have heeded in these days, I think, the roar of flames, or thunders of a flood.

"Listen to me a little," said Giùdettà, and she turned her round on her oaken stool and sat with the sun touching the grated panes above her old white head. She was a little tender old soul, forever chirping on her lonely hearth like a little brown grillo, and very good and patient with me, and I all the while brutally thankless. "Listen a little. You young things think no one was ever born before you; it seems so new to you, all you suffer. You are wrong. Listen. When I was fourteen I was a dancer at the opera-house here;—like these girls I mend for, only I had prettier feet than they. I was a simple, honest, happy thing; dancing for my bread and my mother's, and thinking no harm, and doing none. I danced a couple of years; heart whole and content, though I never got in the front, or made over half a paul a-night.

People all said I was pretty. Perhaps I was, as a robin is. One Carnival night, as I ran home in the snow, I slipped and fell down on Carraria bridge; it was very bad in those days. A passer-by picked me up and carried me home, for I was light of weight, and had sprained my foot, so I could not stand. There was no dancing for me for weeks. He came to see how it fared with me; came often; he was a nobleman, and a soldier; a Francese, too. Before the vines were in flower we had got to love one another. Some people shook their heads at me, but that did not matter; no man had touched so much as my hand till he kissed it. That year—well, I thank the good God for it. One can live on a year. He would have given me all manner of great and rich things. But I said, 'No, no, no; if I take a paul of yours, what shall I be better than the rest?' And all he ever gave me was a few knots of roses. I have got them. They will be put in my coffin with me. When the year was lived out,—I thank the dear God for that year,—there were war and trouble, and that great one they called Napoleone was in his death-struggle, so they talked. Then my love came to me and said, 'See, he was my chief, and I owe him much, and I cannot let him fall and I not there. You are the light of my eyes, Giùdettà, but what can I do when my honour speaks?' I tried all I could to speak to him. For honour—that sounds so hard to us women. We do not see it; and it is always set against us; and we have no share with it; and we hate it, I think. But all I could do did not stir him. 'If I come not back in a year's space I am dead in battle,' he said. Then he kissed me for the last time and went. Napoleone was ruined and put in chains; that they said; but he—he never came back—not at that year's end, nor any other's. And never a word have I had. It is near fifty years now. Never a word—dear God. People made a mock of me, and cried, 'A fine lover!—he was only tired, and fooled thee!' But I never answered them back. I knew he was dead, or he would have come. What use was it to have loved him if one had not such little faith as that?"

Her voice shook a moment, and dropped into silence; it was all still in the chamber; the gold sunbeams shone through the gratings and cast an aureole on her old bent head.

After awhile, she took up her tale again.

"There were times I was mad, and was nigh throwing my body in the river, and making an end, but I thought the good God would not let me meet him in Paradise if I did that. So I went on and on, and bore with my life. I never danced again—no, no,—it was not for others to look on what he had used to call fair. I took to mending the maglié and the hose, as I do now, just getting bread; that was all. My poor old mother lived a long while. She used to fret herself, and curse me. I was good to look at, and there were many men of our quarter here wanted me—all in marriage and honesty. And my mother could not see why I shook them off 'all for a bad man, and a dead one, or as good as dead,' she would say—she did not know. She lived a long while here; —yes, here;—I was born in this room. I shall die in it. He used to want me to change to some fine villa up in the orchards and gardens; but I always said no; —if I had taken an ounce of silver from him, I should have felt he had bought my kisses. I only took the roses,—I have them safe,—they will put them in my coffin with me. So many, many, many years I used to look out at this window to watch for him coming down the street, as he used to do, just at nightfall, as the moon came up over the old palace there. I go and look still—still—and I always think I shall see him just the same, just as young and light of foot as he was then. And it is fifty years ago—fifty years this Carnival."

She was silent; the sunbeams fell through the grating on to the stone floor. She drew her stocking on her arm again, and worked on and on, on and on.

I shivered where I lay.

Fifty years! and always alone thus!

My life looked ghastly to me, seen by the light of this corpse candle that shone over these buried lives.

Should I live to be as old—always alone—always alone—live to tell my tale calmly, sitting in the evening light?

If I had had strength, I think, in that moment's agony, I should have yielded to the temptation that had in her youth beset Giùdettà, and have gone out into the streets, and flung myself into the full flood of the mountain-shed Arno water.

Swift death! fierce death! how fair and pitiful it looked beside these fifty lonely years passed in poverty and pain under the strong summer suns and all the driving winter blasts!

"And did you never doubt him—never doubt that he lived and was faithless to you?" I asked her, roused

out of my apathy and isolation into a faint passing
sense of some human interest.

She looked at me with eyes a little angered and
more surprised, and paused in her work, the stocking
on her arm.

"*Doubt him!* But, bambina mia, you have not
understood. I had loved him and belonged to him;
how could I ever doubt him—after that?"

The answer burnt me with a hot, sharp shame.

She was an old ignorant woman—one of the very
poor; she could not read or write; she had no knowledge of any sort; she had a child's eagerness for
seeing feasts and pastimes; she would gossip by the
hour with the people in the street about any passing
trifle of the town; she was a little homely, harmless,
hard-working body, who went to pray in great white
Santo Spirito in a dumb, dog-like, wistful, pagan sort
of faith; she was the gossip of the washerwoman over
the way, and the crony of the cobbler at his stall in
the road below; she was only old Giùdettà, the mender
of the dancers' magliè; and yet, shut up, unseen in
the rude, wrinkled, weather-worn rind of her rough
life, there was hidden the pure white heart of this
noble and deathless faith!

Beside her I seemed in my own sight to fall away
worthless and rootless—with neither love nor faith.

This was such love as he had dreamed of, there
on the star tower, in the days of spring—the love that
sees as God sees, and, has pardon and pity, wide as
the width of heaven.

It had not been in me; young, with the years Love
loves, and dreaming with glad eyes against the sun,
and fleet feet, light as a blown leaf upon a world of

flowers.   It was in her, poor, old, and utterly alone;
—whose solitary hope on earth was that a dead rose
should lie with her in her grave:—a rose dead fifty
summers.

CHAPTER V.

Under the White Lion.

GIUDETTA found time betwixt the mending of the
magliè to do many a little helpful act for her poor
brethren and neighbours.   She was always moving
about at such times, as the hose she had to mend
were not so many that they occupied all her time
from sunrise on to midnight.   But one August day,
going down the seventy odd stairs of the old house
she dwelt in, she slipped and twisted her foot under
the brass pail that she was carrying for water to the
well below.

She was a helpful, stout-hearted soul, and bore it
well, and contrived to do for herself and me, and
even to make the little frugal meals all the same. But
she could not move beyond the church to which she
went nightly at vespers; and her neighbour's child
had to run hither and thither over the town to fetch
and carry home the stockings that were her only
source of income.

I should have done this, no doubt; but I was too
deeply sunk in the apathy of pain to notice any duty.
Nevertheless, one day, when the little lad was later in
than usual, she so begged of me to take homeward
some magliè, without which the poor dancer waiting
for them would be unable to make her appearance at
the summer theatre that night, that a vague sense of

the shamefulness of my own absorption stirred in me; and, the hour being close on evening-time, and the streets already dusk, I wrapped myself closely in an old dark-hooded cloak of hers, and for the first time in six months and more, went out into the air.

It made me stagger and feel sick.

The owner of the maglié lived beyond the Frediano Gate. The streets seemed all in a tangle of strange unknown curves to me—I, who had known the city, as a child his father's garden-ways, was adrift in it as in a foreign desert place. There was the red evening light everywhere, burning on the black shadows and the grey housewalls. Bells were beginning to toll for vespers. There was the scent of orchards from great mounds of ripe and rotting fruits. There was a loud gay chatter of voices and hurry of feet everywhere. A girl, about my years, leaned from a casement, and threw down a knot of carnations, and pouted, and shook her head ruefully at a young man standing below in a grey shirt and a scarlet cap.

"No chance of a stroll to-night, Agnolo;—mother will not let me stir from the treccià."

She thought it such a hard fate, leaning there, tied to her task of straw-plaiting, with her lover in the street below, unable to get out in the cool summer night, to stray into the woods, and see the lucciolé lighten, and count the nobles' carriages in the wide, moonlit piazzone. She thought it such a hard fate, only able to toss down the carnations—Oh God! she did not dream how hungrily I below there envied her the shelter and the tyranny against which she thus rebelled.

Out by the Frediano Gate there was more light.

The after-glow came in full from the west, across the valdigrève. The cypresses of Oliveto were standing out against a wonderful sky; rose-purple, like the heart of a dahlia flower. The Strozzi lion couched white amongst the hanging woods. Along the road that wound at their base there were some contadini going homewards to the outlying villages.

One of these came towards me on a black mule. She was a little round red-and-brown figure; her panniers were full of market merchandise; before her strutted slowly a flock of young turkeys; she held a long switch, with which she struck at them; the old mule hobbled slowly in their wake; the grey plumes of the birds spread fanlike over the dust of the highway, as they rose and rustled in their wrath.

"Our Lady grant me patience, oh you diavolini!" cried the shrill, swift voice of the market-woman. "The sun is down, and, surely as one lives, you will all go to roost in the hedges—you always do;—just wherever you find yourselves, like the stupid boobies of birds that you are! And what can one do with you, you wretched simpletons?—sit and watch you in the hedge oneself all night, or else not a wing feather of you will there be to be seen in the morning! Such thieves as they all are in this city. That is what comes of buying you of that Pratoese by the barracks. If ever I buy poultry in the street again, may all my eggs be addled! And go to roost you *will*;—and we all these kilometres off home: you must have the tempers of a herd of gipsies in you, you nasty beasts, or you would never squat in any hedge like that, instead of waiting to get to proper perches like good God-fearing fowls——"

The shrill, scolding tones dropped suddenly; then a little frightened shriek broke the silence; her switch fell in the dust, her bridle on the mule's neck. In the warm ruddy light, under the dusky wood, amidst the grey fluttering feathers of the birds, the little round, rosy face of Brunótta looked down into mine, blanching with sudden fear and wonder. Her hands sought the ring of amber beads about her throat, and her lips began to mutter prayers.

Perhaps I looked the ghost of my dead self to her, there, in the shadows and the warmth, perhaps; —I was so changed. And the long, dusky folds of the cloak covered my shape loosely from head to foot, and all she saw were my wide opened, feverish-startled eyes. I did not move. I sat on the stones, and looked up at her. I felt no wonder, no surprise, no passion of any kind; only a dreary desolate disgust and sickliness of great humiliation. He had loved her—this little shrill, scolding, petulant, coarse fool, striking at her turkeys with her switch—that was all I thought of: what better did I know?

The birds fluttered to right and left of her; the mule stood still; the other people had gone on round the bend of the wall; it was quite quiet; there was only the sound of a fisher's feet wading in the river below the bridge.

"Is it you?—is it you, indeed, donzella?" she murmured, timorously, her hands clasping and counting the beads all the while. "I thought you were dead; I always thought so. You look dead now; only your eyes burn. Are you angry? Are you very angry still? Oh, holy Gesù! how you frighten me!"

I made her no answer.

I gazed at her in a sort of dreamy contemplation, in which my disgust of her was lost in deeper scorn for him and for myself. This was the thing that had shared his heart with me; this was the toy that he had dallied with ere he had turned to play in my turn with me! So I thought, poor little, weak, faithless, ignorant soul that I was, knowing nothing of the follies and fancies of men, knowing nothing of how their passion floats over an ocean of froth, that it skims curlew-like till it dives for its one pearl of price in the depths that the storm stirs and opens.

"I was sorry as soon as I had done it," she began to whimper. "But who was to know he was in the Bargello? And who could tell that you would tear away and kill yourself like that? You were handsome, and you said you were illustrious. I thought all would go well with you. And the very next day I went and vowed a necklace to the Virgin, and I gave it, too; a beautiful thing, all real silver, with a moonstone, that that big black Dominic hung round me all for love—he swore it was his mother's; but I believe he pilfered it. Anyway, handsome it was, and the Madonna had it, and she ought to have had a care of you. But if you are not dead, you must be very, very poor—*are* you poor? Will you not say a word? Look you; now it is all over, I am not one that bears ill-will. I would give you a bed and a bit and drop—yes, I would; for Cocomero, he never saw any good looks in you; you were too thin for him; he likes a woman like a juicy apple, all round and rosy, just as I am. And if you like to come home with me, come. You shall be welcome. It is all over with Pascarèl and me, you know; and I have a tidy little place out here, Signa way, and I always was a handy one with poultry——"

"All over!"

I echoed the words, not knowing what I did. What! a creature lived there, rosy, and young, and full of health, and quite content with all her days, who yet could say thus coolly all was over with her love, and could think and know that she would see his face and hear his voice no more, and yet, a moment earlier, had had no care but to drive her grey birds homeward ere the evening fell!

The sound of my voice banished her strange fears of me as an unreal thing. She ceased to cling against her mule, and stepped a little forward in the dust. The sun had set, it was growing quite dark under the shadow of Mount Olivèt.

"It *is* you, then——donzella?" she cried aloud; "and you are here still? and in great straits, I think; for where are your yellow skirts, and your sunny hair, and your proud pretty toss of your head like a princess born? One would think you were a beggar, sitting on those stones there. Yes, it is all over with him and me. After you were gone I did not seem to care—somehow—I had been jealous,—and when he was in prison—it is as if a man were dead, you know. One gets to forget—quite. And I had always liked Coco: he was such a goodnatured simpleton, and just like a baby to manage, and as merry as a dog in a fair. So, when Pascarèl found us out one day in Friuli and offered us this farm here, and said we might go before the priest and syndic and make all straight and right, as if one were a duchess, why, what could one do better? Coco was all for taking no-

thing—men are such fools; but I, I said, 'never turn
your back on a neat little podere, and a mule, and a
poultry-house; when the Madonna sends such things,
we should sin indeed not to take them.'   And, after
all, dancing about in tinsel is merry and good enough
in its way, but one cannot do it for ever, and it is
well to have a roof over one's head, and a fair name
for fat fowls in the mercato; and, after all, say what
you will, it is something to be a wedded wife,—
wedded before syndic and all,—and if you only had
seen the old mother's face the first day I walked into
the hovel in Casentino, and held my hand up to her
with the yellow ring!   It was worth anything just to
spite her, for she had always sworn I should come to
no good, but die in a ditch; and now she would
give her ears for one of my turkeys to fat for Capo
d'Anno."

So her tongue ran, standing there in the white dust,
and ending with a little gleesome laugh that showed
her white teeth from end to end between the ruddy
lips, like daisies set in poppies.

The dusky trees and purple skies, and all the deepening shadows in the bronze and gold of the night, swam
round me in circles of darkness and light.

Brunótta slid herself from the back of the mule
and stood leaning against the animal with one arm
over his neck; a little ruddy figure, scarlet and brown,
with black braids shining, and silver earrings glistening in the sunset, just as I had seen her first of all as
the day had died and the crocus flowers had closed
in the ilex woods to the sounds of the mandoline.

"Are you angry still?" she muttered, piteously. "As
soon as I had told you, I was sorry—yes, I was. I am

not a bad little thing—only I was sick to see him crazed for you, and I wanted you to know—out of spite—yes, out of spite. But as soon as I had done it, I wished it undone. I hammered at the door to tell you so, but you would not listen. You went away through the window, and such a fuss as the padrona made about her rose trees, that were all dragged down and trampled, never was! But how you look! You must be dead, I think. And if you are dead, I will have a mass said for you—two or three masses, if only you will be quiet, and not walk at night!"

She began to sob as her wont was in any fear, or any extremity; her finger in her mouth like a sulking child, and her shoulders shaking against the broad neck of the patient mule.

I did not speak to her; I did not even rise and move away. I sat and looked at her vacantly; while, through the stupor of my thoughts, a shiver of the old scornful, bitter hate began to steal upon and stir in me.

"A wife!" I echoed, dully. "A wife! whose wife?"

I had only one thought. I had gathered no definite sense from her words.

She looked like a humbled chidden child who finds a gilded toy he boasted of is only rag and patchwork after all. Some sense and tinge of shame came on her; she shifted her feet in the dust. There was a sort of exultation and mortification struggling in her as she answered,—

"I am Coco's wife; why not? He is just such a fool as he seems; and he dares not say his soul is his own if I look at him. That is the stuff one wants in a husband. And I always had been fond of him,—that I vow,—always. And when Pascarèl was in prison,—it

was as if he were dead, you know. Of course I did
not mean him to find out, but he overheard one day,
and then he gave us the farm; and Coco, like a little
blind barbaggiano as he is, went and told him I had
driven you away. And then he was in such madness
—such rage—the saints forgive him! I never saw the
like. And we have never seen him since, except I
passed him once on this very Signa road, and thought'
his eyes would have withered me up like a shrivelled
leaf—he can look so, you know. But I bear no malice;
no, not I; and if you want a roof over you, I will give
it you, donzella—oh, yes, willingly; and we will let
bygones be bygones, and be good friends, just as we
used to be; and though you are useless enough, as I
remember well, still there are things that you could do;
and if you could not, I, for one, should never grudge
you anything, and Coco,—whatsoever I tell him he
thinks good, or says he does, which comes to the same
thing; and you could see the house was safe while I
come into the mercato, which one must do most days,
or else lose credit with the buyers. You see I bear
no malice—no, not I,—why should I? I have all I
want. So, if you like to come—come;—and say no
more about it."

She put her hands out as she spoke—rough, brown,
chubby, rosy palms—in token of fair faith and of all
amity. She meant well—oh, heavens, yes! she meant
well, poor little soulless, mindless, empty thing, that
had no force to love or force to hate.

Why did I not strike her? Why did I not kill her!

I moved where I stood in the dust: a convulsive
shudder of longing shook me to hurl her back into the

dust and strike her insult dumb upon her mouth as men may do with one another.

But some strain of an old proud race still ran in me and helped me to keep silence, and gave me force enough to rise quite quietly from the heap of stones on which I crouched, beggar-like as she had said, and look down into her pretty, cunning, timorous eyes, in which the red light was shining.

"You mean no harm," I said to her, "may things go well with you. But, if you are wise, do not let me ever see your face again."

And so I left her, and went back under the olive shadows to the city, and she stayed there, a little frightened ruddy figure, in the glory of the after-glow, and ere I had gone far I heard her calling to her birds that had nestled down by the wayside and folded their russet pinions for their rest, like feathered gipsies and hedgerow philosophers, as their kind have ever been.

The turkeys would roost in the road—that was her trouble; she had forgot all other.

Who will may see her any day sitting underneath her green umbrella, with her fowls clucking loud around her, hard by the old Strozzi pile, and not a stone's throw from what was once the bottega where Benvenuto shaped his Hercules on its field of lapis lazuli, and fashioned in gold, and bronze, and silver, his griffins and cherubs, his lilies and fauns, his wild acanthus wreaths, and his love-legends for his daggers' hilts.

Ah, dear foolish folk that weep for women! to one Gretchen on her prison-bed there are a million, Brunótte at their market stalls.

Some pluck, like her, their speckled hens for a few

soldi; some pluck their golden geese in the great mercato of the world; but their end is all the same, and they are quite content.

I went on past the bridge, where men were wading with great cloud-like nets, and underneath the little church of Santa Maria, whose mellow bells were ringing across the silent water.

The sun had quite sunk; but there was a deep hot glare upon the sky that burnt the water red, the trees that stretch away towards the country were black, and from the full moon that hung in breathless purple skies, a lovely whiteness touched the river here and there, and gleamed upon the old pale walls of Signa, where she crouched to sleep under her feudal hills, scarce changed at all since the days of her many martyrdoms, when she was ever the first and surest mark for steel and torch from every foe who came across the mountains to violate the fruitful and serene loveliness of the olive-wreathed Verzaja.

I paused and looked back at all that evening calm —once—just once. I could still hear the voice of Brunótta screaming to the birds beneath the monastery. I thought of one day, one golden day of the late summer, that we had loitered away in Signa; how we had strayed amongst the tossing millet, and wandered amidst the old monastic walls, and cut reed pipes from the canes by the Greve stream, and quenched our thirst with the sweet green figs as we watched the cloud shadows come and go on the shallow gold of the Arno water, where Hercules had cast down the rock that in later days served to save the fair jewel-hung throat of Fiorenza from the brutal blade of her ravisher Castruccio.

Then I groped my way senselessly through the Frediano Gate, the gate of the green country, as the old City called it.

It was night, though the red tinge was so slow to leave the west.   The bells were tolling everywhere. People were passing through the doors of the churches to vespers.

Great, still, and white the vaulted basilica of the Dove looked like a palace of peace.   There were a few dim lights at its east end.   Scattered in its solitude half a dozen women, poor and old, kneeled in prayer, —dark bent forms against the marble pillars.

I lingered a moment on its steps, wishful to enter and pray likewise.

But shuddering, I looked and turned away—how can one pray when all one cares for on earth and in eternity is dead and gone?

I turned away and dragged my weary feet across the piazza where the moonlight was softly spreading, and under the shadow of the Guadagni Palace, where in the first night that I had laughed in the Wandering Arte the alabaster workers of Florence had borne away Pascarèl upon their sturdy shoulders to the sound of their shouting and singing.

When I had groped my way by the Mouth of the Lion up to the garret of Giùdettà, her lamp was alight; there were swift eager voices in the chamber; the little old woman sitting on her settle gave a little thrilling cry of joy; a shadowy figure sprang to me and knelt at my feet, and kissed my poor dust-covered skirts.

"Ah, dear donzella!" cried the voice of Florio, "is that you?   Is it indeed, you?   How I sought you, all

northward—all on a false trail, and you in wretchedness like this the while! And such news, signorina
mia—such news! The lord, your father, is a great
noble, and a rich one too—this very Capo d'Anno
only; such strange accidents, so many deaths, and he,
whom none would own or look at, called at last to
his fathers' place. Oh you never, never heard—it is
a wonder-story for a child at Ceppò. And then to us
—when we were all in the black north, taking crown
and kingdom as it were—for it is all so great—then
to us all of a sudden when I, amidst our grandeur,
was still thinking and praying for you, though I had
given up all hope—why, all of a sudden, comes to us,
a week ago, a light witted, reckless, wandering scamp
and playactor, who had made me split my sides many
a night in his booth in years gone by in towns and
villages. And he, all travel-stained and tired, with
that wayward, capricious lordly fashion he has with
him—for Pascarèl was always as proud in his ways as
a prince, hedge-stroller though he has been from his
boyhood up—he, I say, my darling signorina, forced
his way to audience with your father, do all one
would, and then and there told him where to find
you; and what more passed between them the saints
only know, but certainly high words of some sort; for
the fellow when he came from your father swung
through us all mute and fierce and with such a scorn
on his face that I was like to strike him, only one
knows he is so very apt to strike back. And a very
little later milordo sent for me and bade me seek you
out here, and I am come, and no empress, oh, my
blessed little lady, shall ever have been greater than
you shall be—if only it had pleased the Dominiddìo

to let dear dead Mariuccia see the day—and have you never a word to cast to your old faithful Florio; but can you only stare at one with those sad blind strange eyes that it half breaks the very heart in one's breast to see?"

I stood and listened: the flicker of the oil-lamp on my face, and on my ear the eager headlong torrent of my old friend's words.

Little by little—very slowly—the truth dawned on me.

My bidding had been done; and fortune came to me.

Then, in a passion of weeping, I wrenched myself from Florio's hands and cast myself face downwards on the bare stones of the floor.

Great? great?

Oh, God! what use was that?

Only to wander once again light of heart and of foot in the sweet Tuscan summer when the magnolias bloomed on the wide hillside and the lilies were blue in the vine-shadowed grasses—only to wander so once again with my hand held in his and his kiss on my cheek! What use were the greatness of kings to me?

I was left that night and day with old Giùdettà, and Florio went and came a hundred times, bringing me silks and satins, and jewels, and sweetmeats, and pretty painted toys, and all manner of rich dainty things, to be a surety to me of my new-won wealth; and he, good merry soul, full of joy and glory to the brim at the wondrous fortunes of the man to whom he had clung through every evil chance of penury and shame, he could not comprehend, but was sorely wounded because I would not look on any of the treasures, but turned my face to the wall and kept crying: "Take me back to dear Mariuccia—take me back."

For it seemed to me, a brave glad child by nature, and therefore the more utterly unnerved and passion-beaten under my great pain, that the only real good that life could do me would be to take me back again to that old innocent despised home, where the lizards had sported under the broken Donatello, and the crack of the bean shells had struck sharp on the silence.

All that I could have any sense to hear was when he spoke of Pascarèl, and this he did often; because the story seemed strange to him.

"It is odd," said he, "that you have chanced on that wild-living fellow. Ah, dear donzella, I knew him so long long ago—when you were not born—a clever rascal, playing with French people who strolled through Savoy. They used to say, even then, that he might be a famous artist, and a rich one, if he chose.

"But he never chose. He is a vagabond at heart. That is certain. But I suppose he dealt with you as well as he could; for my lord, your father, let him go without rebuke, nay—seemed to be rebuked by him, if one might say so without disrespect.

"And of a surety he showed judgment and honour in never letting you be seen on his wandering stage. I suppose he did as well by you as he could, since you do not complain. But it was a terrible fate for a little illustrissima like you. And your father says that you are not to breathe one word of it.

"If you could have seen that fellow Pascarèllo

sweeping through us all as light and as swift and as fierce as a panther, all dusty and travel-stained, and very pale, and with a strange light in his eyes, and calling aloud to see your father, with all haughtiness and insistance as though to be sure he were a prince himself, as some folks say his ancestors were in this Tuscany.

"Yes, to be sure it was strange: to see that clever rogue, last in his booth, in a little sea town on the Corniche making a hundred fisher people split their sides with laughter; and then next to find him a dozen years later calling out like a king to have speech with your father, all that way away in the northern islands —it is strange enough surely.

"And the people were so terrified at him because of his imperious way and his language, that was all unknown to them. But it was good of him, that I will always say, and I think only an Italian would have done it; to take all that pains and trouble to trace your father; and it was no slight work, such a change having come to our fortunes. A selfish man, dear donzella, would have been tempted to keep that pretty face of yours to deck his stage for him; and a mean one would have looked for some vast recompense. But Pascarèl—your father is a great noble now and has been a very bold person always, but I think he would no more have dared to offer a reward to Pascarèllo than a boy would have dared to face the Rè Satana.

"And it is very piteous to see you with your little white handsome face always shivering and weeping, though it is bright sunshine like this.

"Pascarèl said, I think, that he lost you when he

13*

got caged in Bargello; and I suppose, though this good soul has done her best by you, still you have been half starved and very wretched.

"Never mind, carina; you will be so great now—so very, very great, and when we have got the roses back into your cheeks again you will have all the world at your feet. For even miserable as you look, my darling, you are very handsome still—beautiful, if one could get that haunted look out of your eyes."

So he would speak, and I would listen, my heart breaking as I heard. And I could see it all,—so well, so well,—in that dreary misty land that I had never trodden, in those towering castles of my father's race, that were set seawards against the clouds and billows of the vexed Gaelic water. I could see it all, the steel-hued waves, the grey bare country, the towering skies, the heavy pomp, the sullen northern crowds, and amidst it all the proud and wayward grace, the rapid voice, the lustrous eyes, the fearless eloquence of the Italian, dropped amidst them in utter unlikeness like a pomegranate flower shaken down on winter-withered bracken.

I could see it all, and broke my heart with vain-spent weeping at the thought of it.

In face of all my cruel words he had left his country and his people, and his free and simple life, and had gone northward in my service, maintaining himself doubtless by hard toil—for he was poor.

And I had driven him away, and said that I would never see his face again,—for what? For that poor little fickle traitorous thing who had screamed to her roosting birds there at sunset on the Signa road.

When Florio had left me that night in Giùdettà's

garret to sleep my last hours under its kindly shelter, for which I had been so thankless always, I sat and thought, and thought, and thought, till I was mad staring at the blue summer sky above the piled black roof of dark Oltrarno.

Giùdettà came and looked at me and put her hands gently on my bowed head.

"You are going to great people and great things, dear little lady," she said gently; "well, no doubt the world must be very fine for those who are rich and full of might in it. As for me I cannot tell, I have darned magliè here by the Bocca di Lione all my days. But I do not know rightly what is amiss with you. You have never spoken. But if you have ever loved one man do not ever try to love another. No. Not if it be ever so. So only can you ever live and die pure of heart and pure of body. That I know, though I have only mended magliè all my years in Florence."

Then she bade the Mother of God bless me, and left me in the twilight and went to her vespers in the Church of the Dove as her wont had ever been for seventy years at evening-tide, when there was no longer any light to draw together the silken threads.

I was alone, in the shadows that deepened and deepened till the brown front of the palace grew black and the streets had only little gleaming stars of flame where the people's oil lamps flickered.

When it was quite night there came a little knock at the door; a pretty barefooted child stood there with a great knot of roses.

She crossed the floor and brought them to me.

They were the same sweet snowy beautiful things

that had come to me at day-dawn after the Veglione. Round them was a roll of paper, and on it was written only: "Be happy. Farewell."

I crushed them to me as mothers crush their dying children in their arms, and my hot tears burned them like dropping fire.

This was the end? the end of all? Was the old sweet life of that Tuscan summer dead and gone then for evermore? Should never I see a blue lily bloom in its lowly grass nest without this sickness of soul upon me? Should never I smell the fresh scent of the vines and drink the magnolia breaths on a moonlight night, without this madness of memory that is worse than all death. Was this the end? the end of all?

BOOK VII.

THE FIELD OF FLOWERS.

CHAPTER I.

His Story.

THE villa stands amongst the hills.

It is four hundred years old. The broken sculptures on the terrace walls are all the shields of the great race that once reigned here. The chapel is changed into the chief reception room; it is long and lofty, and has a high vaulted ceiling, painted with frescoes of the Paradise; through its one vast window at the end there is a mass of silver shining; it is so beautiful and luminous and strangely white that nothing could compare with it except newly-fallen snow upon the Alps,—yet, go closer and look, it is only the plum trees in blossom there, beyond the wall, above the lily-filled grasses.

Out yonder in the rough simple gardens, where all that whiteness shines, you can see the towers of the city rising amongst the olives far below; nearer glisten the marbles of the old Monte Croce Church amongst the cypresses; farther than all, away there in the north there is Vallombrosa; the pinewoods at that distance are like cool blue shadows, and above them there is still snow, white as these fruit blossoms that the wind shakes against your hair.

A great artist has made his dwelling here; there

under those roof arches of green leaf is his open air studio. On the old stone terrace there is a litter of brushes and sketches, and books open at a verse of Dante or a page of Boccaccio. Beneath, in violet clusters, lies a mandoline. Under the ilex darkness stands a contadino; he has a wreath of golden tinted laurel in his hand; he has been a model for a study from the Decamerone. A window is half open into a chamber within; through the space there gleams the deep rose of a velvet curtain, and the ebony of an old cinquecento portrait frame. Within doors a sweet strong voice is singing half aloud a fishing song of Naples. Who sings like that? oh, only little Gillino, the gardener's lad, who is plucking the dead leaves off the trellis work in the open court there, beyond the doors.

Save for Gillino's singing and a little tremulous note from the mandoline, as a lizard runs across its strings there is not a sound on the sunny stillness of the day.

The artist paints on in silence under the ilex shade; the contadino erect before him with the sun full on his yellow jerkin and his black straight brows, and the tawny leaves of the winter-gilded laurel.

I, Pascarèl, come up through the fields where thousands of yellow daffodils are blowing and the peach blossoms are scattered by millions on the grass; come through the fields and vault the low walls and stand by the painter's side.

"You would make a much better Panfilo," said the artist, looking up with a smile of welcome. "Take Giacone's place and let him go to his vines."

The peasant goes, nothing loth to be liberated,

and I take up the laurel bough and stand with the sun in my eyes.

"I am not young enough for Panfilo."

"You are young enough for anything," says the artist. "You will never be old."

So the painter paints on, and his Pamffilio stands there while the golden daffodils blow in the fields, and the city shines far down below, beyond the light clouds of the olive foliage.

Shall I never be old?—I, Pascarèl? I felt very old to-day before I came up here amongst the white plum trees. I felt very old as I walked through the Frediano Gate this morning, across the Grève river, towards Signa, for where the red roses were nodding over the field walls, I met a little woman on a black mule with a great crate full of cackling poultry, and she was as plump as a guinea-pig, and was hung about with big cabbages in nets, and she screamed shrilly to her mule as she beat him. And she looked at me and started a little and crossed herself, and beat her mule afresh to hurry onward. Then I felt old.

Only the other day it seems she was a little round rosy laughing thing in the boat on the river, when the fireworks flashed red against the blue night sky; then she learned to dance the saltarello with the frolic of a kid, and her lips were like two cherries—only the other day!

Now,—on the Feast of the Dead that November morning, I was heavy of heart as I went along down into Florence. For what could I say, I thought, to my darling whom I had wooed and won? It seemed to me that for an honest man who had tried his best to do right I had come as near to looking like a scoundrel as might be. I would never judge men again, that I swore to myself; for there was I who had suffered more than I cared to confess to myself for the fair face of that child, and had curbed and controlled myself in a way altogether novel to me, here was I who had endeavoured with all my might to do well by her, here was I, I say, become as nearly like a rogue, turn it which way I would, as a man can well become through the love of woman. And what a large latitude that is, all men know without my telling them.

And how I loved her! dear God! Well, what use was that?

I saw my way none the clearer for it as I stumbled down the stony road from Marco Vecchio, not being willing to see the donzella's two soft radiant eyes until I had faced the perplexities before me and solved them.

For how could I tell her the truth? And how could I tell her what was not the truth? One was as hard as the other.

Chance solved the question for me as it does often for most of us.

For when I got down into Florence that day there was a storm in the air. All about old bronze Porcellino, and in the square of the Signoria the people were clustering with dark words and darker brows, and it wanted but a touch of the match to the tinder to have had a day of darkness and bloodshed. There had been aggression and irritation, and they were sharp on the edge of revolt; and I knew the time was not ripe, and that they would only fill the graveyard ınd prison, and I took their leadership, for they always loved me, and one must do one's best for Florence, and I spoke to them from the old Loggia ıs worthier men than I had done in older times; and so held them in hand all that day, and saved, as I nay say without boasting, their bodies from shot and steel, and the city herself from feud and from flame. And at sunset for my pains I was arrested and borne ıway to the Bargello Tower, and when I asked my crime was told that I had harangued the people and incited hem to tumult.

Old Porcellino knew better, but being of bronze ıe could not bear witness, and the people who could vere not listened to; so in the Bargello I lodged that ıight amongst thieves and murderers, not able even o send so much as a word to the Capanna above Marco Vecchio, and fretting my soul bitterly because ıf the trouble I knew must be there on account of ny unexplained absence.

The only thing I could hope was that some noise ıf the tumult and of my own arrest would be taken ıp the hills by some villager or another going home rom the market in Florence.

On the morrow, quite early, they moved me from he Bargello for judgment; and the people wanted to rescue me, and were wild for a little space; but I ıegged of them to keep quiet, for the soldiery were strong, and I wished no Tuscan blood shed about me —a straw, a bubble, a player. The tribunal condemned me to three months of prison.

It was not the first time by half-a-dozen. I had seen the solitudes of Spielberg, and I had heard the water wash the dungeons of Venice, and I had been

quartered with the rats in old Vicenza, and had spent
a few dreary weeks behind the fortress of San Leo,
high above the rent and rocky land, on the bare peak
against the blaze of the skies. For I had never been
behindhand wherever the people had been moved
against the Princes, and for many a rash word spoken
in my Arte the feeble Dukes and the powerful
Tedeschi had alike been adverse to me.

But that day the sentence fell on me like a
thunderbolt. Before, it had been only myself that
had suffered when the prison gates had closed on
me; I was without a tear, without a pang; I laughed
when I went in, I laughed when I came out. What
was I that I should complain of what Boethius and
Tasso had endured? But now—now I fear they saw
that they hurt me, for what could my song-bird do,
homeless and friendless in the snows of the winter,
that were so soon to drive down through the open
gates of the Apennine gorges?

I was heartsick that day as they took me through
the old familiar streets in the noon-day sun back to
the Bargello Tower, and for the moment I was remorseful that I had not allowed those streets to run
with blood at daybreak when the people had
clamoured for me.

For it is a bitter thing—perhaps as bitter as life
holds—when you hear the bolts grate in their sockets,
shutting you out from the living world, and know
that for want of you that world may be worse than
hell itself to some helpless female thing that is all
adrift in it like a young bird in a storm. For there
you are in your iron cage, and your bird may beat

er breast till death release her, and you cannot touch
er through the bars.

For many days I heard nothing and could send
o word, and so fretted my soul in sickly desperation,
s many worthier men had done before me.

Somewhere about the twelfth day little Toccò
ame, having wrenched down a lamp-iron and done
ome other naughtiness to get taken to prison and
ave a chance to be near me—poor dear little lad—
or this was his notion of loving one, and a notion
o loyal that one could hardly believe that he had
ver been born of a woman.

Toccò delivered me many messages from Bru-
ótta, and weeping and frightened brought out from
ound his little brown throat my old onyx ring with
ie Fates.

Then I knew what I had lost; I knew before he
ad told me that the child had fled away, none
nowing why nor whither, in the dusk of that very
ay when they had arrested me in the Loggia of the
'ree Lances.

What had driven her away? I could not tell.
for for one moment did I dream that the sin was
runótta's—men are such fools. I thought that in
ome manner she must have heard of my peril and
ave flown down the hillside in her wild innocent
hildish impulse to aid me, and so had come to some
errible woe in the city; and been killed perhaps—or
'orse. Who could say?

A child like that—sixteen years old—and fearless
ecause knowing no evil, and beautiful in her way as
ie flushed flowers of the rose-laurel.

I dropped like a dead man, they tell me, and when they brought life back to me it came in the form of a raging fever—the only sickness that I ever remember in the whole course of my life.

Little Toccò got leave to tend me, and did it so well that I got over it when the prison leeches had abandoned me as only good for the graveyard. He said that I kept hold of the Fates in my hand all the weeks through; but raved of such a medley of cities and seasons and women's faces and poets' fancies, that none were a whit the wiser for what I said.

By the time I was strong again it was the end of my term of captivity. The lad capered and flung his cap for glee when the gates unclosed for us. But as for me, when that flood of dancing sunshine flashed upon my eyes I reeled like a drunken man. For the first time since I had run barefoot after my father's barrow the translucent living light of my Italy was hateful to me. For how could I tell if the child were living or were dead?

A good and loyal friend of mine was waiting for me, a worker in gold and silver, who dwelt hard by in the old street of the Ghibellines; he lies now in the fields by the village of Magentà.

I staggered into his workshop that day and sat down and felt like a man from beneath whose feet the solid earth splits and opens. I had never suffered greatly in my life before;—except in sympathy for grief outside myself—and be one as philanthropic as one may, one bears the woes of others more lightly than one's own,—but now I was dulled and dazed with the misery I felt. And misery to me meant utter bereavement in a wider sense of desolation than rich men can know. Misery to me meant famine of the body and the soul and the senses. For if I could no longer laugh at Fortune, I must feel her buffets as the galled jade the lash. And if I had not my light heart to wander with, what wealth had I on the face of the earth?—for it is only by gaiety of heart that one can escape the thorns of the rough hedge-school which is only mirthful in one's Maytime when the hawthorn buds are fresh in blossom.

Well, they sent me out of Florence that night and forbade me the city. My friends tried to find trace of the child for me in Florence, and I tried hard in the country. But it was all of no use—no use. Some straw-plaiters in Settignano thought that they had seen a young girl in an amber skirt go down the oakwood-path towards the town one feast-day at early dawn. But that was all; and this slender clue broke in our hands and led us no further than those old oaks under the war-seared Vincigliata.

And the truth of the matter never dawned upon me—never once. All I could think of was that she had heard of my seizure in the Loggia and had tried in her rash innocent fashion to help me, and had so come to some horrible ending by some crime done to her that the guilty doers smothered.

I believe I was quite mad for the time, ranging north and south to find her. But that Brunótta had aught to do with her flight I never thought. Men are such fools.

One day in the spring-time I rested a little in a village in Friuli, whilst I was ranging Lombardy and Venetia in the vague hope to hear or find something of my darling.

Brunótta was nothing to me, but how could I send
her adrift—a little helpless, ignorant creature like that!
She had loved me very much that San Giovanni's day
and every other day afterwards, or at least so she
swore twenty times in as many hours. I did not doubt
the truth of it; perhaps I was too vain and thought
too well of myself to imagine that a little empty-
headed rogue out of the Casentino, who could not for
her life have read or written her name, would ever be
tired of me; of Pascarèl. Anyhow, could I send her
adrift? A poor little simpleton whom I had taken for
my whim and fancy away from her straw-plaiting and
her goat tending, and could do nothing in the world
except hop about on her little plump feet, and that
too clumsily for any greater theatre than mine?

I had always winced at the sight or the touch of
her since I had seen that child's eyes in the Cathedral
square in Verona; but I would not be cruel to her.
I had had so many pleasant sunny heedless foolish
days with her, going over the length and breadth of
the land in our idle gladsome fashion. Men are tender to women for remembrance's sake long after all
love has died out of them. Brunótta to me was like
a little round brown bird out of the woods; I could
not wring the bird's neck just because its homely little
song had lost all music to me; I could hardly even
fling it down the wind to go its own gait away from
me. It was such an innocent little thing, I thought;
and if it fell into the fowler's snare through my abandonment, things would go ill with me.

I joined her and the boys where of their own whim
they had set up the Arte in a Friulian village. I
wandered carelessly, stupidly, wretchedly, seeking only

one thing, and that always vainly. I had ceased to play; the laughter choked me; I did field work when I worked at all, and for the rest I had some few hundred pieces laid by with an old goldsmith in Florence, so that I could keep together the poor little troop, of which the lads and dogs—and the brown-eyed dancing girl too, as I thought—were all dependent on me for every mouthful of bread.

Pepito and Pepita had been poor stray brutes that I had saved from drowning; Toto had been sentenced to death as dangerous when I had cut his halter one day in Pisa, and showed the Guardia that his madness was nothing more than thirst; Toccò I had taken out of the hell of the galleys; Cocomero had been perhaps the most utterly desolate of all when I had found him in the streets; his father had been a clown, called Flageolet, who travelled with a French circus, and had been killed by a horse's kick in the ring that very noonday, leaving his son—without a coin in the world and leagues away from his birth-country—to weep his poor cowardly heart out in the burning sun of grim old Rimini.

We waited the night in a little place where a green bough above the door told us we could get wine and bread. It was only a little mountain village, too poor and small to have any regular place of resting. All Friuli is sad and unlovely; if it were not for the glimpses of the Alps away there towards Venice it would be hateful, that desolate historic land that had every rood of it stamped bare by the iron heel of Barbarossa.

This little village lies flat on the grey slope with nothing to break its melancholy and its barrenness where it is swept by the sharp sea winds. The people were poverty-stricken and scraped the arid soil assiduously to get a bare subsistence from their wines and millet. It has been incessantly a battlefield in the times of the episcopal wars and of the aggrandizement of Milan, and it seems still as if the torch of war had scorched it sear forever.

Still even here the vine leaves were thick and green, and the grapes were budding in the little pergola, which the poor house that entertained us had managed to stretch out between doorway and garden wall in the teeth of the keen breezes that blow from the lagunes and the chain of the Tirol. In the heat of the noon I sat there, glad of the shelter of the leaves; bitterly sad at heart and tortured with a thousand imaginings of all that might have chanced to that young and pretty thing adrift by herself in the width of the world. I had tried all I knew to trace her and had failed; the madness and the suspense of it were eating away all the life of me. I reproached myself for a million things that I had done and had said and for a million things that I had not done and had not said. I seemed to myself such an utter fool; no better than a man who holds a diamond fit for kings in his hands and lets it slip through his fingers into a foul ditch where the toads can swallow it.

I sat there in the scirocco that blew like a furnace blast over the nakedness of the land; the insects were buzzing and booming in the thickness of the vine leaves; it was two o'clock in the day and quite quiet.

Presently in the drowsy stillness there came a murmur of voices; one was Brunótta's. I was so used to hear it humming all the hours through without ces-

sation about millions of little odds and ends that
served her for endless discourse, that I heeded it no
more than a man who lives on a millstream heeds the
noise of the churning water.

The sense of what she was saying drifted to me
without my being aware; I heard as it were without
hearing; I was so used to the sound of all her little
shrill notes piping on by the hour over a mislaid ribbon or a smoked dish of macaroni.

"Pray take more care," it was saying now with a
little stifled terror in it like a scolded child's. "He
would beat me, perhaps, or you, if he got to know.
He can be so violent when he is cheated."

"Why not let us run away?" whispered another
voice, and this time it was the voice of my eighteen-
year-old Coco. "You are afraid of him—afraid of
your ears of him since that dreadful night the donzella
went, and we do cheat him, as you say, and, when
one thinks, it is not well—why not let us run away,
right away?"

"How could we live? We have not a bit of talent
hardly, you and I, and it would be very bad to starve,"
said Brunótta. The practical objection always comes
from the woman.

"But then if you love me?" murmured Coco; the
man, you see, is always such an enthusiast, and always
thinks that love is meat and drink.

"Oh, I love you best a thousand times," cried
Brunótta. "I used to think I loved him, and so I did,
and specially whilst I was jealous of the donzella. But
you see Pascarèl is too great for me. He is always
doing and saying some wonderful thing, and all that
cleverness tires one; it is like walking on the tight

14*

rope—don't you know? I can do that; but I am always so glad to jump down, so sick of being up so
high.   Pascarèl is just like the tight rope to me.   But
you are such another simpleton as myself, as one may
say; and you are just my age, and you like to romp
about and stuff your mouth with fruit and make an
ass of yourself just as I do, and besides you have
sworn you would go before the priest with me, and I
should like to show my old foster-mother the ring on
my finger—just to spite her—and besides I *do* love
you, Coco mio!"

And with that she kissed him where these lovers
stood together upon the other side of the vine leaves.

I thought it time to rise and walk out of the pergola.   Brunótta screamed and dropped upon her
knees.   Coco was as white as his ghost, and his limbs
trembled under him.

I soon put them out of their misery.

"My dear children," I said to them quietly, "instead of cheating me, why not have trusted me? Instead of deceiving me behind my back, why not have
said all this to my face? You are two little fools, as
Brunótta has sensibly said, and you have succeeded
in tricking a man who thinks himself no fool.   The
wiseacre is always served quite rightly in such cases.
How long has this been going on—some months? Oh,
I might have guessed that you had learned too many
comedies by heart not to act them to your own profit
some day.   I might have wished indeed that it had
been anybody but Coco—but after all, that is the
merest sentimentality. You owe me so much? Altro!
what of that? Ever since the world began, that has
been only a reason for the debtor to pay his debts by

making a dupe if he can. If you wish to marry this poor lad, Brunótta, pray do, I will not stop you. It will be very bad for him, but that is his affair—not mine. I have a thousand lire in Florence put by, that I always intended for you whenever we should wish to part company. Set up in life with it as best pleases you both, and only take my advice in one thing— never talk secrets close to a pergola in full leaf."

And they did as I told them, and went before the priest, and bought a little piece of land with my money, two leagues beyond the Frediano Gate by Florence.

Coco indeed crawled at my feet and wept and cursed himself, and was all for not touching one of the thousand pieces. Men have so much more con- science and so much less common sense than women. But Brunótta persuaded him out of those scruples, and chose the little bit of ground herself, and selected as the mission and fulfilment of her life the fatting of the finest turkeys in all Valdarno, which had indeed, she confessed, been all her life-long the secret and chief ambition of her dreams.

No doubt it is a thing to be duly thankful for when a little girl who has helped one to *filer le par- fait amour* for a few foolish seasons takes to so deco- rous an end for herself as marriage and fat turkeys. It is a much more agreeable reflection than the water- lilies of Ophelia or the prison bed of Marguerita are to their lovers; and rids one of all responsibilities clearly. It would be manifestly absurd to reproach a man with having broken his mistress's heart or blasted her youth and her peace, when who will may see her plump and busy jogging on the Pisan road upon her

mule and selling poultry under a green umbrella hard
against the Strozzi pile any market day at noontide.
Still—such is the vanity of man, I suppose—one
scarcely likes a little brown egg-wife to play the traitress to one with a poor scamp like Cocomero. And to
have lost all that I lost through that little silly false-
tongued thing is bitter—very bitter—sometimes.

For, when they were fairly married out of anybody's power to part them, and when the little bit of
land had been made their own where the roses nod
over the high dusty walls as you go up to the place
where Arno's fury overthrew Castruccio's plans in the
old times whilst all the glad Valdarno was a smoking
ruin, when all, I say, was quite safe and sure with
them, Coco, who was not a bad lad at heart, though
timorous and deceitful, as it proved, came and threw
himself at my feet and lay there on the ground as a
beaten spaniel might, and bemoaned himself that he
had got a thing to confess to me.

"Say on," I said to him. "If it be a new villany,
make a clean breast of it. My dogs will not bite me,
but they are the only things whose life one can save
without being made to rue for it."

That was a harsh saying of mine, no doubt, but I
was mad with pain of which I could say nothing to
any creature, at not finding any trace of the donzella,
and even this little miserable treachery of the lad
Coco, whom I had befriended as far as I had been
able ever since I had found him sobbing in the sun
in Rimini, had cut me a little; one is always so weak
in those things.

And then Coco, weeping like a child, confessed to
me with sore terror that it was no fault of his own

that he had now to tell, but one of Brunótta's which he had known long before, but had never dared to relate until she was surely bound to him, being foolishly fond of her, poor lad, and having set his silly heart on having her for his wife and dwelling with her on that dusty rood of land towards Signa. But now that she was fairly his own, and could no more fly away from him than his land could, and he was sensible that he was seeing the last of me, and had broken our fellowship by a piece of ingratitude for which he was sorely repentant, plucked up his heart and told me what he knew, and of how she had betrayed me that autumn evening under the vines below Fiesole. And so I learned at the last why it was that I had received back my onyx. Coco, I think, was terrified at the effect on me of his revelation; for when I came to myself he was grovelling at my feet and beseeching me not to kill Brunótta; and indeed in that moment if she had come before me I could not have answered for myself very surely. These foolish vile things sting so deep—so deep—and then we are to let them alone *because* they are foolish and vile, forsooth! It is hard to hold one's hand sometimes.

He told me word for word as he had overheard it all, that scene under the vine by the Badià; and I needed no more to tell me the reason that the Fates had come back to me. And I had never once in the wildest of my fancies imagined that Brunótta had been to blame. I had never once in my sharpest pain suspected that Brunótta had been lying when she had run weeping out of the Fruilian shadows to lament to me for the loss of the donzella. No, I had never dreamed that her jealousy had been at work, and that her rain of tears was all a lie; never once! men are such fools.

Well, it was over and done, and there was no help for it, and the poor foolish lad crouched aghast at his work at my feet. I bade him never let me see their faces again; and then I turned away and left the village as the sun set; and went where chance might take me. What did it matter?—the world seemed as empty to me as a shrivelled gourd. To me—Pascarèl —to whom the world had always been as full of red colour and of pungent flavour as any pomegranate that one cuts open in the first heats of April weather. The thing was over and done, I say, and as far as I know, the issue of it might have been that the child had already drifted dead down some mountain river, and the fair white body of her have been already thrust unshriven amongst the nameless and the lost in the marble desolation of some Campo Santo.

WE Italians love the soil, I think, more closely than other nations. I, wanderer though I have been all my days, I always want to tread again the grey Macigno after I have had the Alps awhile betwixt myself and Florence. One wants the light too; the dreamful radiance of the skies, that is neither so intense nor so blue, nor yet either so glittering as the poets and painters will make it, but is an endless ecstasy of light —light clear and pure and gentle, always soft, always silvery rather than golden; always tender and dreamful, like the eyes of a woman who lies awake and remembers the kisses of her lover.

So I came back here to the city so soon as my
time of exile was ended, with little hope that she were
living, but solely from long habit and love of the soil.

And as I entered the town, the people got hold of
me, and would fain feast and welcome me, and bore
me in the midst of them all down the old Oltrarno.
And then—up on high, behind a barred casement
against the corner of the Lion's Mouth—I saw her
face, and then—

Well, then the sins and follies of my old life smote
me from the lightning of the child's eyes of scorn;
and she spoke words I merited, no doubt, but still
such words as one cannot hear even from a woman
twice; and so I saw my duty plain before me, and did
it, though late in the day, no doubt.

It was long and tedious labour to find her father,
more especially because I had to earn my daily bread,
whilst I sought for him, by any such handicraft or
labour of the roads as came to my share in the bitter,
joyless, strange countries where the people only saw in
me a travel-stained vagrant with a brown skin and a
foreign tongue.

But I did her will at last, and found her greatness
and fair fortune, and so sent her the roses in farewell,
and knew that she was lost to me for evermore, the
pretty, careless, sunny, wayward thing who had strayed
with me through the Poets' Country whilst the blue
lilies were in bloom. I am glad that I had strength
to do it—yes, glad, surely, for her sake. For even had
she been willing to link her life with mine, it would
have been shame in me to lead her into my obscure
and thorn-set paths of life whilst she was so young—
so young,—and knew not what she did.

Yes, I am glad.

For, though one be but a strolling player, and
never saw one's crown engraven save on a travelling
tinker's old iron pot, still, when one bears a once-
mighty name of Florence, one must needs try to be
worthy of it by some poor shred of honour, at the
least.   Only for me, look you, all the world seemed
dead.

God knows what I might have done in the weary
days when I had sent her my farewell in flowers, and
knew that every year of her life would only serve to
make her higher and higher, farther and farther, away
from me for evermore.

They were long burning days of drought and dust.
The land was white with long thirst, and within the
city the clouds of zanzari hooted all night long. For
the first time in all my years of love for her the face
of my Florence looked without beauty. Is not the
beauty of all things so much within us, and derived
so little from without?

God knows, I say, what evil or mad end to my
life I might not have been tempted to put, in my
heart-sickness and haste, had there not chanced to me
a strange accident.

One blazing eveningtide, just as the sun was close
on its setting, I was walking wearily down the Stock-
ing-makers' Street, thinking of nothing in particular,
when I came upon a little group of people gathered
before the door of a Cantina.

It is a quaint, odd, many-coloured, picturesque
street, as all the world knows; and what with its pretty
crowded gay wares, and its narrowness, and its
popularity, it is a street that will always talk to one;

it has done so much; the blood of Florence has coursed so often down it: and it has been a channel of the full Florence life ever since the Arts and Trades marched along it to set their flags round San Michaele that brave day when Duke Walter was hounded out through the gates.

Calzaioli will always talk if you will listen—here on the stones that are still called the Song of the Lily it has heard the soft footfall of Ginevra's bare and trembling feet; here, where Guardamortà rose, it saw the Lion tremble before a mother's love; here in its workshop the Bronzino dwelt, and here, in its church, his bones were laid to full rest; here Donatello and Michelozzo laboured for the love of arts and men hard by yonder against the little Bigallo; here flame and steel ravaged their worst after red Arbià; here the White Bands shivered and fled before their old hereditary foes; here, on Ascension Day, the Signoria went up with the gold and purple of ripe fruits, to lay them at the feet of that Madonna of Ugolino whose manifold miracles sustained the soul of Florence beneath the Devil's Plague; here, on the Feast of Anna, it saw Walter of Athens driven out of the city, and all good men and true trooping thither to render her thanksgiving, and all the Arts raising in memory the statue of their patron saint and the shields of their blazonries—all these things, and a million more, has Calzaioli seen since its old towers and casements crowded hard on one another, and the destriers and palfreys champed below in the logge, and the painters and sculptors worked high above in the turretted roofs, worked amidst the challenge of silver clarions, and the clangour of brazen bells, the fret of horses' hoofs, and the clash of crossing swords, the saucy laugh of the playing pages, and the sturdy tramp of the marching Trades.

Calzaioli will always talk to you, if you have ears to hear, and it was talking to me then, and I was heeding not at all the living throng around me, when my ear was caught by an air that was being played on a violin where the knot of people stood before the wineshop. I think I have heard most music that has ever rejoiced the earth; and at Pisa, amongst other things, I studied music as a science; but this air struck me at once as unlike anything else that I knew—quaint, delicate, fanciful, mournful, charming, and altogether new. I paused to listen with the rest.

A boy of about fourteen was playing, sitting on an old barrow that stood in the kennel of the street. He was very small and slight and pretty as a child; his clothes were ragged, and he was very pale. It grows dark in Calzaioli long before the light has died in the open contado; there was a lamp lit in the doorway above his head; the great silvery pile of San Michaele loomed beyond, with the saints and prophets white in the darkness. I stayed with the rest of them and listened.

The air had enchanted the people; they were humming it to themselves as it was played; and two country girls had caught it, and were singing to it a first and a second as they plaited on at their hanks of straw. It was just one of those melodies made to be repeated on every lip, and handed from town to town in every land: not because it was catching and common, but because that true divine spirit of music was in it which has an universal tongue and a life eternal.

All of a sudden, as I listened, the music of the violin ceased—snapped, as it were, and ceased; there was a little movement in the group; the musician had fallen backward in the gutter, and the violin had dropped out of his hand.

I pushed the people aside, and lifted his head on my knee. By his looks I thought he had fainted from hunger.

The people, looking frightened, began to edge away, still humming fragments of his melody.

"He does not belong to any of us," they said, with little shrugs of their shoulders.

He did not belong to any one, poor lad; he had been seen in Florence for the first time for what anybody knew, playing along the Arno side for pence that day at noon. The beauty of his airs had drawn a little crowd after him. The people will wander after any harmony hour by hour anywhere over Italy.

Down in the gutter the lad lay, and if one lie there in Calzaioli, one is as sure to have a horse's hoof in one's face as Maytime is sure to bring cherries.

The wineshop people did not much like to let him in; but, nevertheless, as they knew me well, and in the old days of my fooling I had had many an idle night over their chiante, they gave way; and after a while, in their inner chamber, the lad came to himself, and opened great dark bewildered eyes on us. He was as handsome and small as a girl, with curls of Venetian gold lying soft and thick about his throat.

"I was playing—a moment ago?" he murmured, staring up into our faces. "It was in a street—what has happened?"

"You fainted, that is all," I told him. "Was it the heat, or are you ill, or what is it?"

White as he was, and bloodless, he coloured painfully.

"It was hunger, I think," he murmured. "I have eaten nothing for three days but a crust a dog left."

Knowing that, to do for him was easy.

He soon after sank into deep slumber, and seemed likely to sleep all the night; so I would not disturb him; but with the first of the daylight, as soon as the shutters were down, I, watching by him, saw his pretty eyes open; and then he was all for falling at my feet and blessing me, although, poor little lad, I had been St. Michael himself who had called him up into paradise. When he got a little calmer, he told me his story. His name was Raffaello Baptista.

"You see, dear signor," said he, lifting his wistful, pitiful eyes to mine, "I belong to Verona. My mother, who was blind, was very very good, but she died more than a year ago, and I was very unhappy. Because my old master in music was dead too; and there was a lovely little lady who had always been my playmate who had disappeared in the strangest manner possible. She was much above me—oh yes, quite illustrious. Her people, I believe, were very great; only they never took any notice of her, so that it was not any good at all. When she was lost, all Verona said she was dead, because a girl's body was found in Adige, and the face none could see, being gnawed by the rats. But I was always quite sure that the good God had not taken her without letting me see her once more. And little by little I came to think that I would try to find her. My mother was dead and buried, and my

father drinks all day, and old Ambrogio, even, was
gone; and so I thought to myself, no one wants me
here, and I am kicked about like a useless little cur,
and I am quite old now, thirteen come the Day of
Ashes; and I will go and try and find out the donzella,
and I am sure Mariuccia and the Mother will pray for
me. And so off I came the very end of Quaresima,
and I have been wandering, wandering, wandering
ever since then, and never a sight of her face. Only
once, in a hamlet, in the Romagna country, I heard
of a girl who was singing, with hair all gold, like the
wheat in summer, and the people spoke of her as
L'Uccello; and then I took heart of grace to hear the
old dear Veronese name, and I said, 'There cannot
be two like that,' and I kept on and on till I came
into Florence. Her brothers are all dead, and she is
quite illustrious, you know, only so poor, so poor!
And she and I were friends always, and always so
happy together. And she has nobody at all but me;
her old nurse died in the last wintertime, and of her
people nobody knows. Have I money? Oh no. How
should I? You see my legs are bare, and I have only
this little pack—one shirt in it—and my little viol.
But I have wanted for nothing. Nothing, nothing.
Yes, I have come on foot over the plains and the
mountains. What of that? It has only been cold the
last few months, and the people have always been
good. I have played for them at feasts, at fairs, at
bridals, at vintage dances, anywhere, always; and they
have always given me a supper and a bed, and very
often much more than that. Oh, I have not suffered
it all—sometimes just a little, perhaps, from being
tired, or out in the storms; and once some pifferari

set on me, and beat me, and threw me into a ditch, because they thought I was in the way on their rounds; that is all the unkindness I have had. I have been only a fortnight in Florence, and the last three days I have made no money. I have been too weak to play, and I have slept in the grass in the Cascine meadows, and I think I have got a little fever perhaps. To-night I wandered out into the street, and did play a little. You know the rest. I never shall find the donzella now. But—but—if I should die, will you let the poor little viol be buried with me? I should not like it to be burned as waste wood, though perhaps it is worth nothing more."

So he spoke, the poor little Baptista, sitting on the mattress in the inner room in the Cantina, and looking at me with his great pathetic eyes under the auburn tangle of his locks—such a pretty, fragile, heavenly-looking little lad; one would have had him painted as that boy-martyr whose head being severed from his body sang on day and night the sweetest Aves ever afterwards. His whole face breathed music; we have many such faces amongst us. Very often they mean nothing; but his meant all that it uttered.

I seemed to know him well. Had I not heard of Raffaellino scores of times from the mouth of his playmate, as she went with me along the Adda or Arno water? Had I not seen him with his little mandoline, and his bare feet, and his red sash, that first day of Carnival in Verona?

He did not know what the memory was that stirred in me; but it made him like my own son, as it were, to me, and as sacred. Besides, I loved the lad for staying neither for sense nor prudence, but setting forth to find his donzella in that innocent, foolish, childish faith and loyalty.

Now when I found Raffaellino in Calzaioli that night I was very little better off in the world than he; and the lad being very ill and altogether destitute, I had need to cast about me for some surer manner of maintenance, or let him drift away to the hospitals and the sepulchre. It seemed to me that the boy came in my way like a duty there was no means of escaping. My own faulty fashion of living had cost so much anguish to the child that had gone with me through all the fresh green Tuscan summer; and it seemed to me now that to do my best by her favourite playmate was the only sort of poor atonement that ever would lie within my reach.

So whilst Raffaello was stretched on the sacking in an attic amongst the roofs in the Street of the Stocking-weavers, I took thought as to a means of livelihood.

Now I had absolutely nothing.

The little I had saved had gone for that bit of land in the Valdigrève. I could always gain my day's bread and lodging by a turn amongst the vines, or a few hours in the modelling shops, or by taking a fiddler's place in the little opera houses, or by showing the trick of the clay to some young sculptor; for I have a sort of desultory universal talent, which is in a manner the most general curse of my countrymen —an over fertility of invention that is very apt to end in absolute sterility of achievement.

Little Toccò had gone as a pupil and 'prentice to Orfio Orlanduccio, and was thought of good promise in the art, so that I had no soul in the world to work for; and where is the Italian who will work for mere work's sake?

It is not possible to us. Give us an end and we will labour as well as other men; but without some impetus we will not serve that grim and ghostly Northern Thor whose hammer has struck down all the wild roses and tossing hawthorns and sweet sky-larks of the world's soft smiling, useless, leisurely, heaven-sent joys.

If we are happy, let us lie in the sun and dream of it; and if we are unhappy, what else better can we do. For Italians do not kill themselves; why, I cannot say; perhaps from fear of Dante's Circles, or perhaps from sheer love of the mere plant-like sense of living: why, I will not say, but they do not.

The fifth night after I had found him, I went up the dreary Sdrucciolò by the Pitti to get a little fruit for him, and I had nearly resolved to go to Carrara as soon as he should prove able to be moved. The mountain air might do him good, and there was always work enough for any one who knew how to chip marble; and the life there, where all the sculptors' dreams take shape, amidst the white desolation of the quarries, with the keen mountain solitudes all around, was most unlike (and therefore least painful to me of any) the life that I had led with my gay little Arte.

I was known there. It had even happened now and then that, finding some artist struggling with a fine fancy that he could not to his liking embody in the clay, I had had the luck, by a fitful night's work, to call up the Andromeda or the Spartacus that escaped him, and the figure has gone forth—mine, if

I had cared to claim it—and now and then, I have even heard, has made the other man's fortune. What did it matter? it was only an accident, a knack, a turn of the hand, more or less happy, that chanced to put fire into a soulless model. What matter who claimed the statue in its city market-place? When we love Art for Art's sake, we are pained by a line awry, a note discordant, a colour misplaced; but we are not pained by a name being lettered in gold instead of our own?

To Carrara, therefore, I thought I would go. But as fate would have it, as I thus resolved, I ran against, in Sdrucciolò, a little plump, oily Piedmontese, by name Luca Pestrò, who had rolled a good deal of gold together, as the men of Piedmont have a knack of doing, and was the director of the Goldoni Theatre in this city and of another larger one in Turin.

I knew Pestrò very well, he having been a gay, jovial soul before he had taken to money-making, and we had had some merry days together years and years before in France, where he was travelling with a choice company of marionettes, whose joints were as stiff and as dire a trouble to him as the tempers of any living troops of actors.

Pestrò flew across the narrow passage to me, and cast his arms about me, with tears in his eyes and his dress all disordered. I had not met with him for at least five years.

"Pascarèl! oh, Pascarèl! What ever good angel has dropped you here?" he cried, in hot haste, still holding me by both arms, whilst the men and the mules pushed by us. "Do you know Ferraris is dying—struck speechless up at his villa only an hour

15*

ago—and he to play to-night to all the Princes, and I at such expense as never was;—and now all ruined unless indeed you would take the character yourself?"

I told him I had heard it as I came up the Sdrucciolò; people were heavy of heart for it; for Ferraris, though in the decline of his years, was the greatest player that the stage of Italy then numbered amongst its actors.

Well, in a word, he so besought me and wrought on me to take Ferraris's place, that I, thinking of Raffaellino, at last assented.

The doors of the Goldoni opened at eight of the clock. But I needed little preparation; the costumes of Ferraris were about my measure, and for the part I knew it all well: in the old times, with the Zinzara and her people, we had played the "Don Marzio alla Bottega del Caffè" many and many a time in the little sea and mountain towns of the Riviera and the Basque country. A glance, and all the old eloquence came back to me. I heard, as though it had been yesterday, the sonorous roll of the Zinzara's voice as she had first taught me the part by the light of a single candle, in her little attic, with her slender feet bare on the bare bricks, and a red japonica-flower thrust into her rough hair, and a great brown sausage hissing itself solemnly into readiness for supper over the charcoal stove, and through the broken lattice of the garret always the glimmer of the moonbeams and always the shimmer of the sea.

Poor woman! Was she dead? I wondered. It is strange how suddenly they flash into our lives, and how utterly they drift out of it, all these women!

I thought of the Zinzara—of nothing else—as I took the place of Ferraris, and, for the first time since I had played with her in those old dead days, passed on to the stage of a theatre "with a roof to it," as my Piedmontese's phrase had run.

That night was one of the strange accidents which have the force of gods—or devils—to change the tenour of men's lives.

When the curtain fell, my fame was crowned in Florence. I—the people's Pascarèllo—had the ball at my foot to play with it as I would.

The whole city seemed to go mad for me; they took me home to my garret in riotous homage, and stayed under my window half the night singing my Io triomphe.

Much was due to the time, no doubt. I had become to them a sort of incarnation of Free Italy, and I always love to believe that it is less Pascarèl the Player they care for than it is Pascarèl the Patriot; and if indeed it be so, how little, how very little, it matters that one is not likewise Pascarèl the Prince.

From that night my fame spread, and spread, not only in this country but in all others, like circles on water from a well flung stone. In a few months' space every hour of my art could be counted by gold and diamonds. And for Raffaellino I accepted it and worked; the little angelic lad saved my reason certainly, my life perhaps.

For the winter, any or all of the cities hire me, and they bid much higher for me, one against another very often, than I am surely worth; but, when the vines are in blossom, I always come back under the Cross and the Lily, and play all the summer through to my own people in this dear city of mine, a Florentine once more and nothing else.

For the other cities I am the Pascarèllo of the kings, and the wits, and the great ladies, and the pleasure seekers, and I have as many gold boxes and honied words as Marzzoco in the old days had kisses from captives. But here I am the Pascarèl of the people who come trooping to me out of the scorching streets and burning squares, that are even hot when the moon is high, and in from the sun-baked contado, where the grapes burn black in the fierce scirocco.

Here I am myself once more, and I have my own populace about me: and the foreigners seek me with bribes in their hands and say, come with us to Baden, to Monaco, to Belgium, to Russia, to heaven knows where not, and I will not go; I stay here in the summer and play as I choose in the open air theatres with the wings of the swallows over my head, and the eager brown faces of my own people around me.

If half the year I did not hear that deep chested, sonorous vibration of Italian laughter that is like the metal tones of great melodious bells, I should lose heart and manhood. It has been about me all my life, I cannot do without it. It is to me as the trumpet call to the trooper's horse. And there is no laughter like it under the sun; just, so I often think, must the young gods have laughed when Pan piped to them.

And so I have played on from that time until now, for sake of the little tender lad who dreams his days away in music in a little home that I have made for him looking on an old green convent garden behind the Palace of the Torrigianni. Besides, one must do something, or go mad.

And going up under the pale walls where the field roses are nodding, in the sunny road towards Signa, I meet Brunótta on her mule, going to sell her birds in Florence. She is plump, and brown, and cheery: she thrashes her beast, and shrieks shrilly to the fowls in her panniers. And I once cared to caress that little foolish sulky face! Oh God, what fools men look to themselves when they see themselves in the mirrors of their old dead loves! I feel chilly and grown old.

The crickets sing in the canes by the shallow Grève water, and the little red roses are bright on the edge of the grey dusty wall; but for me—I feel old, I say.

What brought me this way to-day?

———— ————

THERE I stand with the laurel wreath in my hand. The laurel is not green, it is yellow from the passing of winter: laurels should always be painted so, for who gathers them in his spring time?

The daffodils blow to and fro by millions, in the fields; the vines are everywhere thrusting out their little tender buds; down there, beneath the shimmer of the olives, lies my City of the Lilies.

My friend paints on at his study of Panfilo, and tells me that I shall never be old; he will have it that artists never are. Perhaps there is some truth in it. In a sense we are children to the end—children who are ready to laugh even in our tears, and whose gayest laughter has always a sob in it; children so, no doubt. Children who after all know that the only real good that can come to them will be to be lulled into forgetful sleep in the arms of the great nursing mother, Death.

The painter rises and breaks off a bough of laurel fully budded, and brings it to me.

"Take this instead," he says; "your laurels are not tarnished nor faded."

For the matter of that I differ with him.

"I prefer those wrinkled ones flaked and crumpled with the winter's frost. They are very much more true, I say.

"Yet I have nothing to do with laurels of any sort, unless I hold them as deputy for Madama Pampinea. Get me those dandelion heads, blow balls as the old poets call them, they are my prototypes, for they are light as feathers, and arrow headed, and all the four winds of heaven toy with them, and no one marks where they fall. If a player is painted with any emblem, he should be painted with those puff balls. Their place in creation is very much about what his own is."

So I say. But he will not paint me with my puff balls; he paints his Panfilo holding a branch of amber tinted laurel. He tells me that I always look as if I had stepped out of the Decamerone; I tell him that every Florentine does the same. We have our father's faces, if not our father's force and our father's florins.

It is absurd to paint me with even a dead laurel; I Pascarèl, a player. I have a sort of fame now, it is true, but what is the fame of a player? I said long ago, the mere breath of a breeze that drives the comets of man's wonder a little before it for one hour, and with the wind sinks to utter silence, and cannot stir so much as a baby's paper windmill were it ever so.

I used to be so happy in the old life of mine. I think few men, if any, lived so long as I and had so little care. Merriment, freedom, air, and pleasure; I had them all, the petals of the four-leaved shamrock, which here and there one in a million finds and gathers, having the wit to know where to look for it, not in kings' gardens, but in little cool, green, darkling nooks of life, that bubble with the waters of content.

I had always been happy from the time that I first ran bare-legged and bare-headed in the Tuscan sun after my father's barrow. I was really and truly the last of the Pascarèl princes; so he said, my poor father, if he were not crazed, and indeed I suppose it is true enough. But what was that to me? It was much more to me that I had the lithest limbs in the Salterrello of any one north of Abruzzi; much more to me that the girls leaning across the rails of the loggia in the summer nights had ripe red lips that always smiled on me. I was happy tinkering the old pots and pans, from the Aquilean marsh to the Sorrentine orange woods; I was happy studying all lore, virtuous and iniquitous, in the sad old ways of Pisa, and following even into occult paths, the steps of Paracelsus and Agrippa; I was happy when I went seaward with the Zinzara and her people, to make sport and laughter all along the bright sea road from Savoy to Basque; and happiest of all when, with no master but my own whim and fancy, I sauntered through the world and

then came home this side the Alps, and set up, year
after year, wheresoever I would, my little wooden
theatre in some silent, shadowy grass-grown square of
any old forgotten city, or amongst the hyacinths, and
the poppies, and the asphodels of any sunny hillside
field; the time when I lived with the country folk and
the craftsmen, and when the very best that could be
said of me was, "There goes that vagabond; some
wit? Oh, yes; over his wine cups, so they say; but
only a stroller, that goes a-foot from place to place
and carries his baggage like a pack horse, nothing
more."

Life was a merry and gladsome frolic, if a sigh
ran under it on occasion; so it seemed to me, I say,
then, when the brown contadina grinned at my mirth,
and the young coppersmith hid his tears at my woe.
But now, when they call me a great genius, and des-
pots laugh and their consorts weep at the things that
I say and the things that I do on the stage of the
world's great theatre, now I feel myself no better and
no wiser than any soap bubble that a child's breath
floats upwards on the air. The heart is gone out of
the jest for me; and as for the pain—well, it lies too
close to me now; so close, that when I make them
laugh at it, I seem to make them mock my own. Can
you understand?

Nay—who should understand an artist? We do
not understand ourselves.

They call me great. Well, so be it, if it please
them. But for me, I know that I was nearer greatness
under my old torn canvas roof. For the artist is only
great when he lives in the ideal life of his imaginations, and when his own heart aches, how can he do

hat well? When the rack of the Real holds him tight
n its iron jaws, how shall he sport and sleep and
smile, in the arms of the Dream Mother?

"Have you seen Pascarèl, the great Pascarèl?" they
all say; and all the world runs to stare.

At times I play my own pieces, and then they say
too, "What a genius he has!"

Nay, it has even so happened that a king has called
me to his seat to give me a diamond box, and that a
great princess has cast to me her own bouquet of orchids in a band of jewels. They run after me in the
streets, and they sell my portrait betwixt the newest
courtezan and the last murderer. Who can want more
than that of Fortune?

Nay, nothing that I know of: only where is the
light heart with which I used to toss down the poor
mountain wine after I had acted to an audience of
stonecutters and vinedressers away there on the grey
Apennines? Ah, light hearts do not tarry with laurels.
This artist friend of mine does rightly to paint the
laurel with edges sear and torn. That laurel that Panfilo held, though gathered in the gardens of delight, it
must surely have borne the taint of the plague somewhere about it. Did the laughter on their lips never
make those storytellers shudder?—I shudder sometimes, now, at mine.

I am a fool: oh, I know that well. What was a
child with a sheen of yellow hair and a voice like a
lute, that she should change the face of the world and
the laughter of men to me?

Nothing in reason, I know, but then reason has
so little to do with one's life, and when one cannot

so much as tell whether the thing one cares for be living or dead;—that is hard, you see.

Pascarèllo! Pascarèl. When a village ran at my heels with welcoming clamour sending my name over the budding vines and the crimson glow of the field tulips, how well it was with me; I asked nothing better of heaven or earth, than just to laugh on in my own fashion through the careless spaces of the happy years. But now, though all the cities cry it out, and men come to me with gold in their hands, where is the charm? I felt old to-day, I say, as I went by the grey Grève water, where the little red roses were all alive and glad in the living sunshine.

And yet it is April too; and I am here in my City of Lilies.

"You waste half your year," said a Frenchman to me the other day. "You fling away on your Florentines in the summer all the fortune you make in the winter in Russia, and Paris, and Rome."

Well, if I do: I love my Florentines better than Russia, or Paris, or Rome: and, what do I want with a fortune?

Besides, I like to be free in the glad summer weather, when the fireflies flash all along the ground and the magnolia trees are all white with flower.

Perhaps I am idle by nature, an Italian is sure to be.

One fierce summer noon I espied a letter-carrier going out for a day's pleasuring at a fair in the contado, and stowing the post-bags of a whole district away in a cupboard behind his house door to await his return on the morrow. I asked him how he re-

onciled the dereliction to his conscience. He looked
t me with wide open innocent eyes of surprise.

"Che diamine, signore! The fair will not wait; if
do not go to-day, I go never. But, as for the letters,
hey will wait very well. No one knows what is in
hem, so no one is expecting anything; and, no doubt,
hey are all bad news, letters always are, and the poor
eople will be all the better for having another day in
eace."

With which he turned the key on the post-bags,
nd jogged happily off on his donkey with red ribbons
lying from its ears.

So on in like manner, I being idle and always at
eart a vagabond, shut the gold bags out of sight and
ome to the fairs in the summer, only instead of sure-
ooted Dapple I have a shying Pegasus; and there are
o red ribbons at its ears, but only the frayed ends
f tattered fancies; and when I get to the fair, the fun
f it is flat and jarred to me now like a bell that has
racked in a fire.

It is odd too. In the old time, when I made a
core of woolcarders weep like children, or a handful
f stonecutters laugh in their dry dusty throats under
hat canvas roof of mine, that blew with the winds,
nd rocked with the rains, and shone yellow with the
sunshine; in that time it always seemed to me that
the Player after all was the greatest artist of them all,
since turn by turn he was a breathing statue, a moving
picture, a poet who spake aloud, and a musician whose
syrinx was no less a thing than the million-chorded
passions of mortals, strung on the echoing shell of
human sympathy. So it always seemed to me in the
old times.

It used to be pleasure enough just to be in the sun and hear the cicale's zig-zig, and watch the big black fortuna buzz amongst the magnolia flowers, and beckon a brown-faced buxom girl up the path under the vines with her arm full of peaches and her lips ready for kisses. It used to be pleasure enough, all that; but now, there is wit enough in the cities, and there are women, handsome enough and ready enough with their laughter, and it is a gay, mad, zestful life, this life in the gas glare, and the masqueing, but still there is not much flavour in it. Perhaps it is because I have won all such graces and glories as there are to win—graces of a string of glass beads, glories of a truncheon of rushes.

Well, say I am great in my fashion, say I write what I please and I say what I please, and I am true to the duties of the Pantomimi and the Pasquin, whom every player worth his salt represents, in thrashing the tyrants with my scourge of asses' tails, and in showing the great world its ridicule in my triangular fool's mirror. Say I am great, so far,—pretty much as is the barber's brass basin which reflects its audience with their faces so lengthened or widened, that they perceive for the first time all that is grotesque in their features. Well, the brass basin only holds soapsuds, and sometimes I think I myself hold nothing better. But whether I am great or little the flavour has gone out of my life.

That is thankless enough. Yes, I know. They call me a wit and a poet, they call me Martial and Plautus, they say I am a Boccaccio in motion, and an Ariosto in motley. Well, it is all very pretty, if it be not all very true; and they know that once down

ere in the cheerless spring of Novara, it was not
ith a sword of lath that my blows were given; they
now that in Pascarèl the Player there is also a little
-just by that saving grace, a little—of Pascarèl the
atriot. And that last title I like much better than
ie old one my forefathers owned of Pascarèl the
rince. But still the flavour is gone somehow.

Now and then, when the lads are around me and
e go by moonlight through the streets, and some
ne strikes a chord from his mandoline and the shrill
esh voices rise, raising the echoes from palace and
rison, the old spirit comes over me, and I drive them
ith words of fire, and I make them laugh, just such
otous, endless, rippling laughter as the torrent laughs
i the sunshine, springing from stone to stone. Then
am the Pascarèl that the people knew, who was gay
ll day long like a grillo. But it will not last now,
nd when I am quite alone it seems to me that the
orld is weary as it seemed to me only to-day down
iere by the grey Grève water.

. "It is the idle hour," says Varkò, the painter,
oing into his room, which is heavy with the scent
om great sheaves of mughetti that fill a score of
Iontelupo bowls and Majolica dishes. "Lie here a
ttle while and smoke, and Ninetta will bring fruit
nd wine; meanwhile do you look at my winter's work,
y Mona Lisa."

"You are profane," I tell him; but he is indifferent
) the thunders of heaven that in justice should smite
im for thus taking in vain the name of a god. He

pushes me gently back into the shadow and then goes across the room and draws back the velvet curtain that is catching the full light on it. As the purple cloud sinks away, the light shines instead on a picture set in a dark frame of cinquecento carving, that is heightened here and there with a gleam of smalto in heralds' devices, and is surmounted by a ducal crown. It is only a woman's portrait.

Behind her there is a scarlet frame of oleander; she leans on a trecento balcony; her dress is of a curious dead gold, it is open at the throat and breast, and against the white skin a knot of vermilion-coloured carnations glow; there is a broken lute at her feet; she does not smile; one would say that she knows why the cords are snapped, why the music is still.

Red and gold! how the picture burns! And the woman's face is beautiful in the midst of all the fire; and one would say that the last love-song she will ever care to hear has been sung on that shattered lute.

Somehow, though it is summer with her, and girl-hood with her, and those oleanders are `flowers of Florence; somehow you know well that there is a great silence round her, a silence as of things that are dead.

It is a strange picture.

I stand before it blinded and confused. What is it I see? I hardly know. In impatience, he asks me what I think; what I think?

Who knows so little as I?

Rudely I tell him that his oleander should not beam so radiant-red as that, Tiziano always painted his summer roses in dull semitones; Tiziano's—beside his woman's cheeks—are cool and pale, and have no flush on them. So I say to Varkò; and all the while my eyes gaze into that oleander glory; and the woman's eyes look back at mine, and all manner of dead dreams raise their heads like little snakes around me.

Varkò is speaking to me, that I know; but the sense of what he is saying is vague and imperfect to me. Perhaps .he is telling me the history of the portrait. What need of that?—there is the broken lute.

"And her name?" I ask him suddenly.

My heart stands still as it were, and a rush of heat and life seems to throb through those Fates, that have been so heavy and so chill on it so long. I ask under my breath, as one speaks of the dead; I know that I am afraid of the answer. Afraid as I never was of that fiery sea of slaughter, down there by the field of Novara.

Varkò laughs aloud: a laugh that seems to me to echo jarringly through the stillness of the lily-scented air.

"Have you heard not a word of all I have been saying?" he cries to me. "It is scarcely a portrait: have you not heard me, indeed? And yet it is herself, just as I saw her in the last summer in Florence; I changed nothing. Nay, the oleanders burned as red as that behind her in the sunset. I know the Titian roses are all pale; but still, I have painted as I saw. It always seems best to me to do so, or try and do so at the least. All that red, all that gold, they would kill any other woman's face, but they do not kill hers. It is an old Florentine dress of cloth of gold, you see.

She was ready for a costume ball. She came out on to the balcony — just so, — the sun was setting. I sketched the scene, and showed it to her on the morrow. So the picture grew. And, now, what shall I call it? Not her name, she will not have it. It might be the 'tanta rossa' of Dante: or, I thought, of the mistress of Giorgione; she might have looked just so upon his balcony in Venice; and the lute is broken —there will be no more music in her life,—a little space, and the red oleander leaves will be falling like rain upon her grave and his. The picture would tell all that Giorgione story, not ill, I think. You see, under that lowest blossom to the left I have put the little arrowy head of an asp that will serve for the symbol of the plague. I asked her once if I might call it so, and she said: 'As you like; only Giorgione's mistress would smile, I think; she would know that death was about to be merciful to them both. But, as you like,' she said; 'as you like.' So I can call it so. And it is more Venetian than Florentine in colour after all. Her name? I wonder that you have to ask. The world knows you both so well. She is often in Florence, but she is not here now. She is the daughter of a great personage, a very great personage."

Then he lets the purple cloud of the curtain fall again over that fire-glow of the flowers, a little angered with the doubt that Titian's roses being pale, he perchance is wrong. But I stand looking at the shadow that had fallen and see still the oleander, and the broken lute, and the eyes of the woman which have no smile in them as the eyes of Giorgione's mistress would have had.

For the face of the picture is to me as the face of one risen from the dead.

A great personage, so he says, leaning there with the gold tissues falling all about her on the marble, and the Florentine carnations in her breast, and the gleam of jewels on her throat and forehead, and at her feet the lute, whose broken chords she, with all her greatness, could not heal again so that they would ever breathe forth the old, sweet, simple, tender notes. A great personage: yet surely also the child that had once gone with me through the lily-whitened grasses and the moon-lightened fields of maize, singing as the birds sang and careless of the morrow.

I feel chilly and grown old, as I felt by the side of the grey Grève water, where the sun had flashed amidst the canes. For there is no ghost whose breath is so cold, as the ghost of a love that is dead; and I have met two this day, this April day, when the soil is all yellow with daffodils, and all the earth is glad.

Would it be better to know her under the dusky marbles of some aisle of graves, in the mouldering heart of some world-forgotten city, or to find her great like this, with jewels in her breast, and that strange haunted look in her eyes?

The lute is broken: does she remember, I wonder?

Has she forgotten the days on the sunny hillsides, by the shallow brook waters, and the leaves of the vines, and beneath the murmuring poplars? Has she forgotten? Has she forgiven? What can it matter—anyway—if she be great like this?

She must be dead to me, you know.

And that living death is worse than the death of

the grave, they say; that living death when the voice speaks still to all others, and only is silent to you. And yet the world is full of these things! One wonders the sun still drags on its way; one wonders all men are not mad.

The seeding grass was wet with torrents of blood down there on the March day of Novara, and the cannon balls, as they swept through the rising corn, did the work of the harvest sickle. How came Fate to miss me amongst the slain? I wonder;—and grow old.

I have tried to love other women; I have told other women I did love them; but I do not think they believed me, and I know I did not believe myself.

And now that I have seen that picture—yes, that is, of course, how she must be; a great lady, with a knot of diamonds in her breast. There is not much left in her of the bold, shy, pretty, saucy child that I walked through Verona with, that night of the Veglione. Nothing left probably, not even perhaps a regret.

A flush of shame at most, perhaps, when this brilliant illustrissima remembers how she roamed the fields and hills with a troop of strolling comedians; remembers too, maybe, now and then, that one of those wandering players set his lips to her cheek and held her little hand in his in the autumn hour, when the wild anemones were all aglow beneath the brown Badià.

Well, no one will ever know that I remember it too. She last and least of all; if ever I should meet her.

There are things one is bound to forget, or, at least, that bind one to live as if they were wholly forgotten.

And what is Oblivion if it be not Age? I feel old, I say, as I felt at noon where the little red roses nod by the Grève stream.

"You are sure there is never a scorpion?" says Astra, the actress, to me this April day, when at sunset we go up together to the great open-air theatre that draws all Florence to it on summer nights where it stands under the pine woods on the hillside beyond the Gate of the Cross.

"You are sure there is never a scorpion?" says Astra to me, bathing her fair face in the lilies and lying breast downward in the grass with the vineshadows playing, as if in love with her, over her soft, indolent, wanton limbs.

I tell her no; but alas! grow the lilies ever so richly there is always a scorpion somewhere for me.

That is just because a man ever desires the thing he has not, you see; most surely desires it of all when that thing is called woman. For the lilies are yellow as soon as gathered, but the scorpion stings on and on, on and on.

I talked with a scorpion once; an old, old scorpion, long as my hand, and hoary as Esau with length of years. I found him, and made his acquaintance in a prison in Venice long, long ago, where the Stranieri lodged me three months or so for having spoken words too strong and too seasoned one riotous Carnival time, when I had rolled my first little Arte under the wings of the Lion.

The old scorpion never hurt me but would lash his tail and talk by the hour together. He had heard the sad tale of the wild Lagoon waters and the sigh of the Gondolier's Stali! for ages and ages and ages there in his sea-girt chambers; since first he had come from the East, no bigger then than a scarabeus, hidden in a fold of gold tissue that one of Dandolo's men had brought with him from mighty Byzantium, and thrown on the couch of his mistress one amorous night in August. The scorpion stung her and she died—-why not? there is always a sting in all love, and perhaps the quickest death to it is the kindliest.

He had seen many things and many centuries this old wise bearded scorpion of Venice, and one day when he sat in his chink,—a black blot in a line with the sun,—I asked him to tell me, since we were good friends together, what was the secret and source of that mystical power for which my human kind was wont to curse him and his; and slay them and embalm them in oil as dead Pharaohs were buried in perfume.

The old scorpion made me answer; he who had lived in the beautiful wanton breast of that Venice, which men have called the harlot of Italy; the old scorpion made me answer.

"What do we slay with? And what is the death in our sting? A venom that is as that fire which no water quenches, and as the grave-worm that no feast of flesh can slake? What is that, you fool, with which we arm ourselves and strike where we will and never fail? Listen here then, and know that this for which you all curse us is born of yourselves, not of us. For in the beginning of time when Death came forth from the gates of hell on the bloodless white horse and was set free to pace to and fro the world, and scatter desolation as he would, Death scattering himself broadcast in many shapes and fashions, Death one night made us the scorpions and set us to run over the earth.

" The first scorpion was only a harmless big beetle at the beginning, ugly, of course, but quite innocent, but Death took it up and steeped it in two human hearts that all bleeding and smoking lay in the hollow of his hand. And from the man's heart the first scorpion sucked desire, and from the woman's heart it sucked jealousy; and when it had sated itself of these to the full, Death set it down on the ground.

"Now be fruitful and multiply," he bade it. "And do your work on the human race, for you have a venom in you that never will die while the world rolls on round the sun."

So the old scorpion talked, blinking at the light from the sea walls in Venice.

And now,—bloom the blue lilies ever so brightly, there is always a scorpion somewhere for me.

For Astra and Poppea there is a great supper spread this April night, under a tent at midnight when our play is over. They have acted superbly, and they have had all the glory their souls could desire, and they laugh à gorge déployée, their red lips parting over their snowy teeth, playing with flowers in bands of jewels that some of the nobles have flung to them. They are famous, and spoilt, and capricious, and cruel sometimes, and jealous always; and like children in their mirth, as all artists are all the world over.

The white folds of the tent flutter, the torches flicker in their brass sconces, the young actors have dressed the canvas with boughs and pennons and fluttering scrolls; where the curtains open there shines the white radiance of magnolia trees that grow just there on the hillside, and whose closed cups are silver in the moon.

There are laughter and jesting, and such amorous follies as women like Astra and Poppea await whenever their eyes may beam upon the sons of men. They lie there like Tiziano's women, and their jewels gleam and their pretty hands crush the bursting fruits; and without, down the hills, the people troop away shadowy, cloud-like, singing as they go, the sweet sounds grow fainter and fainter as they stream farther away under the low stone pines.

We ourselves go down the hill together a little later; it is the fancy of Astra and Poppea to leave their horses champing by the gates and use their own pretty listless lightsome feet.

Their silken skirts shiver over the grasses, sweeping down the lilies; the young men go before them with flute and mandoline singing the Invitation of Paesiello; there are gleams of blue where the iris are growing, the air is full of magnolia fragrance, the night is as clear as the day, it is past one of the clock, Florence sleeps silvery and very still.

A shrouded figure passes us masked, Astra and Poppea shrink a little; it looks dismal in the moon; they take it for some brother of the Misericordia. I see that it is a woman. But why masked, and on the hills too? It is not even Carnival.

We go on through the gates into the silent city, the sleepy guards let us through, the music and the singing wake all the echoes as we pass along the dark old streets and under the Church of the Croce.

The lads sing more sweetly as they go by and their voices drop to a tender minor key; they remember that Michelangelo and Leonardo lie there. Now and then a woman drops a rose to us from her lattice; now and then a lover comes out from some vaulted doorway, looking warily to see if any talebearer be lurking near; now and then a stream of light falls from some balcony where two shadows lean one on the other.

So we go on through the silent city, on into the square of the Signoria, and here, late though it is, there are men grouped together in little knots, murmuring eagerly, with their cloaks cast about them and their faces flushed and dark.

We have left Astra and Poppea at their palace; the youths have ceased their singing; we pause by the Cathedral and look up; someone has set against the bronze Judith a flag of three colours; the red in it glows like blood in the silver glistening cool Florence night.

"What is it?" we ask; we have lost our memory up there on the hills in music, and have forgotten for the moment the storm that hovers northward where the city of Virgil lies.

"What is it?" we ask, whilst the Judith bends her brows against the moon.

They answer us in one word.
"War."

War again away there in the North.

As I go homeward by myself I am glad.

I am tired of Astra and Poppea, of the masquing and the folly, of the paper laurels and the hobble of lead, of the showers of gold and the laughter of fools.

I come upstairs to the broad tapestried chamber where the moonrays lie so white upon the marble floor, and I go to an old chest and I take out the old knapsack and the old musket that I carried years ago over the Lombard fields.

After all, they are the truest friends a man has; after all, when one is a Florentine, one is a soldier before one is anything else.

They lie there in the moonlight, old battered moulded war-worn things; on the barrel of the musket there is red rust, it was a fellow-student's life blood; I never had the heart to touch it. How shabby and broken the knapsack is, too; it was nearly new that day in Pisa when I saw the Zinzara and her people troop by under the old grey walls, and went after them on the same sea road and caught them as they travelled along in the dust, singing and eating their cherries.

There are the cherry stains now on the leather, for she would fill it with fruit, I remember; the stains are black,—a dying man leaned his head on it amongst the crushed grass whilst a burning village smoked in the midst of the millet fields, as Carlo Alberto's hopes died down with the setting sun.

I sit in the moonlight with the old pack in my hands and the musket at my feet, thinking of all the dead years that seem to drift by me one by one as the clouds go by past the casement.

Some friends of mine break into the room, and find me there, the musket at my feet.

They are all breathless and excited talking of the news.

"You are not going, Pascarèl?" they cry to me.

I tell them yes.

"But you are mad!" they say in chorus.

I shrug my shoulders. It is very possible.

"But, with your fame?" they cry.

"Oh, altro! my poor paper laurels—a plaything for a Mardi Gras—what more?"

"But you will be ruined!" they urge.

"That is very possible, too."

"But just when you are great," they cry; "just when the world catches your words as if pearls fell from your mouth—to thrust that all away into a common soldier's knapsack—it is lunacy."

"That is as it may be. Italy wants Venice and Verona."

I rub the old cherry stains on the old knapsack, and think how strange it is that all we students dreamed of in the gloom of Pisa,—and were called mad and worse for so dreaming of as we marched twelve abreast by night through the sombre streets, chanting sonnets of Manzoni,—should now be come and be coming to pass with a precision, and romance, that together make it like the work of magic.

They stay till the day breaks arguing with me—what is the use? The old musket lying there on the marble, seems to suit me better now than the painted bladder and gilded bells of the pantomime. To care for the follies of the carnival fair, one must have a heart as light as the bladder, and mirth that rings like the bells.

Well, I had these longer than most men. If the bladder be weighted with lead and the bells are jangled and out of tune now, at least my measure lasted longer than it lasts for most men.

At length my friends go away; they go sorrowful, and they think me a fool.

The chamber is black and grey around me. The dawn breaks, but breaks slowly.

I felt old to-day as I went by the shallow Grève water.

I felt weary as Astra laughed amongst the lilies.

How still it is!—here,—high amongst the roofs.

I am left alone in the chilly light of the dawn. The shadows are black on the marble floor. A mouse creeps up and smells at the musket where the blood of the dead soldier is crusted on the steel. The knapsack still lies on my knee. I think of Pisa.

How prettily and innocently jealous she was, the donzella, leaning out of the old grated window, because she had heard how, in the student days, the Zanzara had wound a red ribbon to my mandoline. Yet I remember too, how as we went underneath the old palaces, and spoke together of Margherita of France, she marvelled how the princess could wish to

ander with gipsies, and to leave all the pride and
ie pomp of her royalty for mere freedom and mirth
nd the fresh air of heaven. She marvelled, yes,
ıough she had wandered with the Arte and me. She
ould not have been happy with us in other years;
o doubt she is best as she is.

And yet,—does she never, I wonder, think of the
ours when we went together through the trailing
ines light of foot as of heart in the warmth of the
un?

Oh, those old fair dead days! they were so glad
nd so innocent and so simple. Why could they not
ast for ever beneath those blue Tuscan skies?

The city is still asleep.

The first chimes ring muffled through the shadows
if night that still lingers. Good women will rise
rom their beds and will go out into the darkness of
he churches, and will break their hearts in prayer
iver the sons and the lovers who are going out to
var, on the old Lombard battle-fields, where the maize
ınd the vine are green.

I have no one to pray for me.

It is always so, when one has loved too many.
Ve gather the roses too quickly, and the wind blows
he leaves away hither and thither, and our hands are
eft empty.

Well, the musket lies there; and, there is always
Italy.

If the lute be broken and the fool's bells be
angled it is time to die as my fellow-students died
ımongst the trampled corn.

CHAPTER II.

Her Story.

Do you know Sta. Margharità's? the little brown square church with its bell clanging in the open tower, above in the sweet air on the hills?

There is level grass all about it, and it has a cool green garden shut within walls on every side except where a long parapet of red dusky tiles leaves open the view of the Valdarno; underneath the parapet there are other terraces of deep grass and old old olive trees, in whose shade the orchids love to grow, and the blue iris springs up in great sheaves of sword-like leaves.

There are trees of every sort in the cloistered garden, the turf is rich and long, the flowers are tended with the tenderest care, the little sacristy glows red in the sun, an acanthus climbs against it; the sacristan's wife comes out to you plaiting her straw and brings you a cluster of her roses; you sit on the stone seat and lean over the parapet and look down-ward, birds flit about you, contadini go along the grass paths underneath, and nod to you, smiling; a delicious mingled loveliness of olive wood and ilex foliage and blossoming vineyards shelve beneath you; you see all Florence gleaming far below there in the sun, and your eyes sweep from the snow that still lies on Vallombrosa to the blue shadows of the Carrara range.

It is calm and golden and happy here at Sta. Margharità's, high on the fragrant hill air, with the gueldre roses nodding above head, and the voices of

he vinedressers echoing from the leaf-veiled depths
elow.

To live here and dream the years away and only
core the time by the colour of the vines, it would be
rell, I think; very well. Only for such a life one
ust needs be so happy. Happy as one is for an
our, for a day, for a month, but never for longer.
Iappy as one can only be when a great passion is
lose about us, and is past, and present, and future,
; world, and sun, and God.

Sometimes I come up here for quiet's sake and
ean my arms on the red ledge, and wait to watch
he sun sink down behind the deep azure of Carrara
nd change the broad green valley to a sea of molten
old.

I used to come here with Pascarèl—many times,
nany times.

One day in especial I remember. The wooden
Arte had been reared in the village yonder; it was a
;iorno di festa; it was in the April time; we came up
long the narrow road between the high walls, over-
opped with china roses and hawthorn; we came into
he garden by the church and sat down, he on the
arapet, I on the little stone bench in the corner
nder the aloe.

Mass was over; in the sacristan's house they were
;oing to the mid-day meal; they brought food out to
s and would take no denial. We shared the simple
east of soup and bread and salad, there amongst the
;reen leaves and the flowers; we paid them for it
vith the mandoline and many songs of Florence.

We stayed there all the afternoon till the sun set,
nd we heard the Ave Maria ringing from all the

belfries in the valley as we strolled backward along the grass paths of the hills; he gathered the dainty orchids for me under the olive trees; we laughed and jested and made music as we went.

To-day the same scene lies before me in the sun; the old bell in the little square tower strikes the quarters with the same sound; the garden and the church are nowise changed; the sacristan's wife comes out smiling, plaiting her straw, and holding to me a little knot of flowers; she calls me the most illustrious, she gazes with gentle awe at the jewels on my hands; she does not look aged and her husband is stooping over the dark moist fresh-turned earth binding carnations just as we left him on that day.

It is just the same, just the same, only the music is silent.

Only!

I lean on the red edge of the wall and look down; two contadini go by under those old gnarled olives; they are young; he laughs and her cheeks grow red. I would give the world to be the girl, bareheaded there in the sun, poor, plaiting her straw as she goes along over the grass-grown furrows.

For the music is not silent for her. It may only indeed be a homely little pastoral song, only a peasant's stornello, rhymed to the hum of the spinning wheel and the bleat of the goats in the meadow. But it is the song that makes blythe her heart in the ragged bodice and light her feet in the ox-ploughed ways. It is perfect to her, and lips that are eager and tender murmur it low in her ear; she is blessed amongst women, I say. But to me the green earth silent.

Varkò, the painter, made my portrait the other
lay. I stood in the sunset one night in a court-dress
1at pleased him. He brought me an old trecentisto
1te and asked me to sing him some Florence song
s he worked. As I stretched out my hand the lute
ell and broke in two on the marble floor. "Paint it
o," I said to him; he did not know why, but so it
eemed fittest to me.

And the lute is there on the picture, broken—
1eyond the cunning of men to mend. He calls the
ainting Giorgione's Mistress. It seems an ill-chosen
1ame to me. For she must have been happy always;
ll that glad life in Venice that was one long golden
ower-crowned masque, and then the short sharp
leath that did not divide them but wedded them
losely for all time, together forever in the quiet of
he grave and in the memory of the world.

It is so few years, and yet it seems so many ages
ince the white roses came to me in farewell.

There followed on that time a space of absolute
1nconsciousness. It is all blank, all dark to me.

When I awoke again there were no more around
ne the bare Florentine walls, the aromatic pungent
7lorentine odours, the gay vibrating Florentine street
:hatter. I saw no more the old carved window and
he little brown figure of the stocking mender with
he sun on her silver earrings and the silken hose at
1er feet.

It had all faded away as though it had never
1een.

I awoke with gold and silver and fine linen and
:osy hues about me; I awoke with great wide windows
1efore me, through which there gleamed gilded rails

and chesnut trees in blossom, and a light vivacious crowd of children, running hither and thither with lilac in their hands; I awoke with Florio's whispers in my ears.

"Oh, carina mia, you will live? you will live! Only see, this is Paris and we are so rich, so rich. If the donzella like to eat gold she can have it as easily as grapes in vintage time! Oh, carina mia, you will live, you will try a little to live, will you not?"

I looked at him stupidly, pushing the curls from my aching forehead; live? why should I live? the blue lilies were all dead in Tuscany.

One day they set before me great cases of sapphires and diamonds and other precious stones. They were heirlooms, they said.

"You are too young for them," said my father, "but they will become you, as those old yellow and purple velvets used to do in old Verona. Make yourself your handsomest to-night, the world will see you."

I had no choice but to obey.

The world saw me and made itself a fool for me: the great dazzling lawless world of Paris. I stretched my hands to it thankfully, it gave me a feverish forgetfulness; anything was better than to sit and see the chesnuts bud in the cool sunlight and to go mad with longing for the deep vine shadows and the sweet mountain stillness of my Tuscany. Anything was better than to stare till one was blind at the cruel glare on the shadeless pavements, and grow sick with longing for the mere smell of the oak wood fires in the Florence streets.

One day I saw an iris behind a gilded garden-pale;
n iris as blue as my lost heavens—the iris of Dante
1at blooms in millions down the olive slopes and
mongst the maize in Tuscany with the first wakening
f the spring-time sun.

I thought that Dante in his hell had missed the
1arpest torture of it all. Why did he not set a little
alian meadow lily to grow in the darkness of Caina
nd Ptolomea and smile with its azure eyes at the
espair of those for whom the sun of Italy had for-
ver ceased to shine?

Am I not mad? as mad as dead 'Dino's Pazza,
alling on the waters to give up her lover by sad
errara? I call on the dead days, and they are
rowned and mute like 'Dino.

My father is good to me, in his cold idle manner.
Ie is proud because the world calls me so handsome,
nd he fills my hands with riches; I spend in a day
·hen I like what would make this little paese on the
ills here a fairyland for all its people. Men love
1e—or vow they do,—and I play with them, and
1ey say I have no heart. Women envy me as I pass
y, and hate me with that hate which is a woman's
ross of honour. What more can any female creature
vant?

And yet you see one is so thankless. I, who
lreamed ceaselessly of all this greatness, and thirsted
or it lying wide-awake on my truckle bed, and
vatching the moon rise over the Scala's palaces, and
ight the painted loves of Orpheus on the vault above,
often shake the jewels off my aching head and
ling myself down weeping as 'Dino's Pazza weeps be-
ide the riverside, for the time when the wild poppies

were twisted in my wind-blown curls by the hands of Pascarèl.

Many have asked me in marriage. My father looks at me with a curious look often and says, "Gather your roses while you may — that is sound counsel, though a poet's."

But how shall I gather them? I? who only hold a dead rose to my heart that no one sees, as old Giùdettà held hers fifty long years in silence and in faith.

I have no faith; if I had had faith, never had I let so poor and vile a thing as his dead amorous folly stand betwixt me and my belief in him. All that I know; too late, too late.

But so much faith as this I have. He kissed me there, on the dark hillside on the night of the saints under Fiesole. No other shall ever touch me; so much faith as this I have.

A woman who carries lips un-virgin to her husband, what better is she than the adulteress?

So I think at least; old Mariuccia would say so if I could rouse her from her hard-won rest away there where the alpine storm-winds lash the sullen sea-green of the Adige into foam.

There is one who torments me more than all others to be faithless to this single poor shred of human fealty that I treasure.

I have seen him but lately, since we came hither, back into this dear Tuscan land; it is he who in the old villa above Lucca begged me to sing to the mandoline with so insolent an eagerness in his bold eyes.

He is my father's cousin and heir; the likeness in

ı that I saw that night was no chance resemblance.
times I wonder if he recognizes in me the child
t leaned against the screen in the great hall with
 strange masquerade dress of violet and gold: I
ınot tell. He never talks of it; he is a man full of
ce and courtliness, and to all people my father
aks of me as having been reared in a convent of
rthern Italy. No one doubts: why should they?
ly sometimes I think my cousin doubts; sometimes
ıink he knows full well that I was once the little
ndering Uccello of the Arte.

He loves me, or pursues me at the least with a
ɔng ardour and with delicate wiles and ways. My
ıer favours his suit, so far at least as he ever
ıses himself from his voluptuous apathy to urge
ɔn me anything. The man is sole heir to all his
ɔ-come greatness and he would be glad that I
ɔuld bear the mighty name and wear the honour of
ɪlways.

So they talk; so they talk; and my cousin woos me
only men skilled in the world as he is can; he has
· father's beauty and my father's grace and ease;
t I—whilst his words are most eloquent upon my
·, all I can hear is one voice murmuring in its sweet
ıorous Tuscan, "Oh, gioja mia!" in the dreamy
trous midnight when the falling stars dropped over
ite Fiesole.

For how can I forget? how shall I ever forget till
.m dead?

What woman forgets the first kisses that have
rned on her cheek, and throat, unless she grow
ht enough and foul enough to lend her lips to
:sh caresses? And that I am not;—nay, thank God;

—so much of womanhood there is in me, though in so much else, I, the great lord's daughter and the great world's darling, am so far sunk beneath the little simple wayward, fear-innocent less, Uccello.

Yet there must be something more, for in the world there where they sing my praises, they always say "a beautiful thing—but wild—and with an untamed look;" and when I shake off my rich velvets and my priceless laces at the end of the long nights of pleasure, I shiver a little, and in my soul long for the old simple dusty skirts stained with the juice of the trodden grapes, and the play of the bleating kids and the dew of the wind-blown acacias where I ran bareheaded and happy in the summer sun in the wake of the wandering Arte.

For I am so young still, and yet I feel so old; and all that one sweet buried summer time has all my dead youth with it in its grave of withered rose leaves.

"What would Mariuccia say if she came before us now!" cries good, merry, blissful Florio, a thousand times if once: ah, yes! I have all the greatness and the glories that I sighed my soul out for in my ungrateful babyhood, sitting at her feet under the broken Donatello. And what good is it to me? so little good that when I see a little white anemule shine under those olive trees my heart is sick with longing and I am weary unto death.

Is it three years? only three years? It seems eternity since there, by the Mouth of the Lion, the crowd of Oltrarno bore him away on the wild rejoicing night?

Men talk of him; I hear his name and see it on the walls of cities.

"A great genius," they say, "fitful and never to be controlled, but of wit keen as the needle's edge, and of powers varied as the sunset's hues." The fame of him has leapt into sudden light before the world; "a player's fame!" says my cousin with a sneer, "a player's fame! a mushroom's fungus growth that will die down with the first day of rain!"

Does he remember,—my cousin? When he says these things, I think so.

Can I be glad that he has those paper laurels, as he used to call them?

No, for art is a rival longer lived than any woman. Ah, dear heaven! I should have known that a woman's love is worth nothing unless it be doglike and takes good and evil alike uncomplaining? Yes, perhaps; but as it is my heart burns with love still.

Last night, only last night, I was weak enough to wish to see his face again there on the hillside where the great open-air theatre stands, and I left my horses at the base of the slope, and put my mask and domino on, and went upward on foot where the red and white flag fluttered high above the oak woods.

How still the night was; and the great golden moon hung in the silvery air, and the white magnolias gleamed like lamps, and a cloud of rosy oleander leaves was blown in my face by the wind.

Do you know what the night is in Italy? No? Then you do not know how near heaven your earth can be.

It is a great place without a roof, a summer theatre for the people. The grass grows up to the walls and the oak woods are all above. It was quite quiet; there was a sound of dreamlike music sighing everywhere upon the silent and leafy sides of the hills.

There were many doors all open to the air. In one a group of pifferari leaned; next to them was a peasant girl with a bulrush in her hand; next her again a woman who rested her basket of melons on a rail and held a child to her bare breast.

Behind, the little wandering pifferari strayed near the entrance without paying, their eyes aglow under their tangled hair; the metal workers and perfume pressers and mosaic makers from the town leant together with bended brows; the noble stooped his delicate dark head to hearken yet more surely; the proud duchess at his side beat the measure softly with her broad black fan, so they listened, the Tuscan people, with the shadow of the great roofless walls around them and above their heads the blue night skies. And the genius of what they had heard had entered into them, and the sweet sounds of it were sighing in echo from all their mouths, and they laughed aloud in pleasure, while their eyes kindled and flashed through the shadow, and a great shout went up from three thousand voices to the quiet stars where the clouds were floating.

They all cried one name;—"Pascarèl!"

I glided in and stood in the press between a cobbler in his leathern apron who had brought a shoe to sew there and a contadino with his brown cloak tossed over one shoulder and behind his ear a knot of asphodels.

The light and shadows played about them; the oil flames burned clear, the smell of the fresh herbs and grass drifted from the hills without; above head were the purple clouds with the moon a globe of gold, and a great dusky hawk winging his slow way across the face of the sky.

Ah, God! the familiar sweetness of it all! I lost all sense of time and place. I was once more the little wandering Uccello of the Arte, happy because the breeze blew, happy because the sun would rise, happy for every trifle of the day and night, happy as the flowers in the fields.

The people made a little way for me and I sank on the seat that the old cobbler rose to surrender to me. They looked but little at me, they were absorbed in what they had heard, and a woman masked is not so strange in Italy as elsewhere. I sat quite still.

The great circle went round and round before my sight, the lights wavered in the dusky shadows of it, the music sounded like the swell of some far-off sea.

Whether it were harmony or discord I had no perception, nor how long it lasted after my entrance there I cannot tell.

I could feel the wind blowing in my eyes, I could see the hawk hovering above with outstretched wings, I could smell the sweet familiar scents of the wild hillside; that was all.

My consciousness was with the old dead days.

The silence around me was broken by tumultuous shouts; the music had ceased, the people were sending the thunder of their applause up to the quiet darkness where the stars were; the hawk had soared away.

It was all vague and full of fury, like a storm, to me; the waves of sound beat on my ears but I did not hear them.

Then—lightly as a leopard in its own deserts, Pascarèl leaped on the stage with a bound, and thunders of homage echoed through the house, and his eyes flashed over the sea of faces and the clear resonant vibrations of his voice thrilled through the murmuring welcome of the hushing house.

And so I saw and heard him—I—once more; I who had felt his kisses there on the far hillside beneath Fiesole that unforgotten night before the Feast-day of the Dead.

And yet I sat quite quiet, and only drew a little into shadow where the gaslight would not find my diamonds. Women are liars, say you? Well, they need be.

There was silence, tumult, silence, tumult again; then the people streamed away out into the moonlight.

I was left all alone. I could hear them going down the hills playing on their mandolines. The lights were blown out. There was only the white light of the full moon.

Near at hand there was laughter and singing. They sounded strangely, waking all the echoes in the great silent amphitheatre. My life thrilled with sharp sickly pain, as though a snake had bitten me.

I heard the clear vibration of the laugh of Pascarèl, that Italian laugh, like the ring of silver upon stone, which is like no other upon earth. The light merriment of women crossed it, and a burden of a love song followed.

I rose to my feet, and felt my way blindly through the rows of seats to the open doorway, round which the coils of wild vine were blowing in the wind from the mountains.

He was standing on the hillside; his lips laughed, the moonlight fell about him; his mandoline was slung with a scarlet ribbon; against him leaned a beautiful wanton thing with laces trailing in the damp grass, and a white hand that stretched over his shoulder and touched the strings of the lute.

I knew her face; she came of Venice; they called her in her world Poppea.

I went by them, noiseless and shapeless, a dark shadow against the white magnolia blossoms. He started, and a false note shivered sadly from the mandoline.

This was how he remembered! Ah, God! what is it that stays with me still?—it cannot be love—for very shame's sake it must now be hate?

And yet,—and yet,—I envy that peasant girl who goes yonder through the olives with her lover's hand in hers!

CHAPTER III.

The old Sea Queen.

It is not an army that goes out to war. It is a whole people that rises in arms. My birth country alone sends out many thousand Tuscans; all made of the same steel as those who, in the old day held their villa on the Murello slopes there, against all assaults from the stoutest chivalry of England and of Germany.

I come down to Genoa in the fresh May days; along this beautiful sea road that my knapsack and

I travelled so long long ago with the French comedians, eating their cherries and singing their songs, with the blue sky overhead and the blue sea at their feet.

I remember how we came into Genoa then—they and I—in the glad Easter weather, with the white dust on our feet and the ready jest on our mouths. Genoa was in festà that day; and all the ladder-like streets were ablaze with flags, and all the many-coloured flints of the old sea palaces glowed in the fervid noon heats from the sapphire water. And we ate fruits in the quaint old galleries along the sea line; and laughed and chattered down the steep ways where the Doria and their fellows fought so often, knee to knee and knife to knife; and then, at nightfall, we played to a thousand odd sailors and traders of every clime from off the vessels in its harbour, and the theatre over and done with, we strayed out into the moonlight along the sea again, slaking our throats with pomegranates, and waking the echoes of the palaces of the old Sea Queen with the thrill of the mandoline until the dawn broke away there across the waves where Africa was lying.

Ah, Dio mio!—those were goodly days, and gracious in their folly, and sweet in the mouth as the red water melon, if also as swift to melt away and leave no taste, and as little fit for life's real sustenance.

And here is Genoa again in the May time, and this time its music is of drums and bugles, and the roll of cannon and the tramp of soldiers; this May time its waters and skies and air are grey, and full of storm; the rain falls, the shadows of the hills close darkly round; the old palaces lean together, and the

eets are dark as night; there are only the golden
anges and the tricoloured banners that have colour
them, and laugh a little through the gloom.

The city seems to tremble where she sits by the
a, that she wrested in the old old days from bereaved
sa.

Through her streets and down her mighty quays
ere tramp, all day long, thousands and tens of
ousands of tired feet—all Italy and half France are
re.

Through the mists that hang on high, over the
ive woods, there come half muffled cheers. Though
e rain falls the bouquets fall too; fall in showers on
e shining lines of bayonets from the balconies above.
hrough the white vapour from the Mediterranean the
unds of the salutes from the frigates roll heavily and
:ho down the mole. The old archways and the dim
.vernous galleries along the sea line are all full of
e troops, that pause there in a little breathing space
taste the wine and press the fruits into their burn-
g throats. Little children glow here and there out
the fog like little knots of flowers; the smallest of
em have the three colours somewhere on their dress,
d their small shrill voices are all crying vivas for
e King and Italy.

Genoa is for the moment the mouthpiece of the
hole roused nation.

The rain falls—falls all day long; and at night
ims the cressets and clusters of lights that glitter
own the terraces in the old palaces, and puts out the
road flame of torches that glow down the terraces
nd flare on the sculptured fronts and the varicoloured
arvings in all the sloping streets. The rain falls as

though the sky were sold to Austria. But for once it cannot drive the people in; for once, though the flags droop, the hearts do not: for once the eager steps race, and the loud huzzas rise, and the millions of flowers are thrown through the grey sad mist as through the lost gold of the sunshine.

The clouds may gather and the storms may beat as they will, and do their worst; there is a fire alight in Italy that no rain can quench;—nay, not even a rain of blood.

Genoa for the moment is the meeting place of the whole roused nation.

I sit here in the covered places in the galleries fronting the sea.

It is full of many-coloured fruits, and flasks of wine, and piles of polenta. Oil-lamps swing above, shedding a dim light. A handsome brown-faced woman chaffers at the counter, her great gold ear-rings flashing with each movement of her head. Soldiers come and go by scores, by hundreds; Zouaves with the African sun on them, Neapolitans still in their fishing shirts; Tuscan conscripts with the first down on their lips; Cuirassiers with flashing chains and plumes; Italian nobles with Titian faces and slender stately forms in the simple tunic of the volunteer, all coming and going, drinking and jesting, clashing their sabres against the great brass scales, tilting the straw covered flasks to their mouths, tossing their sashes against the baskets of oranges, making, all unwittingly, a thousand studies for Meissonnier, with the dusky light on the white crosses of Savoy and the silver medals of France, whilst out there, beyond the quay, the ι is murmuring, and the vessels are looming like antom ships in the shadows.

The French laugh and chatter endlessly, and our ɔple will not be outdone in lightness of heart; but ery now and then the Italian faces grow very grave d pale a little under their olive brows as their eyes seaward; here it is not a question of a campaign t or won, it is a nation's life or death that is in the lance.

I have come from the Caffè of the Concordia.

It is grander there and stiller amongst its orange ɔves and throngs of staff officers; but I like better be here in this dusky archway with my musket at r knee, and, around, the strong salt smell of the ι.

As I sit here thinking thus, there comes noiselessly ɔ the crowded place a slight small figure, travel-ined and very weary, with a beautiful pale little ɛe under curls of reddened gold. The figure comes me shyly through the noisy soldiers, and takes my nd.

"Dear friend, am I too late? May I go with you?"

It is Raffaellino.

For a while I cannot speak to him, I am so much ιazed. I left him safe in Florence with his genius, the quiet and the sunshine, springing to goodly sta-re like the prophet's gourd.

"You!" I cry to him, making way for him on the ndow settle. "You;—Merciful heaven, you! to ɛe this war? We shall have women and children xt!"

It is brutal of me, but I am rough with him. I

am angered to see him there; a lad no stronger than any reed that blows in Arno water.

"The women and the children will arm, I think, if the men fail," he said, with a gentleness that shames me. "Did you not say yourself—it is not an army; it is a nation in arms?"

I sit silent; I cannot chide him for any love that he bears to Italy, but in my heart I think that the first hour's march under the summer sun under his knapsack will stifle the life and music in him, as a stone will crush a skylark.

As the oil flames flicker in the wind I see that he is very pale, paler even than is his wont.

"Can we not go elsewhere?" he murmurs to me. "It is so full of noise here, and the smell of wine so strong. And I have a thing to tell you!"

It is hard to find quiet in Genoa that night. Every house is full of feasting soldiers, and all along the streets there come bands of them singing and clanking down the precipitous old world ways.

The rain has lifted a little; there is only a sea mist; I go along the mole with him, and when we have got a little away from the clamour we sit down in the shadow of an old boat that is high and dry there up on the flags. The rain does not touch us; and we have the sea in front, with a captured schooner of Galatz at anchor in the gloom.

Then Raffaellino turns his shining eyes on me, and his eager voice trembles.

"Oh, dear friend, she is living after all! I have seen her, I have spoken with her—there in Florence —and she was in the Arte that night and we never knew!"

The grey sea eddies and heaves before my sight. For a moment the schooner's solitary light flashes out of the darkness like a million suns. The ground grows unsteady beneath my feet.

I have no need to ask him whom he means.

The boy leans his head on his hands, silent; the wind blows in from the sea; the lights in the captive ship die out; from the terraces above, where the hills are, there comes a loud sweet echo of men's voices singing; they are chanting the Hymn of Garibaldi.

Then——

"Your donzella?" I say quietly, for it is her secret and must be kept, and the lad knows nothing. "Your donzella? Well! she is not dead, then. But she is dead, no doubt, in another fashion—by all kinds of change."

He looks at me a little bewilderedly. Perhaps I speak too coldly—men do when they are in pain.

"She is changed, and yet she is not," he murmurs; "a hundred times more beautiful, yet quite the same, I think, as when we ran together through Verona. But she is very great, you know—very great and rich, and of high estate, and her own mistress. Changed so; but not in any other way. I think, except——Well, a great countess, you know, and a poor child singing in the Carnival for bread, they are so wide asunder. Yes, you are right—change is a sort of death. Perhaps a sadder one for those it leaves."

"She is married greatly?" I say to him. The words have no sense or reason to me as I say them. I think of my child with the loose golden cloud of her hair blowing in the fresh hill winds, and her hands full of the purple glory of the wild anemones as she came down on the day of the Saints towards the old brown Badià.

I lost her, as one may miss a firefly in a myrtle thicket, one hot June night, in the Florence gardens, and I find her as one may find it another night, set to shine on high in a woman's hair in the palace of a Florence duchess.

The firefly, gathered to play the part of a diamond, and gleam in a palace masque, dies of the honour; the little soul goes forth in fire like other souls of greater martyrs; but what woman ever died of exaltation? They leave such thankless follies to the lùcciole.

It cannot be a second ere he answers me, but it seems a horrible endless space and silence that follows on my own voice; the noise from the city and from the sea blending into a strange dull roar that surges at my ear.

"She is not wedded," says the boy, at last, and my heart leaps like a loosed deer that springs from hunters' nets to woodland liberty—and yet what can it be to me?—to me more than to any one of those careless lads in the streets up yonder, who will find his grave in the ripening wheat of the wide Lombard fields? "No! It is some great title of her father's. Our folk call her contessa, because he is now so noble. I do not know much. I did not listen. I could only think of her. There was some wondrous change of fortune for them—she did tell me, I forget. She was in the Arte that night and—then she saw me in the street and sent for me, and I went—it was the day you left,—she had the great villa under Sta. Margharità on the hill. I went, in courtesy and wonder, to

stranger as I thought, not dreaming—then, when she
retched her hands to me, and cried, "'Ino, 'Ino!—is
erona all forgotten?' she laughing a little, and yet
eeping too, then I knew her, though it was all so
anged, and I fell at her feet, and I forget the rest."

After that he is silent a long time—poor little
nder Raffaellino.

I am silent too.

The rain falls faster, and the wind drives against
e boat, but neither he nor I heed that.

As for me I do not ask another thing. He has
en her, and the world has gone by just the same,—
id she is there in my own city,—and I am here a
mmon soldier with my musket, bound in honour
ot to turn back and look upon her face. For we
e to march at dawn.

I sit still looking into the grey mist of the waters;
the town they are shouting and gathering and sing-
g and drinking, and all the lines of the palaces and
reets glitter in zigzags of light fretfully through the
g, but no one disturbs us under the black shadow
f the old fishing boat.

Raffaellino, after a time, speaks again, his head
ill bent upon his hands.

"I do not think she is changed at heart," he mur-
urs. "The same generous, imperious, tender, wilful,
apricious thing, I think, that used to run with me in
e winter snows and the summer noons, hungry and
appy, about in old Verona. She laughed and wept
ith me; she forgot all her greatness,—she called me
er brother, her playmate, her friend—she, a princess,
s it were, in the north land of her father's. She is
proud, graceful, noble woman now,—a little haughty

of speech and swift in scorn, I fancy, but to me most tender. 'Oh, 'Ino!' she cried, 'if only I were now that merry, naughty, wayward child that ran with you in the old carnival days amongst the merry people!' And then I think she would have fairly wept—only she turned her head and was too proud—but there went a sort of shiver over her, like that which shakes the glacier just before it falls."

I let the boy talk on, the broken phrases of his speech filled in with the fall of the rain, and the sough of the sea in the harbour. I ask no questions. I seem to know it all.

"It was late in the day when I saw her," he goes on after a pause. "She made me stay the evening with her. She lives like an empress. We went out into the gardens as the sun set. Then she would hear my story. Did ever you see her in the world, I wonder?"

I look straight at the sea, and answer "Never,— Why?"

If one be a man, and have a shred of honour, one must lie so often; so seldom is there any other way that serves a woman.

"Only, because, when I spoke of you, and without you I should have no story, she grew quite pale, I thought, and listened with a strange look in her eyes. And when I told her how you had kept me with you all these years, and won your gold and fame for me; her tears fell into a knot of oleanders that she held, and she murmured to herself, 'So like him!—Oh, God—so like!' And when I asked her if she knew you, then she turned all coldly and suddenly, and answered, '—I know what the world says

of him, no more—a great genius—wild and generous
—what can he see in those laughing painted women?
But they say he loves such best.' And then she would
hear no more of you, and then she would hear of
nothing except of you; and when she asked if you
were still in Florence she trembled, or I thought so—
perhaps it was only the flicker of the trees, for it was
twilight then—and when I said that you had thrown
up fame and fortune, and gone off to join the troops
at Genoa, she flashed on me her great proud starry
eyes with such a scorn—it scorched me like a flame
—Ah, heaven! I shall see till I die. 'And you wait
here!' she cried, 'you let him go alone! You!—who
but for him would have died in the Florence streets
of hunger like a dog!' She did not know how much
she hurt, nay, I am sure she did not mean to hurt at
all. I murmured something of the only strength I
had lying in music. But her eyes flashed fire on mine,
though they still were dim. 'What!' she cried, 'does
genius then claim cowardice as its first privilege and
exemption? It was not Lelio Pascarèl who taught
you that!' She did not mean to hurt—oh, no! she
never meant to hurt at all. That I am certain. But
only spoke out her quick proud passionate thought as
was her habit when a little child. But one would
not wait to hear a woman say that twice. And she
was right too, very right, I know. I left her very
soon, and said that I would go to her again. She
gave me both her hands, in our sweet frank Italian
fashion,—she is not changed in any thing of that; I
kissed them, and I left her. And when the morning
came, I offered myself for service with the volunteers,
and they took me, though I am weakly and girlish,

as you say, and they gave me the rough dress and
the heavy musket, and I came to-day to Genoa with
a thousand others. I shall be of little use; but she
was right, you know. If one can only die—one ought
at least die for Italy."

So she cannot have forgotten that sweet year long
Tuscan summer?

And it was she masked on the hillside that night;
and I—I laughed like a fool with Astra and Poppea.
What could she think but that I loved those "painted
women?" Ah, heaven! how sweet that jealous word
to me!

Nay—I know how base my joy is.

What right have I to be glad that my memory
lies like a deep evening shadow across the brilliancy
of the morning of her life?

Of course she cannot forget.

What woman forgets kisses that have burned upon
her lips, unless she grow light enough and base enough
to lend her lips in loves swift-chosen and quick
changed?—and that she will never grow to be my
proud innocent lost treasure.

I know that gladness is base in me.

Yet glad I am—fiercely, madly, heedlessly glad,
though I sit mute here by the sea, and listen with a
cold face lest the lad should think any thought that
may come near the truth. For all I can ever do in
this world for my darling now is to keep her secret
for her—better than she would keep it for herself,
perhaps, if she be indeed so little altered.

After awhile, Raffaellino looks up at me wistful,
"Are you angered with me that I come?—you are so
still. One could not let a woman say that twice."

"That is as one may feel," I answered him, roughly.
f you did not fight for the sake of Italy, what use
fight for the gibe of a woman?"

It is brutal in me, I know that, but I cannot sit
ietly here and hear him talk of her. I rise from
e boat's rest and shake him a little as he leans with
s head upon his hands.

"Dio! you are wet through. Do you want to die
fore you see a battlefield? Get up; you have done
lly enough for one day's work."

He gets up, as I bid him; there is a startled pain
his eyes that moves me with remorse for wounding
m.

I laugh a little that he may see no change in me.

"Nay, 'Ino, you were my nightingale, and belong
me; I am angered to see you come to be shot
wn with all the sparrow-hawks and vultures. A
rl might as well stay a breach with her slender arm
you come out to feed the cannon. Besides, the
usic in you! You should have had pity on your
nius—"

"It was not by pity on their genius that your
lorentines made Florence great in the old days you
ve," he murmured. "And, on your own, what pity
ave you had?"

"Mine! Oh, altro! A trick of imitating any other
eature that I see; and being able to play a little
ith words upon the hearts of a people who laugh or
y without knowing why when I tell them! A fine
ing. But you—who speak in music, that is the very
ice of God Himself amidst men!——Well, now you
e here you cannot turn back. We must do our
est for you. Rise up, and come out of this wild

weather. If you would serve Italy, you must keep your strength."

A gleam of moonlight from a rift in the clouds falls on his face as he lifts it.

"If they kill me, it does not matter," he said softly. "You know I have loved the donzella ever since we sang together in my father's workshop amongst the clank of the hammers; and always, wherever I wandered, I thought of finding her; and always, when I have dreamed of my music, I have heard her voice as it used to sound in the still old square in the summer nights; and when they praised my music, and talked of a great future for me, I thought to myself, perhaps she is in pain and in poverty somewhere, or even perhaps in shame, and I shall lift her up, and crown her with my crown, and give her all that men give me; but now it is over—all over for ever! And now she is set on high there, and she can never be anything ever again to me; and I feel as if I should never bear to hear a note of music; and my music was all my soul, you know. And it is dead."

Ay, indeed, I know; know but too well. When you can solace a mother for her first-born's death, then, and then only, shall you solace an artist for the death in him of his Art.

Then the lad rises up and walks a little feebly along the grey sea line: and we go in silence—perfect silence, backward into the heart of the town.

The rain has lifted a little. The fires of torches and of illuminations light the grim stone heights of the old palaces; we tread on laurels as we mount the steep and crowded streets; from the terraces, where

₂ orange boughs toss in the wind, distant voices
me chanting still the "Fuori il Stranier!"

Raffaellino turns to me a moment with his tender
le face in a sudden glow from the warmth of the
ldened lights in a gallery above.

"You hear them?" he says, softly. "Nay, she was
ht—so right. What can one ask better than to lay
wn one's life for Italy?"

CHAPTER IV.
In the Land of Virgil.

It is not an army, I say, that goes out to war, it
a nation in arms that sweeps across the Mincio to
ipple with the old hereditary foe. When one heart
ats in the million breasts of a nation, the nation is
vincible. Man cannot hurt her, and God will not.

Every square inch of this soil, through whose
lden harvests the child Virgil once ran with fleet
et chanting strophes to the great Ceres Mammosa,
s been thrashed through and through by the iron
il of man for twice a thousand centuries.

The struggle is so old, so old—older than the old
in crown of Lombardy. Down from the dreary .
stnesses of the Dolomite, the imperial eagle has
ooped so many times to fasten beak and talons
the fair eyes of our Italia.

Against the empire! It is the old old war-cry.

No doubt it was grander work going out across
e green Valdarno, with the red Carroccio and the
ilkwhite oxen, and the banners of the Silver Dove
id the Silver Temple; no doubt it was grander; but
erhaps we are not altogether unworthy our forefathers

as we toil through the hot sun and the blinding dust, with the mosquito in our flesh, and the regulation knapsack heavy on our shoulders. One is only a volunteer; but still, if one does one's best——

The other day, after a toilsome march, some of us bivouacked in sight of Mantua; our arms were stacked, and our tents set up where there were old grey crumbled ramparts just on the very edge of the lake. Some young soldiers, who were students from Ravenna and comrades of mine, cared for such old things, and spent their leisure in tracking out the line of the fortifications beneath the rank grass and the wild tulip roots that grew so thickly beside the water, where the castello with its village clustering beneath it had stood in the bygone times of Bonacolsi and Avvocati. And amongst other marks and sculptures on the fallen stones they found most often a prince's coronet, and two hawks fighting, and dates of that old old time, when the Lake-city yonder, in the midst of its melancholy waters, had quivered under the velvet hands in their gloves of steel of Beatrice and Matilda.

I said nothing to the lads as they scraped the grass away with their swords off the crown and the two hawks, but I knew the cognizance well, it had been carven in many a razed fortress and ruined town over the Tuscan fields and the Aquilean marches, in the sign manual of the Pascarèlli. If I had had all those old fiefs and that crown, perhaps;—poof! it was the first time that I had ever wished for them. But the Fates lie like lead on my heart,—mine; to whom the three grim Parcæ had ever been up to that time of the Feast of the Dead only only as three gladsome

.idens that only summoned me to dance whilst they
ıg.

As it is, I go the next day into Alessandria, and
officer, seeing me, and wanting his horse held,
ows me the bridle, with a word of command.

I walk up and down with the horse over an hour.
ıen the general comes out of the house he had
:ered he looks over me with a steady glance: "A
lunteer?"

I salute, and assent.

"What do you get?" he asks.

"A musket and twenty-five centimes a day."

"You are a noble?"

"No."

"What then?"

"A vagabond."

He smiles and throws me, instead of the bridle, a
ldo, and so rides away. I keep the coin.

A copper coin for holding a horse; well, the Pas-
rèllo Princes in their graves there, under the ruined
:tress, could not be ashamed.

In its way that copper coin is worth the ducal
ɔwn.

It is fierce and dark work here in this fruitful
ıd of Virgil. The world has got so tired; it has
ɛn so much of heroism and carnage; it has grown
d and dull, and would scarcely open its drowsy
rs at a noble deed, though the note of it were loud
 that bugle blast of Orlando which made the birds
op dead in all the forests of Roncesvalles.

Else the world has seldom seen anything finer
an this fiery torrent of national life rushing to the
ains of the Mincio as fast and as furiously as Mincio

in time of flood can rush from her Mother of Garda
The noble fights beside the populano. The young
marquis leaves his marble villa, as the cobbler his
board at the street corner. The prince strides through
the millet, shoulder to shoulder with the coppersmith
and the mosaic-maker. This is the reason that we
are so strong in this summer-season; strong as a
chain of which every link has been proved in the fire.

The men who march and fight with me have
laughed and frolicked with me a thousand times in
the masquerades and sweetmeat showers of the Carnival, and I can do them some little good. Even Italians find it hard to raise a jest sometimes, plodding
through the rain-soaked earth in autumn with only a
muddy blood-stained brook to drink at, and the ants
settling by the score in the gaps of half-healed wounds.
Even Italians feel their hearts a little heavy, straining
under the weight of rifle and knapsack over the
parched ground in the scorch of noon, with comrade
after comrade falling out of the ranks from sunstroke,
and the mosquitos buzzing horribly where the sword-
slash is still unclosed. I can do some little good,
perhaps, raising their courage with a strain of Leopardi
or Giusti, or taking them back to their village under
the vines by some burden of a country-ritornella,
sweetening their hard black bread with a tale out of
Boccaccio, and making them forget their ague on the
marshy ground by some one of the infinite jests in
the old comedies, of which my brain is full, and their
ears are never tired.

I strive to keep up my mirth for their sakes;—at
night lying round the fires that we light to keep off
the marsh fever, or by day tramping along the dry,

ite, tiresome roads with the clouds of gnats at our
rching throats.

But it is hard to do it, sometimes. War is sickly
rk at its best; and life, I say, is weary. So it seems
me as I go to-day—alone, for once,—through the
iling country where the maidens pluck the mul-
rry leaves as though no such things as flame and
·el were as near them as the vines are near.

My heart is heavy as I pace between the lines of
ves and watch the runlets of water glisten in the
ıss.

Poor little Toccò has died here.

He volunteered with me, poor dear little lad, only
venteen then, and merry as a lark; leaving the bot-
ʒa and the work he loved, and the fun and frolic
 the Florentine street life; and in the very heart of
agenta, as we marched through the standing corn,
ɪder the hail of iron, a bullet struck him, and he fell.

I could not stay to see for him then; the sea of
ood swept me away, a league away, as it seemed, in
second, and all the day long it was as much as we
uld do to keep our feet amidst that trampled wheat
ɪder that fierce red sun.

But when old Mars, who ever loved Florence, had
rned the balance in our favour, and the carnage
ıs over and done, and the sun was gone down west-
ard, there beyond the Apuleian Alps, then I had
ne to seek for him, and after long search I found
m; one amongst so many other simple brown-eyed
ds in their rough coats of blue, and their little
:aked caps, and their straps and their belts, lying
rn and crushed and nameless and forgotten, down
ere amongst the summer harvest.

He was not quite lifeless.

He took a drop of water, and lifted his eyelids, and smiled; he knew me, though it was quite night, and he was nearly dead.

"It is a great thing—to die for Italy," he said gently, with a light like morning on his little parched sad face; then a shiver shook him, and his hand tried to fold itself in mine, and he stretched his limbs out, and all was over.

He was only a sod of clay that cumbered that harvest field.

Ah, Dio mio!—the world is weary after all.

I go through the green glad country.

Who could tell that death in its most ghastly shapes walked here with every day and night?

It is all so peaceful.

The white road runs straight and shining in the sun. The red roofs of the farmhouses glow through chestnut woods and olive orchards. The mighty river glistens here and there where a break in the vines shows its course. Away in the shadows are the towers of Pavia; and, beyond, the beautiful snowy sea-like surge of the Alpine crests where Milan lies. Near me girls are putting mulberry leaves into great baskets, chatting the while; and through the vineyards gentle white oxen drag the lumbering waggons.

Only now and again there is some headless helmet in the grass, or the dogroses blossom above a dead warhorse; or a cherry tree, red with fruit, lies on the ground, its stem broken under a rain of bullets.

I walk on, and think of another sad thing that I saw yesterday.

It was by the wayside in a little village. There

d been a short sharp struggle between Tirolese,
ιo held the street, and Bersaglieri who wanted to
eep it clear. The Bersaglieri won, and carried the
sition. The little narrow road all green and golden
th fruit trees, where the women were wont to sit
t at their thresholds at evening spinning and sing-
ʒ in unity, was strewn with dead and dying.

I had helped the Bersaglieri—being in the way;
d when all was over tried to help the wounded.

I carried one Tirolean into a cottage. He was a
.l, strong, and very handsome man; a mountaineer;
d he had been shot through the head, and had but
lf an hour to live.

I soothed that half-hour for him as well as I was
le; he lying on the mud floor of the hovel with
e door wide open, and through it shining the glory
 the afternoon sun, and the whiteness of a late
wering peach-tree. He had been unconscious since
e time the shot had struck him; before death his
ason came to him—it is often so.

His hand sought his chest feebly and uncertainly,
ɩe the hand of a blind man.

"Do not take it away," he muttered, with his wist-
l beautiful frank eyes looking with passionate prayer
to mine—his enemy's. "Do not take it away—it is
l I have. She laughed, you know—but she did not
ean to hurt—oh, no, oh, no. Look at that white—
that snow? We must bring the cattle down from
e mountains. Yes—I am in pain; a little pain. Do
ɔt tell my mother—nor Anton. Lift me a little, so
can see the hills —she laughed, you know, but then
ɩe did not mean to hurt. Do not take it away—it is
.e only little thing I have."

And so gazing at the whiteness of the fruit blossoms in the open door, and thinking it the lustre of the virgin snow upon his own eternal hills, he shuddered a little and turned wearily on his side, and so looking up at me like a dog in pain, drew his breath with a sigh and died.

When we stript to bury him his right hand was on his chest, and on it was a little tuft of the wild grass that is called the maiden's hair.

We laid him to rest in the little garden under the fruit trees, with his face turned to his own mountains.

His name I never knew.

His is one of the many million nameless graves that strew all that green country betwixt Alp and Apennine. But I have no doubt that if it could be known we should find it to be—Marco Rosas.

Away in a chalet of Unterinnthal the good mother will sit and spin and pray; and the cattle will come from the grass lands in autumn, and the sun and the clouds will play on the broad snow fields, and the calves will low at the barred byre door, and the seasons will come and go till the Alps are once more smiling blue as the eyes of a northern child, with the gentian flowers and the hyacinths of the spring.

But always in vain will the old mother pray, and never again will the feet of her first-born come over the mountains.

CHAPTER V.

The Song of the Grilli.

I HAVE kept the dear little Raffaello beside me as much as possible.

Every soul treats him tenderly, as if he were a irl. There are hundreds of lads as young as he; ut there is something in his pretty innocent face with s curls of Giorgione's gold, and its clear, wondering, istful eyes that wins the heart out of the toughest eteran and wildest trooper.

The boy looks so astray in it all.

His soul is in music. This thunder of cannonade, nd screams of dying horses, and clash of crossing teel, and falling trees and burning houses, must be a ell to him. He has always a startled look.

Yet he is brave in his way, this little dreamer, who nly the other day was a barelegged child, singing rhile the robins sang in the garret of Ambrogiò Lufi.

He is brave in his way, though he clings so closely o me, and will hardly quit my shadow.

One day I found him hidden by the high yellow orn, listening—listening—listening with an intent and rondering face. I spoke and roused him, and forced iim away; for a battery of the Austrians commanded hese very fields, and their fire was raking through the ending wheat not ten yards off him.

"What were you doing there?" I asked him in ome wrath.

"I was hearing what the grilli said," he answered ne; and then he got out his little trecento viol which ies always in his knapsack; and began to echo out on it the story of the grilli; the little brown grilli singing so happily here in joy of the sun and the summer, amongst the yellow corn stalks and the flame of the tossing poppies; the poor little grilli caged for Christ's sake on Ascension Day, and singing still on and on in the little prisons till their life grows out of them, whilst every hut and homestead on the olive hills and in the vine-lands sets bread and wine on its threshold and hangs out a lanthorn to guide the steps of Christ who walks that night on earth.

Raffaellino played the plaint of the grilli that day, whilst a score of rough soldiers stood round, he nothing noting them, and not a few of them had their fierce eyes dim with tears. Then all in a moment he broke it off suddenly,. and thrust the viol behind him, and went away by himself into the little bare plaster cottage, where a dozen of us were quartered.

When I followed him he was crying like a child.

"What is it?" I asked him.

He hid his face shyly, as a girl may do.

"Only—only—I have loved my music for itself, you know, and it was quite enough for me. But now I do not know—I think the things and feel them, and I can make others feel them too, but all the harmony is gone out of it for me. In all I do, I only see her face, I only hear her voice. My music is like the grilli's in the cage; it is my nature—and so it will not leave me—only I am faithless to it, so I die. She will never be anything to me, you know; how should she? great like that, and I a little beggar? Oh, I know, I know it is my folly; but you see in old Verona she had no one else but me, and so——"

And so the gentle heart of the little lad is half broken; a childish love and as innocent as ever this impure earth ere saw, but still one that has killed art in him, and made the adder of memory hiss in every sweet note that was once his solace.

He is no more fit for the fiery furnace of war than

are those delicate heads of the millet, that blow like a girl's auburn curls upon the summer wind. Nevertheless, the battle does not spare the frail maize feathers, but sweeps them aside, and treads them down, and tramples them in blood. Nor does it spare Raffaellino.

The next day after he has listened to the grilli's chaunt in the cornfields, there is bitter struggle over all this fertile smiling land, with its festooned vines and its leaf-hidden watercourses, that is like one vast sheet of verdure enrolled between the far mountains.

It is a struggle that is called, later on, the Field of Montebello.

"We go in black with powder; we shall come out red with carnage," says one of its soldiers, and it is true that we do. We dip the scarlet lilies of Florence and the white cross of Savoy in blood till they are both of one colour. We strangle the black eagle that day, down there amongst the tangled vines and the full-eared corn in the country of Virgil.

It is a hot and blinding day.

The sun lies heavily on all the white roads. The bruised vines, and trodden corn, and ruined orchards, are sad to see.

At intervals here and there, on the green face of the country, there are dusky clouds of smoke and dark small masses slowly moving. There is a battle scattered over the great plain. The fine ethereal lines of the mountains are delicate as gossamer against the summer sky. So they looked when Theodoric and Otho fought here. They have seen so many millions of men slaughter one another here, since the far ages when men were not, and all this laughing land of the

19*

vine and the pomegranate was only a primæval valley
of ice.

How the battle goes elsewhere I cannot tell. Where
I am, we hold a villa and its courts and gardens
against the Austrians.

It is a rambling old place, with great walled gardens, and great echoing chambers, and great discoloured frescoes peeling in the sun.   Its owners have
fled long before.

There is only an old man, a gardener, who sits by
a well in the central court while the struggle goes on
round him, and stares and looks stupid, as though
his wits were gone.

God knows how we fight—I do not.   There are
some fifty of us and a handful of Bersaglieri—that
is all; and the Austrians are very numerous.   They
held the position early in the day, and we took it
from them at noon; and we have held it against the
worst that they can do until it is now four by the
sun-dial on the wall where the great mulberry grows
and a cherub's head is painted.

The musketry rolls; the smoke is thick; the dead
men fall down the broad stone steps, and lie under
the red oleander flowers.   The staircase is disputed
step by step.   The pavements are all wet with blood.
The din is horrible.   Amidst it all I know I hear, in
a moment of stillness, a little bird singing.   I look up
and see it above my head, on a tendril of a vine that
comes through the large unglazed window.

There is a young face lifted to listen to it.   It is
innocent and heavenly looking, like the cherub's on
the frescoed wall.   It is terribly out of keeping with
the ghastly scene around.   It is quite white, even to

the lips; but they are firmly closed, although so pale, and Raffaellino has not left my side to-day.

The sun-dial points four in the afternoon.

We have looked for reinforcement, but none comes. How the battle goes elsewhere we cannot tell. The enemy are strong here still and keep pressing upward through the courts and gardens.

All the later half of the bitter burning day our own men seem to close round me, and look up to me as their leader. I do not think how or why it is—whether all those in command are dead or not. I lead them because it comes naturally—I, a mere volunteer, a common soldier, like the rest of them, with nothing but my musket.

As the bird sings, and a little lull comes in the strife, as such a pause will, even in the fiercest struggle, I look around me anxiously. My clothes have been shot through and through, but, strangely enough, nowhere is the flesh grazed or the bone broken. Yet men have fallen round me like chestnuts in the autumn forests.

We are very few.

However the day go elsewhere in the plain, here it goes against us.

Jägers have joined the Whitecoats, and are pressing up through the ilexes.

We hold the staircase and the inner court still;—but for how long?

If I could send word to the head of the bridge, a mile off, the Sardinians are there, and might spare men. Raffaellino, watching my face, in that one little moment as the bird sings, reads my thoughts, and whispers to me through the din—

"If I crept through the laurels and ran, the poplars would shelter me; once by the river-side, to the bridge is not far?"

I do not answer him.

The lad is dear to me. Did I not see him first, the pretty child, touching his little viol that carnival day in the cathedral square where grim Roland keeps watch and ward?

The passage to the bridge is possible; but whosoever makes it—being seen—will surely meet his death. For all the way is set thick with Tirolese, who mark their men as on the hills they mark their chamois.

"No, it is too dangerous," I say to him abruptly. "No; I forbid you."

Raffaellino lifts his golden head; the sun coming through the open window makes an aureola round it. A little feverish flush comes on his cheeks.

"And I—disobey you!" he said quickly. "Even before you—Italy!"

And then he runs out swiftly, and through the window I see him in the open air, and then I lose him underneath the leaves, and have only space to breathe for him that half-unconscious prayer which the most reckless men will cling to by an instinct; for the lull is over, and the Jägers are in the inner court, and a ball has struck down the old man sitting at the well, and I have to draw my comrades closer round me, and hold the hall as best we can with a raking fire that makes the Tedeschi reel and scatter as they come.

Then follows the fiercest, hottest, darkest, dreadest moments of my life.

The shadow on the sun-dial creeps on; it is a

quarter past four and more. My little troop is only half in numbers what it was when the bird sang. The grape-shot falls like hail. Unless the Sardinians come quickly——

The shadow on the dial creeps onward.

It is no longer mere firing and counter-firing; it is a hard, devilish, hand-to-hand, throat-to-throat struggle on the marble stairs and pavement that is all slippery with carnage.

Some of the Jägers have found a second stairway on the other side of the villa, and so have crept up unseen by us, and pour out on to the head of the great staircase, and thrust us downward, so that we are between two forces, as in a vice. We are some thirty men in all—not more; and many of us are wounded, and very weak from long thirst and the heat of the day.

Caught between these two, the Jägers pressing on us from behind, the Tirolese forcing us backwards on to their comrades' steel, we struggle, God knows how, in a horrible crush and medley, across the court and into the green grass-lands of the gardens, where the ripening grapes are hanging on all the trellised vines.

Here, if the Sardinians do not come, we must be butchered like so many sheep. Yet all the while it is hardly of the Sardinians that I think; it is of the dear little lad making his perilous way through the canes underneath the poplars; and every now and then, even in the fellness and ferocity of the struggle, I turn my head to look beyond the laurels to the grassy stretches across which he must return.

The brutes hem us in on both sides. The men

go down like corn under the sickle. I and the few who remain contrive to force a little breathing space, so that we have our backs to the villa gates and get clear a moment of one half the pressure.

At that moment I see Raffaellino.

He is running, not creeping fox-like, as he should do, for the canes to shield him; but running erect, his feet are bare as in his childish days over the stones of Verona, that he may speed himself the quicker; his fair tangled hair is blowing back from his face. He has picked up a shattered standard somewhere, and the colours of Free Italy float from him as he comes.

He waves it and cries aloud to me, the dear, rash, impatient, unselfish little lad; because he knows that, in such straits as ours, hope, being a moment delayed, may be too late forever.

He cries to me, the little dear, brave lad—

"Hold out ten minutes, and they are here."

Then, as he speaks, there is a shower of green leaves above his head; he throws his curls back with a strange dizzy gesture; then he stops short there in the grassy path, with all the vines and the rose-laurels close about him; then down he falls, face forward, on the turf.

They have shot him from behind the laurel-hedge.

What it does to me I know not; I only know that all the rage of desert lions wounded, and all their strength with it, seems to pour into me.

Seeing the child fall there, I only know that I pierce the storm of shot, and cleave the pressure of the Austrians with a fury before which all is borne down as before the rush of a mountain tempest.

I only know that so do the agony and vengeance
n my soul set light to the passions of every Italian
rith me in that hour, that, ere the ten minutes are
pent, ere the Sardinians are with us, we—not thirty
ıen in all, and faint and bleeding, and far out-
ıumbered—have driven the foe out from the courts
nd gardens, and hurled them on to meet their death
nder the hewing steel and trampling hoofs of the
ıardè horsemen as they sweep up to aid us by the
iver's course.

And then—when it is all over, and the place is
lear, and over the broad plain all men know that
taly has won—then I go and find the dear child,
here where he fell, with the torn flag under him, and
he rosy laurel flowers hanging their clusters over his
ıretty head.

Is he quite dead?

Not quite. When I lift him, his heavy, blue-veined
ids raise themselves, and his eyes smile. But I, who
ıave seen so many men die, know that this is Death,
hough the strong sun still shines so clearly and the
ose-laurels blow in the wind.

"Give it me," he says softly; his voice is barely
ıudible.

They have shot him in the chest, and he bleeds
.o death internally.

I know what he means.

I unstrap his knapsack and take out the little viol
hat he used to play on in the moonlight in the arch
ɔf the coppersmith's door in sad Verona.

He thanks me with his sweet, wistful, shining eyes,
ınd tries to touch the chords.

It is of no use; he has no strength left. He tries

no longer; his hand falls, and he sighs a little, whilst
the rose-laurels brush his curls.

"Take it to her from me," he murmurs. "Perhaps
she will remember a little—now and then."

Then he lifts his face, like a tired child, and kisses
me on the cheek, and smiles against the sun.

"Do the dead grilli sing where God is?" he says;
and then the breath quivers a moment on his mouth,
and the eyelids fall, and I know that he sees the sun
no more.

     *   *   *   *   *

At evening on that day all men praise me, and
they speak great things of my leadership whereby the
villa was won; and even my king gives me brave words
upon the field; and I, Pascarèl, the player, have won
a name as a soldier of Italy that is not unworthy the
dead Pascarèlli who live in stone in the crypts and
the cloisters.

But I hear it all as in a dream; I see it all as
through half-blind eyes.

What I hear is the song of the grilli that is silent
for evermore with all the rest of the sweet wild music
that lived in that innocent soul. What I see is the
tender body of Raffaellino, where we have laid it in
the silent hall of the villa, with the moonbeams shining white about his head, and on his breast a knot of
the red rose-laurel.

Ah, God! it is as cruel as to wring the throat of
a bird in full song. Ah, God! the fair dawn that will
have no noon; the sweet blossom that will have no
flower!

CHAPTER VI.
Red and Gold.

My father tells me to put on that cinquecento
ess of red and gold, and set the rose-diamonds he
ve me in my breast and hair, and be ready for a
eat masque at a great palace to-night, when all
lorence is mad and drunk with joy.

Here in the stillness of the villa gardens, up where
a. Margharità lifts her little bell-tower to heaven,
en here, though so high in the hills, the sound of
e people's rejoicing comes to me all the day long,
; the heavy sough of a distant sea rolls up to those
ho sit on the cliffs above.

I have told them I am tired and so cannot see the
ty in her festivity to-day. But it is not true. The
uth is, that I shudder from the shouts of homage
nd the sight of mirth.

For he is not dead; he has even done great things
pon those terrible plains—so rumour says; giving
im the green bay of the patriot in lieu of the paper
urels of the player. But I cannot go down into his
lorence, this the first day her troops return to her.
cannot risk to see his face as strangers see it, and
ok upon him in the press of the glad streets, maimed,
erhaps, war-worn, dust-covered, lame with long
arches in the summer suns—as heaven knows I
ay.

And little 'Ino; my rash words must have sent him
o the front, for they know nothing of him in that old
ool cypress-shaded chamber behind the Torrigianni
'alace; and I can hear nothing of him—a mere little

lad, a mere grain of dust in the great plains, a mere drop of blood in the vast sea of carnage.'

Men make no account of him. I cannot hear if he be living or dead; my poor little bright playmate, who stood and sang with me that day of carnival in old Verona. And whatever his fate be, I sent him to it.

Ah! why do we frail, foolish, fire-filled things that they call women live only to hurt and kill?—all heedlessly as children catch at flies?

My heart is heavy as I sit within all the long luminous Tuscan day, and hear the echo of the people's mirth, the thunder of the guns, the tramp of marching columns, the roll of beaten drums that comes dulled by distance up the olive slopes upon my ear.

But when the day is dead I cannot have the sad luxury of solitude longer. My father and cousin will not be denied. I put on the masque dress with the diamonds that Varkò painted, and I make ready for the festa of the night.

It is a wonderful and costly thing, this dress; I have not worn it yet in public. The train is cloth of gold, and the scarlet skirts beneath are sown with little diamonds. It was my father's fancy, copied from some old Florentine picture that he has.

It is very beautiful and rare, and lights me like a robe of flame, and makes my eyes gleam black as night, and my rebellious hair all shine like crisp new gold.

And yet—and yet—I fancy I looked better in the old yellow and purple skirts, with my hands full of poppies and my curls caught with the wild vine.

I lean on the terrace balustrade, and, despite my wealth of diamonds, am sick at heart.

My cousin joins me: he is courtly and full of
ace; but a great distrust of him is always on me,
d some memory that I hate, yet cannot disentangle,
ises in me always with the sound of his voice—a
ice ever harsh, however skilfully modulated.

This evening, while the sun is sinking over Car-
ra, he urges, for the twentieth time, his love upon
e.

He is in earnest, that I think. He seeks me with
ssion and purpose; and my father has more than
ice sought to persuade me that the destiny of my
ture years lies here, in all this man can give.

This evening, while the sun is red, my cousin
esses his prayer on me until I turn in weariness and
bellion.

"Once for all," I say to him, with a tired im-
tience of his honied phrases that sound so poor
d pale beside the memory of those words amongst
e golden vines under Fiesole. "Once for all, will
u not take my answer? I have said it often—no!
! no!"

"I am then quite hateful to you?" he asks, very
w.

I look him full in the eyes, and answer straightly.

"Well, you are."

No milder way will end his importunity.

Then the veiled evil in him wakes.

"That is your last word?" he asks.

"My very last."

"Well then," he says, and smiles a little cloudy as
e speaks. "Well then, I have a tale to tell you. I,
raying about in this dear Italy of yours, found
yself, of a winter's night, in old Verona. There

was a masked ball. I went to it. Amongst the crowd there was a beautiful wild, naughty thing who had broken loose from home and took her pleasure there. I paid her entrance-money; so I know——"

He checked with a gesture the cry that escaped me, as the memory which had pursued me in the sound of his voice rose clear.

"Nay, hear me. I will make my story brief. I had no thought who the girl was—a pretty, foolish, feather-brained fierce thing; but as time went I found she bore, rightly or wrongly, the name I bore myself. I lost her in Verona, and in the summer of the self-same year I saw her wandering with some strolling players, and let her go, for what was she to me! A little while, and, through many deaths and strange accidents in my family, the lands and the titles fell on one who had been disowned by all his race for his loose living—a worn-out gambler, to whom fortune came at last in much magnificence. I came to know him, since I was next of kin, and in his daughter I discovered my waif and stray of the Verona carnival. And then,—foolishly, no doubt,—I grew to love her. Ay, I do love her, that I swear; and all a gentleman can offer to the woman he loves I offer now to her. But if she turn against me, if she say me no in her haughty, pretty fashion, that is half wild still, then let her beware. For, though she holds herself so royally, she is but a bastard born. For, though none knows it but myself, her mother, the Florentine singer, was no wife."

The blood leaps into my face, and seems to sting me like a thousand vipers. Not knowing what I do,

I strike him hotly in the eyes with a bough of the pomegranate that I hold broken in my hand.

"It is a lie!" I cry against him.

He recoils a moment, pale as death. Then, bowing low, he says,—

"Go,—ask your father."

"You dare me to that!"

"Go,—ask," he says to me calmly, with a quiet smile.

I go.

My father is there in the great dusky white room that the sunset is touching to all kinds of tender hues, like those that fall through the painted casements of great churches.

I go to him swiftly across the vast glistening floor, very silently; yet he looks up with a startled glance in his cold clear eyes.

Perhaps I look strangely; I do not know; my mouth burns and my face is flushed. I feel lost, and amazed, and feverish, and vaguely frightened, as I did when I was astray in the press and fury of the Veglione.

"Is it true?" I ask him.

He looks me full in the face, and smiles a little—slowly.

"Is what true?"

"That my mother was not your wife?"

The smile lingers on his mouth. It is very cruel though so slight.

"What does it matter? Mariuccia thought her so; think you so if you like."

My own voice seems to choke me as I say—

"Mariuccia thought so? Yet it was a lie. Is that your answer?"

He looks at me coldly, full in the eyes—

"She was a singer. I never married her. Why should I? You had never known it, had you been wiser and listened to your cousin. These things can be kept unseen in the same family. But with another there would be trouble; one would need to tell the truth. What can it matter? You have all you want. You are called a great lady, and no one has looked too closely—yet. Some money I can leave you, and you are rich in jewels. For, in a way, I love you, 'Nella; you are beautiful, as a picture is, and your wild grace is charming, and you fool men with true woman's skill. But if you be wise, you will wed with your cousin. No questions then, and the old name your own, with no bar sinister. Mariuccia was a poor old purblind fool; she thought your mother was a wedded wife, and who should undeceive her! Pshaw! why look at me like that? I never told you any lie—not I. Go and marry with your cousin, and who will know it then? It rests with you."

I am silent.

My father rises, with a certain trouble on his face that for once clouds its cool serenity. He tries to touch my hair, but I avoid him by a gesture that makes him shrink a little.

"Nay, 'Nella, why take it to heart like that!" he says, with a tone in his voice that is half pity and half derision. "You thought your mother married; well, that was Mariuccia's fault, not mine. I never told you so. And, indeed, to quiet her, she passed as my wife, to others, for most of the few short years she lived. What had you to complain of?—nothing surely. Most men would have put you in a convent or had you taught some useful trade, or left you as a model to your friends the painters. But I have dealt with you as though you were my heiress. And I—I promised your mother when she died—I have told no one, have told no one: not even your friend the vagabond player, when he upbraided me for my neglected duties with a *furia* only possible to a flame-tongued Italian. No one knows it, save your cousin; and he, you should be told, found it out long, long ago, from following you one night in old Verona, when you broke away from home and ran in mischief to the Veglione. You never saw his face that night, but he remembered yours. Now see you this, 'Nella, if you be wise, your secret is his; wed with him. He has a great passion for you, and is sincere,—so far, —but if you cross him what can I do for you?— Nothing. He can strike you with that sole sure weapon—truth. And you will feel your fall. For you have wasted wealth as though you were an empress born; and you are one of those wild, wayward, graceful, useless, pretty things, with nothing but a picture of a face and a bird's trick of song. You are one of those who will not like the world, carina mia, unless its soil be velvet to your foot. Be wise while there is time, and rest a great lady always. Wed your cousin."

And with that my father rises and leaves the chamber, already weary of a theme that has no pleasure in it. I stand in the red sunset light, looking out blankly on the glory of the oleander flowers that fill the open casement with their fire.

Is all the world a lie?

CHAPTER VII.

The broken Bubble.

WHAT is it I feel?

I scarcely know. I act without knowing— only stung into a bitter, burning, all-corroding shame, that drives me like a whip of scorpions.

Oh, poor little fool, who sat upon the broken stairs shelling the beans at Mariuccia's feet, and prattled of a great past and a great future alike allied to me by the golden and magic chain of birth! Oh, poor vain, baby dreamer, idler than the child that blows soap bubbles in the sun, who had come hither across the mountains, with my golden florins for all my store, doubting not that the purples of some mighty destiny would enfold me as soon as I should open the gates of the south!

Was ever anything more pitiful, more foolish, more pathetically lonely, more grotesquely fooled than I? Was ever any hapless idiot, thinking himself the sovereign of the world, under a crown of straw, more deluded and more desolate than I have been when I have played at greatness?

A withering shame consumes me; the humiliation clings to me like Glauce's web of fire.

My poor poor mother too! In the scorch and fury of my own wretchedness tears well into my eyes as I think of her—think no blame; ah no! heaven forbid! Doubtless her fault of love was purer and more innocent by far than my rank greed of self.

My cousin's hand puts asunder the oleander flowers. He comes and looks me in the face.

"Well?" he asks, softly. "You see I told you truth. Is it now yes or no?"

I turn on him as a leopardess turns on her pursuer. The longing thrills in me to strike him in the eyes, as I had done that winter's day at dusk in the Verona streets.

"No!" I cry to him. "No! a million times! What! you think my fear is greater than my hate? Sir,—you mistake, then. No, I say. No, no, no. Do you hear? No—if I die for it."

In that moment I am all again the passionate outraged child who had fled from him in the Veronese twilight.

The years, the dignities, the tranquil scorn of my late life drop from me; I become again only the fierce, fearless, thoughtless, haughty little waif and stray whom Pascarèl had rescued on the Veglione night.

I leave him standing there against the red oleander, dazed, as it were, with the fire of my eyes and speech; then, without another word, I sweep to my own chamber, lock myself in from him and every other, and tear off, like a frantic creature, the gold and red of my perfect masque-dress. The shining skirts fall in a crushed heap; the costly train is crumpled up like wind-blown leaves; I shake the jewels from my breast and hair; I pluck the great rose-diamond from above my ear.

The things are to me hateful, horrible, vile: my father's gifts, indeed—ay, and so far justly mine; but they are accursed to me like the wages of my mother's shame and death.

I do not reason; I can only feel.

20*

As my father denied me when I stood before him with my poor little sceptre of the peacock's plumes, so I deny him now.

There is no tie between us.

As the law yields me no rights on him, so I will yield him no rights on me.

My heart burns that I have ever eaten his bread and ever spent his gold.

A madness of determination comes to me. I will not stay for the smile and sneer of the women I have reigned over, of the men I have made my slaves. I will not stay an hour more in this, the second paradise of lies, that has lulled me to sleep sweet as the lotus, deadly as the upas.

I am useless; ay, indeed; but still I have my voice. It can charm courts, let it charm nations. I can be once more the people's Uccello.

Ah, no! never again that. Never again the light-hearted and thoughtless child that sang to the listening Tuscans when the lùcciole lit the plains. The best that can be before me, if a life of triumph, yet must be a life of utter loneliness.

My heart grows sick with dread and longing.

I do not reason; I can only feel.

Between my father's life and mine there is a deep gulf fixed. It is the darkness of my mother's grave.

It is evening. The sun is gone. The shadow of night is here, even on these heights by Santa Margharità.

I leave aside every coin, every gem, every trifle of luxury or cost I ever have possessed. I leave aside all my splendid costumes and my priceless diamonds. I wrap myself in a dark cloak, and cast a veil about my head, and, without the value of a copperpiece upon me, I undo the bar of a side door that looks upon the gardens and pass out. On the threshold I linger and look back.

Lights are burning in the wide chamber. The glittering things I have thrown down catch the reflection; sumptuousness, grace, ease — all are symbolised in them.

Am I unhappy because I leave them? No.

My whole life is on fire with shame, and my whole soul is sick with falsehood. But amidst it all a strange sweet thrill stirs; for I am free.

It has been but a gilded slavery, this grand and gorgeous pageantry of the great world.

I long for the breezy downs, and the wild hillsides, and the sweet liberty of untrammelled movement, and the peaceful sleep of healthful tired limbs. And yet —oh, God! I shudder as I think—my life will be alone, all alone always.

What beauty will the daybreak smile on me? What fragrance will the hill-side bear for me as I roam?

I shall see the sun for ever through my tears. Around me on the summer earth there will be forever silence. For Love has left me.

CHAPTER VIII.
The Lily and the Laure.

I UNBAR the door and pass into the coolness of the early night. Down there where Florence lies it seems alive with fire. The people rejoice for their heroes.

Without any thought or measure of what may befall to me, or whither I, penniless and defenceless, may hereafter go,—I leave the gardens by the path that passes through the olive woods, and once more drifting like a snapped flower on the wind, I set my face towards the city.

The night is perfect.

All the hillside is hushed to an intense stillness. The olive woods upon Arcetri are white as silver in the moon. The hills are steeped in radiance. The roses underneath the vines are bright as in the day.

From the depth where the massed lights of the town are shining there come sounds of music, outcries of the populace, deep shouts that rise and lose themselves like echoing thunder amongst the mountains lying round. Florence rejoices in her strength; to her, as her dower, Hercules gave the dragon's teeth, and she has sown them on her sacred soil, and they have sprung up armed men who have held her own again and again against the world, and have not failed her now.

I go down the old green familiar ways; the field-mice run from my feet amongst the tulip roots; just so, down this very path stole Lucrezia to Fra Lippi, but I am alone—all alone.

They will think I am safe in my chamber. They will not seek for me to-night. And by morning I must be away somewhere; away seeking for work.

I have nothing even to buy bread with on the morrow.

It is no worse with me than it was in this very city when under the old trees I had sat and wept my heart out because I was a beggar. And yet how much poorer I am! for then I had all my dreams, and all things were possible to me. But now I have nothing, not even a hope, only a dead rose on my heart that I shall ask them to bury with me as old Giûdettà asked.

Fifty years she lived with one memory shut in her soul, darning the dancers' magliè, and thinking of the love of her youth. Oh, God!—is that all the Future holds for me?

I tremble and grow sick with fear as I thread the olives and vines to the city.

But I never pause and look back, not once; I seem to hear Mariuccia say in the still cool night, "Live on the shame and the sorrow of your mother? nay, anima mia, be strong and die first."

Is it a folly that?—I do not know. I do not think, I say; I only feel; and I keep my face straight to the city.

The masque dress I threw aside was put on for a palace festa. The whole town is wild with jubilee. The shouts roll deep like the war-cry of lions.

All down the water side the lamps and the torches burn by millions. The bridges are lines of fire. Great Vecchio glows like a lighted beacon against the clouds. The river is a sea of flashing colour, from the many-hued globes of the illumined boats. Laughter and music, and the ring of choruses, and the call of trumpets, and the surge-like sound of an ever moving mass of men grow nearer and nearer, as I pass through the gates, and into the Street of the Maytime.

Everywhere the night is bright as the day. Long garlands swing from one side of the street to the other

The old grim iron-bound houses are hidden in flowers and foliage. Under the feet are dropped blossoms, and above head is a maze of roses. Not a single casement, not the poorest, but has hung out its basket of flowers; great lilies, wild poppies, tuberoses, coils of vine, trails of ivy, leaves of arums, everywhere in the streets they are shedding their sweet woodland dews on the stones.

The reign of feasts and of flowers has followed the season of death. All Florence is out to-night, drunk with freedom and crowned with victory.

Everywhere the great arched house doors stand open. Everywhere groups of soldiers are drinking or dancing. Arms are piled in the squares. Women waltz down the grim passage-ways singing.

Conscripts war-stained and dust-covered tell tales to a wondering crowd.

Tables are spread under the stars; under the garlands that the wind tosses hither and thither.

Bells are pealing; cannon are firing; great sheaves of coloured fires are launched to the clouds. In the churches they chaunt orisons. In the palaces they will dance till the dawn.

In the woods by the river the troops are bivouacked; and there in the fields the men and the maidens reel and spin, and leap and laugh, to the wildest mirth and melody.

For in the Field of Flowers, for the hundredth time, they have planted the Laurel.

The gladness makes me colder and wearier as I go. The light and laughter would drive me home-ward in desolation, had I a home to shelter me.

Vaguely I feel that the people look upon me in

wonder. I, a dark, veiled, shivering thing, a blot on the endless radiance—Ginevra, in her cere-clothes, amidst the mad masquing of an universal Carnival.

But they part in reverence before me, and are a little quiet as I pass them; they think that I mourn some dead soldier lying in the maize-fields beneath the shadow of the Alps. I mourn the dead, indeed; dead days, dead love, dead liberty.

But my dead I slew with my own hand, all witting what I did. That I am now alone is just—quite just.

But justice is hard.

It presses on my life like lead. I shut my eyes to shut out from me the frolic and the brilliancy around, and stumble on with little thought or purpose across the river and into the heart of the city.

What can I do? I know no more than knew Ginevra; homeless and denied, with every heart and every house closed against her. But Ginevra had one refuge—I have none.

As I go the throngs grow thicker, they push more eagerly. Their passionate dark faces glow; their voices pour forth torrents of joyous words; their holiday dresses gleam gaily against the shadows and the stone fronts of the buildings; they dash the tears from their eyes for the dead; they laugh with proud joy in the living. And from mouth to mouth, as in the night of the Carnival Fair, one name runs more audible than any other:—

"Pascarèl! —Il Pascarèllo!"

I catch the flying skirts of a woman as she hurries by me.

"He is here! Pascarèl?"

She twitches her garments from me in good-humoured haste.

"Ay! He talks to the people on the Place of the Signoria. He has done great things in the war, they say."

Without well knowing what I do, I too follow with the pressing crowds who are hastening under the Arches of the Uffizii, where the red and white banners are tossing as in the midnight of the Carnival Fair.

As we go under the arcades we pass a little contadina in all the bravery of festal ornament; great beads glitter at her throat; golden pins shake in her hair; all colours vie as in the rainbow in her skirts; she laughs, and shows her white teeth, grinning as she sets them in the velvet skin of a peach; she pushes a young slim stripling before her, and scolds him with shrill laughter, mocking at a tremor that shakes his limbs, and a pallor that blanches his cheek.

"To let a look at his face unman you like that, you simpleton!" she cries; and drives him before her, crushing out the juice of the peach between her rosy lips.

It is Brunótta.

So well goes life with the Unfaithful.

I draw my veil closer about my head, and am borne by the strong swift tide of the hurrying crowd into the Place of the Signoria, by the Loggia of the Lances, under the Palace of the People, where the baby Cellini used to sit throned on his servant's shoulders, to sing his little song and pipe his little carol to the grave ears of the great Gonfalonière.

The square is packed close with a listening

people. Their faces are all upturned like the ears of
wheat that a strong wind lifts to heaven. All the lines
of the mighty building are traced out by running
lines of fire. Jets of flame, and garlands of flowers,
and blazonries of shields, and folds of standards, all
shine together against the moon.

On the steps of Orcagna's Loggia, whence of old
the magistracy were wont to harangue the city, with
their faces set to the mountains, and the keen hill
winds blowing their robes of office, on the steps betwixt the two lions, Pascarèl stands, and speaks to the
Florentines.

There is the red-cross banner above his head; he
wears the simple garb of the Tuscan volunteer, on
his chest there is the cross of valour, and on the
stones at his feet there lie laurel crowns and clusters
of lilies that the people have flung to him.

The moon shines upon his delicate dark face;
his straight, poet-like brows; his dreaming eyes, that
have at once the scholar's sadness and the soldier's
passions.

The multitude is hushed to perfect stillness. They
love him too well to lose a single word.

He is telling them a legend in that fantastic
humour which has flashed for so many centuries
from beneath the tri-cornered hat of Tuscan Stenterello.

Dear to them before, he is now to them sacred;
he who has come forth from the heat and the dust
of those fields of bloodshed with the splendour of
great and daring deeds to lend their lustre to his
name, and twine the bay-leaves of the patriot round
the harlequin's wand of the player.

I crouch down in the deepest shadow on the
lowest step, and gaze upward at him, and drink in
the sweet and silver sounds of his voice, until the
love I bear him, and the loss of him, make me mad
as 'Dino's Pazza was, calling for ever on the grave to
yield her dead.

He was all mine;—all mine;—dear God! Mine
all the rich, glad, fearless freedom of his life; mine
all the rapturous caressing, priceless passion of his
love;—mine all! And I have lost them.

The war has left him life, but he is dead to
me.

And yet I listen as he speaks to the people. I,
athirst for the mere echo of his step as dying men in
deserts for the fountains of lost lands.

"You know how S. Michael made the Italian!"
he is saying to them, and the clear crystal ring of the
sonorous Tuscan reaches to the farthest corner of the
square. "Nay?—oh, for shame! Well, then, it was in
this fashion; long, long ago, when the world was but
just called from chaos, the Dominiddio was tired, as
you all know, and took his rest on the seventh day;
and four of the saints, George and Denis and Jago
and Michael, stood round him with their wings folded
and their swords idle.

"So to them the good Lord said: 'Look at those
odds and ends, that are all lying about after the
earth is set rolling. Gather them up, and make them
into four living nations to people the globe.' The
saints obeyed and set to the work.

"S. George got a piece of pure gold and a huge lump of lead, and buried the gold in the lead, so that none ever would guess it was there, and so sent it rolling and bumping to earth, and called it the English people.

"S. Jago got a bladder filled with wind, and put in it the heart of a fox, and the fang of a wolf, and whilst it puffed and swelled like the frog that called itself a bull, it was despatched to the world as the Spaniard.

"S. Denis did better than that; he caught a sunbeam flying, and he tied it with a bright knot of ribbons, and he flashed it on earth as the people of France; only, alas! he made two mistakes, he gave it no ballast, and he dyed the ribbons bloodred.

"Now S. Michael, marking their errors, caught a sunbeam likewise, and many other things, too; a mask of velvet, a poniard of steel, the chords of a lute, the heart of a child, the sigh of a poet, the kiss of a lover, a rose out of paradise, and a silver string from an angel's lyre.

"Then with these in his hand he went and knelt down at the throne of the Father. 'Dear and great Lord,' he prayed, 'to make my work perfect, give me one thing; give me a smile of God.' And God smiled.

"Then S. Michael sent his creation to earth, and called it the Italian.

"But—most unhappily, as chance would have it— Satanas, watching at the gates of hell, thought to himself, 'If I spoil not his work, earth will be Eden in Italy.' So he drew his bow in envy, and sped a poisoned arrow; and the arrow cleft the rose of paradise, and broke the silver string of the angel.

"And to this day the Italian keeps the smile that God gave in his eyes; but in his heart the devil's arrow rankles still.

"Some call this barbed shaft Cruelty; some Superstition; some Ignorance; some Priestcraft; maybe its poison is drawn from all four; be it how it may, it is the duty of all Italians to pluck hard at the arrow of hell, so that the smile of God alone shall remain with their children's children.

"Yonder in the plains we have done much; the rest will lie with you, the Freed Nation."

———

A shout from the people drowns his voice and stays it for a moment, the shout of assent and of homage, of love for him and of love for the country.

For a while I hear nothing.

I weep as women must weep by the grave of some noble dead thing they have lost. All my soul goes forth to him on fire. All the passion that he taught me that night of the saints, amongst the golden vines beneath Fiesole, burns in me and consumes me with its longing and despair. Not knowing what I do, I stretch my arms to him and moan aloud;—none hearken.

For a little space I fail to see or listen; I hear only a dull sound, as a drowning thing may hear the sighing of waters that devour it; 'when sense comes back to me he is still speaking to the people; but far more gravely now; his eyes kindle, his face flushes, his voice has in it all the yearning of a mighty love; his words fall without thought into the cadence of the terza rima.

He speaks thus:

"All greatest gifts that have enriched the modern world have come from Italy. Take those gifts from the world, and it would lie in darkness, a dumb, barbaric, joyless thing.

"Leave Rome alone, or question as you will whether she were the mightiest mother, or the blackest curse that ever came on earth. I do not speak of Rome, imperial or republican, I speak of Italy.

"Of Italy, after the greatness of Rome dropped as the Labarum was raised on high, and the Fisher of Galilee came to fill the desolate place of the Cæsars.

"Of Italy, when she was no more a vast dominion, ruling over half the races of the globe, from the Persian to the Pict, but a narrow slip bounded by Adriatic and Mediterranean, divided into hostile sections, racked by foreign foes, and torn by internecine feud.

"Of Italy, ravaged by the Longobardo, plundered by the French, scourged by the Popes, tortured by the Kaisers; of Italy, with her cities at war with each other, her dukedoms against her free towns, her tyrants in conflict with her municipalities; of Italy, in a word, as she has been from the days of Theodoric and Theodolinda to the days of Napoleon and Francis Joseph. It is this Italy—our Italy—which through all the centuries of bloodshed and of suffering never ceased to bear aloft and unharmed its divining rod of inspiration as S. Christopher bore the young Christ above the swell of the torrent and the rage of the tempest.

"All over Italy from north to south men arose in the darkness of those ages who became the guides and the torchbearers of an humanity that had gone astray in the carnage and gloom.

"The faith of Columbus of Genoa gave to mankind a new world. The insight of Galileo of Pisa revealed to it the truth of its laws of being. Guido Monacco of Arezzo bestowed on it the most spiritual of all earthly joys by finding a visible record for the fugitive creations of harmony ere then impalpable and evanescent as the passing glories of the clouds. Dante Alighieri taught to it the might of that vulgar tongue in which the child babbles at its mother's knee, and the orator leads a breathless multitude at his will to death or triumph. Teofilo of Empoli, discovered for it the mysteries of colour that lie in the mere earths of the rocks and the shores, and the mere oils of the roots and the poppies. Arnoldo of Breccia lit for it the first flame of free opinion, and Amatus of Breccia perfected for it the most delicate and exquisite of all instruments of sound, which men of Cremona, or of Bologna, had first created, Maestro Giorgio, and scores of earnest workers whose names are lost in Pesaro and in Gubbio, bestowed on it those homelier treasures of the graver's and the potter's labours which have carried the alphabet of art into the lowliest home. Brunelleschi of Florence left it in legacy the secret of lifting a mound of marble to the upper air as easily as a child can blow a bubble, and Giordano Bruno of Nola found for it those elements of philosophic thought, which have been perfected into the clear and prismatic crystals of the metaphysics of the Teuton and the Scot.

"From south and north, from east and west, they rose, the ministers and teachers of mankind.

"From mountain and from valley, from fortress smoking under battle, and from hamlet laughing under vines; from her great wasted cities, from her small fierce walled towns, from her lone sea-shores ravaged by the galleys of the Turks, from her villages on hill and plain that struggled into life through the invaders' fires, and pushed their vineshoots over the tombs of kings, everywhere all over her peaceful soil, such men arose.

"Not men alone who were great in a known art, thought, or science, of these the name was legion; but men in whose brains, art, thought, or science took new forms, was born into new life, spoke with new voice, and sprang full armed a new Athene.

"Leave Rome aside, I say, and think of Italy; measure her gifts, which with the lavish waste of genius she has flung broadcast in grand and heedless sacrifice, and tell me if the face of earth would not be dark and drear as any Scythian desert without these?

"She was the rose of the world, aye—so they bruised and trampled her, and yet the breath of heaven was ever in her.

"She was the world's nightingale, aye—so they

burned her eyes out and sheared her wings, and yet she sang.

"But she was yet more than these: she was the light of the world: a light set on a hill, a light unquenchable. A light which through the darkness of the darkest night has been a Pharos to the drowning faiths and dying hopes of man."

———————

His voice rings like the call of a trumpet over the hushed and awe-touched multitude.

Then it sinks low as a summer wind that steals over a tideless sea; and falls upon the silence with a sound in its gentleness and its solemnity that moves men like a prayer.

"We are Italians," he says, slowly. "Great as the heritage is, so great the duty likewise."

Then he uncovers his head and stands a moment silent in the moonlight. The people are silent too, and many kneel and pray.

CHAPTER IX.

Love is enough.

He comes down from the highest steps of the Loggia, his hands full of the lilies and the laurels. A mighty shout goes forth from all the city, such a shout as a populace can only give when a great faith beats in ten thousand breasts with the same pulses.

As he passes me, I catch his hand and touch it with my lips.

I worship the greatness in him; I know it all too late; when he was mine, I had cast him from me, now that I am nothing, less than nothing, I cannot even lift my eyes to his. I cannot claim a memory;—that would be charity.

So many touch him as he goes, he does not note my kiss from any other's; a dark veiled figure crouching at his feet; how should he see me in the blaze and stir, and tumult and triumph of this festal night in Florence?

Ginevra was happier than I.

He passes by, not knowing; ah, dear heaven!— can one be so near to any man one hour, and then so utterly a stranger, and more alien to him than the stray dog that brushes by him in the street?

He passes by me; and the crowds seize him, weeping and laughing, and lift him up on their shoulders, and bear him across the great piazza, shouting, with the white cross flags tossing above their heads and women raining roses in the moonlight.

He has his art; his eloquence; his power of the tongue and sword; and all his city's love and loyalty. How natural it is he should forget!—most natural.

But I!—

I crouch down where I first dropped to rest, on the lowest step of the Loggia. The bright bold Perseus keeps watch above, and the black brows of the Judith frown against the stars.

The square is left quiet. The people have flocked elsewhere. The sounds of music and of mirth are still loud over all the town, and the coloured fires flame against the sky. There is a sweet odour heavy

21*

on the air; the stones are strewn with flowers, and they lie dying underneath the moon.

I am half conscious of it all; and yet it all seems far away, so very very far.

I am so young, and yet my life is dead.

The deep chimes toll the hour more than once; it is near midnight; Florence is still light as at noontide. Still the noise and the mirth of the people are at their height. It is only the flowers that fade; the flowers that are trodden on the stones.

I sit with my head on my hands, crushed, and broken, and bruised, like one of the trampled lilies.

I do not think of my fate or my future. All I hear is the echo of his voice; all I see is the life lost forever. If I had been patient, if I had been true, if I had been faithful!—but I thirsted for greatness, and it has failed and fooled me. And I have touched his hand, I have looked on his face, I have been close to him, as the dust beneath his feet; and yet I can never claim a look or word again from him. Never,—whilst our lives shall last. For what would any love of mine seem now save like the prayer for alms of any homeless beggar?

The night flies on; the square is almost empty; the flowers are dying fast. I sit there, stupid with my wretchedness; the laurels lie scattered on the steps above.

A footfall comes near.

I shiver and look up; I see him in the moonlight, as so many times I saw him in that glad summer time coming through the silent streets of old forsaken cities, or the poppy-sown breadths of the cornlands.

But now his head is drooped; his face is pale and dark: and, as he goes, instead of the notes of the mandoline there is the clash of his sword on the stones.

He comes across the piazza; he is all alone. As he passes me he pauses and looks; it is his nature to be pitiful to all things. He only sees a human thing bowed down and solitary, mourning where all others feast.

He stops before me, deeming me a stranger.

"What ails you," he asks, "that you sit so while all the town rejoices?"

I cannot answer him. I would rise and flee from him, but my feet feel chained to the marble.

He touches me with gentle compassion.

"Are you a woman and young?—you sorrow for some dead soldier?"

With a great cry I clasp his knees, and lean my head against him.

I sorrow for the dead indeed.

By some instinct or thought of the truth he tears the veil from me, and lifts my face to the light of the moon.

Then—ah, then!—I hunger no more for the sweet hillside on the night of the saints under white Fiesole.

––––––

"But I am nothing—nothing—nothing?" I murmur to him, an hour afterwards, as his embrace enfolds me, when all my tale is told.

He answers me with a smile.

"And I have nothing! So we are equal, my treasure! Ah, donzella mia! you have learned then to think with me that these are the fairest things, after all, that the world can give us,—a little laughter and a little love?"

I wind my arms about him where we stand, and lean my cheek on his:

"Say rather only, a little laughter—and a great love."

This is enough indeed: enough, here and hereafter. A love greater than death, great as eternity itself; a love that shall leave earth with us when our souls leave our bodies, and reach its uttermost perfection in other lives, in other worlds; a love that time cannot chill, nor any woe appal, nor God himself unsever.

THE town is white against the shadows of the night. The river breaks with sea-like sound against the piles of the old grey bridges. The red cross banners slowly swing their white folds on the wind; the populace has grown quieter.

The shields of the old republic brighten their blazonries in the moonbeams. The lions, white amidst a green wealth of forest laurel, guard the place of the public liberties.

The roses and the lilies lie on the stones as on a palace-floor. By the water the people are singing, untired with joy and with triumph.

Is it not ever with such things that one thinks of Florence?

A cloud of blossoms, the notes of a lute, the ripple of a little laugh; the deeper joys of sighs that die in a caress; the far-off echo of a gay glad nation's mirth; a sea of yellow moonlight, broad and cool; the stone faces of fauns and griffins coiled about with acanthus foliage; the sculptured shapes of saints and prophets reigning over a frolic of masquers; the fragrance of sea and mountain blown on fresh winds through shadowy marble ways; and in the sacred stillness of the night, in gardens where the fountains fall, or casements where the lucciole are gleaming, the soft fast throbs of quickened pulses, the touches of lovers' lips in the silence—these things are its breath and its life, the City of Lilies, the Amorous City; built in a field of flowers, on a midsummer night, by the Slayer of the Lion, for the mother of Eros; Florence, the daughter of gods and the queen of the freedom of men; Florence, the poetess and paradise of

L O V E.

PRINTING OFFICE OF THE PUBLISHER.

June  1873.

Tauchnitz Edition.

Each volume 1/2 Thaler = 2 Francs.

CONTENTS:

Sold by all the principal booksellers on the Continent.

June 1873.

Tauchnitz Edition, Latest Volumes.

The Pillars of the House by Miss Yonge, vol. 1 & 2.

The New Magdalen by Wilkie Collins, 2 vols.

May by Mrs. Oliphant, 2 vols.

History of two Queens by W. H. Dixon, 3 vols.

A Vagabond Heroine by Mrs. Edwardes, 1 vol.

The Coming Race by Bulwer (Lord Lytton), 1 vol.

Collection of British Authors.

Rev. W. Adams:
Sacred Allegories 1 v.

Miss Aguilar:
Home Influence 2 v.   The Mother's Recompense 2 v.

Hamilton Aïdé:
Rita 1 v.   Carr of Carrlyon 2 v. The Marstons 2 v.   In that State of Life 1 v.   Morals and Mysteries 1 v.

W. Harrison Ainsworth:
Windsor Castle 1 v.   Saint James's 1 v.   Jack Sheppard (w. portrait) 1 v.   The Lancashire Witches 2 v.   The Star-Chamber 2 v. The Flitch of Bacon 1 v.   The Spendthrift 1 v.   Mervyn Clitheroe 2 v.   Ovingdean Grange 1 v.   The Constable of the Tower 1 v.   The Lord Mayor of London 2 v.   Cardinal Pole 2 v.   John Law 2 v.   The Spanish Match 2 v.   The Constable de Bourbon 2 v.   Old Court 2 v.   Myddleton Pomfret 2 v.   The South-Sea Bubble 2 v.   Hilary St. Ives 2 v. Talbot Harland 1 v.   Tower Hill 1 v.   Boscobel; or, the Royal Oak 2 v.

"All for Greed,"
Author of—
All for Greed 1 v.   Love the Avenger 2 v.

Miss Austen:
Sense and Sensibility 1 v.   Mansfield Park 1 v.   Pride and Prejudice 1 v.   Northanger Abbey, and Persuasion 1 v.

Nina Balatka 1 v.

Rev. R. H. Baynes:
Lyra Anglicana, Hymns and Sacred Songs 1 v.

Currer Bell
(Charlotte Brontë):
Jane Eyre 2 v.   Shirley 2 v.   Villette 2 v.   The Professor 1 v.

Ellis & Acton Bell:
Wuthering Heights, and Agnes Grey 2 v.

Isa Blagden:
The Woman I loved, and the Woman who loved me; A Tuscan Wedding 1 v.

William Black:
A Daughter of Heth 2 v.   In Silk Attire 2 v.   The strange Adventures of a Phaeton 2 v.

Lady Blessington:
Meredith 1 v.   Strathern 2 v. Memoirs of a Femme de Chambre 1 v.   Marmaduke Herbert 2 v. Country Quarters (w. portrait) 2 v.

Miss Braddon:
Lady Audley's Secret 2 v.   Aurora Floyd 2 v.   Eleanor's Vic-

The price of each volume is ½ Thaler = 2 Francs.

tory 2 v.   John Marchmont's
Legacy 2 v.   Henry Dunbar 2 v.
The Doctor's Wife 2 v.   Only a
Clod 2 v.   Sir Jasper's Tenant
2 v.   The Lady's Mile 2 v.
Rupert Godwin 2 v.   Dead-Sea
Fruit 2 v.   Run to Earth 2 v.
Fenton's Quest 2 v.   The Lovels
of Arden 2 v.

Shirley Brooks:
The Silver Cord 3 v.   Sooner or
Later 3 v.

Miss Rhoda Broughton:
Cometh up as a Flower 1 v.   Not
wisely, but too well 2 v.   Red as
a Rose is She 2 v.   Tales for
Christmas Eve 1 v.

John Brown:
Rab and his Friends, and other
Tales 1 v.

Eliz. Barrett Browning:
A Selection from her Poetry
(w. portrait) 1 v.   Aurora Leigh
1 v.

Robert Browning:
Poetical Works (w. portrait) 2 v.

Bulwer (Lord Lytton):
Pelham (w. portrait) 1 v.   Eu-
gene Aram 1 v.   Paul Clifford
1 v. Zanoni 1 v. The Last Days
of Pompeii 1 v.   The Disowned
1 v.   Ernest Maltravers 1 v.
Alice 1 v. Eva, and the Pilgrims
of the Rhine 1 vol.   Devereux
1 v.   Godolphin, and Falkland
1 v.   Rienzi 1 v.   Night and

Morning 1 v.   The Last of the
Barons 2 v.   Athens 2 v.   The
Poems and Ballads of Schiller
1 v.   Lucretia 2 v.   Harold 2 v.
King Arthur 2 v.   The new Ti-
mon; St Stephen's 1 v.   The
Caxtons 2 v.   My Novel 4 v.
What will he do with it? 4 v.
The Dramatic Works 2 v.   A
Strange Story 2 v. Caxtoniana 2 v.
The Lost Tales of Miletus 1 v.
Miscellaneous Prose Works 4 v.
The Odes and Epodes of Horace
2 v. Kenelm Chillingly 4 v. The
Coming Race 1 v.

Henry Lytton Bulwer
(Lord Dalling):
Historical Characters 2 v.   The
Life of Henry John Temple,
Viscount Palmerston 2 v.

John Bunyan:
The Pilgrim's Progress 1 v.

Buried Alone 1 v.

Miss Burney:
Evelina 1 v.

Robert Burns:
Poetical Works (w. portrait) 1 v.

Lord Byron:
Poetical Works (w. portrait) 5 v.

Thomas Carlyle:
The French Revolution 3 v. Fre-
derick the Great 13 v.   Oliver
Cromwell's Letters and Speeches
4 v. The Life of Friedrich Schiller
1 v.

The price of each volume is ½ Thaler = 2 Francs.

"Chronicles of the Schönberg-Cotta Family,"

Author of—
Chronicles of the Schönberg-Cotta Family 2 v. The Draytons and the Davenants 2 v. On Both Sides of the Sea 2 v. Winifred Bertram 1 v. Diary of Mrs. Kitty Trevylyan 1 v. The Victory of the Vanquished 1 v. The Cottage by the Cathedral 1 v.

Coleridge:

The Poems 1 v.

Wilkie Collins:

After Dark 1 v. Hide and Seek 2 v. A Plot in Private Life 1 v. The Woman in White 2 v. Basil 1 v. No Name 3 v. The Dead Secret 2 v. Antonina 2 v. Armadale 3 v. The Moonstone 2 v. Man and Wife 3 v. Poor Miss Finch 2 v. Miss or Mrs.? 1 v. The New Magdalen 2 v.

Fenimore Cooper:

The Spy (w. portrait) 1 v. The two Admirals 1 v. The Jack O'Lantern 1 v.

Mrs. Craik (Miss Mulock):

John Halifax, Gentleman 2 v. The Head of the Family 2 v. A Life for a Life 2 v. A Woman's Thoughts about Women 1 v. Agatha's Husband 1 v. Romantic Tales 1 v. Domestic Stories 1 v. Mistress and Maid 1 v. The Ogilvies 1 v. Lord Erlistoun 1 v. Christian's Mistake 1 v. Bread upon the Waters 1 v. A Noble Life 1 v. Olive 2 v. Two Marriages 1 v. Studies from Life 1 v. Poems 1 v. The Woman's Kingdom 2 v. The Unkind Word 2 v. A Brave Lady 2 v. Hannah 2 v. Fair France 1 v.

Miss Georgiana Craik:

Lost and Won 1 v. Faith Unwin's Ordeal 1 v. Leslie Tyrrell 1 v. Winifred's Wooing, and other Tales 1 v. Mildred 1 v. Esther Hill's Secret 2 v. Hero Trevelyan 1 v. Without Kith or Kin 2 v.

Miss Cummins:

The Lamplighter 1 v. Mabel Vaughan 1 v. El Fureidîs 1 v. Haunted Hearts 1 v.

De-Foe:

The Life and surprising Adventures of Robinson Crusoe 1 v.

Charles Dickens:

The Posthumous Papers of the Pickwick Club (w. portrait) 2 v. American Notes 1 v. Oliver Twist 1 v. The Life and Adventures of Nicholas Nickleby 2 v. Sketches 1 v. The Life and Adventures of Martin Chuzzlewit 2 v. A Christmas Carol; the Chimes; the Cricket on the Hearth 1 v. Master Humphrey's Clock (Old Curiosity Shop, Barnaby Rudge, and other Tales) 3 v. Pictures from Italy 1 v. The Battle of Life; the Haunted Man 1 v. Dombey and Son 3 v. David Copperfield 3 v. Bleak House 4 v. A Child's History of England (2 v. 8° 27 Ngr.) Hard Times 1 v. Little Dorrit 4 v. A Tale of two Cities 2 v. Hunted Down;

The price of each volume is ½ Thaler = 2 Francs.

The Uncommercial Traveller 1 v. Great Expectations 2 v. Christmas Stories 1 v. Our Mutual Friend 4 v. Somebody's Luggage; Mrs. Lirriper's Lodgings; Mrs. Lirriper's Legacy 1 v. Doctor Marigold's Prescriptions; Mugby Junction 1 v. No Thoroughfare 1 v. The Mystery of Edwin Drood 2 v.

B. Disraeli:

Coningsby 1 v. Sybil 1 v. Contarini Fleming (w. portrait) 1 v. Alroy 1 v. Tancred 2 v. Venetia 2 v. Vivian Grey 2 v. Henrietta Temple 1 v. Lothair 2 v.

W. Hepworth Dixon:

Personal History of Lord Bacon 1 v. The Holy Land 2 v. New America 2 v. Spiritual Wives 2 v. Her Majesty's Tower 4 v. Free Russia 2 v. History of two Queens 3 v.

Miss Amelia B. Edwards:

Barbara's History 2 v. Miss Carew 2 v. Hand and Glove 1 v. Half a Million of Money 2 v. Debenham's Vow 2 v. In the Days of my Youth 2 v.

Miss M. Betham Edwards:

The Sylvestres 1 v.

Mrs. Edwardes:

Archie Lovell 2 v. Steven Lawrence, Yeoman 2 v. Ought we to Visit her? 2 v. A Vagabond Heroine 1 v.

Mrs. Elliot:

Diary of an Idle Woman in Italy 2 v.

George Eliot:

Scenes of Clerical Life 2 v. Adam Bede 2 v. The Mill on the Floss 2 v. Silas Marner 1 v. Romola 2 v. Felix Holt 2 v.

Essays and Reviews 1 v.

Estelle Russell 2 v.

Expiated 2 v.

Fielding:

The History of Tom Jones 2 v.

Five Centuries

of the English Language and Literature 1 v.

A. Forbes:

My Experiences of the War between France and Germany 2 v. Soldiering and Scribbling 1 v.

John Forster:

The Life of Charles Dickens v. 1-4.

"Found Dead," Author of—

Found Dead 1 v. Gwendoline's Harvest 1 v. Like Father, like Son 2 v. Not Wooed, but Won 2 v. Cecil's Tryst 1 v. A Woman's Vengeance 2 v. Murphy's Master 1 v.

Frank Fairlegh 2 v.

Edward A. Freeman:

The Growth of the English Constitution 1 v. Select Historical Essays 1 v.

Lady G. Fullerton:

Ellen Middleton 1 v. Grantley Manor 2 v. Lady Bird 2 v. Too Strange not to be True 2 v. Constance Sherwood 2 v. A stormy Life 2 v. Mrs. Gerald's Niece 2 v.

Mrs. Gaskell:

Mary Barton 1 v. Ruth 2 v. North and South 1 v. Lizzie Leigh 1 v. The Life of Charlotte Brontë 2 v. Lois the Witch 1 v. Sylvia's Lovers 2 v. A Dark Night's Work 1 v. Wives and Daughters 3 v. Cranford 1 v. Cousin Phillis, and other Tales 1 v.

Goldsmith:

Select Works: The Vicar of Wakefield; Poems; Dramas (w. portrait) 1 v.

Mrs. Gore:

Castles in the Air 1 v. The Dean's Daughter 2 v. Progress and Prejudice 2 v. Mammon 2 v. A Life's Lessons 2 v. The two Aristocracies 2 v. Heckington 2 v.

"Guy Livingstone,"
Author of—

Guy Livingstone 1 v. Sword and Gown 1 v. Barren Honour 1 v. Border and Bastille 1 v. Maurice Dering 1 v. Sans Merci 2 v. Breaking a Butterfly 2 v. Anteros 2 v.

Mrs. S. C. Hall:

Can Wrong be Right? 1 v.

Bret Harte:

Prose and Poetry 2 v.

Sir H. Havelock,

by the Rev. W. Brock, 1 v.

Nathaniel Hawthorne:

The Scarlet Letter 1 v. Transformation 2 v. Passages from the English Note-Books 2 v.

Sir Arthur Helps:

Friends in Council 2 v.

Mrs. Hemans:

The Select Poetical Works 1 v.

Mrs. Cashel Hoey:

A Golden Sorrow 2 v.

Household Words

conducted by Ch. Dickens. 1851-56. 36 v. NOVELS and TALES reprinted from Households Words by Ch. Dickens. 1856-59. 11 v.

Thos. Hughes:

Tom Brown's School Days 1 v.

Jean Ingelow:

Off the Skelligs 3 v.

Washington Irving:

The Sketch Book (w. portrait) 1 v. The Life of Mahomet 1 v. Successors of Mahomet 1 v. Oliver Goldsmith 1 v. Chronicles of Wolfert's Roost 1 v. Life of George Washington 5 v.

G. P. R. James:

Morley Ernstein (w. portrait) 1 v. Forest Days 1 v. The False Heir 1 v. Arabella Stuart 1 v. Rose d'Albret 1 v. Arrah Neil 1 v. Agincourt 1 v. The Smuggler 1 v. The Step-Mother 2 v. Beauchamp 1 v. Heidelberg 1 v. The Gipsy 1 v. The Castle of Ehrenstein 1 v. Darnley 1 v. Russell 2 v. The Convict 2 v. Sir Theodore Broughton 2 v.

J. Cordy Jeaffreson:

A Book about Doctors 2 v. A Woman in Spite of herself 2 v.

The price of each volume is ½ Thaler = 2 Francs.

Mrs. Jenkin:
"Who Breaks—Pays" 1 v. Skirmishing 1 v. Once and Again 2 v. Two French Marriages 2 v. Within an Ace 1 v.

Edward Jenkins:
Ginx's Baby; Lord Bantam 2 v.

Douglas Jerrold:
The History of St. Giles and St. James 2 v. Men of Character 2 v.

Johnson:
The Lives of the English Poets 2 v.

Miss Kavanagh:
Nathalie 2 v. Daisy Burns 2 v. Grace Lee 2 v. Rachel Gray 1 v. Adèle 3 v. A Summer and Winter in the Two Sicilies 2 v. Seven Years 2 v. French Women of Letters 1 v. English Women of Letters 1 v. Queen Mab 2 v. Beatrice 2 v. Sybil's Second Love 2 v. Dora 2 v. Silvia 2 v. Bessie 2 v.

R. B. Kimball:
Saint Leger 1 v. Romance of Student Life abroad 1 v. Undercurrents 1 v. Was he Successful? 1 v. To-Day in New-York 1 v.

A. W. Kinglake:
Eothen 1 v. The Invasion of the Crimea v. 1-8.

Charles Kingsley:
Yeast 1 v. Westward ho! 2 v. Two Years ago 2 v. Hypatia 2 v. Alton Locke 1 v. Hereward the Wake 2 v. At Last 2 v.

Henry Kingsley:
Ravenshoe 2 v. Austin Elliot 1 v. The Recollections of Geoffry Hamlyn 2 v. The Hillyars and the Burtons 2 v. Leighton Court 1 v. Valentin 1 v. Oakshott Castle 1 v.

Charles Lamb:
The Essays of Elia and Eliana 1 v.

Mary Langdon:
Ida May 1 vol.

"Last of the Cavaliers,"
Author of—
The Last of the Cavaliers 2 v. The Gain of a Loss 2 v.

S. Le Fanu:
Uncle Silas 2 v. Guy Deverell 2 v.

Mark Lemon:
Wait for the End 2 v. Loved at Last 2 v. Falkner Lyle 2 v. Leyton Hall 2 v. Golden Fetters 2 v.

Charles Lever:
The O'Donoghue 1 v. The Knight of Gwynne 3 v. Arthur O'Leary 2 v. The Confessions of Harry Lorrequer 2 v. Charles O'Malley 3 v. Tom Burke of "Ours" 3 v. Jack Hinton 2 v. The Daltons 4 v. The Dodd Family abroad 3 v. The Martins of Cro'Martin 3 v. The Fortunes of Glencore 2 v. Roland Cashel 3 v. Davenport Dunn 3 v. Con Cregan 2 v. One of Them 2 v. Maurice Tiernay 2 v. Sir Jasper Carew 2 v. Barrington 2 v. A Day's Ride: a Life's Romance 2 v. Luttrell of Arran 2 v. Tony Butler 2 v. Sir Brook Fossbrooke 2 v. The Bramleighs of Bishop's Folly 2 v. A Rent in a Cloud 1 v. That Boy of Norcott's 1 v. St. Patrick's Eve; Paul Gosslett's Confessions 1 v. Lord Kilgobbin 2 v.

G. H. Lewes:

Ranthorpe 1 v. The Physiology of Common Life 2 v.

Longfellow:

Poetical Works (w. portrait) 3 v. The Divine Comedy of Dante Alighieri 3 v. The New-England Tragedies 1 v. The Divine Tragedy 1 v.

Lutfullah:

Autobiography of Lutfullah, by Eastwick 1 v.

Lord Macaulay:

History of England (w. portrait) 10 v. Critical and Historical Essays 5 v. Lays of Ancient Rome 1 v. Speeches 2 v. Biographical Essays 1 v. William Pitt, Atterbury 1 v.

George MacDonald:

Alec Forbes of Howglen 2 v. Annals of a Quiet Neighbourhood 2 v. David Elginbrod 2 v. The Vicar's Daughter 2 v.

Mrs. Mackarness:

Sunbeam Stories 1 v. A Peerless Wife 2 v. A Mingled Yarn 2 v.

Norman Macleod:

The old Lieutenant and his Son 1 v.

Mrs. Macquoid:

Patty 2 v. Miriam's Marriage 2 v.

"Mademoiselle Mori,"

Author of—
Mademoiselle Mori 2 v. Denise 1 v. Madame Fontenoy 1 v. On the Edge of the Storm 1 v.

Lord Mahon: *vide* Stanhope.

R. Blachford Mansfield:

The Log of the Water Lily 1 v.

Capt. Marryat:

Jacob Faithful (w. portrait) 1 v. Percival Keene 1 v. Peter Simple 1 v. Japhet 1 v. Monsieur Violet 1 v. The Settlers 1 v. The Mission 1 v. The Privateer's-Man 1 v. The Children of the New-Forest 1 v. Valerie 1 v. Mr. Midshipman Easy 1 v. The King's Own 1 v.

Florence Marryat (Mrs. Ross-Church):

Love's Conflict 2 v. For Ever and Ever 2 v. The Confessions of Gerald Estcourt 2 v. Nelly Brooke 2 v. Véronique 2 v. Petronel 2 v. Her Lord and Master 2 v. The Prey of the Gods 1 v. Life of Captain Marryat 1 v.

Mrs. Marsh:

Ravenscliffe 2 v. Emilia Wyndham 2 v. Castle Avon 2 v. Aubrey 2 v. The Heiress of Haughton 2 v. Evelyn Marston 2 v. The Rose of Ashurst 2 v.

Whyte Melville:

Kate Coventry 1 v. Holmby House 2 v. Digby Grand 1 v. Good for Nothing 2 v. The Queen's Maries 2 v. The Gladiators 2 v. The Brookes of Bridlemere 2 v. Cerise 2 v. The Interpreter 2 v. The White Rose 2 v. M. or N. 1 v. Contraband; or A Losing Hazard 1 v. Sarchedon 2 v.

The price of each volume is ½ Thaler = 2 Francs.

Meredith (Hon. R. Lytton):
Poems 2 v.

Milton:
Poetical Works 1 v.

Miss Florence Montgomery:
Misunderstood 1 v. Thrown Together 2 v.

Moore:
Poetical Works (w. portrait) 5 v.

Lady Morgan's
Memoirs 3 v.

My little Lady 2 v.

New Testament [v. 1000.]

Mrs. Newby:
Common Sense 2 v.

Dr. J. H. Newman:
Callista 1 v.

"No Church," Author of—
No Church 2 v. Owen:—a Waif 2 v.

Hon. Mrs. Norton:
Stuart of Dunleath 2 v. Lost and Saved 2 v. Old Sir Douglas 2 v.

Not Easily Jealous 2 v.

Mrs. Oliphant:
Passages in the Life of Mrs. Margaret Maitland of Sunnyside 1 v. The Last of the Mortimers 2 v. Agnes 2 v. Madonna Mary 2 v. The Minister's Wife 2 v. The Rector, and the Doctor's Family 1 v. Salem Chapel 2 v. The Perpetual Curate 2 v. Miss Marjoribanks 2 v. Ombra 2 v. Memoir of Count de Montalembert 2 v. May 2 v.

Ossian:
Poems 1 v.

Ouida:
Idalia 2 v. Tricotrin 2 v. Puck 2 v. Chandos 2 v. Strathmore 2 v. Under two Flags 2 v. Folle-Farine 2 v. A Leaf in the Storm; A Dog of Flanders & other Stories 1 v. Cecil Castlemaine's Gage 1 v. Madame la Marquise 1 v. Pascarèl 2 v.

Miss Parr
(Holme Lee):
Basil Godfrey's Caprice 2 v. For Richer, for Poorer 2 v. The Beautiful Miss Barrington 2 v. Her Title of Honour 1 v. Echoes of a Famous Year 1 v. Katherine's Trial 1 v.

Mrs. Parr:
Dorothy Fox 1 v.

"Paul Ferroll," Author of—
Paul Ferroll 1 v. Year after Year 1 v. Why Paul Ferroll killed his Wife 1 v.

Miss Fr. M. Peard:
One Year 2 v. The Rose-Garden 1 v. Unawares 1 v.

Bishop Percy:
Reliques of Ancient English Poetry 3 v.

Pope:
Select Poetical Works (w. portrait) 1 v.

The Prince Consort's
Speeches and Addresses 1 v.

The price of each volume is ½ Thaler = 2 Francs.

Charles Reade:

"It is never too late to mend" 2 v. "Love me little, love me long" 1 v. The Cloister and the Hearth 2 v. Hard Cash 3 v. Put Yourself in his Place 2 v. A Terrible Temptation 2 v. Peg Woffington 1 v.

Recommended to Mercy:

Author of—
Recommended to Mercy 2 v. Zoe's 'Brand' 2 v.

Richardson:

Clarissa Harlowe 4 v.

Rev. W. Robertson:

Sermons 4 v.

Charles H. Ross:

The Pretty Widow 1 v. A London Romance 2 v.

J. Ruffini:

Lavinia 2 v. Doctor Antonio 1 v. Lorenzo Benoni 1 v. Vincenzo 2 v. A Quiet Nook 1 v. The Paragreens on a Visit to Paris 1 v. Carlino and other Stories 1 v.

G. A. Sala:

The Seven Sons of Mammon 2 v.

Katherine Saunders:

Joan Merryweather and other Tales 1 v.

Sir Walter Scott:

Waverley (w. portrait) 1 v. The Antiquary 1 v. Ivanhoe 1 v. Kenilworth 1 v. Quentin Durward 1 v. Old Mortality 1 v. Guy Mannering 1 v. Rob Roy 1 v.

The Pirate 1 v. The Fortunes of Nigel 1 v. The Black Dwarf; A Legend of Montrose 1 v. The Bride of Lammermoor 1 v. The Heart of Mid-Lothian 2 v. The Monastery 1 v. The Abbot 1 v. Peveril of the Peak 2 v. The Poetical Works 2 v. Woodstock 1 v. The Fair Maid of Perth 1 v. Anne of Geierstein 1 v.

Miss Sewell:

Amy Herbert 2 v. Ursula 2 v. A Glimpse of the World 2 v. The Journal of a Home Life 2 v. After Life 2 v.

Shakespeare:

Plays and Poems (w. portrait) compl. 7 v. (*Second Edition.*)
Shakespeare's Plays may also be had in 37 numbers, at 1/10 Thlr. each number.
Doubtful Plays 1 v.

Shelley:

A Selection from his Poems 1 v.

Nathan Sheppard:

Shut up in Paris 1 v.

Sheridan:

Dramatic Works 1 v.

Smollett:

The Adventures of Roderick Random 1 v. The Expedition of Humphry Clinker 1 v. The Adventures of Peregrine Pickle 2 v.

Earl Stanhope:

History of England 7 v. The Reign of Queen Anne 2 v.

The price of each volume is ½ Thaler = 2 Francs.

Sterne:

The Life and Opinions of Tristram Shandy 1 v. A Sentimental Journey 1 v.

"Still Waters," Author of—

Still Waters 1 v. Dorothy 1 v. De Cressy 1 v. Uncle Ralph 1 v. Maiden Sisters 1 v. Martha Brown 1 v.

Mrs. H. Beecher Stowe:

Uncle Tom's Cabin (w. portrait) 2 v. A Key to Uncle Tom's Cabin 2 v. Dred 2 v. The Minister's Wooing 1 v. Oldtown Folks 2 v.

Swift:

Gulliver's Travels 1 v.

Baroness Tautphoeus:

Cyrilla 2 v. The Initials 2 v. Quits 2 v. At Odds 2 v.

Colonel Meadows Taylor:

Tara: a Mahratta Tale 3 v.

H. Templeton:

Diary and Notes 1 v.

Tennyson:

Poetical Works 7 v.

W. M. Thackeray:

Vanity Fair 3 v. The History of Pendennis 3 v. Miscellanies 8 v. The History of Henry Esmond 2 v. The English Humourists 1 v. The Newcomes 4 v. The Virginians 4 v. The Four Georges; Lovel the Widower 1 v. The Adventures of Philip 2 v. Denis Duval 1 v. Roundabout Papers 2 v. Catherine 1 v. The Irish Sketch-Book 2 v.

Miss Thackeray:

The Story of Elizabeth 1 v. The Village on the Cliff 1 v. Old Kensington 2 v.

A. Thomas:

Denis Donne 2 v. On Guard 2 v. Walter Goring 2 v. Played out 2 v. Called to Account 2 v. Only Herself 2 v.

Thomson:

Poetical Works (w. portrait) 1 v.

F. G. Trafford
(Mrs. Riddell):

George Geith of Fen Court 2 v. Maxwell Drewitt 2 v. The Race for Wealth 2 v. Far above Rubies 2 v.

Trois-Etoiles:

The Member for Paris 2 v.

Anthony Trollope:

Doctor Thorne 2 v. The Bertrams 2 v. The Warden 1 v. Barchester Towers 2 v. Castle Richmond 2 v. The West Indies 1 v. Framley Parsonage 2 v. North America 3 v. Orley Farm 3 v. Rachel Ray 2 v. The Small House at Allington 3 v. Can you forgive her? 3 v. The Belton Estate 2 v. The Last Chronicle of Barset 3 v. The Claverings 2 v. Phineas Finn 3 v. He knew he was Right 3 v. The Vicar of Bullhampton 2 v. Sir Harry Hotspur of Humblethwaite 1 v. Ralph the Heir 2 v. The Golden Lion of Granpere 1 v. Australia and New Zealand 3 v.

T. Adolphus Trollope:

The Garstangs of Garstang Grange 2 v. A Siren 2 v.

The Two Cosmos 1 v.

"Véra,"

Author of—

Véra 1 v. The Hôtel du Petit St. Jean 1 v.

Eliot Warburton:

The Crescent and the Cross 2 v. Darien 2 v.

S. Warren:

Passages from the Diary of a late Physician 2 v. Ten Thousand a-Year 3 v. Now and Then 1 v. The Lily and the Bee 1 v.

Waterdale Neighbours 2 v.

Miss Wetherell:

The wide, wide World 1 v. Queechy 2 v. The Hills of the Shatemuc 2 v. Say and Seal 2 v. The Old Helmet 2 v.

A Whim

and its Consequences 1 v.

Mrs. Henry Wood:

East Lynne 3 v. The Channings 2 v. Mrs. Halliburton's Troubles 2 v. Verner's Pride 3 v. The Shadow of Ashlydyat 3 v. Trevlyn Hold 2 v. Lord Oakburn's Daughters 2 v. Oswald Cray 2 v. Mildred Arkell 2 v. St. Martin's Eve 2 v.

Elster's Folly 2 v. Lady Adelaide's Oath 2 v. Orville College 1 v. A Life's Secret 1 v. The Red Court Farm 2 v. Anne Hereford 2 v. Roland Yorke 2 v. George Canterbury's Will 2 v. Bessy Rane 2 v. Dene Hollow 2 v. The Foggy Night at Offord etc. 1 v. Within the Maze 2 v.

Wordsworth:

Select Poetical Works 2 v.

Lascelles Wraxall:

Wild Oats 1 v.

Edm. Yates:

Land at Last 2 v. Broken to Harness 2 v. The Forlorn Hope 2 v. Black Sheep 2 v. The Rock Ahead 2 v. Wrecked in Port 2 v. Dr. Wainwright's Patient 2 v. Nobody's Fortune 2 v. Castaway 2 v. A Waiting Race 2 v. The Yellow Flag 2 v.

Miss Yonge:

The Heir of Redclyffe 2 v. Heartsease 2 v. The Daisy Chain 2 v. Dynevor Terrace 2 v. Hopes and Fears 2 v. The Young Step-Mother 2 v. The Trial 2 v. The Clever Woman of the Family 2 v. The Dove in the Eagle's Nest 2 v. The Danvers Papers; the Prince and the Page 1 v. The Chaplet of Pearls 2 v. The two Guardians 1 v. The Caged Lion 2 v. The Pillars of the House v. 1 & 2.

Series for the Young.

Kenneth; or, the Rear-Guard of the Grand Army. By *Miss Yonge* (Author of "the Heir of Redclyffe"). With Frontispiece, 1 v.

Ruth and her Friends. A Story for Girls. With Frontispiece, 1 v.

Our Year: A Child's Book, in Prose and Verse. By the Author of "John Halifax, Gentleman." Illustrated by Clarence Dobell, 1 v.

Ministering Children. A Tale dedicated to Childhood. By *Maria Louisa Charlesworth.* With Frontispiece, 1 v.

The Little Duke. Ben Sylvester's Word. By *Miss Yonge* (Author of "the Heir of Redclyffe"). With a Frontispiece by B. Plockhorst, 1 v.

The Stokesley Secret. By *Miss Yonge* (Author of "the Heir of Redclyffe"). With a Frontispiece by B. Plockhorst, 1 v.

Tales from Shakspeare. By *Charles* and *Mary Lamb*. With the Portrait of Shakspeare 1 v.

Countess Kate. By *Miss Yonge* (Author of "the Heir of Redclyffe"). With Frontispiece, 1 v.

Three Tales for Boys. By the Author of "John Halifax, Gentleman." With a Frontispiece by B. Plockhorst, 1 v.

A Book of Golden Deeds. By *Miss Yonge* (Author of "the Heir of Redclyffe"). With a Frontispiece by B. Plockhorst, 2 v.

Moral Tales. By *Maria Edgeworth.* With a Frontispiece by B. Plockhorst, 1 v.

Friarswood Post-Office. By *Miss Yonge* (Author of "the Heir of Redclyffe"). With Frontispiece, 1 v.

Cousin Trix and her welcome Tales. By *Miss Georgiana Craik.* With a Frontispiece by B. Plockhorst, 1 v.

Three Tales for Girls. By the Author of "John Halifax, Gentleman." With a Frontispiece by B. Plockhorst, 1 v.

Henrietta's Wish; or, Domineering. A Tale. By *Miss Yonge* (Author of "the Heir of Redclyffe"). With a Frontispiece by B. Plockhorst, 1 v.

Kings of England: A History for the Young. By *Miss Yonge* (Author of "the Heir of Redclyffe"). With Frontispiece, 1 v.

Popular Tales. By *Maria Edgeworth.* With a Frontispiece by B. Plockhorst, 2 v.

The Lances of Lynwood; the Pigeon Pie. By *Miss Yonge* (Author of "the Heir of Redclyffe"). With Frontispiece, 1 v.

The price of each volume is ½ Thaler = 2 Francs.

Collection of German Authors.

On the Heights. By *B. Auerbach.* Translated by F. E. Bunnett. Second Authorized Edition, thoroughly revised. 3 v.

In the Year '13: By *Fritz Reuter.* Translated from the Platt-Deutsch by Charles Lee Lewes, 1 v.

Faust. By *Goethe.* From the German by John Anster, LL. D. 1 v.

Undine, Sintram and other Tales. By *Fouqué.* Translated by F. E. Bunnett, 1 v.

L'Arrabiata and other Tales. By *Paul Heyse.* From the German by M. Wilson, 1 v.

The Princess of Brunswick-Wolfenbüttel and other Tales. By *H. Zschokke.* From the German by M. A. Faber, 1 v.

Nathan the Wise and Emilia Galotti. By *G. E. Lessing.* The former translated by W. Taylor, the latter by Charles Lee Lewes, 1 v.

Behind the Counter [Handel und Wandel]. By *F. W. Hackländer.* From the German by Mary Howitt, 1 v.

Three Tales by *W. Hauff.* From the German by M. A. Faber, 1 v.

Joachim von Kamern and Diary of a poor young Lady. By *Maria Nathusius.* From the German by Miss Thompson, 1 v.

Poems from the German of *Ferdinand Freiligrath.* Edited by his Daughter. Second Copyright Edition, enlarged. 1 v.

Gabriel. A Story of the Jews in Prague. By *S. Kohn.* From the German by Arthur Milman, M.A., 1 v.

The Dead Lake and other Tales. By *Paul Heyse.* From the German by Mary Wilson. 1 v.

Through Night to Light. By *Karl Gutzkow.* From the German by M. A. Faber, 1 v.

An Egyptian Princess. By *Georg Ebers.* Translated by E. Grove, 2 v.

Flower, Fruit and Thorn Pieces: or the Married Life, Death, and Wedding of the Advocate of the Poor, Firmian Stanislaus Siebenkäs. By *Jean Paul Friederich Richter.* Translated from the German by E. H. Noel, 2 v.

Ekkehard. A Tale of the tenth Century. By *J. V. Scheffel.* Translated from the German by Sofie Delffs, 2 v.

The Princess of the Moor [das Haideprinzesschen]. By *E. Marlitt,* 2 v.

The price of each volume is ½ Thaler = 2 Francs.

Dictionaries.

Dictionary of the English and German languages
for general use. Compiled with especial regard to the elucidation of modern literature, the Pronunciation and Accentuation after the principles of Walker and Heinsius. By *W. James.* Twenty-third Stereotype Edition, *thoroughly revised and greatly enlarged.* 8vo sewed 1⅓ Thlr.

Dictionary of the English and French languages
for general use with the Accentuation and a literal Pronunciation of every word in both languages. Compiled from the best and most approved English and French authorities. By *W. James* and *A. Molé.* Eleventh Stereotype Edition. 8vo sewed 2 Thlr.

Dictionary of the English and Italian languages
for general use with the Italian Pronunciation and the Accentuation of every word in both languages and the terms of Science and Art, of Mechanics, Railways, Marine &c. Compiled from the best and most recent English and Italian Dictionaries. By *W. James* and *Gius. Grassi.* Seventh Stereotype Edition. 8vo sewed 1 ¾ Thlr.

New Pocket Dictionary of the English and German
languages. By *J. E. Wessely.* Fourth Stereotype Edition. 16mo sewed ½ Thlr. bound ¾ Thlr.

New Pocket Dictionary of the English and French
languages. By *J. E. Wessely.* Fifth Stereotype Edition. 16mo sewed ½ Thlr. bound ¾ Thlr.

New Pocket Dictionary of the English and Italian
languages. By *J. E. Wessely.* Second Stereotype Edition. 16mo sewed ½ Thlr. bound ¾ Thlr.

New Pocket Dictionary of the English and Spanish
languages. By *J. E. Wessely* and *A. Gironés.* Second Stereotype Edition. 16mo sewed ½ Thlr. bound ¾ Thlr.

Technological Dictionary in the French, English and
German languages, by *Alexander Tolhausen,* of the Patent Office, London. Revised and augmented by *Louis Tolhausen*, French Consul at Leipzig. In three Parts. 8vo. Part I. French, German, English. sewed 8 Marks (2⅔ Thlr.) = 10 Francs = 8 Shillings. In the Press: Part II. English, German, French. Part III. German, French, English.   7 -   **11**

BERNHARD TAUCHNITZ, LEIPZIG;
AND SOLD BY ALL BOOKSELLERS.

CPSIA information can be obtained
at www.ICGtesting.com
Printed in the USA
BVHW041426150819
555988BV00011B/458/P